For
O.

Contents

I

BROADWAY

1900–1918

ERA OF
GOOD FEELINGS

In this book Broadway refers not to the long thoroughfare but to the theater district in midtown Manhattan. The thoroughfare extends 146 miles from Bowling Green near the tip of Manhattan Island to Albany. The theater district known as Broadway is a minute fragment of the thoroughfare. In 1900 it was one and one-half miles long; it was less than half that length in 1950; it was six blocks in 1970. In 1900, sixteen of the Broadway theaters were located on Broadway; in 1950, only three were located there; in 1970, two. Most of the houses for legitimate theater are on side streets; they are known as Broadway houses, for it is not in the nature of the theater to be literal.

The story of a half century of Broadway falls into three overlapping stages. From 1900 to World War I, it was provincial and parochial; it bore no serious relation to art or life. Between the two world wars, it was bursting with energy and enterprise; the new dramatists, of whom

Olga Nethersole and Hamilton Revelle in *Sapho* (1900).
(*The New York Public Library*)

there were many, and the people of the theater were full of hope and fresh ideas and were enthusiastic about new styles of craftsmanship. During those dynamic years, Broadway was a brilliant center that influenced the theater of the world. During World War II, and indeed a few years before the war broke out, Broadway began to lose originality and drive; the new dramatists were less numerous, and the competition of motion pictures and later of television became increasingly burdensome. Some theaters were pulled down, making room for parking lots; many others became motion-picture houses. The legitimate theater no longer dominated Broadway.

Although the Broadway of 1900 and of the first decade of the twentieth century was artistically trivial, it had charm and a kind of disarming simplicity. The population of New York was three and one-half million—up from two million in the previous decade. Broadway attracted large audiences of middle-class people who paid $1.50 or $2.00 for the best seats and were in search of amusement, excitement, and romance. They were the despair of serious theater people from abroad, but they were a comfort to American producers.

In 1900, the theater district began at 13th Street, where the Star was located. Henry Irving and Ellen Terry had played there. Julia Marlowe began her New York career on that venerable stage where Lester Wallack and Laura Keene had made stage history in the nineteenth century. In 1900, the Star housed a melodrama called *A Great White Diamond*, which has left no mark on the literature of the stage. Broadway extended as far north as 45th Street, where the New York Theater was located. In 1900, the New York Theater had two bookings—*The Man in the Moon, Jr.*, and *Broadway to Tokio*, neither of which aspired to immortality.

The intervening thirty-two blocks contained other productions and stars that have not been entirely forgotten and that give an impression of the pleasant casual tastes of the period. *Way Down East*, which portrayed the essential goodness of country people, in the highly profitable vein of James A. Herne's *Shore Acres* and *Sag Harbor*, was at the Academy of Music on 14th Street, the home of many famous New York events. *Ben Hur* was racing its clattering chariots across the stage of the Broadway Theater at 41st Street. William Gillette was introducing America to his *Sherlock Holmes*, which would not be forgotten as long as he lived. The chivalrous John Drew was playing the chivalrous *Richard Carvel* at the Empire at 40th Street. That admirable Polish actress, Helena Modjeska, nearing the end of her career, was playing repertory at the Fifth Avenue

Theater, which was not located anywhere near Fifth Avenue but on Broadway at 28th Street.

Maude Adams appeared in two productions that year—first at the Criterion at 44th Street as Lady Babbie in Barrie's *The Little Minister*, which had made her a star in 1897, and then as Napoleon's little son in Rostand's *L'Aiglon* at the Knickerbocker Theater at 38th Street. The affable Nat Goodwin and his stunning wife, Maxine Elliott, had just finished playing *When We Were Twenty-one* there. Julia Marlowe had also appeared that season at the Criterion, in Clyde Fitch's *Barbara Frietchie*, in which, after weeks of coaching, she suavely fired a rifle. Her sedate audiences were thrilled by her manual dexerity. Weber and Fields were simultaneously burlesquing her play as *Barbara Fidgety* in their flourishing music hall at 29th Street. In the Metropolitan Opera House at 39th Street, Emma Calvé, Nellie Melba, and Lillian Nordica were singing grand opera at a $5.00 top. The yellow brick pile of the Met looked a good deal more elegant than it did nine years later when Gatti-Casazza stuck two or three more stories on the daintily balustraded roof. But the Met, as always, was leading a life secluded from the theater because opera and drama never mix and because the golden box holders dominated the Met. During performances of Wagner operas, they talked so loud that music lovers in other parts of the house could not hear the singers. The theater did not have box-holder troubles until the New Theatre was built in 1909—by the kind of people who instinctively buy boxes.

During the 1899–1900 season, Mrs. Fiske acted her most famous part in Langdon Mitchell's *Becky Sharp* at the Fifth Avenue Theater, after Madame Modjeska had finished her repertory there. Mrs. Fiske was rudely evicted in the midst of a profitable run because Klaw and Erlanger, producers, had placed her on their blacklist. Other productions of merit that season included Mrs. Leslie Carter's sizzling reappearance in Belasco's *Zaza*, also at the Criterion; Henrietta Crosman in *Mistress Nell* at the Savoy at 34th Street; James A. Herne and Lionel Barrymore in Herne's *Sag Harbor*, which opened Oscar Hammerstein's beautiful Republic Theater on 42nd Street, adjoining the open area known then as Longacre Square. Two versions of *Quo Vadis?* by different adaptors opened in different theaters the same evening. The one adapted by the more cultivated writer was the one that failed.

All these productions suited the respectable New Yorkers who found Broadway exactly to their taste. But there were two productions that raised scandals. The Madison Square Theater at Madison Square and 24th Street was housing a "carnival of adultery . . . reeking with suggestiveness" called *Coralie & Company, Dressmakers*. In that brothel epic, a white male was discovered in bed with a Negress. A Brooklyn clergyman with a knack for fine measurement said that immoral plays of this kind "put the doors of the box office and the gates of hell a short yard apart."

And Clyde Fitch's *Sapho* was arousing the libido of the populace at Wallack's Theater at 30th Street. At the end of the second act, Hamilton Revelle, a manly actor, carried the voluptuous Olga Nethersole upstairs to an unseen bedroom where, many people thought, a terrible sin occurred at every performance. One critic with 20–20 vision and personal enthusiasm said he could see Miss Nethersole's dimples through her gauze nightgown. Despite her amorous beauty, or perhaps because of it, the police closed *Sapho* after the first performance, although they permitted it to reopen later by popular demand. In New Haven, the police had been more constructive. They closed *Sapho* until Mr. Revelle could learn how to carry Miss Nethersole upstairs "in a chaste and orderly manner" in which the implication of sin would be totally eliminated.

In January of 1901, Sarah Bernhardt introduced a dash of cosmopolitanism to Broadway by arriving for her sixth American tour with fifty trunks, five servants, one secretary, the great Benôit Constant Coquelin, a troupe of supporting actors, and a formidable repertory consisting of *L'Aiglon, Cyrano de Bergerac, La Tosca, La Dame aux Camélias,* and *Hamlet*. Since she played in French, few people knew what she or any of her actors were saying. Once she skipped a whole scene, though no one in the audience realized it. But Broadway audiences were sufficiently familiar with *Hamlet* to say some very harsh things about the imperious French lady who had the effrontery to emasculate *Hamlet* at $5.00 a ticket at the Knickerbocker Theater.

In *Hamlet*, Coquelin was obliging enough to play the First Gravedigger, although Madame had brought him to Broadway to play his greatest part, Cyrano, when the Rostand play turned up in the repertory. He was as good a Gravedigger as the French language permitted. But Bernhardt failed as Hamlet. Everyone denounced her performance indignantly: "a farce"; "in every way she is unfitted to Hamlet"; "the grandeur of the play is lost." Norman Hapgood, the most flexible and civilized of the critics, was more precise. He described her Hamlet as "a pert, ill-mannered, spoiled, bad-tempered boy with little sense and a theatrical temperament," which sounds suspiciously like a portrait of Bernhardt.

Other disastrous things happened on that ill-fated sixth tour. One hotel would not evict a guest to make room for Madame's pet dog. A Harvard professor was impudent enough to say that *L'Aiglon* was inferior French poetry. In New Orleans, a writer for the *Picáyune* reported that Madame's voice had gone, she was overaged, and her audiences had been "dull, apathetic and unresponsive." In May, Madame left New York for France with a bag full of American gold and an angry declaration that she would never visit America again. She kept her vow until 1906.

In this era of good feelings, the relationship between audiences and actors was on the whole cordial and unsophisticated. Mrs. Leslie Carter said that audiences invariably greeted the star with applause on her entrance. They applauded at the end of every act. If the performance pleased them they clapped, whistled, and stamped their feet at the final curtain. In melodramas, it was standard practice to hiss the villain and warn the hero or heroine of impending disaster.

Audiences were inclined to talk during performances. Richard Mansfield, Margaret Anglin, and Eleanor Robson on occasion stopped their performances and refused to continue until the audience was silent. They rebuked chatty audiences directly across the footlights. Matinee girls also had a reputation for bad manners. During the performance, they giggled and chatted with their friends and made audible comments about the actors: "Isn't she just darling?" and "I think he's the handsomest man I've ever seen." During the last act, the matinee girls disturbed their neighbors by putting on their hats, veils, and jackets and rushing out of the theater as soon as the curtain came down. They were in a hurry to get their ice-cream sodas before the calamity of having to go home.

There were some civilities about playgoing that have disappeared. No respectable theater would be without a pit orchestra to play before the show began, during the intermissions, and after the final curtain. The musical selections were refined and cheerful: "Dream of the Rarebit Fiend," by Thurban; "Spring, Beautiful Spring," by Licmke; Chopin concertos, Herbert's "American Heiress," Schubert's "Rosamunde." Between acts, "little nigger boys," in the phrase of a visiting actress, handed around glasses of water. It was a civilizing experience to go to the Broadway theater, where the patrons were treated like ladies and gentlemen.

Broadway had a local flavor all its own. Electric street lights—the successors to arc lamps and gas—were laying the foundation for the Great White Way. (That phrase, by the way, was devised in 1901 by O. J. Gude, a designer of advertising displays.) Two-wheel cabs—"han-

View of 42nd Street and Broadway in 1898. The building on the right was replaced by the Hotel Pabst, which was in turn replaced by the Times Building. (*Culver Pictures, Inc.*)

soms"—provided most of the transportation, although automobiles were beginning to appear. Broadway cable cars passed the Hotel Vendome at 41st Street. Browne's convivial Chop House stood next door to the Empire Theater and opposite the Metropolitan Opera House until the curse of prohibition destroyed it thirty years later. Stanley's celebrated restaurant was located between 42nd and 43rd Streets.

On the northeast side of 43rd Street, the homey Barrett House, where Eugene O'Neill was born, had just merged with an adjoining structure and rechristened itself the Cadillac Hotel. Rector's stood next door; behind a solid façade and canopy, it remained cheerfully lighted until early morning for the convenience of theater people and their bedazzled patrons. Five large globes mounted on lamp-posts at the curb made Rector's look official. It was the Sardi's of its time. To dine at Delmonico's, where the steaks and oysters were superb, a gourmet had to go over to Fifth Avenue, next-door to Richard Canfield's gambling emporium.

In the winter, ladies wore long, heavy coats, bustles, and tall hats, and they stuffed their hands in muffs to keep their fingers warm; men wore derby hats, and gentlemen—this included some producers—wore silk hats. The constabulary wore tall, gray helmets made of felt. Vendors of roasted chestnuts rolled their smoking carts through Longacre Square. O. Henry said that at night Broadway was crowded with shopgirls, panhandlers, confidence men, and actors—he seemed to be making no real distinction. He said that visitors from out-of-town were always in a hurry, but native New Yorkers had time to loiter around construction sites and gape at the wonders of Broadway. Only the out-of-towners were sophisticated, according to O. Henry, who was not.

The Broadway summers seem idyllic in retrospect. Dray horses wore straw bonnets; men wore flat straw hats called skimmers or boaters. Men took off their jackets and starched collars and walked around in shirt sleeves. Women wore fluffy, transparent gowns and carried white parasols to shade their complexions. A bemused columnist in *The New York Dramatic Mirror* reported that the summer grooming of the ladies gave enchanting glimpses of pretty necks and arms—"Venuses rising in all

Robert Frazer and Virginia Howe in *Ben Hur* (1900). (*The New York Public Library*)

Sarah Bernhardt leaving her private railroad car with her manager, Edward J. Sullivan, 1911. (*The New York Public Library*)

The Empire Theater, with John Drew starring in *My Wife* (1910), and, next-door, Browne's Chop House. (*Seidman Photo Service*)

Rector's restaurant in Times Square, the symbol of glamour and sin. (*Seidman Photo Service*)

their loveliness" from asphalt that boiled at 100-degree temperatures.

Despite the wilting heat, *Florodora* continued to flourish at the Casino in the drooping summer of 1901. It gave its 350th performance in August. For the benefit of suburbanites, the local railroads ran "Florodora Expresses" at hours printed in large type and red ink in the timetables. Francis Wilson, the comedian, was playing in *The Strollers* next-door at the Knickerbocker. Some of his actors used to linger on the fire escape, which was cooler than the dressing rooms. They could and in fact did peep into the dressing rooms where the Florodora girls were getting ready to look ravishing. To defend their modesty, the girls discharged syphons of seltzer and vichy at the boys next door. *Florodora* upset the self-control of the entire neighborhood. After one performance, the girls were delayed a half-hour while the police disciplined youths who were bombarding the Casino stage door with firecrackers.

The section of Broadway between 37th Street and 42nd Street was known as the Rialto. Theater people gathered there or promenaded there. Producers could sometimes cast a play by looking over the actors loitering on the Rialto; and out-of-town managers, gazing out of office windows, could book tours by seeing who was available.

Broadway was gay. It did foolish things with enthusiasm. The Hippodrome press department on Sixth Avenue organized a party of showgirls to be drawn up Broadway on sleds by elephants. An ostrich drew a light runabout through the streets. A baby elephant climbed five flights of stairs to take tea with Edna Wallace Hopper. The Hippodrome organized a sightseeing trip in a huge open bus for a tribe of Indians in full regalia. It was good for everybody, including the producers.

In the season of 1899–1900 there had been 87 productions. There were about 70 productions in the season of 1900–1901, not including the shows at seven vaudeville and six burlesque houses. The year 1900 came to a bountiful close with five openings on New Year's Eve. (For comparison: in 1927–1928 there were 254 productions; in 1950–1951, there were 87; in 1968–1969, 42.) Thirty-three theaters for legitimate productions were not enough, and new building began at once and continued for fifteen years. Five new theaters were built in 1903—the new Lyceum in 45th Street, the Drury Lane at 34th Street and Eighth Avenue, the Hudson in 44th Street (Ethel Barrymore opened it in *Cousin Kate*), and the luxurious New Amsterdam and the distinguished Lyric in 42nd Street. With the addition of several other theaters built there later, the New Amsterdam and the Lyric made the block between Seventh Avenue and Eighth Avenue one of the finest in the city and a splendid part of the theater district. People treated the block with considerable respect. They dressed for opening nights. They arrived ceremoniously. Even the ushers were splendidly bedizened.

There was no Times Building to give Longacre Square architectural distinction until 1905. A provincial and hospitable-looking building called the Pabst Hotel stood on that site, dispensing beer and general well-being. In the summer, the windows were shaded by striped awnings, and the whole building looked festive. The Astor Hotel was nearing completion at 44th and 45th Streets.

In 1905, Adolph S. Ochs, publisher of *The New York Times*, endowed Longacre Square with a distinguished building that transformed a ramshackle neighborhood into an impressive plaza. He set the tone for the area for the next forty years. Having a sense of civic responsibility as well as pride in his newspaper, he commissioned C. L. W. Eidlitz and Andrew McKenzie to design a beautiful building in the style of a soaring Giotto tower in Florence. During the two years while the tower was being constructed, Mr. Ochs frequently took a room in the Cadillac Hotel across Broadway to watch this charming masterpiece reach 375 feet above the skyline. It also rose above the deepest hole ever dug in New York City until then, for the new Interborough Subway was being dug at the same time, and Mr. Ochs had to sink the Times pressroom below the subway station. On April 9, 1904, Longacre Square officially became Times Square —an uncluttered esplanade stretching from 42nd Street to 47th Street. In less than a decade, the street and subway traffic made the tower an impractical newspaper plant, and Mr. Ochs moved his newspaper to The Times Annex on 43rd Street. But his Times Tower continued to set a standard of taste and good citizenship for the Broadway district. Whatever else happened on Broadway, the slender Times Tower dominated the neighborhood and acted as a courtly host to the carnival crowds on New Year's Eve, when a ball of light descended from the flag pole on the dot of midnight.

Although the surfaces of Broadway were innocent and beguiling at the beginning of the century, something very ugly was going on in the business offices. A group of six businessmen, dominated by Abraham Lincoln Erlanger, had formed a Syndicate that came close to establishing a rapacious monopoly. Since bookings, particularly outside New York, were made inefficiently at that time, the Syndicate was a constructive idea when it was organized in 1896 to book shows systematically. By 1900, it had accumu-

The Times Building under construction, 1904.
(*Seidman Photo Service*)

The Hotel Pabst, torn down early in 1902 to make way for the Times Building. (*Seidman Photo Service*)

Abe Erlanger. (*Culver Pictures, Inc.*)

lated power that was approaching absolute. If a star actor or a producer did not sign an exclusive contract, the Syndicate made it difficult for him to get a theater on Broadway and almost impossible for him to organize a national tour. It harassed and persecuted actors who tried to remain independent.

Erlanger was a fat, squat, greedy, crude egotist who had no interest in the theater as an art or as a social institution. He was a dangerous enemy. The honor roll of stars who resisted him included Mrs. Fiske, Joseph Jefferson, Nat Goodwin, James K. Hackett, James A. Herne, James O'Neill, and Sarah Bernhardt. When the Syndicate boycotted Bernhardt by closing theaters to her on the road, she played in a circus tent, with a roar of success that pleased audiences as well as the actors.

The Syndicate bought so much advertising that it influenced newspaper coverage. It sometimes succeeded in getting critics dismissed if their reviews were negative. It bribed critics by such trite devices as hiring them to rewrite plays or paying them "consultation" fees. Friendly critics praised Syndicate productions and ignored or criticized other productions. The Syndicate could be quite Jovian. In an attempt to silence Harrison Grey Fiske, a publisher (and the husband of Mrs. Fiske) who campaigned against the Syndicate in every issue of his *Dramatic Mirror,* the Syndicate posted a notice on the call boards of the theaters it controlled: "Notice is hereby given that under pain of dismissal members of the cast are forbidden to advertise in, buy or read *The New York Dramatic Mirror.*" Maurice Barrymore read this arrogant notice on the call board of the Hollis Street Theater in Boston. He sent a telegram in reply: "Have rarely read a dramatic newspaper but will read the *Dramatic Mirror* regularly hereafter." He was not dismissed.

Times Square in 1909, looking north from the Times Building. At the New York Theater, the marquee reads "Jardin de Paris Revue: Follies of 1909." At the Criterion Theater, "Elsie Janis in *The Fair Coed.*" At right center is Rector's. (*Culver Pictures, Inc.*)

Eventually the power of the Syndicate was destroyed by three young brothers—Sam, Lee, and Jacob Shubert—who came from Syracuse and set up a rival powerhouse. But Sam, the most engaging of the three, died in a grisly railroad accident near Harrisburg in 1905 when he was twenty-nine. Lee, his close associate, was so depressed by this family disaster that he considered liquidating the family business, and he went to Erlanger to discuss an arrangement. One of Lee Shubert's principal terms was that Erlanger fulfill a contract that Sam had made with Belasco. Erlanger hated Belasco, who had challenged the Syndicate monopoly. He answered Lee with a crude remark that, in view of Sam's recent death, wounded

Lee deeply. Erlanger said: "I do not honor contracts with dead men." Lee departed offended and determined for revenge. His brother Jake agreed with him: "We'll kill the son of a bitch," he said. That was the emotional impetus for the bitter competition that broke out between Erlanger and the Shuberts. In the end, the Shuberts destroyed the Erlanger empire, and they presided over the theater with many of his primitive methods. But if the brothers were less rapacious than the Syndicate it was because Lee Shubert loved the theater. Erlanger loved nothing but the box office. In the early years of the century, the Syndicate was the unseen monster that hovered over Broadway and preyed on theater people.

The corner of Broadway and 43rd Street in 1909. (*Culver Pictures, Inc.*)

Most people outside the theater knew nothing of this. The pleasantest period in the history of Broadway for the theatergoers coincided with the Syndicate. Photographs of Times Square show the crossroads of two great streets with no mall to break the open center; there were bright streetlamps, trolley cars, many cabs, and—near Hammerstein's Theater—a row of parked automobiles with flat tops and ungainly bodies. The headlights of moving vehicles were polite and weak. A string of dainty lights ran around the roof and cornices of the resplendent Astor Hotel, which was advertised as the "most electrified hotel in the world." At the head of the square, the single word "Studebaker" appeared in lights, with "Trimble Whiskey" in lights just below. "Roller Skating 50 Cents" was the rubric over another building that is impossible to identify now. The New York Theater advertised "25-50-75-$1" in a conspicuous horizontal sign. There was a huge sign on the top of Hammerstein's Theater that read "Roof Garden." Where the Paramount Building now stands, at 43rd Street and Seventh Avenue, the six-story Putnam office-building was erected in 1909. Among its remembered tenants were the United Booking Office, the Orpheum Circuit, the Bijou Circuit, A. H. Woods, Milton Aborn, Percy G. Williams.

About this time, the famous spectacular signs began to appear. The first had been mounted in 1891 on the nine-story building that stood where the Flatiron Building now stands at 23rd Street and Broadway. In 1906, the success of *The Red Mill* was partly ascribed to the fact that it had one of the first moving electric signs on Broadway. When the Great White Way was solidly established, some charming and famous signs faced Times Square and beguiled the whole community—a nimble kitten that chased a spool of silk to advertise the Corticelli Silk Company, the White Rock nymph leaning over a pool of sparkling water, the Heatherbloom Petticoat Maid, a Roman chariot on the Normandie Hotel at Broadway and 38th Street.

In 1910, there were forty first-class theaters in the Broadway district, and the phrase "42nd Street and Broadway" stood for revelry and delight. Since the theater is a public institution, no realist expects it to be predominantly refined. But the men who were building the theaters then respected Broadway as an institution. The buildings they commissioned represented the good taste of professional architects. Maxine Elliott's Theater in 39th Street was built in 1908, the most costly theater of its time—and it was a gem of comfort and décor. The Gaiety, built the next year on Broadway near 46th Street, was designed in Louis Quinze style and had an interior color scheme of blue, gray, and gold. It was opened by John Barrymore in *The Fortune Hunter*. Next door, the Astor Theater represented similar elegance. A *Midsummer Night's Dream* and *Cymbeline* were its first two productions.

The producers instinctively kept Broadway outwardly respectable. Promenading up and down Broadway, looking at the carrousel of electric lights, staring at the houseboards of the theaters and also at the carriage trade, people could go about their affairs without fear or misgivings. The dramas were trivial, but Broadway was solid, the safe refuge of New York's good-humored burghers.

THE HAPPY
WORLD OF STARS

It was an actor's theater because, on the one hand, no one took the drama seriously and, on the other hand, some very interesting actors with broad styles and vivid personalities dominated the stage. Plays were not inquiries into the nature of life or discussions of ideas but vehicles designed to present the stars triumphantly. In the autumn of 1900, James O'Neill, who had been playing in *The Count of Monte Cristo* since 1883, found Broadway audiences delighted enough with his old warhorse to support eighty more performances. The old thrills satisfied the same people year after year. Denman Thompson spent most of his adult years touring in a piece of bucolic hokum called *The Old Homestead*. It made him so rich that he and his wife once had the distinction of being robbed of $60,000 in stocks and bonds and jewelry worth $10,000 when they were on a tour of one-night stands between Elmira, New York and Albany. If Thompson had appeared in a new play in which he did not

Holbrook Blinn and Mrs. Fiske in *Salvation Nell* at the Hackett Theater (1908). (*The New York Public Library*)

wash his face in a tin basin and slobber noisily, the public would have repudiated him. Clara Morris, a highly emotional actress, said that the public
would not accept her in any play in which she did not shed tears. When
she tried something less lachrymose, her public said in effect: "Yes, it's all
very fine, but she does not make us cry. Give us the old plays where we
can weep for four of the five acts."

In Boston, a good critic, Henry Clapp, remarked that "Our drama has
no permanent literary value and produces nothing that is going to remain
in the intellectual stock-in-trade of our race," and Broadway proved his
point. Plays were not so much written as assembled; and the writers for
Broadway thought in terms of the melodramas or the sentimental romances
that had sufficed throughout the nineteenth century, when, in Thornton
Wilder's later opinion, the middle class controlled the theater and would
not accept plays that were not flattering and soothing. An actable script
included the "obligatory scene" designed to overwhelm the audience.
Power, passion, sacrifice, romance, salvation were the chief ingredients of
the plays that worked. It was as if the realities of American life were too
terrible to be faced. Audiences were content with stage fare that was
familiar.

This must have been because the actors played on a heroic scale, out
of a feeling of self-confidence. Emotions that would be guffawed off the
stage in the twenties were accepted as the essence of theater; and sentimental artifices that have become too cloying to be endured were relished
by the public then. Charles Frohman, the busiest as well as the most ingratiating producer of his day, believed in the supremacy of the actor, and
he had a gallery of fine actors to prove his point—John Drew, Ethel Barrymore, Maude Adams, Marie Doro, Viola Allen, Julia Marlowe, Henrietta
Crosman, William Faversham, Margaret Anglin, May Robson, Otis
Skinner, any one of whom could make the audience believe the impossible.
Frohman stated his case as follows: "We regard the workman first and
the work second. Our imaginations are fired not nearly so much by great
deeds as great doers." The stars led lives of affluence and conspicuous waste
because they had devoted followers who paid top prices to see them in
anything, at least once, and also because there were no income taxes then.

Nothing vanishes into nothingness so completely as a stage performance. Even when there is some sort of record of it—as in the cases of
Edwin Booth and Joseph Jefferson; even when there is an abundance of
scene photographs like those that make the files of *Theatre Magazine* invaluable—a contributory element of great importance is missing: the frame
of reference, the life of the times, the code of values, the habits of thought.

We have no way of understanding the relevance of James O'Neill's romantic style to the society of his time. Great acting affects the manners of society, but the manners of society also affect great acting by giving sanction to endemic styles. Actors are indeed the abstracts and brief chronicles of their time. Today we cannot sit comfortably in judgment on the broad, swaggering, sentimental acting of 1900 because our society is wary, self-conscious, and squeamish, and reluctant to suspend the capacity for disbelief.

But there are some things that we can assume: for instance, that in all ages actors are more interesting than most people. Even when the writers are hardly more than mechanics, the actors are qualified to keep the theater alive because they are dramatic people. They are wittier and more alert than most people; they are observant and responsive; they are independent and individualistic; they are original and free of bourgeois cant. They also know the most important thing in any civilized community: they know how to get along with other people. What they were playing at the turn of the century seems negligible and silly today. But we can assume that they made it interesting to their audiences because they were interesting people.

Like Richard Mansfield, for example. His contemporaries were reluctant to use the word "great" in the comments on his acting. When he died in 1907, *Theatre Magazine* described him as "a clever, versatile and highly-cultivated eccentric comedian, which we sometimes call a character actor." The judgment of his contemporaries has to be respected because they saw him act. But if he was not great, he was nevertheless ambitious and less provincial than any other male star on Broadway. He acted in two Bernard Shaw plays (*Arms and the Man* and *The Devil's Disciple*) when Shaw was considered more of a nuisance than a dramatist, and his last production was Ibsen's *Peer Gynt*, which is anything but conventional.

Nowadays the record of his career seems astonishing for its range, intelligence, and industry. Beginning with light comic parts in Gilbert and Sullivan, he moved on to heroic parts like Napoleon, Don Juan, Beau Brummell, Ivan the Terrible, Don Carlos, Henry V, Brutus in *Julius Caesar*, Richard III, and Alceste in Molière's *The Misanthrope*. His chief romantic parts were in *Cyrano de Bergerac* and *Monsieur Beaucaire*. His *Dr. Jekyll and Mr. Hyde* was a famous tour de force, and is still part of the cultural heritage of people who never heard of Richard Mansfield. If Mansfield was not a great actor he was certainly no hack.

In the last half of the century, it is difficult to visualize the scale on which theater stars lived in Mansfield's time. His colossal ego gave him an extra dimension. There is a photograph of him seated on a horse near his Riverside Drive home—very upperclass indeed; and another of him stand-

Richard Mansfield on horseback on Riverside Drive. (*The New York Public Library*)

ing nonchalantly at the steps of his private railroad car—very grand. He earned about $75,000 a year net profit. In addition to his townhouse, he owned a summer place in New London, Connecticut, and a private yacht of princely dimensions. The royalty of the screen do not live today on a more patrician scale than this stage interpreter of Henry V and Don Carlos.

Physically, he was a comparatively small man—five feet, seven or eight inches (the records are not clear). To maintain the illusion of grandeur, he was careful not to stand close to actors taller than he was. His ego was so massive and his temper so quick and savage that some people suspected that he was insane. In rehearsal and on tour, he behaved like a member of royalty. He spoke to no one at rehearsals; he treated all his actors as if they were serfs. If he was pleased with a scene or an actor, he said nothing; that was the most to which a good actor was entitled. If he was not pleased, he denounced actors with humiliating ferocity. "Hopeless, hopeless," he would roar at even the older members of his company. Sometimes he got into such rages in rehearsals that he would fire the whole company on the spot and stride out of the room. The company learned that it was prudent to remain, for Mansfield invariably returned and took up the performance where he had left off. This seems not to have been a trick, as it was with Belasco. Mansfield had an ungovernable temper.

On tour, he played God. He lived and took his meals in his private car, from which other members of the company were excluded. He regulated the speed of the train. There was a gauge in his car. If the speed rose above forty miles an hour, he would send an order to the engineer to go more slowly. If members of his company got into trouble on the road or became ill, he was generous with money which he sent through an emissary. But he would not deal with them in person. When he was walking on the street one day in a city outside New York, a member of his company whom he had helped stopped to thank him. Mansfield would not recognize him or speak to him. Through a secretary, he sent word to the actor that he was not to be accosted on the street.

Although he was neither loved nor liked, he was respected by other actors because of his skill, knowledge, and taste. His productions and performances were so famous throughout the nation that he could and did treat local managers contemptuously, and he would not play in a theater that did not meet his terms exactly. Obsessed with his own interests, he once betrayed his colleagues in a shocking manner: when actors and managers were defying the Syndicate, he stood on their side and made speeches about the Syndicate's ruthlessness and malignance. He arranged with the other dissidents to meet in his business office to draw up papers for an organized opposition. The others assembled at the appointed time. Mansfield never appeared. He sent a message to say that he had just signed a contract with the Syndicate—on very handsome terms, incidentally.

Offstage Mansfield was intolerant and intolerable. But long after he died, people kept saying: "You should have seen Mansfield's Cyrano" or "You should have seen Mansfield's Peer Gynt." Onstage he was superb.

The most unlikely actress became the most legendary. Offstage, Maude Adams was not beautiful in any of the conventional ways. Offstage, she was without personality or distinction. In 1910, after she had been a star for eighteen years, she had difficulty in establishing her identity in a Fifth Avenue shop. She had just returned from a lucrative national tour and went skipping around town on a shopping spree. A slim, apologetic figure in an old brown traveling coat and a small hat, she looked insignificant. Since she had not brought either cash or a checkbook with her, she asked the manager of a store to have some clothes sent to her home C.O.D. He hesitated when he considered the shy, colorless woman who was asking for service. The name "Maude Adams" meant nothing to him. She did not look to him like a woman who could pay for good merchandise. In another shop the same day she bought a sable hat for $1500, to be paid for by check when it was delivered. She could afford anything that struck her fancy.

The theater was her whole life. She was born in 1872 in a Mormon community, daughter of a woman who was a member of a Salt Lake City stock company. Little Maude Adams Kiskadden was carried onstage in a platter when she was nine months old—the platter being an essential prop in an obscure stock play. When her mother moved to San Francisco to join a stock company, Maude was a conspicuous success at the age of five in a play called *Fritz*. A precocious boy actor named David Belasco was in the same cast.

When she came to New York, she had an undistinguished career. She puzzled some of her fellow players by her apparent lack of knowledge about acting and her helplessness. There was a good deal of puzzled apprehension when Charles Frohman made her John Drew's leading lady in *The Masked Ball* in 1892. She played the part of a gentlewoman who drank too much at a party. When she made her exit after a scene in which she had to balance her gentility against her state of intoxication, the applause made her a potential star. In 1897, Charles Frohman made her a genuine star in Barrie's *The Little Minister*. She earned $50,000 the first year. Her blue eyes, luminous skin, delicate features, and her enchanting voice gave her a unique and irresistible stage presence. After triumphing in the Barrie play, she played a listless Juliet that was generally regretted, and L'Aiglon, in which her refinement and gentility emasculated a vivid character. (Sarah Bernhardt played the same part triumphantly the same season.)

But her success in *The Little Minister* began a long series of associations with Barrie, a playwright whose literary manners were identical with hers. She was also successful in Rostand's *Chantecler*—which gave her personal pleasure because the part was not typical of her style. Once Maude Adams became a star, she earned vast sums of money. She had a private house on 41st Street, a farm at Lake Ronkonkoma, Long Island, and a house in Onteora Park in the Catskills. When she was playing in New York, a special train stood by in Long Island City on Saturday night to take her to Lake Ronkonkoma and return her on Monday. Her St.

Bernard dog accompanied her. Her railroad car cost $30,000. It included a small stage on which she rehearsed her company when on tour. To say that she worked like a trouper was a literal statement of fact.

All her most enchanting and most memorable qualities came into perfect focus in her performance of Peter Pan, in 1905, and that was the chief factor in the legend of Maude Adams. At the time, Barrie was not a name to conjure with. "A sugar-coated Shaw," one commentator thought. Nor was Maude Adams regarded as an actress of the first rank. She is "too frail to be a great actress," the *Theatre Magazine* critic wrote. "But she has a sweet, lovable personality, which fascinates and endears her to audiences." He might have added that she had a formidable knowledge of the stage; she always knew exactly what she was doing and what the other members of her company must do in support of her. *Peter Pan* was—and is—one of the theater's most disarming and improbable treasures. For many years, it compelled American theatergoers everywhere happily to suspend their common sense. When a young woman thirty-three years of age advanced to the footlights and asked the audience if it believed in fairies, it invariably roared "yes." The audience warned Peter that the Pirate was coming. The audience cried "Hurry, Peter!" when the chase began. Peter Pan was accepted as a living person. A child who lived at 255 West 95th Street invited Peter for luncheon and pointed out as an added inducement: "You can fly here and save carfare."

As a human being, Maude Adams was something of a mystery; only a few people penetrated the wall of air with which she surrounded herself. She probably lacked self-confidence. But she undertook stupendous projects when she was challenged. In the summer of 1909, she played Saint Joan in a spectacular outdoor production in the Harvard Stadium. It sounds impossible now, and certainly outside the range of an elfin-like person of decorous habits. She made her entrance riding a horse (dubbed by her "The Great White Peril" because she was afraid of him), and rode into the massive amphitheater, supported by a cast of 1,400 members of the Massachusetts National Guard, many of them riding horses. How could the audience have heard the lines this frail woman spoke in this unroofed space? Perhaps the spectacle was enough.

Maude Adams was generous with her associates. She gave handsome presents to members of the stage crews who had been particularly helpful. Out of her own income, she raised the salaries of some of the actors in her companies. Thus, in her private life she exercised some of the happy prerogatives of the fairies in *Peter Pan* and of the heroines she played. After crowning her career with a beguiling performance in Barrie's

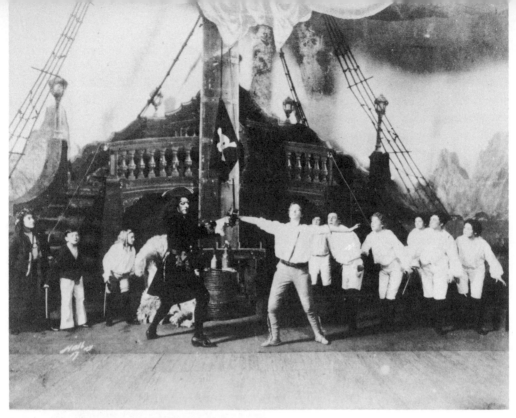

Ernest Lawford and Maude Adams in *Peter Pan* (1905).
(*The New York Public Library*)

A *Kiss for Cinderella,* she retired from the stage in 1918, taught acting and stagecraft in a small Middle Western college, and spent a lot of money and time trying to perfect what she expected would be a revolutionary stage electric light. In 1931 she returned to the stage to play Portia to Otis Skinner's Shylock—a drab performance and production that never got closer to New York than Newark. In 1931, she toured summer theaters as Maria in *Twelfth Night*—a small part in an undistinguished production. But she could not renounce the stage. Apparently the discipline and the excitement of many years in the theater could not be discarded permanently.

On the stage, Maude Adams had a soft, elusive charm that could not be analyzed or resisted. Acting the part of Maggie in Barrie's *What Every Woman Knows,* she spoke three famous lines: "Charm is the bloom upon a woman. If you have it, you don't have to have anything else. If you haven't it, all else won't do you any good." In the latter half of the twentieth century, that may sound too pat and sentimental. But it states a fact; and Maude Adams was the fact it stated.

On Broadway stages, there were no more cultivated and dedicated idolators of Shakespeare than Julia Marlowe and E. H. Sothern. They set the standard for Shakespearean production until they began to retire in 1915. In the theater, retiring always takes time. In those days, Shakespeare

E. H. Sothern and Julia Marlowe in *Much Ado About Nothing* (1903). (*The New York Public Library*)

was the one classic that everyone accepted as both proper and enjoyable, and there were many good Shakespearean actors. Ellen Terry and Sir Henry Irving were the greatest from abroad. But everyone who pretended to be a serious actor played some Shakespeare—Ada Rehan, Helena Modjeska, Maude Adams, Viola Allen, Julia Arthur, Henrietta Crosman, Annie Russell, Richard Mansfield, William Faversham, Otis Skinner, James K. Hackett—even John Drew, who played in Shakespeare in his apprentice days, though not after Charles Frohman put him into a three-piece suit and cast him as a gentleman. Drew's Petruchio, which he had played in London as well as New York, was held in high repute everywhere.

Before World War I, some theatergoers and especially some actors who remembered the masters of Shakespearean acting gave Sothern and Marlowe secondary ranking. But to most American audiences, they were synonymous with Shakespeare, and for very good reasons. Julia Marlowe, who was something of a prodigy, became infatuated with Shakespeare when she was a girl, and all through the rest of her life she was a formidable student of Shakespeare. Sothern had played *Hamlet* with his first wife, Virginia Harned, in 1900. According to Norman Hapgood, the critic, Sothern brought grace and scholarship to the production, but Hapgood thought the scenery was too realistic as well as ponderous and imposing, and most people thought Sothern was too light an actor for classical tragedy. (Hapgood thought Miss Harned's Ophelia was "hopeless.") Sothern was best known for his sword-and-tights dramas, like *The Prisoner of Zenda* and *If I Were King*. His speech was dry and crisp in comparison with Miss Marlowe's, which was rich and melodious. They began to play together in 1904 in *Hamlet*—a notable production. She spent $2,201.60 on the costumes for Ophelia. After they settled down to co-starring they occasionally played in non-Shakespearean plays, like Percy MacKaye's *Jeanne d'Arc*, in 1907. (As an added inducement to attendance at that production the theater provided uniformed guards to take unaccompanied women home after the performance.) Sothern and Marlowe were as solid as gold; everyone trusted them. After the customary divorces, they were married in 1911 and lived happily ever after, fulfilling the disciplines of Shakespeare's romances though not of his adult tragedies.

As a girl, Julia Marlowe was not only abnormally bright but abnormally self-confident—a trait she never lost. Born Sarah Frances Frost, she was brought up in Cincinnati, Ohio, where her mother, separated from a footloose husband, ran a boardinghouse. As a child, Julia Marlowe played in a troupe of child actors in *H. M. S. Pinafore* and had minor parts in a Shakespearean company that toured the Middle West. She seemed to have such a remarkable understanding of Shakespeare that her neighbor and patroness, Ada Dow, sister of the owner of the Cincinnati Opera House, took her to New York, rented an apartment near Broadway on 35th Street, and devoted the next three years to preparing her for the stage.

Their work schedule sounds awesome—body and mind training through most of their waking hours, and an unwavering discipline that only a fanatical young lady could have endured. In 1887, they engaged a company of actors from those at liberty around Union Square and toured *Pygmalion and Galatea* through a long list of New England towns. With that experience as a background, they booked the Bijou Theater in New York for an exhibition matinee performance of a German drama called *Ingomar*. Julia was nineteen. Managers and critics were invited; many of them attended. The matinee was such a great success that one overwrought drama critic jumped onto the stage to lead the applause at the end.

After her successful exhibition performance, Julia Marlowe proceeded to tour her own company in *Romeo and Juliet, As You Like It, Much Ado About Nothing, Cymbeline, Pygmalion and Galatea, Ingomar,* and *The Love Choice* for several years, coming no closer to New York than Brooklyn. She felt uneasy about Broadway. Among the theatergoers who admired her acting was the great agnostic and Shakespearean scholar, Colonel Robert Ingersoll, who advised her, promoted her, helped finance her, and took charge of her during one critical illness when the preservation of her beauty was as important a medical factor as the saving of her life. After she was recognized in New York as a star, she played in a dramatization of *When Knighthood Was in Flower* so successfully that she became independently wealthy within two years. But she could not be diverted from the chief end of her life. Her economic security assured, she devoted the rest of her life, with very few interruptions, to producing Shakespeare.

E. H. Sothern, the talented son of another celebrated actor, E. A. Sothern, was also looking for the kind of parts that an educated man could respect. Co-starring with Julia Marlowe turned out to be ideal for both of them. They studied together and acted together for the rest of their lives. The Klaw and Erlanger Syndicate paid them $115,000 a year. But the Syndicate lost them by the crude business methods it instinctively cultivated. When Miss Marlowe sprained her ankle on tour, the Syndicate applied the penalties it invariably held in reserve for any actor who was not earning money for them. Sothern and Marlowe then went over to the Shuberts, who increased their income by paying them a percentage of the gross. In a crisis involving money the Shuberts had more charm than the Syndicate. Sothern and Marlowe were first-rate actors with excellent minds, inexhaustible enthusiasm for their work, and a sense of responsibility to both Shakespeare and the public. Sothern was an exacting workman with great personal charm. Julia Marlowe was not only beautiful but had a musical voice that she knew how to use. Their performances were never stale. They did not act *Macbeth* until 1910, six years after they had first appeared together. But there was nothing routine about the production. *Macbeth* was regarded as their finest work, and Julia Marlowe's sensual Lady Macbeth was not only original for its time but her masterpiece.

They had one unhappy experience. In 1909, they were given the honor of opening the New Theater, and they produced *Antony and Cleopatra* for the occasion. Everyone was disappointed with it, including Sothern and Marlowe. It was dull; it lacked magic. Many people thought it was unnecessarily immoral. There were so many things wrong with the New Theater, including its grandiose auditorium and its society audience, that Sothern and Marlowe did not have to shoulder all the blame for a pedestrian production. As soon as they decently could, they went back to the Shuberts and to their loyal audiences all across the land. They never had the nature of pioneers.

Despite the depth and breadth of their knowledge, they represented the conventional attitudes that prevailed in their time. Their scenery was ornate and overblown, and the staging was literal. Now it seems odd that they never experimented with an apron stage, as William Poel was doing in England. Since 1894, he had been mounting Shakespearean productions in what he believed to be the "Elizabethan manner." Knowledgeable people already knew that pictorial productions of Shakespeare on proscenium stages were spurious. John Corbin, a critic with an extensive knowledge of Shakespeare, had already taken a stand. He characterized Sir Henry Irving's staging as wrong-headed—the pictures made by the scenery being false, and the essential spirit of Shakespeare being swamped by décor. And Sir Beerbohm Tree was drowning Shakespeare in the same kind of productions at the same time.

The Elizabethan style in production was not new. In 1910, there was a production in that manner at the New Theater, of which John Corbin was literary advisor. Edith Wynne Matthison, Rose Coghlan, Ferdinand Gottschalk, and Albert Brunning appeared in *The Winter's Tale* without scenery, and everyone was impressed with the speed and spontaneity of the performance. During World War I, Forbes-Robertson played *Hamlet* on an open stage at Harvard, and it was brilliantly successful.

But Sothern and Marlowe were creatures of their time, obsessed with respectability and middle-class good taste. Percy Hammond, a shrewd, acerbic critic, felt that they patronized Shakespeare as well as himself. They eliminated bawdy speeches and tried to keep Shakespeare a respectable writer. Once Julia Marlowe described her creed: "The purpose of theater," she said, "is to free the audience from the burden of existence. The land of Romance—for that I was bound and desired those who were tired and troubled to follow me." That bland creed was alien to the recklessness and despair of much of Shakespeare's best work.

Sothern and Marlowe concluded their stage career in 1926 by staging ten of Shakespeare's plays at the new Memorial Theater in Stratford-on-Avon, England, and donating all the proceeds to this institution. They represented admirably the manners, beliefs, and intentions of their day. Not very many actors or producers on Broadway had their integrity of purpose, style, and skill. But they came at the end of a genteel and empty tradition.

There was one exception to the mindlessness of Broadway. Mrs. Fiske, a red-headed, mettlesome actress, was not afraid of plays that said something. She was short of stature and hardly a beautiful woman in any conventional sense. But she had a stubborn chin, which was a mark of character, and she was tireless, animated, and determined. She was also married to Harrison Grey Fiske, who managed her career and had a major influence on her taste. Some of her contemporaries were glamorous; some of them were more conspicuously dazzling. But none of them had such a firm command of the theater as a forum for ideas. At the time when Ibsen was hated in America as immoral, morbid, and subversive, Mrs. Fiske played several of his plays, not only well but profitably. Even Ibsenites nowadays might regard *Rosmersholm* as rather dreary. But the production Mrs. Fiske acted in and staged had 199 consecutive performances and earned a net profit of $40,000. Embattled by critics and clergymen who were horrified by Ibsen, she nevertheless argued that Ibsen was the genius of the age and that no dramatist or actor could escape his influence.

Every other theater person in the first part of the century has stature only if he is judged by the provincial standards of the time. If it were not for the uninspired tone of the theater of 1910, Edward Sheldon might have been a dramatist of first rank, and if it were not for the numbing gentility of the time Julia Marlowe might have been as transcendent as Eleonora Duse. No such allowances have to be made for Mrs. Fiske. She was modern at a time when nearly everyone else on Broadway was Victorian.

The theater was her life. Daughter of a theatrical agent in New Orleans, she appeared on the stage at the age of three as Little Minnie

Maddern. At five she appeared in New York in *Uncle Tom's Cabin*, *Richard III*, and *King John*. The vivacity of her acting made her a popular star in New York when she was in her teens. She was sought after, courted, and wooed. After divorcing the superfluous husband she had married when she was seventeen, she married Harrison Grey Fiske, editor and owner of *The New York Dramatic Mirror* and reputed to be a millionaire as well. Out of respect for his social standing, she did the decent thing: she retired from the stage and proceeded to live like a lady of leisure. But even a lady is permitted to act in public for charity if she accepts no fee. In 1894, during her polite retirement, Mrs. Fiske played Nora in Ibsen's *A Doll's House* in a benefit performance for a hospital. Modjeska and Réjane had failed as Nora; they seem to have succumbed to Ibsen's lugubrious style. But Mrs. Fiske's modern, dry, intelligent, ironic performance brought both Ibsen and the play alive, and Mrs. Fiske immediately acquired the standing of "great actress."

Soon after that startling event, she abandoned the role of lady of leisure and plunged into all aspects of the theater with a vigor, insight, and tenacity that still seem remarkable. She understood the whole of the theater. In addition to several parts in Ibsen plays, she was bold enough to defy criticism by playing unconventional parts, like the immoral Tess in Lorrimer Stoddard's version of *Tess of the D'Urbervilles* and the deceitful Becky in Langdon Mitchell's version of *Vanity Fair* and the parish scrub-woman in Sheldon's *Salvation Nell*. "I consider the most vicious influence of the day is the chambermaid-society drama," she said (although she appeared in a few at the end of her career when realistic acting was no longer a novelty). She was against cant of all kinds in a day when cant was one of the common amenities of life as well as the theater.

Mrs. Fiske's long war with the Klaw and Erlanger Syndicate was characteristic of her. In twelve years of continuous warfare she never surrendered a point. The editorial offices of Mr. Fiske's *Dramatic Mirror* were located at Broadway and 40th Street. In 1893, Mr. Fiske and his weekly newspaper found themselves surrounded on two sides by Mr. Frohman's new Empire Theater, which was wrapped around their plant. Since Frohman was a member of the Syndicate, they must have had a feeling of entrapment by the enemy. But *The New York Dramatic Mirror* kept up a steady drumfire against the viciousness and mendacity of the Syndicate; hardly a week went by when the *Mirror* did not denounce the enemy with solemn indignation, and Mrs. Fiske denounced them repeatedly in addresses to civic and social organizations. Once when Mr. and Mrs. Fiske were strolling down the street they met Mr. Erlanger coming in the opposite direction. As he passed, he made some derogatory remark about Mrs.

Fiske. Handing his cane, gloves, and hat to his wife, Mr. Fiske struck Mr. Erlanger and they brawled until the police hauled them off in the paddy wagon. Most of the other stars of the time eventually went over to the Syndicate, but Mrs. Fiske never lowered her guard. After the Syndicate had evicted her from the Fifth Avenue Theater at the height of her run in *Becky Sharp*, Mr. Fiske bought the Manhattan Theater at Sixth Avenue and 33rd Street, the site now occupied by Gimbel's. He renovated it in a glowing color scheme of dark green, bronze, and gold, with the chairs upholstered in red—a stunning modern theater. Mr. and Mrs. Fiske inaugurated the custom of giving the audience free programs. Although Mrs. Fiske played there for several years when she was in New York, the Manhattan Theater became an economic liability. It was a large factor in the collapse of Mr. Fiske's fortunes. After the death of his father, Mr. Fiske discovered that he was not the millionaire he thought he was. In 1915, he filed a voluntary petition for bankruptcy—liabilities, $94,198; assets, $78,-794. Mrs. Fiske kept barnstorming for years to help pay the bills. Her letters to her husband during this dark period preserve the gallantry of her spirit.

It must have comforted her to be able to count on good notices in the *Dramatic Mirror*, which was invariably abject and rhapsodic about her. In 1901, for instance, the author of *The Unwelcome Mrs. Hatch* is mentioned only once in passing in the *Mirror's* hysterical review. (Mrs. Burton Harrison was the author.) But Mrs. Fiske's "great" acting is praised lavishly and ecstatically in every paragraph. When Mrs. Fiske acted the death scene in which she faced upstage and died with the eloquent elocution of her back, "women in the audience were in tears and men choked back sobs." That was theater.

Her acting was often criticized for its lack of gesture and its cold businesslike speech and unintelligibility—"bad diction," as this fault is ungrammatically defined. Franklin Pierce Adams, columnist on the New York *Tribune*, once wrote an amusing verse about Mrs. Fiske's speech:

> Somewords she runstogether,
>   Some others are distinctly stated.
> Somecometoofast and s o m e t o o s l o w
>   And some are syncopated,
> And yet no voice—I am sincere—
>   Exists that I prefer to hear.

Mrs. Fiske was never much concerned with what people said about her. She was only interested in putting on good plays with good casts. She got the best supporting actors that were available. John Mason, Walter Hampden, Tyrone Power, Sr., Dudley Digges, Forbes-Robertson, George Arliss, Holbrook Blinn appeared with her, and so did her talented niece, Emily Stevens. At a time when everyone else was swooning over establishing a repertory company in an art theater, Mrs. Fiske called it an "outworn, impossible, harmful scheme." She thought the best performances were by actors cast for their parts. In 1906, Mrs. Fiske appeared in the one American play of that period that retains some of the humor it must have had originally—Langdon Mitchell's comedy about divorce, *The New York Idea*. Mrs. Fiske's swift, hard acting must have been particularly enjoyable in that tart comedy. The dialogue is still lively, and the idiocies of the characters are still pertinent and belong to the long tradition of drawing-room comedy. It differs from the chambermaid-society comedy that Mrs. Fiske despised by being satirical and not snobbish.

The amount of work Mrs. Fiske poured into the theater over a period of sixty-three years is awe-inspiring to contemplate now. Apart from her passionate crusades against the killing of wild animals for fur and of birds for feathers (she took an active part in these humane causes), she had no life outside the theater. Her marriage, which was a fundamental part of her life, was blighted by her implacable industriousness in the theater, and her interminable tours—and also by her husband's flagrant infidelities. Her last years were undistinguished and a little desperate. She appeared in a succession of potboilers. But her total career was one of the most honorable on Broadway. At a time when nearly everyone else was content with humbug, she acted on the stage in a sharp, naturalistic style, and she was the champion of intelligence in the theater. Since she did what she wanted to do, it would be patronizing to feel sorry for her, particularly at the end. But as she hurried around the country, rehearsing her company almost every day and playing almost every night, she surrounded herself with loneliness. A brilliant public figure had a joyless private life and few of the comforts of companionship and devotion.

If the Broadway theater had been less banal, Laurette Taylor might have made an indelible impression on it. Many people thought she was the greatest actress of her time. To begin with, she had a winning personality. Born Loretta Cooney in Mt. Morris Park, Manhattan, she charmed everyone with her sparkling eyes, uptilted nose, golden hair, humorous mouth, and joyous manner; and she lost none of these distinctions when she grew tall enough to become an actress. But she was more than a personality. Ever since she was a child, she had been infatuated with acting. Her

childhood really consisted of a succession of fantasy parts that she instinctively played at home, in school, or in the neighborhood. When she
was in her teens, she went on the stage and learned her craft in mechanical
melodramas, like *Rags to Riches,* in which she acted in 1903. If she succeeded in subduing audiences in melodramas or other pieces of claptrap,
she had no reason to think that she was not fulfilling her responsibilities
in the theater. She accepted the commercial theater uncritically.

Acting was her only reality; she was not much interested in life offstage.
By the time she was in her late teens, she had created a highly individual
technique of acting that was spontaneous and eloquent; it consisted of
variations in tempo, tentative movements that were not quite completed,
quizzical glances, absorption in what other actors were saying, and, of
course, a warm, expressive voice that always seemed to be addressed directly
to the individual theatergoer. "Luminous" was the word most frequently
used about her performances. In her early career, some people thought she
was not acting; she employed none of the ritualistic mannerisms or extrava-
gances of the conventional acting of her day. After years of obscure and
often mortifying experiences as a trouper, she became a star in 1910 in a
now-forgotten play called *The Girl in Waiting.* Then everyone understood
that her spontaneity behind the footlights was indeed acting, and perhaps
the most original and virtuoso acting of the time.

There was nothing in her family background or her own experience to
convince her that great acting needed great parts—like those her counterpart in dramatic acting, Alla Nazimova, was playing with great success.
Nazimova had a background in European theater, which was more mature
than Broadway. In Laurette Taylor's lexicon, parts were vehicles. When
she married a gentlemanly English playwright, J. Hartley Manners, who
was steeped in the trivia of the popular theater, she played a long list of
parts that he wrote especially for her. In 1912, he wrote a part that made
her the most generally worshiped star of her time, and made him about
$10,000 a week. The play was *Peg o' My Heart.* She opened the new Cort
Theater in 48th Street as Peg in 1912 and played it for 607 performances
—the longest run of any dramatic play up to that time. She would have
played it as long or perhaps longer in London if the Zeppelin bombing
raids had not put an end to the engagement in 1915. After so many years
in one part, she was glad to finish with it: "We've made a lot of money,"
she said, "but even money gets very monotonous."

Peg was an example of the Cinderella formula: an Irish girl inherits a
fortune from her father and moves to London, where her artless simplicity
proves to be more practical and wholesome than the artifices of her

snobbish London relatives. This was the formula that kept her and the public contented for many years. It was also the formula for *Out There*, a war play that opened on Broadway in 1917, two days before the United States declared war on Germany. In *Out There*, an obscure Cockney waif raised herself to the status—with uniform—of a Red Cross nurse by patriotism and idealism. She relieved the suffering of wounded English soldiers by attending to them professionally and by charming them in person. One line from that play appeared on recruiting posters: "If I go, will you go?" And thousands of dazed American civilians answered "yes." After a successful Broadway engagement in *Out There*, Laurette Taylor joined an all-star cast, including Mrs. Fiske, George Arliss, George M. Cohan, Chauncey Olcott, Julia Arthur, James K. Hackett, and De Wolf Hopper, that toured America in *Out There* and raised $683,632 for the Red Cross. No one could prove that she was squandering her talent in a play as successful as that. In 1918, she continued with the Cinderella formula in a play her husband called *Happiness*. It was a sentimental comedy about a Brooklyn errand girl who taught a rich customer the secret of happiness; and, as usual, the formula was successful.

But some of her admirers were becoming restless over the undistinguished quality of the plays her husband wrote for her. John Corbin, then critic for *The New York Times*, said that she "had probably the greatest talent, the highest spirit of our times," but he complained that both were "subdued to the level of J. Hartley Manners' improvisations." In the twenties, public taste was also changing; it was more mature than the tastes of Miss Taylor and her husband. In an attempt to answer the growing criticism of her choice of vehicles, she appeared in 1922 in a serious play, *The National Anthem*, in which her husband rebuked and denounced the jazz generation. But neither Mr. Manners nor Miss Taylor was prepared to contribute anything except an expression of distaste to a subject that had more profound meanings and was better analyzed by others. The play failed; only professional moralists supported it, and they were neither numerous nor influential enough to sustain it. After the failure of a play that had such high motives Miss Taylor never again appeared in a play by her husband.

From this time on, many other things went to pieces in her life for many sad reasons, including the death of her husband who had been her most stabilizing influence for more than a decade. She became an alcoholic. Many wretched years went by before she was sufficiently in command of herself and her talent to play the dowdy Mrs. Midget in a deeply moving revival of Sutton Vane's *Outward Bound* in 1938, and the complacent

Mrs. Wingfield in Tennessee Williams' *The Glass Menagerie* in 1944. Given one touching part in a wistful reverie about death and one overwhelming part in a beautiful drama of nostalgic poetry, Laurette Taylor played magnificently. She looked into the dark corners of two human hearts and flooded them with the light that had always radiated from her acting. She was worshiped again on a different level of sensibility. It was almost too late. But when she died in 1946, she knew that she had won an agonizing personal battle. The public knew it had lost an inspired actress, who had squandered most of her career on merchandise below her artistic level.

PERSONAL STYLE
IN PRODUCING

Most of the early producers were showmen who regarded the theater as a good gamble, as it was. Successful shows made fortunes for producers as well as for stars on a scale and at a speed that seem incredible in our heavily taxed era. The good showman was the producer smart enough to buy a salable script and to hire smart people to stage it.

But at least three of the early producers were businessmen who genuinely loved the theater—Dan and Charles Frohman, brothers, and David Belasco. Dan Frohman, the elder of the brothers, had begun his theater career as business manager for Steele MacKaye, the poet and dramatist. Steele MacKaye should be remembered as a brilliant actor and theater man who developed a theory of acting at a time when most actors learned their craft haphazardly. When Steele MacKaye founded a stock company at the old Lyceum, Dan Frohman became the manager. Dan Frohman employed as his stage manager a plausible and indefatigable

Charles Frohman. (*The New York Public Library*)

young man from San Francisco, David Belasco. At the old Lyceum, after Steele MacKaye left it, Dan Frohman managed a famous stock company that included E. H. Sothern, Mrs. Thomas Whiffen, Effie Shannon, Henry Miller, James K. Hackett, Henrietta Crosman and May Robson, all of whom became independent stars, no doubt because of their superior training in stock.

In 1903, Dan Frohman opened the new Lyceum Theater in 45th Street with Ethel Barrymore in *Cousin Kate*. For many years, he continued putting on plays there with taste and with conspicuously talented actors. A tall, grave man who wore high starched collars and looked forbiddingly formal, he had a sense of responsibility about the theater as a profession. He consistently supported and promoted the Actors' Fund for indigent actors, which has never had a better friend, and he took an active interest in the American Academy of Dramatic Arts, which had developed out of Steele MacKaye's principles of acting at the old Lyceum. Dan Frohman carried on a fine tradition.

His Lyceum Theater still has the warmth and hospitality of a cordial era. In the wall above the theater, it retains a peephole where Dan Frohman, sitting in his office, was able to keep one eye on his business affairs and the other on his actors. He did not have the panache of his younger brother, Charles, but he had a civilized sense of acting values and was dedicated to the best interests of the theater.

As a boy, Charles Frohman was fascinated by the theater. As he grew older, he fell in love with it and loved it so successfully that he owned one theater, which he built, controlled five others, and was the manager of twenty-eight stars. When he died, he left a net estate in the United States of $451. This tiny estate was significant: as a businessman, he could have looked after his affairs more successfully if making money were his first consideration. But he illustrates one of the most winning aspects of the theater—it can transform the people who go into it. In the case of Charles Frohman, it transformed an eight-year-old boy who sold souvenir programs for *The Black Crook* into the foremost producer of his time, the friend and manager of most of the contemporary stars and a man who met death with a cavalier gallantry that still seems remarkable.

Charles Frohman, his brother Daniel, and David Belasco all came into the theater at about the same time, determined to succeed. In the 1880s, when the theatre industry was totally disorganized and it was difficult to arrange road tours efficiently, Charles Frohman booked shows throughout the country. During his apprentice days, Charles had been advance man for traveling companies, and he had learned more about the theaters and theater audiences throughout the nation than anyone else in New York.

He was one of the charter members of the Syndicate, and he was cordially hated by some theater people in New York for that reason. Although his part in the Syndicate became ambiguous after he settled down as a producer, he never withdrew from the Syndicate. He had come into the theater as a huckster.

He was a huckster when, in 1889, he produced his first drama— Bronson Howard's immensely successful *Shenandoah*—at the Star Theater. At that time, Frohman had no reputation for taste. But it is interesting to note that he booked his first production into a theater that had prestige because many of the finest actors had appeared there, and his first cast included some of the best—Viola Allen, Effie Shannon, Henry Miller, and Wilton Lackaye. Net profits—$200,000. On January 25, 1893, he opened his own theater, the Empire, just south of 40th Street on Broadway. It had the finest auditorium of any theater of its time, the largest and most hospitable lobby, and all the comforts of a cultivated institution. The ticket-taker wore full dress and a silk hat. The Empire retained its prestige long after Charles Frohman died. He built so well that the pride and luster of his theater outlived him.

In view of the Empire's subsequent reputation, Frohman's choice of play for the opening seems ludicrous now. The play was *The Girl I Left Behind Me*, written by David Belasco—a ham—and Franklyn Fyles—a hack who reviewed plays for *The Sun* and could never find anything unpleasant to say about a production managed by the Syndicate. Although Frohman's taste in stars was excellent, his taste in plays was indifferent. He had no intellectual curiosity; there was always a fundamental core of show business in his attitude towards the theater. He detested Ibsen and most European plays. He was prudish and chauvinistic. He said that eroticism and decadence are "foreign to us because, as a people, we have not felt the corroding touch of decadence. Nor is life here all drab. Hence, I expect lights as well as shadows in every play I accept." Some of his actors rebelled against his preference for the ephemeral. Margaret Anglin, Annie Russell, and Viola Allen left his management because they felt frustrated by the trival parts he put them in. But he always had a glamorous star chart—John Drew, William Gillette, Maude Adams, Ethel Barrymore, Billie Burke, Marie Doro, Elsie Ferguson, and many others. Some of them were associated with him for particular dramas, but many of them remained with him as long as he lived.

It was a gay and pleasant life in the happiest tradition of that period. As a playwright, Barrie was just right for Frohman. Frohman had seen stage possibilities in Barrie's novel, *The Little Minister*, and had persuaded Barrie, against his best judgment, to make a play out of it. From that time on, Barrie and Frohman were close friends. In 1905, most people thought that the script of *Peter Pan* was a case of mental derangement. But Frohman understood its stage possibilities at once. By casting Maude Adams as Peter Pan, he made theater history, to say nothing of a fortune for Miss Adams, Mr. Barrie, and himself.

Although Frohman loved the theater genuinely, he did not regard himself as an artist or creator. Unlike his brother Dan and David Belasco, Charles Frohman did not stage plays. They were staged by the craftsmen he employed. He did not participate in a production until the end of the rehearsal period.

Since he thought that mystery was one of the theater's most valuable assets, he encouraged his stars to lead secluded lives and not to frequent public restaurants or make public appearances. This business principle coincided with his own personality. He was shy. He never appeared on the stage to take curtain calls as others did. (David Belasco's timid, obsequious curtain calls were his best performances.) Some of the people who worked for Frohman never saw him and would not have recognized him if they had. A bachelor, he lived at the Hotel Knickerbocker, only two blocks from the Empire Theater. Like all successful producers, he went abroad frequently. In 1910, he founded a repertory theater in London at the Duke of York's Theater and produced, among other plays, Elizabeth Baker's *Chains*, which is still famous as an early realistic play about lower-middle-class life. Barrie lost a million dollars in Frohman's repertory theater. No one knows how much Frohman lost, but this attempt to put the theater on a high level of art and culture made him content with treating the theater as a form of show business afterwards.

In the early stages of World War I, Frohman did not go abroad as frequently as usual. But in 1915, he responded to one of Barrie's persistent invitations and booked passage on the *Lusitania*. Some of his friends urged him not to go in wartime—especially John Drew, who took the threat of German submarine warfare seriously. Drew sent Frohman a departure telegram that sounds grisly now, but must have sounded clever at the time: "If you get blown up by a submarine I'll never forgive you." There is a famous photograph of Frohman on the deck of the *Lusitania* before she got under weigh—an amiable, roly-poly man with a big starched collar, a double-breasted suit on a wide, chunky body and a walking stick. No one would have suspected that he was the leading American producer. Among the other passengers were Charles Klein, author of *The Lion and the Mouse*, and Rita Jolivet, an actress. When the *Lusitania* was off the coast of Ireland, the German government fulfilled the threat it had made before the ship left New York. A German submarine torpedoed her. There were not enough life belts for all the passengers. Klein was among the passengers who went down with the ship. Frohman helped Rita Jolivet with her life preserver and quoted a line from Barrie: "Why fear death? It is the most beautiful adventure in life." Those were the final statements of a good friend, a lover of the theater, and a former huckster who was a gentleman at the moment that counted most. After the death of Charles Frohman, the barbaric reality of a savage world tore into the provincial make-believe of Broadway.

David Belasco was the master of mediocrity. From the time when he was a boy in San Francisco, where he acted professionally and wrote successful melodramas, to his late seventies, when he kept his theater busy in New York, he was obsessed with the theater, worked at it with unparalleled fanaticism and left almost nothing that anyone remembers except his personality. He left the scripts of two extravagant melodramas that Puccini made into operas—*Madame Butterfly* and *The Girl of the Golden West*. But what else? The elaborate production of *The Merchant of Venice* in 1922 with David Warfield as Shylock? It was costly and inert. Warfield broke with Belasco after that production which he said Belasco had misdirected, although Warfield was not a great actor. Lillian Russell said Warfield could cry on cue more copiously than anyone she knew on the stage, but his taste was no more discriminating than Belasco's. Belasco trained some memorable stars—Blanche Bates, Mrs. Leslie Carter, Frances Starr, Lenore Ulric, and Ina Claire, who were the most admired. But he seldom presented them in dramas of genuine distinction. He was a showman masquerading as an artist. To him, the theater was on a higher plane than the tent-show or the carnival but essentially the same thing.

When James Gibbons Huneker, the critic, was living in the boarding-house run by M. and Mme. Felix on 23rd Street in the 1890s, he used to take midnight walks with Belasco, who also lived there. At that time, Belasco was stage manager and producer for the Frohmans. According to Huneker, Belasco thought of nothing but the theater. That was true to the end of his life in 1931. He even dramatized himself. He wore the collar and the dress of a priest, which was another one of his countless impersonations because he was neither a Christian nor a man of holy orders. He acted on Shakespeare's premise that all the world's a stage and all the men and women merely players. He played the part so vehemently that he could not tell the difference between illusion and reality.

After serving a long and notable apprenticeship in San Francisco and

Daniel Frohman, David Belasco, Billie Burke, and Gilbert Miller. (*The New York Public Library*)

New York, Belasco became a producer in his own right just before the new century. At one time, he used two theaters in New York, the Republic and the Lyceum; and in 1907, he moved into a theater he built for himself and used consistently for more than twenty years. Originally it was the Stuyvesant–Belasco, but it became the Belasco soon after it opened. A pioneer in stagecraft, Belasco equipped the theater with a lighting system that was well in advance of its time. He liked the big gesture, and assumed that electric light had been invented especially for him. In the early part of his career, he wrote—or, more often collaborated on—spectacular plays that had big scenes and the surfaces of grandeur— *The Heart of Maryland, Zaza, DuBarry, The Darling of the Gods, The Rose of the Rancho, The Return of Peter Grimm, The Music Master, The Auctioneer*—all of them sweeping and grandiloquent. Everything was spectacular; everything was elementary; everything was in falseface.

Although Belasco was often sued for plagiarism, he was never convicted. He could prove that the Belasco stamp was unique. Once he did contribute a series of learned articles about acting to *The Booklovers*

Magazine. It turned out that they had originally appeared in England under the signature of George Henry Lewes, an eminent British critic. Belasco explained that his name on the article was a clerical mistake made by a subordinate who had since disappeared. Just a regrettable oversight in Belasco's opinion.

He measurably improved the standards of stage décor by his ingenious use of lighting and his meticulous attention to the details of scenery. He was the first manager to conceal footlights in the interest of reality. He was one of the few men in that time to understand the importance of direction. He rehearsed his companies remorselessly. He did not so much interpret as invent and mold performances. He tortured his actors. He stuck a pin in Frances Starr's beguiling behind to make her scream dramatically. In the heat of a rehearsal, he sometimes threw his watch on the floor and stamped on it. It was a dollar watch that he kept in stock for the purpose, but the gesture was sobering.

All the actors whom he took in charge were gratified. He expected to take charge of them in every part of their lives. When Mrs. Leslie Carter married for the second time without telling him, Belasco excommunicated her and never saw her again, although she kept on writing to him and hoping for a reconciliation. He was a tyrant and an artist manqué.

In the middle of his long career, realism came into style. Henrik Ibsen, August Strindberg, Tom Robertson, Emile Zola, Henri François Becque, Arthur Pinero, H. A. Jones, G. B. Shaw, and Oscar Wilde were turning the theater away from bombast and romantic trumpery and trying to make it look like life. That was the advance-guard movement of its day. As a producer, Belasco went further than anyone else. To give *The Easiest Way* (1908) a look of verisimilitude, he bought the interior of a dilapidated theatrical boardinghouse—broken furniture and gas fixtures, threadbare carpets, faded wallpaper—and transferred it to the stage intact. To make *The Governor's Lady* (1912) look authentic, he bought the tables and equipment of a Child's restaurant and set them up on the stage, not forgetting a coffee urn that spread a delicious coffee odor through the theater. He could buy the materials of reality.

It was paradoxical, nevertheless, that the truth of reality escaped him. He did not believe in reality. He believed in stage buncombe, in the shabby materials of the artless dramas of his youth—heroism, sacrifice, villainy, purity, immorality, voluptuousness; also retribution, sweet tears, kindly laughs, noble sorrow. Life never got inside Belasco's head or heart. All he knew was theater.

THE
READY-MADE
PLAY

It is difficult to account for the torpor of American playwriting at a time when American life was dynamic. Fresh ideas were abundant, and thousands of people were interested in them. The vitality of the decade may have been a reaction to the stupidity, cant, and jingoism of the Spanish–American War, which had debased the tone of American life two years earlier. William McKinley had justified the seizure of the Philippines by formulating a sanctimonious purpose—"to educate the Filipinos and uplift and Christianize them" (shooting at them first, of course); and Theodore Roosevelt felt "bully" about charging up San Juan Hill in Cuba and killing the Spanish. A lot of respectable Americans were appalled by this combination of seedy ethics, childlike bombast, and military ferocity. If it had happened in the second quarter of the twentieth century, Broadway playwrights would have crusaded against the responsible for such a moral disaster.

lyde Fitch at home in his library. (*The New York Public Library*)

Once the Spanish–American War was out of the way, however, the public mood changed, and one of the liveliest periods in American history began. It was a time of optimistic reform—regulation of banking and industry, concern for the poor, the immigrants, the Indians, and the Negroes, control of child labor, exposure of political corruption, improvement in the standards of public health and education. After Roosevelt doffed his campaign hat and field leggings, he also became a moral crusader, like Robert La Follette, William Jennings Bryan, Albert J. Beveridge, Gifford Pinchot—all of them hopeful. Men of conscience in and out of the government applied the principles of democracy to areas of life that had been ignored or forgotten. Jacob Riis wrote *How the Other Half Lives,* meaning the slum dwellers. Jane Addams brought light into the slum life of Chicago by founding Hull House. Crusading writers, whom Roosevelt peevishly called "muckrakers," dug into the accumulations of power, corruption, and indifference in city governments and corporations. The popular magazines became spokesmen for reform and addressed themselves to the general public. *Everybody's, Cosmopolitan, Collier's, McClure's Magazine, The American Magazine* represented the public interest and raised the cultural level of the entire country. Ida Tarbell's *History of the Standard Oil Company,* written in installments for *McClure's Magazine,* analyzed the practices of a huge corporation and set ethical standards appropriate to the conduct of big business. Similar books were written about the beef trust, the life insurance companies, and Wall Street.

Although Roosevelt often spoke loud and carried a small stick, ("speak softly and carry a big stick" was his professed motto) his zest for the strenuous life, his native bravado, and the breadth of his point of view shook America out of provincialism. At home, he reformed the civil service, altered the relationship of labor and management by supporting the miners against the mine owners, and he took concrete action to conserve natural resources—chiefly the forests. Under his administration, the Standard Oil Company was fined $29,240,000 for violations of the Sherman Antitrust Act (but a higher court courteously set the verdict aside). Roosevelt was anything but provincial. He inaugurated international jurisprudence by giving the Hague Tribunal its first case. He brought the Russo-Japanese War to an end. He profoundly altered the life of the world by getting work started on the Panama Canal.

Broadway was not only untouched by this political and cultural dynamism, but it was also unaffected by the vigor and diversity of the other arts. In literature, Edith Wharton, Theodore Dreiser, Henry James, William Dean Howells, Hamlin Garland, Henry B. Fuller, Ambrose Bierce, Stephen Crane, Edwin Arlington Robinson were writing vigorous and enterprising books about human beings; and in painting, John Sloan, William Glackens, Ernest Lawson, George Luks, Robert Henri, and Everett Shinn were portraying many aspects of American life with enthusiasm and independence. And in England, Europe, and Russia, the theater was rapidly emerging from a century of staleness. Ibsen and Shaw were dramatizing ideas. Chekhov, Gorky, Strindberg, Rostand, Schnitzler, Hauptmann and Sudermann were discussing truths of life or were writing with the imagination and virtuosity of poets. Some of the best dramas of the modern era were available, but Broadway either ignored most of them or denounced them as immoral. Broadway was contented with second-rate authors like Pinero. The literary equivalent of the Broadway theater were the novels of George Barr McCutcheon, Gene Stratton Porter, Robert Chambers, and Zane Grey.

How could Broadway have been so insensible and elementary? Bernard Shaw said that the British theater was twenty years behind the times. That was the case also in America. Plays were contrivances composed of standard parts—the first and second leads, the soubrette, the villain, the lover, the landlord, the lawyer, the poor relative, the rich relative, and similar stereotypes. If the hero triumphed and the villain perished, the play was a drama. If the villain triumphed and the hero perished, the play was a tragedy. Plots were manipulated on the assumption that all people were identical organisms, and in identical circumstances all of them were amorous, revengeful, heroic, noble, jealous, shrewd, crafty, or pious and uplifting, without individuality. Effective scenes were transposed from one play to another, like the candle in the window to guide the wandering boy home. Although American playwrights may have been intelligent and attractive people, they wrote mechanical devices that could be exploited by actors whose personalities and styles were familiar to the public.

Managers were inclined to be wary of American playwrights. Daniel Frohman once remarked that he wouldn't take the risk of producing even a good script by an American, although he later changed his mind.

But in the season of 1900–1901, Clyde Fitch made a sensational breach of the barrier against American playwrights. Four plays written

Elsie de Wolfe and Frank Mills ride across the stage in *The Way of the World* at the Victoria Theater (1901). (*The New York Public Library*)

by him were on the stage simultaneously. One commentator said that future generations would never believe that such a thing could happen and would have to turn back to "musty records" to confirm it. (There was a later time when five of Fitch's plays were running simultaneously.) In December of 1900, Fitch was a very busy man. He rehearsed Amelia Bingham in *The Climbers* from 10:00 to 2:30. From 2:30 until 6:00, he rehearsed Ethel Barrymore in *Captain Jinks of the Horse Marines*. His two other plays that season were *Barbara Frietchie*, in which Julia Marlowe was acting, and *Lover's Lane*, which had a less distinguished cast.

Once Clyde Fitch got his foot in the door, he dominated Broadway drama. Having had four plays on view simultaneously in the season of

1900–1901, he had three on view simultaneously in the autumn of the next season: *The Way of the World*, with Elsie de Wolfe; *The Girl and the Judge*, with Annie Russell; and *The Marriage Game*, with Guy Bates Post, Junius B. Booth, and Winchell Smith. Fitch knew his stars and contrived to present them attractively. Since Miss de Wolfe was famous

Clyde Fitch directing Maxine Elliott and Charles Cherry in *Her Own Way* at the Garrick Theater (1898). (*The New York Public Library*)

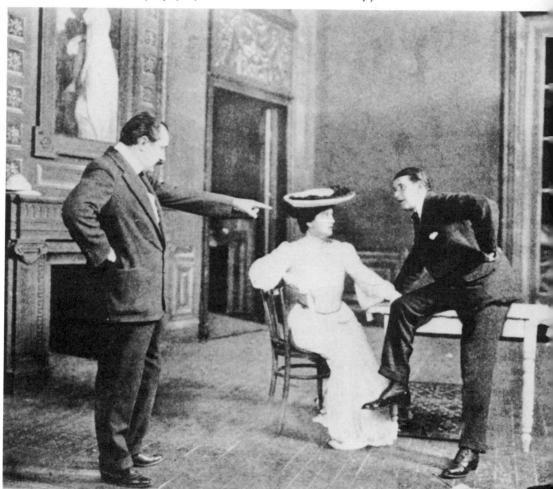

for her neighborly habit of nodding to her friends in the audience, Fitch wrote one scene in which she appeared to be riding in an automobile through Central Park. As the automobile (a very smart prop in those days) gave the illusion of puttering along, Miss de Wolfe nodded to her friends without getting out of character.

Fitch had a special talent for writing female characters that female stars could act agreeably. Maxine Elliott, known as "Venus de Milo with arms," was the most sensationally beautiful woman on Broadway. She was the wife of Nat Goodwin, who had such good taste in women that he married several of them. The Goodwins lived at 326 West End Avenue, which was so far from the theater district that Miss Elliott was compelled to drive her own car back and forth. As she bowled up Fifth Avenue seated at the driver's tiller she lifted up the spirits of the masses, who recognized her and saluted her. It grieved many of her admirers that she had little talent for acting. But in 1903, Clyde Fitch took care of that. He wrote her a comedy called *Her Own Way*, in which for the first time she looked like an actress. She was grateful. Even in the rehearsals, she said, she knew what she was doing.

Clyde Fitch was a charming, modest man whose many letters to his many friends preserve the loyalty and generosity of a gentleman. Everything about him remains attractive to this day—except, unfortunately, his plays. Before he died in 1909 at the age of forty-three, he had written thirty-three original plays and twenty-two adaptations and dramatizations.

Fitch was born in Elmira, New York, and educated at Amherst College, where he dazzled his fellow students with his flair for dress and his virtuosity as an amateur actor. Among other parts, he played Lydia Languish in *The Rivals* and Peggy Thrift in *The Country Girl*.

At the suggestion of E. A. Dithmar, then drama critic of *The New York Times*, Richard Mansfield put Clyde Fitch on salary in 1889 to write a play that turned out to be *Beau Brummell*. It was written for Mansfield at a time when stars habitually supervised the writing of scripts to suit their talents. Since *Beau Brummell* was one of Mansfield's greatest and most memorable successes, the truth of the authorship provoked a controversy that lasted until after Fitch's death. William Winter, the pious and vindictive critic of the *New York Tribune*, claimed credit for having suggested the play to Mansfield, and he refused to credit Fitch with any part of the authorship. In an appendix to his omniscient and sanctimonious life of Mansfield many years later, Winter declared that

Beau Brummell was written by Mansfield "with the clerical cooperation of another hand." Years before that snide comment, Fitch had been, as usual, amiable about the whole situation. "The idea of a play on 'Beau Brummell' is, I believe, Mr. William Winter's. The execution of that play—Mr. Winter claims it has been an execution in more senses than one—some of the business and the great bulk of the dialogue are mine. The artistic touch, some of the lines in the comedy (not the important ones) and the genius that has made it a success are Mr. Mansfield's." One cannot read Fitch's letters and the many records of his life without having a great liking for a sensitive and overburdened man.

Outwardly Fitch was the epitome of success. Once his career had started moving, it mushroomed and he indulged his love of luxury on a fabulous scale. But he kept on working vehemently, as if he were afraid to stop. Archie Bell remarked that he "lived like a sultan and worked like a dock laborer on an eighteen-hour shift." A dapper, fastidiously-groomed man with a guard's moustache, he had a town house at 113 East 40th Street and two country estates—one in Greenwich, Connecticut, the other in Katonah, New York. In New York City, he was so busy that people had to make an appointment twenty-four hours in advance to talk to him on the telephone. His desk was so cluttered with photographs, souvenirs, geegaws, and trays of unanswered letters that he hardly had room to write. His library was described by one interviewer as "Psychological"; it included *Twelve Bad Men, Twelve Bad Women, Famous Crimes,* and *Celebrated Poisoners*—clues to his point of view about the theater.

Every summer, Fitch traveled abroad, but not for rest, apparently. He worked at sea; he worked on land. He wrote one of his two most famous plays, *The Truth,* while floating in a gondola on the Grand Canal. His friend, Robert Herrick, who went abroad with him one summer, reported that while they were driving through the blossoming Sicilian countryside, Fitch wrote on a pad of paper on his knee. He seems to have been psychotic about writing; he did not dare stop. Some scribbler in *The Sun* illustrated his speed in a sequence of verses labeled "A Hustling Histrionicus":

> Swat,
> And out of the glittering social grot,

> Of the very Fitchiest, fetchingest lot,
> Stirred in the scorching society pot,
> Hot,
> He plucks a wild, weird name and plot;
> Whiz!
> Through all the scenic mysteries,
> The gayly appareled fantasies,
> Likewise the dramatic unities,
> He shoves his pen until he makes it sizz.
> Biff!
> Act I,—Act II,—Act III, as if
> The thing were a cigarette to whiff.
> Slambang,
> The word goes to the Broadway gang;
> Hooray!
> Clyde Fitch has written another play!

Most of the plays were ephemeral commercial shows written at top speed for the Broadway market. Even the best of them, *The Truth* and *The City*, were hackwork by the standards of a half century later. Fitch shared with his Broadway contemporaries a lack of interest in first causes—in God, in fate, in the loneliness and defenselessness of human beings in an ambiguous world, or whatever the primary subjects of art and philosophy may be. Like the theater of his time, he had a superficial attitude towards life. When he chose a good subject, as in his two best plays or in *The Climbers*, he did not contribute much that was original or decisive. The comparison with Edith Wharton in the novel is pertinent. She, too, had a limited range of themes and of personal experience, but in her best novels she made vigorous statements. In *The House of Mirth*, which Fitch dramatized, and in *The Age of Innocence*, she wrote out of strength and conviction about the superficiality, the narrowness and smugness of society. She was in complete command of the medium. She dominated it because her mind was clear.

But Fitch never escaped from the scheme of the popular play that followed the melodramatic formula—all the material having been arranged to build a strong last act. It was the day of the "obligatory scene." If a play "worked," it fulfilled its purpose. When Fitch introduced something that was scandalous, like the suspicion of the clandestine affair between a married woman of high social standing and a society rake in *The*

Truth, or like the inadvertent marriage of a drug addict to his half sister in *The City,* he and his audience felt that the requirements for a good play had been met. Lucile Watson, Walter Hampden, and Mary Nash acted in Fitch's *The City* in 1909, and the reviews were exuberant. Audiences gasped in the last act when the rebellious daughter of the family found that she had married her half brother. Women in the audience shrieked; men shouted with horror, or so it was reported. *The City* was founded on the myth that the country is pure and the city evil. When, in the last act, the son discovered that his father had died in a squalid family brawl, he was not surprised. "It means New York for me," he said scornfully. He had known that the city would corrupt the entire family. In *The City,* as in the typical play of that period, a strong last act was the real point of the play, whatever the truths of life might be.

Fitch resented being called superficial. Although he was sensationally successful—perhaps because he was sensationally successful—he was touchy about criticism. His anguish is contained in one letter he wrote to John Corbin, critic at that time of *The New York Times,* and a personal friend. For some reason that cannot be defined now—a stricken conscience? a sense of betrayal?—Corbin sent Fitch the advance proofs of an article he had written for *Scribner's Magazine.* Among other things, the article stated that Fitch was a superficial playwright who had written some offensive plays and that he had had the greatest number of failures of any contemporary writer. Naturally, Fitch was grievously wounded. Only a priggish critic would expect a friend to acquiesce in hostile criticism. In a mild but somber letter, Fitch replied that Corbin had become a harsher critic of his plays after the two men got on a friendly basis. "Deliver us from our friends," Fitch retorted. Although his letter is polite and forbearing, it contains the grief of a man who has been deeply hurt. There are subsequent letters to both Mr. and Mrs. Corbin, and they are invariably affectionate and appreciative. Although Fitch was a superficial playwright, he was not a superficial friend.

Since he was accused of being a trifling writer, he was once gratified to be invited to speak about the state of the drama to an audience at Harvard. The address illustrates the subtleties of social demarcations of the time, as well as the thinking of a man who was serious about his profession. Fitch made social and intellectual distinctions between the downstairs and upstairs audiences that today seem patronizing and artificial. He referred to "the plush audiences downstairs and the up-holstered hearts in the gallery" as if the people who bought cheap seats had less taste than those who paid top prices. He called them the "long-distance trolley audiences" that flocked to such plays as *The Christian, Ben Hur, Way Down East, The Servant in the House,* and the Ben Greet Players. "They are the old-time Lyceum lecture audiences," he said, and he seemed to think that they were ridiculous.

But his maxims of playwriting are still acceptable. He said that good technique never kept a play alive—although he was pre-eminently a technician. He said that a good playwright must create good characters and leave the course of the play to them—still an acceptable maxim, and one that he was unable to follow. "American audiences say 'Show us our social predicament,'" he declared, and that is sound doctrine today, including the word "predicament," which is still part of the acceptable academic vocabulary. In the back of his head, Fitch had an enlightened notion of the artist's milieu. But it is symptomatic of his taste that he thought that Eugene Walter's maudlin and melodramatic *Paid in Full* was "probably the most perfect play written by an American." That argues Fitch's modesty. He himself wrote several plays better than *Paid in Full.*

In the winter of 1908–09, Fitch was in bad health. He was advised to stop working and take a long rest. That was impossible for him to do, although he did curtail some of his activities. He felt, or thought he felt, better in the spring, and he went abroad, as usual. While he was traveling in France, he had another of his recurrent attacks of appendicitis. This one was serious. He went to the hospital at Châlons-sur-Marne for an operation on August 28, 1909. He died there alone on September 4. Since trans-Atlantic mails were slow in those days, many people in New York had the poignant experience of receiving cheerful postcards and stimulating letters from him long after his death. Many of the letters, particularly those to Lucile Watson, were concerned with *The City,* which he expected to stage as soon as he returned from Europe. It was staged by others, on December 21 of that year, in the beautifully appointed Lyric Theater, and it was received with excitement. It had the sort of sensational success that Fitch would have reveled in. He had been unfairly accused of being unable to write women characters, but the women in *The City* were highly esteemed as characters. "Perfection of artistic growth," said Arthur Hornblow in *Theatre Magazine.*

The next year, Walter Prichard Eaton, an excellent critic, made some comments on Fitch that are still pertinent. Although he recognized the hackneyed elements in Fitch's plays, he said that Fitch made American themes respectable, that he raised the cultural level of the theater, and that he also raised the level of staging by his meticulous personal direction. In 1910, there were more American plays than foreign plays on Broadway stages. Eaton thought that the pioneering work of Fitch was responsible and that, for all practical purposes, modern American playwriting began with him.

THE PROBLEM OF

BERNARD SHAW

Since Bernard Shaw was not a mediocre writer, he outraged the hucksters of Broadway, to say nothing of Police Magistrate William McAdoo and various men of God. But Broadway can take credit for having discovered Shaw as a man of unique talents. And his earliest admirers were not confined to what became the Shaw cult. No American playwright at that time and few foreign playwrights could hold a candle to this witty intellectual. Before English and European audiences had accepted him, Broadway realized that he was not a freak.

Richard Mansfield, originally a comedy actor, introduced Shaw to Broadway before the turn of the century. In 1894, he played *Arms and the Man*—the first Shaw production in America. In 1899, he had a sensational success with *The Devil's Disciple*. Thanks to Mansfield, Shaw began to earn enough money from the theater to think of himself as a professional dramatist. But Mansfield was too much of an egotist to

Richard Mansfield in *The Devil's Disciple* (1896).
(*The New York Public Library*)

capitulate to another egotist. He rejected *Candida* as being a wordy sermon and not a play; he rejected *Caesar and Cleopatra*, *The Philanderer*, and *You Never Can Tell*. Although Shaw wrote *The Man of Destiny* for Mansfield, he reserved it for Ellen Terry and Henry Irving at the time when Mansfield was being patronizing towards Shaw. The association of Shaw and Mansfield was pleasant in the beginning, but it got chilly when Mansfield decided to have a life of his own. Shaw was not only prolific but voracious; he consumed useful people.

It was Arnold Daly who established Shaw on Broadway as a man of sustained talent. Daly was an impulsive actor, born in Brooklyn and originally an office boy for Charles Frohman. He first appeared on Broadway in a dramatization of *Puddin'head Wilson* and acted with Julia Marlowe in *Barbara Frietchie*. He read the Shaw plays in *Plays, Pleasant and Unpleasant*. He was fascinated with the text of *Candida*. In 1903, when he was acting in Clyde Fitch's *Major André*, he and Winchell Smith pooled their resources of $350 to put on *Candida* for a trial matinee at the Princess Theater. Much to their delight, *Candida* was popular immediately. After presenting a few more matinee performances, they moved it to the Madison Square Theater where it began a long run. Daly then gave his audiences a bonus by playing the one-act *The Man of Destiny* on the same bill—wrecking his health without increasing his profits. Shaw then wrote *How He Lied to Her Husband* as a companion piece to *The Man of Destiny*, and Daly had another success. In 1905, he produced *You Never Can Tell*—successfully; then *John Bull's Other Island*—unsuccessfully. "A thick glutinous and imponderable four-act tract," said Alan Dale, critic for the Hearst papers; the audience was "bored to utter extinction," said Acton Davies of *The Evening Sun*.

About this time, an English actor, Robert Loraine, read *Man and Superman* on a railroad journey through the United States. His wife later wrote that, after reading the text, he "danced a jig of delight up and down the corridor of the train, elated beyond bounds by the brilliance of the book itself, and rejoicing at the prospect of producing and acting in a masterpiece." After several managers in America had refused to produce it, Charles Frohman produced it for Loraine at the capacious Hudson Theater, where it was immediately successful.

Up to this time, Shaw had been dismissed as the foible of a cult. But now it was apparent that the general public liked him. *The Evening Post* welcomed him as a writer who not only had a mind of his own but also assumed that the audience had minds. Now the newspapers and magazines were full of articles about and by this startling prodigy. Shaw reveled in it. He became an unfailing source of outrageous opinions, insults to America, and boasting. Interviewers from the American press who visited him at his flat in Adelphi Terrace came away with bright bundles of his iconoclasms and braggadocio. To judge by the correspondence in newspapers and magazines, people were startled, stimulated, and skeptical.

But Shaw affronted the people of propriety. They complained that he knew nothing about human nature and that his characters were "idea units." "Play cobbler," "cynic," "perverter of the truth," he was called. William Winter made a magisterial judgment: Shaw is a "man of very little importance. . . . I do not care to waste thought on him." When *Man and Superman* became a success and the great mob started to go to it, *Theatre Magazine* warned Shaw that if he took liberties with his audiences, "he would learn a thing or two." Police Magistrate McAdoo declared that there was no room in New York for a play that ridiculed marriage, because Theodore Roosevelt had just pointed out that marriage was the basis of any healthy civilization. At the same time, McAdoo also stated his own credo for drama criticism. He said that he preferred the "old melodrama where the hero was a gentleman, the villain everything that should be hissed, and everything came out right at the end." The New York Public Library put *Man and Superman* on the restricted list to keep it out of reach of young, untutored minds that might enjoy it. Confronted with the principle of the Life Force and eugenics in *Man and Superman*, the *Cosmopolitan* magazine said that the "stock breeder" was "well enough in its place, but he must not supplant all the noble ideas which up to the present time have distinguished man from his quadruped brethren." Augustus Thomas, ever the defender of banality, publicly doubted Shaw's sincerity.

Shaw was delighted by all such evidences of bigotry and stupidity. "Comstockery," he cried, thus creating a word that Anthony Comstock, the purity crusader, did not wholly appreciate. Shaw went further. He said that America was provincial—a charge that hurt because it was true. He declared that he would never visit America until it reached maturity. At the age of fifty, when most men would have begun to settle down, Shaw was just getting under way and he was full of enthusiasm, wit, and heresy.

Then Daly produced *Mrs. Warren's Profession*. Broadway was scandalized and thrilled. In New Haven, where the trial performance was staged, the police commissioner had threatened to cancel the license of the theater if the performance were repeated. Two weeks before the opening performance at the Garrick Theater in New York, all the tickets were sold and speculators were getting $30 to $40 for tickets on the black market. Magistrate McAdoo could get nothing better than a balcony seat, although he was moved downstairs when his presence became known. After the performance, reporters from *The World* polled the first night audience about the fitness of the play: 304 of the first-nighters thought it was "fit"; 272 said "unfit."

But the cast was trundled off to the precinct station in the paddy wagon and charged with disorderly conduct, and the production was closed. Except for one favorable review in the *Staats-Zeitung*, the press exploded with shock, disgust, and rage. A drama about the economics of prostitution seemed to them to be pornography. Pinero's *The Second Mrs. Tanqueray* and *The Notorious Mrs. Ebbsmith* had discussed the economic basis for sexual and social immorality, but with such a sanctimonious tone that the public felt happily uplifted. The unemotional tone of Shaw's discussion of the economics of prostitution shocked theatergoers; they expected that the brothel-keeper in the play would be—one must not say unfrocked—but at least humiliated and punished. Dr. C. H. Parkhurst, the eminent divine, called it a "heap of moral rot." Dr. Felix Adler, of the Society of Ethical Culture, pronounced the play immoral and expressed alarm over the presence in the audience of young people with no experience in the economics of lechery. After brooding for eight months, the Court of Special Sessions acquitted Daly of the charge of disorderly conduct with an opinion that put the values of art in order: "If virtue does not receive its usual reward in this play, vice at least is presented in an odious light and its votaries are punished. The attack on social conditions is one which might result in effecting needed reforms. The court cannot refrain from suggesting, however, that the reforming influence of the play in this regard is minimized by the method of the attack."

In October 1906, a year after the infamous opening, *Mrs. Warren's Profession* was put on again, but no one seemed much interested this time. "A dull, uninteresting play on a theme obnoxious to every healthy-minded theatergoer," said *Theatre Magazine*, meanwhile warning Shaw to mind his own business. Since America was a big country, the magazine announced that America didn't need any help or instruction from Shaw.

But Shaw continued to be popular with people who went to the theater. In 1906, Forbes-Robertson and his wife, Gertrude Elliott (Maxine Elliott's sister), were enthusiastically received in *Caesar and Cleopatra*—a sardonic play that might be expected to have upset idolators of Shakespeare, who had written a serious play on a related subject. On Broadway, Shaw was among friends at a time when cant ruled the rest of the theater. In the year of *Caesar and Cleopatra,* James J. Corbett, the ex-champion prize-fighter, played Cashel Byron in *Cashel Byron's Profession,* made from Shaw's novel about the inconstancy of life in the ring. The play collapsed —under the weight of Corbett's acting, someone said. In the last act, Corbett was on his feet, but Shaw was flat on the canvas.

But the derision was genial. In its most sluggish, commonplace period, Broadway was enthusiastic about the most original, impudent, and revolutionary dramatist in English letters. There was a cult that expressed contempt for Broadway by hero-worshiping Shaw. The respectable, pleasure-seeking theatergoers who are always the backbone of the theater knew that Shaw was a remarkable man and acted accordingly. In the bright period of the twenties and thirties, Shaw had his loyalest advocate in the Theater Guild. It staged the world premières of *Back to Methuselah, Heartbreak House,* and *Saint Joan.* Shaw abused the Guild, teased it, poked fun at it, upbraided it. But the Guild took his quirks of temperament in good part and performed a priceless service in promoting the giddy plays of the sanest of men. The story of Shaw and Broadway is a charming one.

PLAY CARPENTERS

In 1905, a foreigner who was visiting Broadway was quoted as follows: "Are you all children in America? There is not a serious thought, not a suggestion of intellect in anything I have seen. I predict that there will be no dramatic art in America for another twenty years."

He was wrong about the date. By 1925, several American playwrights, beginning with Eugene O'Neill, had written a number of plays of artistic or intellectual merit. But he was dismally right about the first ten or fifteen years of the century. At a time when English, European, and Russian dramatists were writing like men of talent and ideas, even the best American plays contained a large infusion of claptrap, and were accepted as art because they obviously had nothing to do with life.

The season of 1906–1907 was notable because for the first time Broadway presented the scripts of several American playwrights. Clyde Fitch's *The Truth* and *The Straight Road*, William Gillette's *Clarice*, David

Otis Skinner as he appeared in *The Honor of the Family* (1908).
(*The New York Public Library*)

Belasco's *The Rose of the Rancho* (based on *Juanita*, by Richard Walton Tully), George Broadhurst's *The Man of the Hour*, Charles Klein's *The Lion and the Mouse*, Langdon Mitchell's *The New York Idea*, William Vaughn Moody's *The Great Divide*, Percy MacKaye's *Jeanne d'Arc*, and Rachel Crothers' first play, *The Three of Us*, were produced that year. *The Great Divide*, *The New York Idea*, and *Jeanne d'Arc* represented attempts to shake the Broadway theater out of its insularity. They were the most independent, the least mechanical American plays of the season. But since they were written in an environment of hokum, bits of hokum inevitably adhered to them.

Moody's *The Great Divide* contrasted the freedom of the West with the cautious piety of New England, which was a valid point of view at the time. But as a work of art, it was flawed by the primitive craftsmanship of that era—melodramatic villainy in the first act and a kind of mawkish reward for virtue at the end. The original cast was vigorous and colorful—Margaret Anglin, Henry Miller, Laura Hope Crews and Mrs. Thomas Whiffen, all of whom were forceful and accomplished actors. And the critics were appreciative. John Corbin described *The Great Divide* as the best American drama up to that time; he was favorably impressed by its fullness, wholesomeness of feeling, and technical firmness; and Walter Prichard Eaton described it as the first drama "to find the American soul." These were perceptive observations that must not be taken lightly more than a half century later. For Moody, a teacher of English at the University of Chicago, was an exceptional individual by the standards of Broadway. He was scholar, poet, man of independent thought, an optimist and idealist. *The Miracle Man*, which Henry Miller produced in 1909—the year before Moody's untimely death—communicated his religious exaltation in the high-minded manner of *The Servant in the House* and *The Passing of the Third Floor Back*. But both *The Great Divide* and *The Miracle Man* lack the rigorous style and boldness of thought that characterize genuine achievements in the theater. Moody's talent was limited by the mediocrity of the theater of his time.

Percy MacKaye, son of Steele MacKaye, the enterprising nineteenth-century actor and producer, was also a poet and man of letters, and he was profoundly disenchanted with the Broadway theater. He thought it was cheap and trivial. To escape the monotony of Broadway, he resorted to literary themes, and he wrote some of his plays in verse. The *Jeanne d'Arc* that was produced in 1907 had Sothern and Marlowe in the leading roles, and it was more successful than spectacular dramas by Hauptmann and Sudermann that year. MacKaye wrote on other literary themes—*The Can-*

terbury Pilgrims, Sappho and Phaon, and *The Scarecrow*, which was based
on a story by Nathaniel Hawthorne. During his long career, which lasted·until
1949, when the Pasadena Playhouse produced his mammoth drama based
on *Hamlet*, he wrote an occasional play for the commercial theater, notably
Anti-Matrimony, which was a satire on radical ideas about marriage es-
poused by the plays of Ibsen, Shaw, and Hauptmann. He also wrote several
pageants for community celebrations. But MacKaye did not have much
success in either the commercial or non-commercial theater. Perhaps because of his preoccupation with medievalism, and his contentment with
library themes, he never really came to grips with the realities of life. Even
in *The Scarecrow*, which was done in Europe as well as in America, his
characters were elusive and his story precious and ephemeral. His poetic
mood became a denial of theater.

Langdon Mitchell's *The New York Idea* was a sophisticated comedy of
manners. It was superior to the plays of Arthur Pinero and Henry Arthur
Jones that came to Broadway with the considerable cachet of success in
London. No one expected an American writer to be cleverer than most
West End dramatists, but Mitchell was. He was the son of an eminent
Philadelphia physician and writer, Dr. S. Weir Mitchell. In 1899, he had
dramatized *Becky Sharp* from Thackeray's novel for Mrs. Fiske. He also
wrote *The New York Idea* for her. It satirized the follies of men and
women of wealth and social eminence who divorced one another frivolously.
Although the title contained the words "New York," Mitchell said that the
characters were based on people he knew in Philadelphia. In print, the play
now seems a little too ingenious, the characters a little too broad, and the
craftsmanship too intricate and clever. But actors can frequently improve
the tone of an author's work, and the actors who first played in *The New
York Idea* in 1906 had vivid personalities—Mrs. Fiske, Emily Stevens,
Dudley Digges, and George Arliss. All of them were young and must have
given stunning performances.

When *The New York Idea* was acted in Chicago, Percy Hammond in
the *Chicago Post* said that Mr. Mitchell's "merry comedy romps away
from Mr. Clyde Fitch in shining small talk, breezes past Mr. Augustus
Thomas in creating the atmosphere of the same environment, is closely
bunched with Mr. Pinero and Mr. Henry Arthur Jones in the perfection of
its craftsmanship and is in a fair way to gallop home with season's first
money." Not everyone felt so gay about it. *The New York Dramatic
Mirror*, published by Mrs. Fiske's husband, unctuously observed that
divorce was not a funny subject, although Mr. Mitchell managed to make
it seem so. James Metcalfe, drama critic of the original *Life* (a humor

Henry Miller and Margaret Anglin in *The Great Divide* (1906). (*The New York Public Library*)

magazine) took a highly responsible moral attitude towards Mr. Mitchell's frisky comedy: "Gentlemen like Mr. Mitchell," he wrote, "do not appreciate perhaps the power of the medium they command, and, therefore, do not stop to think that they should be careful, very careful, how they use it, lest they sow evil in minds not able to understand the good they intend." Since 1906, divorce has become common in America. Did Mr. Metcalfe put his finger on the man who was to blame?

Probably Mr. Metcalfe would have had more confidence in the works of George Broadhurst, Charles Klein, and Eugene Walter, who had a knack for the sort of melodrama that poses as a serious study of morals. Except in one notorious case, virtue triumphed in the last acts of their plays. Klein's *The Lion and the Mouse* recorded the gratifying triumph of the daughter of an old judge who had been ruined by a business tycoon. By anonymously getting a job as secretary of the vicious tycoon, she was able to steal "the papers" and vindicate her father. The character of the villain was based on John D. Rockefeller, a man of considerable craft and substance, and one of the actors was made up to look like H. H. Rogers, a Rockefeller associate and, incidentally, the financial advisor to Mark Twain. *The Lion and the Mouse* was all craftsmanship. Klein defined his principles of playwriting after the success of his *The Music Master*, which had been produced in 1904. When he began to write a play, he said, his characters were only "mental abstractions." The mechanics of the play

Garraway-Byron, Robert Homans, Oswald Yorke, and Guy Bates Post in *The Nigger*, by Edward Sheldon, at the New Theater (1909). (*The New York Public Library*)

came first: "The characters are mere puppets, bobbing about at the will of the monarch Mechanics."

Eugene Walter's most spectacular success was *The Easiest Way*, produced by David Belasco in 1908 with Frances Starr in the leading part. *The Easiest Way* was a scandal, a sensation, and a success—the three bright "S's" of show business. It told the story of a mediocre actress who was an accomplished mistress but had the misfortune to fall in love with a virtuous newspaperman who despised sin. She made a valiant attempt to go straight on a limited income. Walter's great achievement in *The Easiest Way* was his flouting of the formula. Virtue did not win. The mediocre actress returned to vice, to which she knew herself better suited. "Dress up my body and paint my face. Yes, I'm going back to Rector's to make a hit and to hell with the rest," Frances Starr recklessly announced at the end of the play. This shocking defiance of the melodramatic formula was as celebrated in its day as Nora's slamming of the door in the last act of Ibsen's *A Doll's House*. Inadvertently, it made a lot of Broadway's bright people feel very self-conscious about dropping into Rector's after the show. Five years later, this cheerful, brightly lighted, sophisticated theater restaurant went into bankruptcy.

The Easiest Way gave the critic of *The New York Dramatic Mirror* a perverse thrill. He doubted that such a wicked play should be seen in public, but praised it as flawless work. He regarded this hocus-pocus story as "disgustingly true." Most of the hits were less radical than *The Easiest Way*. In Walter's *Paid in Full* (1908), an unimaginative clerk stole $19,000 from his employer. His wife told the whole truth to the employer. Instead of punishing the clerk, the employer let him resign because it was worth $19,000 to find an honest woman. In Walter's *Just a Wife* (1910), a wife defeated her husband's mistress by being patient, selfless, and noble. This was more than the mistress could stand; she disintegrated physically as she had already disintegrated morally. In George Broadhurst's *Bought and Paid For* (1911), a poor telephone operator married a rich man who was also a heavy drinker. In the second act, she refused to perform the foremost duty of a wife because he was drunk. She locked the door to her bedroom. At the end of the second act, he broke down the door and poured himself in, intent on legal lechery. The scene was sensational. No one had realized that rich men acted that way. In the last act, the husband, now sober and perhaps suffering from a hangover, swore he would never drink again, and his wife felt very happy. Virtue triumphed, as in real life.

This was the era when Augustus Thomas was at the peak of his long career. His *The Witching Hour*, which is included in many standard texts of the American drama, was produced in 1908, with John Mason, a gentlemanly actor, playing the part of a gambler of superior breeding. Thomas, born in 1857, was a bluff, hearty, good-humored journeyman of the theater. In a career that lasted from 1875 to 1934, he wrote fifty-seven plays. A Middle Westerner, he had a broad and practical experience in railroading, reading law, managing a theater, and acting in amateur theatricals, and he brought to Broadway a wealth of knowledge about American life that no other playwright had.

In no sense parochial, he took an active interest in politics. In the same year that *The Witching Hour* was produced, he seconded the nomination of William Jennings Bryan for president at the Denver convention. It tells something of the geniality of his personality that he was a popular toastmaster. Since his memory went back to the Civil War, when he was a boy, he had constructive ideas about American life, and he wrote several regional plays that dealt with national attitudes and local characteristics— *Alabama, In Mizzoura, The Capitol, Arizona, Colorado, Rio Grande,* and others. He was a homespun American writer.

It is characteristic of his point of view as a writer that *The Witching Hour* derived from some experience he had had in his youth as advance-man for a mindreader with the imposing name of Washington Irving Bishop. *The Witching Hour* was a drama about telepathy, spiritualism, and hypnotism. A weak young man inexplicably murdered a man who had showed him a cat's-eye ring. Later it appeared that a cat's eye had been an evil talisman in the emotional life of a previous generation in his family, and so the young man could not be considered responsible. That was one theme. Another involved the gambler's gift for hypnotism: he hypnotized the public into controlling the minds of a jury. He hypnotized the villain into dropping his revolver ("You can't shoot—that gun—you can't even hold it"), and at the end he confessed that he had probably caused the murder by having previously imagined it. In 1908, the play was a sensation. Now it seems mindless and crude. The stilted dialogue of the period is indicated by an exchange between Lew, an attendant in a gambling house, and Alice, a lady of refinement:

Lew: Why, that's the damndest thing. (*To Alice*) I beg your pardon.
Alice: Don't please—some manly emphasis is a real comfort.

Thomas' *The Copperhead*, which was produced in 1918 with Lionel Barrymore and William Morris, illustrated his interest in themes involving American patriotism. Dramatized from a story by Frederic Landis, *The*

Copperhead chronicled the ordeal of an Illinois farmer who posed as a Southern sympathizer in order to transmit intelligence to the Union Army. His mother, his wife, his son, and his neighbors despised him for his loyalty to the South, not only during the Civil War but for twenty years afterwards. In the "obligatory scene" in the last act, he translated himself out of perfidy into heroism by belatedly telling everyone that he had spied for the union and by invoking the personality of Lincoln. Like most of his contemporaries, Thomas approached the theater as a form of buncombe. It is significant of his taste that he once said scornfully that he never felt impelled to see more than one play by Ibsen or one play by Shaw. He felt more comfortable with the mumbo-jumbo of the commercial theater. As a good citizen, he led an honest life; but, like most Broadway people, he saw nothing inconsistent in playing the drama with marked cards.

It is not surprising that the hacks should have flourished on Broadway. They have always flourished there. Nine of every ten plays are not only

financial failures but failures of thought and style. But in the first two decades of the century mediocrity went further. The hacks tainted talented writers who might have accomplished something of permanent significance if the standards of the time had been more discriminating. A case in point was Edward B. Sheldon, a legendary character in the Broadway theater, less because of what he wrote than what he was. He was an attractive, brilliant, gregarious, wealthy young man who was fascinated by the theater when he was a youth in Chicago and was precocious about the theater when he went east to Harvard. Years later some of his classmates remembered that Sheldon was the one student who had the knowledge, the taste, and the manners to entertain Mrs. Fiske when she visited Harvard to speak on the "Ethics of the Theater." He arrived a little late to the party,

Madge Kennedy, Ralph Morgan, Hamilton Revelle, Janet Beecher, and John Cumberland in *Fair and Warmer* (1915). (*The New York Public Library*)

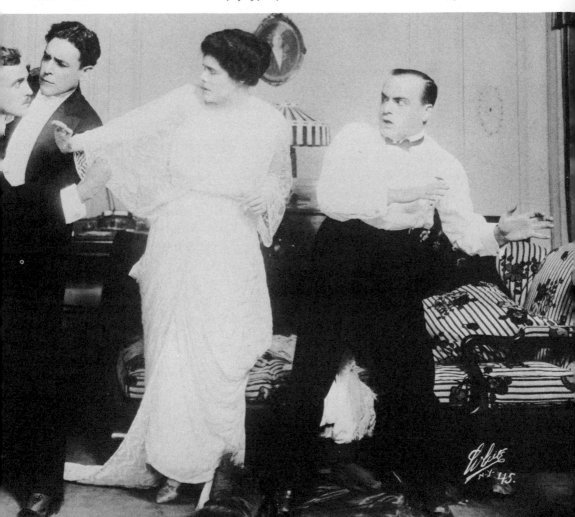

but he presented Mrs. Fiske with a bouquet of flowers and could talk to her about the theater like a professional. He knew all about her career and the affairs of Broadway in general. He also knew that she was a crusader against cruelty to animals.

After he graduated from Harvard in 1907 ("A pink-cheeked boy," Mrs. Fiske said), he wrote *Salvation Nell,* in which she acted in 1908, and he became a celebrity overnight. He lived extravagantly, had many friends to whom he was wholly devoted, and worked on more than one script at a time. He lived in a luxurious apartment in Gramercy Park. John Barrymore, also a brilliant man about town, was one of his cronies. During the rest of his brief career, Sheldon wrote *The Nigger* (1910), which was the only American play included in the first season of the New Theater; *The Boss* (1911); and *Romance* (1913), which he gave to Doris Keane, an actress he loved and admired. She played it all over the world with great success. These were his most important plays. But he later adapted Sem Benelli's *The Jest* for John and Lionel Barrymore and collaborated with other playwrights—*The Bewitched,* with Sidney Howard (1924); *Lulu Belle,* with Charles MacArthur (1926); *Jenny,* with Margaret Ayer Barnes (1929); and *Dishonored Lady,* with Mrs. Barnes (1930).

Since Sheldon was an educated young man with a genuine understanding of the craft of the theater and cultivated standards of taste in literature, he was qualified to write on a higher level than his contemporaries. But, like them, he thought of plays in terms of craftsmanship. He was not motivated to write by what he saw and experienced in life. He wrote on plausible topics that might produce a hit. *Salvation Nell,* which had forty-two characters and a naturalistic setting in the Belasco style, was a compilation of clichés—maudlin, sentimental, melodramatic. Nell was a noble, humble little drab with a heart of gold who remained loyal to her brutal lover, who was in jail at the moment. Faced with having to make a choice by the hard circumstances of her life, she chose to work with the Salvation Army instead of leading the lazy life of a brothel. "You wonderful little wisp of humanity," said a rich young man who had fallen hopelessly in love with her. The first act ended with Christmas carols, the second with the Lord's Prayer, and the third with prayer and hymns. Sheldon had accumulated his local color by attending Salvation Army meetings in disguise. He wrote *Salvation Nell* from the outside, like a tourist.

The Nigger, which Sheldon wrote from a magazine article, was a melodrama about a Southern governor who was trying to control rioting against Negroes. In the last act, the governor found that he was part Negro —grandson of his grandfather's Negro mistress. Now *The Nigger* seems naïve and sophomoric, but it alarmed some of the citizens in 1910 who felt touchy about such topics. *Theatre Magazine* observed by way of prudence that, if the Negro had his full rights in the South, the whites would disappear into "the black quicksand"; it predicted that "the races will be kept apart." *The Boss*, also written from a newspaper article, was a melodrama about a vulgar, ruthless political boss who forced the daughter of a rich contractor to marry him. *Romance* was a rueful tale about a randy parson who was smitten with a lady of easy virtue, who in turn preserved his virtue despite himself. It was all very educational and uplifting.

At the peak of his success in 1917, Sheldon was stricken with arthritis; it gradually and irrevocably petrified him. He lived until 1946—paralyzed, blind, immobile, a living mummy, but one who grew tall and sweet in spirit by devoting the rest of his life to his friends. The more humiliating and crippling his physical condition became, the more exalted became his influence on other people. He was wealthy enough to maintain a comfortable establishment and complete independence. In his last years, he looked like a wax image on a catafalque. But he lived in other people. He kept intimately in touch with them, thought about them, counseled them, gave them ideas, and inspired them. The stricken comforted the well. During the ordeal of this most baffling and cruel of afflictions, Sheldon flourished spiritually. If he had written plays on that level, he might have left his mark on the literature of the stage. He lived his life valiantly; he did not write it.

It was a happy time for Owen Davis and Avery Hopwood, playwrights who were content to write potboilers. Of all the journeymen at that time, the ablest, the most prolific, and the most disarming was Owen Davis, who was also one of the most delightful men on Broadway. He regarded Broadway as a pleasant place to earn a living. He is reputed to have written over 300 plays. But he thought that 150 to 200 would be nearer the mark. Never having had time to keep records, he could not be sure. At one time, seventeen of his plays were being acted somewhere simultaneously. His plays ranged in style from the most lurid melodramas, like *Her One False Step* and *Nellie, the Beautiful Cloak Model*, to serious dramas, like *The Detour* and *Icebound*, which won the Pulitzer Prize in 1923. After World War I, the Broadway theater began to mature, and Owen Davis, tired of trash, had the talent and the experience to keep pace with it.

For a routine playsmith in the early years of the twentieth century, he was unusually well educated. Born in Maine in 1874, he studied at the University of Tennessee and Harvard College. When he had finished college, he was better known as an athlete than a man of letters. The Charles Frohman reader who returned a report on Davis' first script wrote:

"You are strong and husky with, I have learned, some reputation as an athlete. Why don't you take this play of yours and see how far you can throw it." Davis signed his first contract with Gus Hill, a swinger of Indian clubs, who had never met an author before and was as startled as Davis was. Gus Hill was an amiable and persistent peddler of theater goods, who in the course of time trained and helped a lot of performers. He made an encouraging success of Owen Davis' first play, which was entitled *Through the Breakers*.

There was nothing pretentious about Owen Davis. He did not think of himself as either an artist or an intellectual, nor was he emotionally involved in movements to raise the cultural level of the theater. He noted that, at the Hollis Street Theater in Boston, the ushers quit because they could not understand the high-minded plays by William Dean Howells and Frank Stockton that were sponsored by the Society of Arts for audiences densely populated with Harvard professors. Owen Davis' principles of playwriting were simple. He thought that there were three basic themes: the Prodigal Son, Cinderella, and Mary Magdalene. Noting that the success of a melodrama depended largely upon the title, he never started to write a script until he knew what the last act was going to be. He obeyed certain sensible rules: Act 1, start the trouble; Act 2, here things look bad—the lady, having left home, is quite at the mercy of the villain; Act 3, the lady is saved by the stage carpenter. (The big scenic and mechanical effects were always in the third act); Act 4, the lovers are united and the villains are punished.

Davis could write a play overnight. When he was the manager of a stock company in Rochester and losing more money than he had, he happened to see a copy of *Under Two Flags* on a bookstand. He dramatized it before the next day and earned $10,250 from it in four weeks. When business got bad, he always wrote a new play.

The pitch of excitement whipped up by competent melodramas could sometimes produce anticlimaxes more notable than the climaxes. In *Nellie, the Beautiful Cloak Model*, the tireless villain went from one barbaric situation to another in an unforgiving attempt to remove Nellie from society. He threw her under a descending elevator—unsuccessfully. He tossed her off Brooklyn Bridge—still with no luck. He tied her to the railroad tracks—getting nowhere. In the last act, he trapped her in her bedroom. She tried to escape from him. "Why do you fear me, Nellie?" he inquired wistfully, as if he had not spent the whole evening trying to kill her. This is one of Owen Davis' imperishable lines.

He was a mild, modest man who was devoted to the theater, its people and its causes. In the twenties, when Broadway started to emerge from provinciality, he was able to write in the somber style that was leading to a new theater. He drew on memories of his boyhood in Maine to create authentic characters and to present them in elementary situations that portrayed their experience and attitudes. In 1921 with *The Detour*, he started to write on an entirely new level, and he might have won the Pulitzer Prize for *The Detour* if O'Neill's *Anna Christie* had not been produced that season. The next year, he did win the prize for *Icebound*—a competent run-of-the-mill drama based on the reading of a will. Although the characters were vigorously written by Davis and graphically stated in the acting of Phyllis Povah, Edna May Oliver, and Robert Ames, the plot came out of old-fashioned melodrama.

In later years, Owen Davis and his son Donald Davis turned Edith Wharton's *Ethan Frome* into a memorable tragic drama, in which Ruth Gordon, Pauline Lord, Raymond Massey, and Tom Ewell acted magnificently. Everyone was delighted to find the talents of a Broadway artisan so effectively put to the service of a moving theme. In his early days, Owen Davis accepted Broadway as the mart of show business, and he performed many chores there with craft, humor, and enjoyment. When he died in 1956 at the age of eighty-two, he was one of Broadway's grand old men. He had never been a cynic, even in those youthful days when he was writing claptrap.

In the early years of the century, the standards of prudery and decorum were high. The Puritan abhorrence of the theater, which began in Shakespeare's time, extended into New York in the twentieth century. In 1912, an audacious Methodist layman challenged the establishment by proposing that the church abandon the Methodist code, which prohibited dancing, games of chance, theatergoing, horse races, and circuses. To thousands of Americans, the theater was a scarlet woman. In Maine one summer, the director of a church choir asked a Broadway actress, who was sojourning in the neighborhood, to help with the singing of a complicated piece of music the next Sunday. When the elders heard about it, they revoked the invitation; an actress was not a suitable person to be admitted to a choir loft.

Hypocrisy was both petty and silly. When the New Theater had the temerity to produce H. Wiers-Jenssen's *The Witch*, *Theatre Magazine's* custodian of morals protected the public by the following bit of ingenious sophistry: "Guilty love is as old as Greek drama, but only with the aid of operatic music can its sentiment be made to prevail over the universal sense of social preservation." In other words, only bad acting of an evil theme and pompous music would keep society pure.

Joseph Pulitzer, publisher of *The World*, was anything but a sanctimonious man. But in 1911, when he came to write the terms for the
Pulitzer Prize, he automatically dropped into the moralizing unction of
the time: "For the original American play, performed in New York, which
shall best represent the educational value and power of the stage in raising
the standard of good morals, good taste and good manners." Nothing about
truth.

Ibsen and Strindberg outraged the morals of the orthodox. "Great as
the power of Ibsen and Strindberg may be," wrote one alarmed college
professor, "they present those facts of life which men must forget if life is
to be noble or even endurable." Truth could not set this academician free.

When Strindberg died in 1912, *Theatre Magazine* was unable to
eulogize him enthusiastically. It regretted that his view of life "was quite
subversive to progress." Since the editors of *Theatre Magazine* knew numbers of noble and lovely women, they could not tolerate Strindberg's pessimism about the women he knew. They thought that the most Strindberg
had accomplished was to provoke the rest of the world into taking issue
with him. His screams of rage over the first two of the three startled women
who had married him offended the gentlemen of Broadway.

But people who went to the Broadway theater were willing to laugh at
the facts of life. Avery Hopwood, a brilliant and prolific writer of farce,
regarded the conventional objection to "risqué" (his word) plays as a hangover from the Puritans, who frowned on anything enjoyable. Since the
racy aspects of life that were generally regarded as risqué were timeless and
universal, he declared that he would keep on writing about them. Some
risqué situations that he introduced into *The Demi-Virgin* got him to the
police court, but he suffered no permanent damage, and his play became a
resounding hit as a consequence. Hopwood was no man to be intimidated.

He was a man of his time. The mechanical formula for playwriting
that made the value of American drama negligible was perfect for Hopwood, and he developed it with the skill and polish of an ingenious workman. He wrote most of the funniest farces of his day—*Fair and Warmer,
The Gold Diggers, The Bat, Ladies' Night (in a Turkish Bath), Why Men
Leave Home, Naughty Cinderella, Getting Gertie's Garter,* and many
others. He wrote his first play, *Clothes,* after reading Carlyle's *Sartor
Resartus* in his English class at the University of Michigan. Grace George
starred in it in 1907, and it was a hit immediately. He collaborated with
Mary Roberts Rinehart on his second play, *Seven Days,* which was also a
hit. These two plays made him independently wealthy for life. After seeing
one of Hopwood's early plays in 1909, *This Man and This Woman,* Clyde

Fitch said that, if it had appeared with his name on the house boards, the critics would have called it his masterpiece. Clyde Fitch was always a gentleman.

Hopwood was a winning young man with an independent mind. He was tall. He had blue eyes and light hair. He looked grave. A first-nighter said that when he walked down the aisle he looked like a minister officiating at a funeral. Ever since his boyhood in Cincinnati, where the other boys found him odd and incomprehensible, he had been obsessed with writing. It was the only thing in life that he believed in. When he became a professional in New York, he wrote from nine to five, seven days a week, like an industrious clerk. Once, four of his plays were running on Broadway simultaneously. He was earning about five thousand dollars a week on Broadway in addition to his income from plays on the road.

He was one of the best-educated people in the American theater. But to him, playwriting was not an art; it was a craft. He thought that showmen were the best writers for the theater because they were realistic enough to give Broadway what it wanted. *The Gold Diggers* (1919), for instance, sprang out of an item he wrote in his notebook about a chorus girl who knew how to manipulate her men friends into giving her costly presents. "Gold digger" was a term that chorus girls used among themselves; Hopwood's play turned those two words into a national idiom. On this and most occasions, Hopwood wrote to order. After David Belasco had approved of the idea, Hopwood planned the farce scene by scene, arranging for breezy exposition, for climaxes for every act, building up artfully to the peak of suspense, according to the textbook rules for the well-made play. He always wrote the dialogue last; to him, the chief parts of the play were finished before he began the dialogue. It took Hopwood five weeks to write *The Gold Diggers*.

Since he had a genius for farces and since farce is a fundamental part of the theatrical process, Hopwood did not have to justify himself. But like many writers with humorous styles in all periods of the theater, he regarded comedy as the aristocrat of the drama, and he resented the prestige that automatically accrued to serious plays. Serious plays were the easiest to write, in his opinion. There is a comic as well as a tragic catharsis, he believed. To many writers of comedy, the prestige of serious drama is an affectation that enables authors, critics, and the public to flatter themselves into thinking they are intellectuals. Hopwood thought the writers of serious drama were not serious thinkers but poseurs. In his work, he consciously avoided anything heavy, tedious, or philosophical; he ruled out of his plays the kinds of characters that the public would not enjoy meeting in real life. The result was a whole sheaf of hilarious farces spiced with hints of wickedness. The bourgeoisie was scandalized and delighted.

Towards the end of a convivial, amiable life, Hopwood became a heavy drinker. One evening in 1928, he walked into the surf in Nice when he was drunk. He drowned. Hopwood left a large sum of money to the University of Michigan for an annual award to promising playwrights. Among those who have received a Hopwood award is Arthur Miller, a serious thinker, a serious dramatist, and currently the leading exponent of tragedy. Everything has worked out as Avery Hopwood, a gay cynic, thought it would.

William Gillette's family must have thought that he was defecting to the gypsies when he chose the theater as a career. They were very proper citizens of Hartford, Connecticut; his father had been a United States Senator. But there was nothing gypsy about Gillette. He was a cool-headed craftsman who understood his limitations and stayed within them. Without truckling and pandering to the great public, he became an immense success. In the midst of success, he stated his position candidly as follows: "I'm a pretty fair stage carpenter, and not altogether bad as an actor, after I have written myself a good part that suits me." That may sound like modesty, and perhaps it was in an institution like the theater that is always bursting with ego. But the statement expresses exactly Gillette's unique gift. He turned underplaying into a triumph. At a time when actors were bellowing and posturing, he spoke quietly in a small, dry voice and made no superfluous gestures. He made talent look like genius.

Gillette was born in 1855 in the midst of the bravura theater that derived from Forrest, Macready, Wallack, E. A. Sothern, Barrett, and Adah Isaacs Menken, who seduced the nation. Gillette was a cultivated man with the correct manners of good society. There was no place in the theater then for a man of that style. Now it is amusing to record that one of his earliest appearances at the age of twenty was in a romantic piece of gibberish called *Faint Heart Never Won Fair Lady*—in Boston, no less. In his spare moments in Boston, Gillette studied graver topics at Boston University and Massachusetts Institute of Technology, although he never stayed in one place long enough to get a degree.

He was a tall, lean, lank man with a detached personality. He brought an analytical mind into the theater; his brand of well-made play fabricated emotion but did not state it. In the late nineteenth century, he wrote *Held by the Enemy* and *Secret Service*, which were melodramas based on the Civil War, and *Too Much Johnson*, a farce he made from a French comedy. Sitting at a desk in The Players club in 1899, he wrote *Sherlock Holmes*, the play that made him famous all over the western world for the rest of his life. Arthur Conan Doyle's mystery stories about Sherlock Holmes were then in vogue. When Gillette proposed to make a play out of them he asked Doyle how much liberty he could take with the character of Holmes. "Marry him, murder him, do anything you please with him," Doyle replied. Those were the literary terms under which Gillette designed an exciting script about the imperturbable Holmes, who outwits the infamous Professor Moriarty and wins the humorless, sycophantic admiration of Dr. Watson. In Gillette's play the good guy struggles with the bad guy to get hold of "the papers"—one of the most banal quests in the mercantile theater.

Sherlock Holmes opened in New York at the Garrick Theater on November 6, 1899. Reading tea leaves as usual, William Winter said the play "had no value whatsoever . . . trivial at the beginning and feeble at the end," thus ensuring its popular success. For *Sherlock Holmes* played at the Garrick until the next June, a long run at that time, and then traveled around America and overseas to Britain. The play never became obsolete. When Gillette was in his late seventies, he toured in it from 1929 to 1932 under the management of George Tyler. A detective play of terse dialogue, great sleight-of-hand, at least one novel device (the red tip of a lighted cigar in a pitchblack room), and terrific excitement, *Sherlock Holmes* was ideal for Gillette—and vice versa.

Secret Service and *Sherlock Holmes* are the plays by Gillette that are best remembered and that best illustrate his laconic method and personality. But he acted in plays by other people, and he wrote other plays, too. In 1903, he acted in Barrie's *The Admirable Crichton*—made to order for a man of intellect and dignity. In 1919, Gillette made a memorable appearance in another Barrie play, *Dear Brutus*, with Helen Hayes, just beginning her career. No one who saw the production will ever forget the dramatic contrast between the tall, thin, sedate man and the exultant sprite—illustrating two lines by Shakespeare quoted in the last act:

> The fault, dear Brutus, is not in our stars
> But in ourselves, that we are underlings.

By background and experience, Gillette was no hack. He brought into the theater an alien mind, but it was a first-rate mind, and he used it superbly for theatrical purposes. Accepting the literary standards and social precepts of his days, he contrived plots that set up interior tensions that in turn excited the nerves of the audience. He said that what his characters did and how they behaved were more significant than anything they said. He rejected rhetoric. He also believed in type-casting: "Actors of recent

George Wessels and William Gillette in *Sherlock Holmes* (1899). (*The New York Public Library*)

times who have been universally acknowledged to be great have invariably been so because of their successful use of their own strong and compelling personalities in the roles which they made famous. And when they undertook parts, as they occasionally did, unsuited to their personalities, they were great no longer and frequently quite the reverse." That is why Gillette never played Romeo or Don Carlos or *The Prisoner of Zenda*.

Because of the nature of his talents, his dramatic principles and his views on acting were rationalizations; what he believed illustrated what he could do and could not do. "He could not voice moral precepts and was not a good lover," a contemporary critic remarked. Since Gillette was a cultivated man, an amateur painter, and a professional member of the American Academy of Arts and Letters, did it ever distress him that he could not try the great parts? Technically he was the opposite of his fellow player, Otis Skinner, who had very little talent for modern parts but could make the world tingle and dance when he acted in *The Honor of the Family* or *The Taming of the Shrew.*

Gillette's knowledge extended far beyond his abilities. But he made a less permanent mark on the theater than many of his intellectual inferiors. If he was ever disappointed, his success must have compensated him enormously. From 1900 to 1910, his average annual income was $200,000 (the days before the income tax). He could afford to spend $1,100,000 building an eccentric castle in Hadlyme, Connecticut, and $50,000 on a three-mile private railroad that he operated for his personal amusement. He had a big yacht called *Aunt Polly*—in honor of a South Carolina woman who had kept up his spirits when he was trying to recover his health there in a convalescent community. His Connccticut estate is now a state park visited by hundreds of people who must wonder what eccentric millionaire built such an unconventional place.

When William Gillette died in 1937 at the age of eighty-two, he could take sardonic satisfaction for several reasons: although he was threatened with tuberculosis—and perhaps was infectcd with tuberculosis at one time —he worked hard and lived long; although he did not have a theatrical personality, he had a conspicuous theatrical success. He was born a gentleman and remained a gentleman. Although his personality was reserved, he delighted and stimulated thousands of people.

A SCOURGE
OF CRITICS

In 1900, there were fifteen newspaper drama critics in New York, and Broadway took the normal theatrical attitude towards them—it disliked them. Maxine Elliott complained that critics made jokes at the expense of the theater. *Theatre Magazine* thought that too many of the critics were "shallow, ignorant, conceited, flippant, spiteful and tawdry." Producers were dissatisfied because the theater spent ten times as much money for newspaper advertising as baseball did but got only a tenth as much space in the newspaper. In New York, the producers did not indefinitely penalize a newspaper for publishing unfavorable opinion, but they had ways of exerting influence. The critic of *The New York Herald* was fired for writing an interview with Mrs. Fiske, who was anathema to the Syndicate. In Philadelphia, the drama critic of the *North American* resigned after the Syndicate removed its advertising because he was tired of this old wrangle. He said: "The average critic outside New York is

James Huneker. (*Culver Pictures, Inc.*)

entirely subservient to the business office and the theatrical advertising."

Broadway regarded the critics as instruments of the devil. Commenting on Alan Dale, for many years the insolent critic for the Hearst papers, a writer in *The New York Dramatic Mirror* declared: "When he takes pen in hand, the playhouses throughout the land tremble upon their foundations and the faces of actor folk burn white with fear."

It is obviously unfair sixty or seventy years later to judge the opinions of the critics apart from the social conditions of their time. Until World War I shook America out of its complacence, Broadway was a stuffy and bigoted midway. In every period, newspaper critics are traditionalists who resent and resist new ideas and new styles. But it is difficult not to raise an eyebrow over some of the judgments of the early critics because of their moral ferocity. When Shaw's *Mrs. Warren's Profession* was produced in 1905, *The Evening Post* called it "a mean and dirty action"; *The Sun:* "An insult to decency. It glorifies debauchery. It besmirches the clergyman's calling"; *The New York Times:* "Whatever its merits or demerits as a play for the closet, it has absolutely no place in a theater before a mixed audience"; *The New York Herald:* "You cannot have a clean pigsty. The play is an insult to decency."

But it is fair to point out that there were a few critics—two, certainly—with independent minds and judgments that continue to seem reasonable many years later. Norman Hapgood was one. In 1900 he was thirty-two years of age. From 1897 to 1902, he was critic for the *New York Commercial Advertiser* and *The Bookman*. Apart from his thoughtful and discriminating reviews of contemporary actors, dramatists, and producers (he thought Belasco was in large part humbug), he wrote some well-documented articles about the infamy of the Syndicate. In addition to his courage, he had enough political knowledge to understand the corruption the Syndicate imposed on the theater and the nation.

When Hapgood's articles appeared in London as well as New York, the Syndicate removed its advertising from the *New York Commercial Advertiser* in an attempt (which failed) to get Hapgood removed as critic. What he revealed about the power and evil tactics of the Syndicate provoked a storm of indignation in England and in some of the American newspapers, particularly those outside New York.

In judging the ability of critics in the first decade of the century it is inevitable that their attitudes towards Ibsen and Shaw be regarded as reliable evidence, for both Ibsen and Shaw were new influences that had not yet been absorbed into the culture of the day. Hapgood recognized

Ibsen's stature at a time when most critics were in a state of shock. He called *The Master Builder* a "great play." Although he did not wholly admire *Hedda Gabler* and *Ghosts*, he understood Ibsen's place in the theater: "No other living dramatist raises so keen an intellectual interest."

Hapgood was more cautious about Shaw. He admired *Mrs. Warren's Profession* when he read the text in book form before it had been produced in New York, but he thought the subject of a brothel would bar the play from performance on the stage. He said that Shaw's dialogue in *You Never Can Tell* was in the brilliant style of Congreve, and he regarded *The Man of Destiny* as the best one-act play that had been written for a long time. He also acknowledged Shaw's "sparkling wit" and "flashes of wisdom." But he believed that Shaw's didactic point of view and style would deny him a permanent place in the theater. Like other people then and later, Hapgood seems to have been irritated by Shaw's egotism and obsession with promoting himself.

James Gibbons Huneker, born in Philadelphia and bred to the piano, became a drama critic in 1902 at the age of forty-two. He was primarily a music critic. But he was a virtuoso writer ("I am Jack of the Seven Arts, master of none"), and he took an enthusiastic interest in literature, art, and the drama. "Jim the Penman" was the sobriquet he adopted from a popular novel of the time. The sobriquet recognized the nature of his profession, which was to write on any subject that interested him. He was the most cosmopolitan critic in America. In American journalism, he was the advance man for such European writers as Flaubert, Baudelaire, Sainte-Beuve, Brandes, Anatole France, Huysmans, Nietzsche, Strindberg, Gorky, Hauptmann, Sudermann, as well as Ibsen and Shaw. At a time when most American critics felt uncomfortable about the most individualistic foreign writers, Huneker was exploding with knowledge and praise—writing a crackling, highly compact, richly allusive style that cannot be imitated, since it was a vivid expression of a vivid personality. When Franklin Fyles, drama critic of *The Sun* and a persistent spokesman for the Syndicate, had to retire because of bad health, Huneker was assigned to replace him, at a salary of $125 a week, high pay in those days. His first assignments were to review Duse in *La Gioconda, Francesca da Rimini,* and *La Città Morta*—plays he was already acquainted with because of his assiduous theatergoing abroad. He praised the performances like a man of taste and cosmopolitanism.

More than any of his contemporaries, Huneker could have been censorious, omniscient, and condescending if he had wanted to be. He knew more than any of his fellow critics, and his taste was broader and more discriminating. It tells something of his stature that he believed "a little humility in a critic is a wise attitude." "Be charitable, be broad— in a word, be cosmopolitan," he said. The man who knew the most was the least pompous.

Huneker was never in doubt about Ibsen's stature. "In his bones he is a moralist, in practice an artist," he wrote of Ibsen in 1905. "His power is that of the artist doubled by the dramatist; the crystallization in the plays of these antagonistic qualities constitutes the triumph of his genius." Ibsen's attacks on middle-class morality were right down Huneker's alley.

He was also temperamentally able to cope with Shaw at a time when Shaw confused most of the critics he did not enrage. Speaking as a trained musician, Huneker catalogued Shaw's musical criticism as the work of an amateur, which was probably true. His 1906 introduction to Shaw's collected drama criticism, *Dramatic Opinions and Essays*, stands today as an intelligent and lively appreciation of an exuberant dramatist who had not yet written *Saint Joan, Heartbreak House, Major Barbara, Androcles and the Lion,* and other major works. In 1905, he described Shaw as "moralist, Fabianite, vegetarian, playwright, critic, Wagnerite, Ibsenite, jester to the cosmos and the most serious man on the planet." *Mrs. Warren's Profession* he regarded as Shaw's biggest, and also his most impossible, opus. The blatancy of Shaw's egotism eventually annoyed Huneker, as it had annoyed Hapgood. After having been one of Shaw's early champions, Huneker was piqued by some of Shaw's jeering rebukes in personal correspondence in later years. Shaw seemed to be— and no doubt was—outrageous, belittling, and overbearing. In 1920, when Huneker looked back on his prickly relations with Shaw and the patronizing things Shaw had said, his comments sounded bitter and disillusioned. He remarked that Shaw had no vision, never had an original idea, and thought only of the box office. Since Huneker was not interested in politics, he was immune to Shaw's principal motivation. But Huneker had been one of the first critics to appreciate the erratic genius of Shaw when Shaw bored, irritated, shocked or bewildered most theatre people.

Tall, portly, with a massive head on powerful shoulders, active, restless, responsive, witty, Huneker had a gigantic appetite for food, beer, wine, women, art, and conviviality. James Gibbons Huneker was the best critic Broadway has ever had.

The best-known critic was the most virulent—William Winter, born in Gloucester, Massachusetts, in 1836, and critic for the *New York Tribune* from 1865 to 1909. The older he became, the less tolerant, the more petulant, the more vindictive, sanctimonious, and prudish. He came to have a proprietary attitude towards the theater, as if he thought it should conform to his knowledge and taste—and to his prejudices, which were massive.

When he resigned from the *New York Tribune* in 1909, he was seventy-three. He had a scowling face with drooping lines, a long scraggly white moustache, and long white hair that was carelessly combed. He looked like a surprised but doleful dolphin. "Weeping Willie" was what Huneker called him. He wrote an imposing, rolling style, with occasional words and phases that were self-consciously bookish, and a general impression that life was so common that writing about it had become an intolerable duty. His principal reviews were about 3,400 words in length, set in small type in double-column measure. They looked like proclamations sent down from heaven, which indeed they might have been if God had not had a sense of humor. Since Winter never had an office, he wrote his reviews standing up in the *New York Tribune* business office. He always wrote sections of his reviews before the opening night performances—having read the script, perhaps, or having attended a rehearsal. He was paid $50 a week—the smallest salary paid to the head of a drama department in any New York newspaper. To make a living and to support his family in Brighton, Staten Island, he wrote long polemics for magazines, and wrote several books, generally in two fat volumes. In his solemn prose style with its rare and haughty phrases ("impartment of predestinate evil"), in his intolerance of new ideas in the theater, in his thunderous vituperation over what he regarded as indecent or radical, he represented the ponderous cant of his time. Immorality became a vice of hideous mien in his writing. Of *Salvation Nell* he said: "Those persons who wish to have their minds dragged through the gutter and drenched in the slime of the brothel can gratify their desire at the Hackett." Harrison Grey Fiske said that Winter could "unearth impurity from the quotations of the stock market and wantonness from the Declaration of Independence."

In 1909, the *New York Tribune* gradually made life so intolerable for Winter that he resigned. It was a strange and embarrassed conclusion to a long career. Since the *New York Tribune* did not announce Winter's resignation, he announced it himself in an advertisement for which he

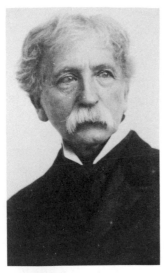

William Winter. (*The New York Public Library*)

paid $7.20. Presumably the Syndicate had put pressure on the *New York Tribune* to get rid of an abusive critic. But perhaps the *New York Tribune* was bored with a headstrong, testy old man who reviewed the theater as if he were a headmaster or an evangelist.

Although his reviews of performances of Shakespeare were magisterial, his descriptions of the acting of Charlotte Cushman, Edwin Forrest, Henry Irving, Ellen Terry, Edwin Booth, and other distinguished Shakespearean actors of his time contain detailed information that is invaluable, if rhetorical. Description was Winter's forte. The reviews do contain much of the mind and style of star actors who are gone. In Shakespeare, he felt safe; Shakespeare was a respectable subject, although it would be interesting to know how he rationalized Doll Tearsheet, Cressida, the depraved villains of *Measure for Measure* and *All's Well That Ends Well*, or even the obscenities of Hamlet's prose style. Shakespeare was never a prudish man. There is reason to think that some of Shakespeare made Winter uncomfortable. After reading a letter that Winter had written to Mansfield about Falstaff, Mrs. Mansfield urged her husband not to act that "disgusting old man." Among the many qualities Winter lacked was a sense of conviviality.

He adored English actors, but he was otherwise ludicrously provincial. Duse, Réjane and Bernhardt he referred to as "foreign strumpets." He handed down a stern manifesto when it was rumored that Duse would be accompanied by her notorious if talented lover, D'Annunzio, on her next visit. In a discussion of Bernhardt's acting, he remarked that "at social dinners Madame Bernhardt rouged her face and painted her lips." Since he regarded her as a "deplorable influence," he wished that she did not act morbid parts so well. He declared that she had no talent for acting "the woman essentially good and noble," but he acknowledged that she did have talent for acting "women who seek to cause physical infatuation and who can generally succeed in doing so." In other words, strumpets.

He excepted the Polish Helena Modjeska, not because she was a magnificent actress, but because she was a devout Christian. He did plead with her not to play the sinful Camille—a vain plea, as it turned out—but he exempted her from the purgatory he maintained for other foreign geniuses.

Ibsen stimulated Winter's talent for calumny and malevolence. He described Ibsen as a "reformer who calls you to crawl with him into a sewer, merely to see and breathe its feculence" (a good example of his stately style. He got credit for sanctity by using imposing literary words to allude to nasty subjects). He denied that the theater was a place for social views, especially those that would disrupt society: "Why inflict the theatre with inquiry as to 'original sin,' or the consequences of ancestral wickedness or the moral obliquity resultant from inheritary disease or the various forms of corruption incident to vice and crime?" When he disliked a play he was likely also to dislike the audience. When Mrs. Fiske acted *Hedda Gabler* he described the opening night audience as composed of "long-haired men and flat-chested she-goats of women"— the opinion of an overaged mammalian.

Because his salary was so meager, he did odd jobs around the theater to supplement his income, under the impression no doubt that a man of his towering saintliness could not be corrupted. In 1902, he accepted a commission by Mr. and Mrs. Fiske to adapt Paul Heyse's *Mary of Magdala* from the German. His English text was to be anonymous. When the play opened, his conscience permitted him to review it. He wrote two solid columns of praise of Mrs. Fiske's acting and of the play, without of course noting that he had written the English text. His vocabulary rose grandly to this auspicious occasion. "This original and singular fabric of the German Muse," he wrote, "stood revealed as a spectacle of solemn splendor. . . . Every impartment of it is vital with the sovereign Christian motives of charity, purity and hope. . . ." He saluted the "moral grandeur" and "beautiful womanhood" of Mrs. Fiske's acting.

John Corbin of *The Sun* did not know who had made the adaptation. But he described the English text as "rather solemn blank verse, much addicted to 'Thou hadst' and 'Thou wert.' " That sounds plausible. As a poet, Winter was in the Shakespearean tradition. He had contributed some original verses for Jessica to sing in Mansfield's *The Merchant of Venice*—thus repairing a grievous oversight in the original text of Shakespeare.

At the opening of *Mary of Magdala*, Winter was gratified to find the audience "remarkable for intellectual character." But, in his opinion, most audiences did not measure up to this standard. He characterized the typical audience as a "miscellaneous multitude." Some of the people were "largely unaccustomed to the use of soap." They were "vulgarians"; they knew nothing about art or literature; they cared "for nothing but the solace of their common tastes and appetities." The commonness of some of the actors also offended him. When he thought that Julia Arthur had read her lines incorrectly in *Twelfth Night,* he called it "a foolish and vulgar mistake," "an error indicative of a coarse taste and dull mind," although it turned out that the reading he denounced as a mistake was correct by the text of the First Folio. Producers were likely to be beneath his contempt—"sordid, money-grabbing tradesmen," "greedy ministrants of gross sensuality," "unscrupulous panderers to folly and fad," "Hebrew theatrical speculators" who have "orientalized the stage." (A touch of anti-Semitism here.)

As the years went by, Winter became more and more self-righteous and abusive. But the theater is by nature a magnanimous institution. After the *New York Tribune* had made life intolerable for Winter and he had resigned, the theater gave him a testimonial dinner at the Lotos Club. In 1916, when he was eighty, the theater staged a benefit performance for him at the Century Theater and raised more than $5000. Victor Herbert conducted the orchestra. Julia Arthur, whom Winter had insulted, Elsie Ferguson, Leo Dietrichstein, Blanche Bates, James O'Neill, Walter Hampden, Clarence Derwent, and others performed for him. Mrs. Fiske, incidentally, refused to participate. In the program book, the list of signatures began with Woodrow Wilson. Edwin Markham, a Staten Island neighbor, wrote and read a poem for the occasion. The scroll was full of unctuous praise: "To the honored veteran of our Literature; the Critic, Journalist, Scholar and Poet, who has so long and so nobly labored for the dignity and purity of our Letters and our Drama."

For forty-four years, Winter had written about the theater as if he owned it and only he knew how plays should be written and acted. He had fought tirelessly for all that was stuffy and obsolete. But at the end of his life, the theater treated him with generosity and kindness. As an institution, the theater is not petty: it has a nobler nature than he had.

FOR THE FAMILY
AND ITS TIRED
BUSINESSMAN

The Broadway theater of escape was best served by the musical stage and the vaudeville theaters, both of which were and are fantasy media. In 1900, the principal vaudeville theaters were Keith's at Broadway and 14th Street, Koster and Bials at Broadway and 34th Street, Proctor's at 23rd Street near Sixth Avenue, Proctor's Palace at Third Avenue and 58th Street, and the legendary and joyous Tony Pastor's on 14th Street near Third Avenue.

Musical plays had a standard style. In the days of flashlight photography, the casts of the musical shows had to assume a deliberate pose before the flashlight powder exploded, and that may be why they all look alike in the publicity photographs. They all seem to have consisted of one coy male actor flanked by coquettish chorus girls leaning forward in a wanton crouch, or one arch actress flanked by obsequious chorus boys with a smile of conquest on their lips. Vaudeville and musical

Weber and Fields. (*The New York Public Library*)

comedy were the natural medium of Broadway before World War I.

Even the starchiest people at the turn of the century agreed that the most jovial place on Broadway was the Weber and Fields Music Hall at 29th Street. It was the home of low comedy with a dash of criticism. Weber and Fields dressed and looked like buffoons and were buffoons. Lew Fields was the tall one; Joe Weber, the short one. Both wore prop chin whiskers. They also wore flamboyant costumes after the manner of stage mountebanks—grotesque plaid suits, checked pants, flat derbies, plug hats. It is said that in order not to confuse the ladies who came regularly they wore the same or similar costumes every week, but photographs do not confirm this. They seem to have dressed with a good deal of variety. In addition to the photograph on page 96 (and many others) there is a famous one that shows the tall Fields in a flat derby and the short Weber in a monstrous stovepipe hat that sits on his shoulders. They had the courage of their buffoonery.

They began their career in 1877 as juvenile comics. In the day of heavy Jewish immigration, they created the mythic character of the "Dutch" (or German-Jewish) comedian, who still murders the language in the modern theater (Jack Pearl having been their most virtuoso successor). Their dialogue had an immediate pertinence that is impossible to recreate today. "What's your name?" "My name is Solomon Yankle." "What is it in English?" "Reginald." (Explosions of laughter.) Weber and Fields are credited with two other inventions that have become standard practice or standard humor—the custard pie in the face and the joke that begins: "Who was that lady I seen you with last night?"

If Weber and Fields are still one of the basic traditions of Broadway and if their brand name is still the symbol of good knockabout humor, there are at least two reasons. In their category, they were artists. They kept the standards of their Music Hall performances high. Their support- ing actors included some of the most talented people of the day—Marie Dressler, David Warfield, Fay Templeton, Willie Collier, De Wolf Hopper, Sam Bernard, Louis Mann.

When the incomparable Fay Templeton decided to leave their cast (she appeared in George M. Cohan's *Forty-five Minutes from Broadway* and later became the most famous Little Buttercup *H.M.S. Pinafore* ever had), Weber and Fields met what they regarded as a crisis by booking the most beautiful and widely adored singing actress of the time—Lillian Russell, whose plump figure and sweet good nature represented the contemporary ideal of American womanhood. Among the Weber and Fields productions in which she appeared were two that bore the char- acteristic titles of *Fiddle-de-Dee* and *Whoop-de-Doo*. Neither she nor her employers were distressed by the newspaper rumor that they paid her $1,250 a week, but they could not have paid that much out of their modest grosses, for their Music Hall seated only 665 people. Although the box seats sold for $1.50, the rest of the house was scaled from 25¢ to $1.00. In order to increase their income, Weber and Fields employed their own ticket speculators to exploit their own black market. They made most of their money from the four or five touring companies that carried their gags around the country.

There is a second reason why their name symbolizes excellence today. They became the recognized court jesters of their time. They ad-libbed satiric comments on productions in other theaters. Their regular shows, which ran eight weeks, consisted of two parts. The first was musical vaudeville—songs, patter, and horseplay. But it was the second act that was the big event. The second act was a burlesque of some popular current Broadway show, and the titles of the burlesques were derisive—*Cyranose de Bric-a-Brac* for *Cyrano de Bergerac*; *Sapolio* for *Sapho*; *Barbara Fidgety* for *Barbara Frietchie*.

It was a mark of distinction (like being mentioned in a Broadway column) to be lampooned by Weber and Fields. Since their own schedule was onerous, producers of other shows were willing to put on special performances to accommodate Weber and Fields. Richard Mansfield was a regular patron at the Music Hall openings. To assist Weber and Fields in preparing a burlesque of his *Cyrano de Bergerac*, he invited them to rehearsals, and the burlesque opened at their Music Hall soon after his production opened at his Madison Square Theater. Weber and Fields, clowns and hokum harlequins, were respected members of the Broadway community.

Backstage at the Music Hall, the mood was not so jovial as it might have seemed to be from the front. Tensions were becoming intolerable. Rumors began to spread around town that Weber and Fields were quarreling. To demonstrate to the public that the rumors were untrue, Weber and Fields spent one afternoon seated side by side in a state of brotherly love on a Broadway bootblack stand, joking with the public. But the rumors were true. By 1902, they were still occupying the same dressing room, but they were no longer speaking to each other. No one knew exactly what the quarrel was about.

There was another factor in the decline of the Music Hall. After the disastrous Iroquois Theater fire in Chicago on December 30, 1902, the New York Fire Department inspected all the New York theaters and condemned the Music Hall as a fire hazard. The cost of remodeling seemed to be prohibitive in view of the limited weekly grosses.

Public taste was also changing. The big audiences were more en-

George M. Cohan with chorus in *George Washington, Jr.* at the Herald Square Theater (1905). (*Culver Pictures, Inc.*)

The Red Mill, with Fred Stone and David Montgomery (1906). (*The New York Public Library*)

thusiastic about George Ade's *The Sultan of Sulu*, Victor Herbert's *Babes in Toyland*, Gustav Luder's *The Prince of Pilsen*, and the two most popular comedians became David Montgomery and Fred Stone in *The Wizard of Oz*. Weber and Fields closed their cheerful Music Hall on January 30, 1904. Twelve years later they returned in a typical show at an uptown theater, and they were received rapturously by hundreds of theatergoers who had happy memories of the old days. But before the season was over, two things were obvious: the uptown theater was too big for the congenial humor of Weber and Fields, and the format was old-fashioned. Broadway was no longer in the mood for the old comic routines and for satirical cartoons drawn with a slapstick. The Weber

The Florodora Sextette—Marjorie Relyea, Agnes Wayburn, Vaughn Texsmith, Marie L. Wilson, Margaret Walker, Daisy Greene—and escorts. (*Museum of the City of New York*)

and Fields era was over, although Lew Fields went on to produce *Hit the Deck, A Connecticut Yankee,* and other modern musicals; and he left children who were steeped in show business all their lives—Herbert Fields, Joseph Fields, and Dorothy Fields. Sometimes together, sometimes not, these three Fields children wrote the books and lyrics for epochal musicals like *Annie Get Your Gun, Present Arms, Wonderful Town, Gentlemen Prefer Blondes,* and many others. They carried on a tradition of the musical stage that is at least ninety years old.

When *Florodora* opened in London, one of the reviewers warned his readers that it belonged to "the class of entertainment known as 'musical comedy.' " He seemed to be supercilious about the form, as if it were vulgar or infantile. When it opened in New York at the Casino in November 1900, no one felt supercilious about any part of it for more than 500 performances. It was so popular that it became a rosy part of the mythology of Broadway.

In Owen Hall's text, "Florodora" was the name of a perfume manufactured by a rich American rascal on a mysterious island in the Philippines. The basic story of *Florodora* was concerned with the familiar problem of getting the right young women betrothed to the right young men. To give it the proper glamour, the betrothals were arranged in a Welsh castle where a titled lady could be on hand. Never bother about logical transitions on the musical stage.

But one of Leslie Stuart's songs became a classic. In the second act, six young ladies in full-length skirts with flounces, shirtwaists with ruffles, and hats with ostrich plumes looked down mercifully on six young men who were wearing silk hats and gray morning coats and carrying walking sticks and who were submissively sunk on bended knees —"modern walking dress," a worldly reviewer called it. "Tell Me Pretty Maiden" was the title of the song. No one seems ever to have been much interested in the young men who sang half of it. But every civilized American took a proprietary interest in the romantic life of the six young women. They were Marjorie Relyea, Agnes Wayburn, Vaughn Texsmith, Marie L. Wilson, Margaret Walker, and Daisy Greene. Everything they did and said was reported throughout the country. In 1900 and 1901, thousands of Americans could sing the first four lines of the maidenly tune composed by Leslie Stuart with coquettish words written by Ernest Boyd-Jones and Paul Rubens. Here are the first four lines and a lot more:

Men
Tell me, pretty maiden
Are there any more at home like you?

Girls
There are few, kind sir,
But simple girls, and proper too.

Men
Then tell me pretty maiden,
What these simple girlies do.
Then tell me pretty maiden what the girlies do.

Girls
Kind sir, their manners are perfection,
And the opposite of mine.

Men
Then take a little walk with me,
And then I can see,
What a most particular girl should be.

Girls
I may love you too well, to let you go,
And flirt with those at home, you know.

Men
Well, don't mind little girl,
You'll see I'll only want but you.

Girls
It's not quite fair to them,
If you told them that you were true.

Men
I don't care a pin for your sisters if you love me.

Girls
What would you say if I said I liked you well?

Men
I'd vow to you on bended knee.

Girls

On bended knee,
If I loved you, would you tell me what I ought to do,
To keep you all mine, alone, to always be true to me?
If I loved you, would it be a silly thing to do?
For I must love someone.

Men

Then why not me?

Girls

Yes, I must love someone really
And it might as well be you.

One of the standard showgirls in *Florodora* was a stunning girl of sixteen from Tarentum, Pennsylvania—Evelyn Nesbit. She was adorable onstage but more renowned offstage. In 1906, when she was attending the opening night performance of *Mamzelle Champagne* in the roof theater of the Madison Square Garden, her husband, Harry Thaw, shot and killed her most versatile lover, Stanford White. Evelyn's succinct comment on that unusual episode is worth recording. "Good God, Harry," she exclaimed. "What have you done!"

On Broadway, the musical theater, like the dramatic theater, was an escape from reality into a never-never-land of innocent snobbery and bountiful wealth. Many of the plots adhered to the ancient principle of the miraculous coincidence, in which, for example, the enchanting waitress turned out to be a princess in disguise and therefore better at her job than a commoner could be. Although George M. Cohan's bustling shows were indigenously American, most of the other important musicals were European operetta. The new composers, Victor Herbert, Rudolf Friml, and Sigmund Romberg, grew up in Central Europe in the period of Johann Strauss, Oscar Straus, and Franz Lehar. And Jerome Kern, who was born in New York City, studied music in Europe and heard the same music. All these men were trained musicians, familiar with counterpoint and instrumental and vocal music, and they had something else in common: they wrote melody; they thought in terms of melody; melody was their vernacular.

No one expected the stories of these operettas to be reasonable or the characters to be human beings. Frank Pixley's narrative for the endlessly popular *The Prince of Pilsen* in 1903 was jocose gibberish about a Cincinnati brewer who, while traveling through some mythical country in Europe, is mistaken for the Prince of Pilsen. But the important fact was that Gustav Luder's music was agreeably melodious and included the standard drinking song. (Note also "Nut Brown October Ale" in Reginald De Koven's *Robin Hood* in 1890 and Romberg's jovial drinking song in *The Student Prince* in 1924.) When Mr. Pixley was asked to account for the popular success of *The Prince of Pilsen,* he itemized the fundamentals of his production as follows: an operetta would have to appeal to the eye, ear, and intelligence of the public; it could not be set in America because the costumes would be dull; it needed a soprano, a tenor, and a comedian and, he added, "the bizarre, the unique." Actually, nothing was unique in the American musical theater until Jerome Kern started to write his famous Princess Theater musicals in 1915.

Since the early composers were musicians rather than songwriters, they should probably not be faulted for being satisfied with trivial and silly librettos. But it is the librettos that have made their operettas unacceptable to modern theatergoers. Victor Herbert was a professional musician. He was first cellist in the court orchestra of Stuttgart, Germany, where he was brought up, and it was as a cellist that he came to America for the Metropolitan Opera Company when his wife signed a contract to sing at the Met. A man of prodigious energy, Herbert wrote concert music in addition to playing it. At a time when he was composing scores for operettas, he was also conducting the Pittsburgh Symphony orchestra. The theater was secondary to his vocation in the world of music.

But all his operettas contained at least one memorable song: *Babes in Toyland* (1903) contained "I Can't Do the Sum"; *Mlle. Modiste* (1905) contained "Kiss Me Again" and "Sweet Summer Breeze, Whispering Trees," sung by Fritzi Scheff of the Metropolitan Opera; *The Red Mill* (1906) contained "When You're Pretty and the World is Fair"; *Naughty Marietta* (1910) contained "Ah, Sweet Mystery of Life" and "The Italian Street Song," sung by Emma Trentini of the Manhattan Opera Company; *Sweethearts* (1913) contained the title song "Sweethearts," sung by Christie MacDonald. If the rest of the theater had not grown up, Victor Herbert's operetta music would be as vital a part of theatrical literature as *Porgy and Bess* or *Carousel,* which have stimulating plots and characters as well as beautiful scores.

Gilbert and Sullivan flourished in America as well as in England. In Herbert's day, there was no other precedent for the literate libretto.

The chorus of the *Ziegfeld Follies of 1915*, representing the twelve months of the year. (*Culver Pictures, Inc.*)

The Ben Ali Haggin tableau of Lady Godiva in the *Ziegfeld Follies of 1919*. (*The New York Public Library*)

George M. Cohan in a revival of *The Song-and-Dance Man* at the Fulton Theater (1930). (*Culver Pictures, Inc.*)

Realism may have been the ideal for Ibsen or the shibboleth of Pinero, but it had no friends on the musical stage. Franz Lehar's *The Merry Widow*, produced in 1907, had a profound influence on the Broadway musical stage because it ran for 416 performances. The story it told of Sonia, the widow, and Prince Danillo in Paris was cloying and witless, but the music was entrancing. Oscar Straus' *The Chocolate Soldier* (1909) had a libretto based on Shaw's *Arms and the Man*; but it ran for only 296 performances. After the success of *The Merry Widow*, with its famous waltz tune and its infantile book, no one wanted to wake up from the operetta dream.

Rudolf Friml was not prepared to depart from tradition. Born in Czechoslovakia, he studied composition under Antonin Dvořák. Until he was in his middle thirties, he was a practicing musician. The New York Symphony Orchestra, under the direction of Walter Damrosch, played one of Friml's piano concertos—with Friml at the piano—in Carnegie Hall. In 1912, Arthur Hammerstein was looking desperately for someone to write a score for a new musical in which Emma Trentini would appear. He had expected Victor Herbert to write it, but Herbert refused after Mme. Trentini had publicly insulted him, or so he thought. At a special performance of *Naughty Marietta*, when Herbert was conducting, she had refused to sing an encore of his "Italian Street Song." He handed the baton to the assistant conductor and left the theater in a rage. That is why Hammerstein was looking for another composer and that is how Friml got the commission.

The story of *The Firefly*, compiled by the industrious Otto Harbach, was standard stuff, but as in the case of the Herbert operettas, the score was rich in melody—"When a Maid Comes Knocking at Your Heart" and "Sympathy" being the best remembered. After World War I, Friml wrote three swashbuckling operettas that were fabulously successful —*Rose Marie* (1924), which contained "Indian Love Call"; *The Vagabond King* (1925), which contained "Some Day" and the "Song of the Vagabonds"; and *The Three Musketeers* (1928). Dennis King, a lively singer and a dashing actor, appeared in all three operettas. Continuing the tastes and moods of 1900, *The Vagabond King* was based on Justin McCarthy's *If I Were King*, a sword-and-plume fable in which E. H. Sothern had dazzled the public. The adapters for the musical stage were Brian Hooker and W. H. Post, whose romanticism was dynamically pompous:

Onward! Onward! Swords against the foe!
Forward! Forward! the lily banners go!

"When I write music for the theater I like books with charm in them,"
Friml remarked. "And charm suggests old things—the finest things that
were done long ago. I like a full-bodied libretto with luscious melody,
rousing choruses and romantic passions." The public thoroughly agreed
with him.

When Sigmund Romberg was a boy in Hungary, he was steeped in
the same kind of music that Victor Herbert had known in Germany. He
came to New York at the age of twenty-two on a sightseeing tour that
never ended because he never went home. He became an American
citizen and carried on the European tradition so successfully that he
composed or helped to compose fifty-six musical shows, some of which,
like *The Student Prince* and *Desert Song*, will outlive the internal com-
bustion engine and the portable tape-recorder. The librettos were uniformly bogus. The scores were spuriously artistic. But, long after the
rest of the theater had come of age, the American public adored Romberg's
orotund banalities, like "Deep in My Heart, Dear" and "Stouthearted
Men."

In his early years on Broadway, Romberg was a staff musician for
the Shubert brothers and wrote the kind of music they ordered—including
innocuous music intended not be noticed. But among many things he
wrote in 1917 was an operetta that established him permanently—
Maytime, in which Peggy Wood and Charles Purcell sang "Will You
Remember?" and "Road to Paradise" month after month at the Shubert
Theater. *Maytime* was so popular that the Shubert brothers opened a
second company at the 44th Street Theater across the street. There was
no reason for Romberg to doubt the soundness of the formula. In later
years, when theater music was becoming querulous or brassy or mocking,
Romberg declared his loyalty to the eternal principles: "Melody is still
melody," he said. "Romantic music will never die because deep at the
roots of all people is the theme of love." During the thirty-seven years
of his career, Romberg successfully ignored the disillusionment of the
world outside his studio.

Jerome Kern was the composer who put melody to modern uses. He
had a modern point of view. Born in New York, raised in Newark, New
Jersey, educated at the New York College of Music, he completed his

musical training in Europe, where he heard the same music that Herbert, Friml, and Romberg had absorbed before they came to America. Kern's first jobs in New York were songs that he contributed to musicals written by other people. In 1904, he revised the score of an English musical to suit Julian Eltinge, a female impersonator much admired before male transvestitism was regarded as a perversion. Kern's first unforgettable song, "They Didn't Believe Me," was interpolated into a forgotten British musical called *The Girl from Utah*. Kern continued to work as a musical jack-of-all trades until 1915, when something happened that was of primary importance to the musical theater. He and Guy Bolton, later joined by P. G. Wodehouse, broke with the European operetta, eliminated the formula, and invented small, artistically integrated musical plays at the Princess Theater, which seated 299 people. *Nobody Home* was the first. The others were *Very Good Eddie* (1915), *Oh, Boy!*, *Leave It to Jane*, and *Miss 1917* (all in 1917), and *Oh, Lady! Lady!* (1918). The stories were humorously contemporary; the songs defined character and carried the story forward without relinquishing Kern's genius for melody. Kern established a style that was spirited and independent, dry and brisk. Since the Princess had a limited seating capacity there was no margin for the failures that are always inevitable, and the project was ultimately abandoned. But the Princess shows were the proving ground for *Show Boat* (1927), which told an American folklore story in musical terms and created a Negro character who sang out of his own experience rather than the white man's mythology, and the Princess shows were the proving ground also for *Music in the Air* (1932). "Ol' Man River," "Can't Help Lovin' That Man," "Bill," "Why Do I Love You," "I've Told Every Little Star" came from those two glorious scores. Oscar Hammerstein II, a genuine poet and a man of wide social interests, was a strong influence on *Show Boat* and *Music in the Air*. As author of the librettos and the lyrics, he put Kern's melodies to cultivated use. But the Princess shows had done the pioneering; and this short, slender, bright, animated little man, whose head rang with melody, established the principles of the modern American musical theater, and made most of the other popular shows look thin and empty and the European-style operettas impossible. Kern wrote other shows with librettos no better than the hackneyed ones he had made obsolete. But the inept librettos for *Roberta* (1933) and *Very Warm for May* (1939) confirmed the fact he had already established —that trite books destroy melodies.

In 1901, Broadway had no idea of what was going to happen to it when it ignored a comedy called *The Governor's Son.* But George M. Cohan did. Twenty-two years old at the time, he knew what was going to happen to Broadway. He was going to overwhelm it.

The next season, Broadway rejected his second play, *Running for Office,* and it did not have much enthusiasm for his third, *Little Johnny Jones,* when it opened in 1904. But Cohan refused to accept a third failure as final. Taking *Little Johnny Jones* on tour with his mother, father, and sister in the cast, he rewrote it extensively, and brought it back to Broadway. On the return engagement, he got what he always knew he deserved: he got success. His story of an American jockey unjustly accused of dishonesty in England proved to be acceptable, since it was essentially jingoistic, and since two of Cohan's songs suited New York audiences completely—"I'm a Yankee Doodle Dandy," and "Give My Regards to Broadway," in which he took the liberty of writing like an established Broadway celebrity. He was twenty-six years old. For the last four years, Broadway had been brushing him off. But in 1905, he gave his regards to Broadway as if he were one of its most familiar inhabitants:

> Give my regards to Broadway,
>   Remember me to Herald Square,
> Tell all the gang at 42nd Street
>   That I'll soon be there.
> Whisper of how I'm yearning
>   To mingle with the old-time throng,
> Give my regards to Broadway
>   And say that I'll be there.

The lyrics expressed a sentiment that may have been presumptuous in 1905. But in the immediate years that followed, he fitted them. He became the king of Broadway. Broadway was his favorite subject—in *Hello, Broadway!, Broadway Jones, Forty-five Minutes from Broadway,* and *The Man Who Owns Broadway.* He had a profound influence on the popular theater for the next fourteen or fifteen years.

Since he wrote comedies, musical shows, and songs, and since he staged them and acted in many of them, it is impossible to classify him neatly. He was a virtuoso theater man. His combination of facility and energy suited the contemporary taste. His shameless flag-waving, his sentimentality, his electricity, his rhythm, his noisiness, his brash personality were the essence of show business. In 1955, Oscar Hammerstein II accounted for Cohan's immense popular success by observing: "A song writer's genius, or rather Cohan's genius, was to say simply what everybody was subconsciously feeling." Cohan's songs, both words and music, were sublimations of the mood of their day. They said what millions of people would have said if they had had Cohan's talent.

George Michael Cohan was born on July 4, 1878 (skeptics maintain that the birthday was actually July 3), in Providence, Rhode Island, into a family of vaudeville performers. He had very little formal schooling and no life outside the theater. He was abnormally bright, ingenious, energetic, and self-confident, and spectacular success was not his hope so much as his obsession. "I'm a freak figure in the theatrical game," he remarked when people started to inquire into the mystery of his success. He was a freak only because his instincts for show business were uncannily shrewd. Ten years after his first show was staged on Broadway, he built a large theater on Broadway between 42nd and 43rd Streets, with his name over the canopy. It was decorated with American flags and other symbols of his career. No one ever made it so big so rapidly. There may have been something significant in the fact that he opened his own theater with his own adaptation of *Get Rich Quick, Wallingford.*

Onstage his personality could not be ignored. He rolled his eyes and dropped his eyelids with a confidential grimace that seemed to be directed at individual members of the audience; he sang through his nose, carried a jaunty cane, wore his hat on the side of his head, and danced exuberantly. Since he was a short man, he avoided standing near taller people and wore thick heel lifts that added about an inch to his stature. But no one was likely to notice details because he was overpoweringly loud and busy. He invented a type of musical show in which everybody talked at the top of his voice, everybody sang full out and danced ferociously. Once Cohan established his style, he adhered to it. H. T. Parker of the *Boston Evening Transcript* said that Cohan impersonated himself.

He could write as fast as he could dance. Working at night, after the rest of Broadway had gone to bed, he was able to write 140 pages or so at one sitting, afterwards reducing the 140 to about 45, or one full act. If he could not get the seclusion he needed at home or in a hotel, he would take a drawing-room in a Pullman car en route to any city far enough away to give him the time he needed. He wrote his songs after he had written the books for his musical plays. Instead of writing the music, he whistled the air to someone who transcribed it. Between 1905 and 1912, he wrote twelve musical shows, in addition to some straight plays. He could write to order easily. When Fay Templeton, a well-loved singing actress, was on his payroll but doing nothing, he wrote *Forty-five Minutes from Broadway* for her (and also for Victor Moore, who was in the cast). Two of the songs for that show became classics, and still are: "Mary Is a Grand Old Name" and "So Long, Mary."

He said he wrote for Joe Blatz—his stereotype for an average audience. Joe Blatz, Cohan said, had the "two-dollar heart." "What the fifteen-year-old, clean-faced, fresh-minded, full-of-life American boy or girl likes, the average American audiences will like," he believed. Joe Blatz, according to Cohan, liked clean plays with a dash of melodrama, fast dancing, and easy, lilting tunes. Cohan was contemptuous of the academic discussion of "audience psychology." He said he "would rather make one man laugh than one thousand cry." He did exactly that in about fifty comedies and musical productions. The level of his personal taste is indicated by the fact that he thought George Ade's *The College Widow* was the greatest play he had ever seen.

When he was still in his thirties, he was both rich and generous. He was idolized as not only the cleverest but the most charitable star in the profession, and he was a frequent guest of honor at testimonial dinners. In 1912, he led off the campaign for the Titanic Fund by giving $500 for the survivors of the Titanic sea disaster. He gave an elderly actor $10,000 to pay his expenses in a nursing home, with a promise of more money if needed. At one banquet the toast to him consisted of a song:

> If every person you have helped
> Should drink a toast to thee
> In one small glass of wine tonight
> Why, no more wine there'd be.

Although he was charitable, he was not generous-minded. A kind of shallow egotism made him a difficult companion, and his brash temperament could be abrasive. "There's one thing I can say about you, George," Gus Williams, a comedian, once declared. "You have convinced me that capital punishment is absolutely necessary." Cohan's career on Broadway began to deteriorate in 1919, when he took the side of the managers and theater owners against the actors in the Actors' Equity strike, which was one of the fundamental events in Broadway history. Although he had begun as an actor and often continued to be an actor and although he belonged to a family of actors, he opposed the strike of actors, not passively but actively. He organized Actors' Fidelity in opposition. He issued defiant statements. "Every dollar I have, and I have a few, is on the table in this fight against the actors who have been misled," he said. "The actors have overlooked one important thing, and that is me." When the managers and theater owners surrendered and signed the Equity contract, Cohan remained unreconciled. He said he would never sign an Equity contract, and he never did. He continued to produce plays and musicals, and occasionally he appeared himself, but only because Actor's Equity was more magnanimous than he was. It gave him a special dispensation.

The rest of Cohan's career was less triumphant. In 1920, with his co-producer, the obliging Sam Harris, he produced a burlesque melodrama, *The Tavern*, which delighted the public, and *The Song-and-Dance Man*, two years later. In 1933, he had a new and happy experience. For the first time, he played in a drama written by someone else and produced by someone else—Eugene O'Neill's *Ah, Wilderness!*, produced by the Theater Guild. As the puzzled parent of two disorderly adolescent boys, he gave a soft, winning, and memorable performance unlike anything he had done on his own. In 1937, he humorously impersonated Franklin Delano Roosevelt in a musical cartoon, *I'd Rather Be Right*, written by George S. Kaufman and Moss Hart, with a score by Richard Rodgers and Lorenz Hart.

Cohan's success in a new style of theater confirmed the authenticity of his stage talent. Although the style had changed, he was still a first-rate actor. In 1939, President Roosevelt, whom Cohan had caricatured the year before, gave him a Congressional Medal in recognition of the national value of two of his war songs—"Over There" and "It's a Grand Old Flag." Cohan died on November 5, 1942; the funeral at St. Patrick's Cathedral acknowledged his eminence as a citizen of Broadway. The mark he had made on the theater was thus impressively commemorated. Seventeen years later, a statue was erected to him at Broadway and 46th Street, after a campaign initiated and conducted by Oscar Hammerstein II. Cohan is the only theater man who has been honored by a statue on Broadway.

In the Calvinist America of the first decade of the century, the *Ziegfeld Follies* gave an opulent illusion of sin. For a quarter of a century, the *Follies* represented the businessman's ideal of the perfect harem. Everything about the *Follies* was beautiful, plump, mysterious, and equivocally erotic. Ziegfeld created the formula; no one could make it work after he went.

Florenz Ziegfeld was to the musical stage what Belasco was to the dramatic stage—a clever showman. The theater happened to be the me-

dium he used. He could have used politics or public relations just as successfully. Born in 1868, he served his apprenticeship to show business as a
sharpshooter in Buffalo Bill's Wild West Show, although he had never been
closer to the plains than Chicago. During the World's Fair in Chicago in
1893, he promoted the career of Sandow, the celebrated strong man, who
appeared on the stage as naked as was then possible, displaying the wonderful rippling of his muscles and other aspects of his spectacular equipment. Sandow was, indeed, a strong man. In Ziegfeld's view, he was a
superman. Ziegfeld's program called attention to a long list of Sandow's
assets, including "Abdominal muscles when tense, producing the wonderful
checkerboard arrangement of fibers, existence of which modern anatomists
deny, being plainly visible at a distance of 300 feet." The press complimented Ziegfeld for such encouragement of "physical development as
Sandow's performance produces." Like Barnum, the good showman invariably turns out to be a benefactor of humanity.

Ziegfeld found his real benefactress in Paris in a *Folies Bergère* show.
She was Anna Held, five feet of sizzling personality. She had a figure that
began with a massive bust, featured a set of broad thighs and ended with a
pair of tiny feet. Ziegfeld not only imported her but married her and put
her on the stage in *Papa's Wife* at the Herald Square Theater. She drove
men crazy with her French accent in two ingenuous songs: "Won't You
Come and Play wiz Me" and "I Just Can't Make My Eyes Behave." To
preserve the texture of her exquisite skin, Anna Held was also compelled
to take milk baths, though, of course, not onstage. Some privacy was absolutely essential.

Since Paris was the reputed capital of wickedness, Ziegfeld used it as
his frame of reference. Anna Held was more French on Broadway than she
had been in Paris. The word "revue" was French. The Broadway word
"follies" derived from the French *folies*. And the roof garden where Ziegfeld produced his first *Follies* in 1907 was called the "Jardin de Paris,"
although it really consisted of hard, folding chairs and a tin roof on top
of the New York Theater at Broadway and 45th Street. The first Ziegfeld
girls were called "Anna Held girls" in the program. Broadway was provincial, but Ziegfeld was not. Anna Held divorced him in 1913, and he married
the charming Billie Burke in 1914.

In time, the *Ziegfeld Follies* became the most glamorous series of
shows that Broadway has ever had. They were founded on girls and
extravagance. Half of the cost or nearly half of the cost of the productions
went for the costumes that, in Ziegfeld's phrase, glorified the American
girl. The costumes cost $123,000 in one edition that was produced for a

total of $300,000. Although the girls were luscious, they maintained on-stage a certain reserve that was artfully coquettish. They slouched across the stage, dragging one foot. They kept their mouths slightly open, reveal-ing wonderful teeth and an imitation of passion. They hardly smiled. Dolores, the greatest of the Ziegfeld girls, never smiled in her decade with the *Follies*, although she could and did smile offstage. (In her first appear-ance she was billed as "The Discourager of Hesitancy," which illustrates the ambiguity of Ziegfeld's style in seducing audiences.)

The costumes the girls wore were ornate, fantastic, and in many cases enormous and heavy. But when Ben Ali Haggin, a society painter, began to pose the girls in living tableaux, the costumes became less burdensome and more revealing, for the living tableaux were "art," as the program credits to Mr. Haggin clearly stated, and art need never be prudish. Zieg-feld had a rule book for the choice of his girls: native refinement, poise, health, strength, symmetry, spirit, style, appeal to both sexes, femininity, and glory. Among the hundreds of showgirls who passed this test were

"The Land of Happiness" number from *Good Times* at the Hippodrome in the 1920–1921 season. (*Museum of the City of New York*)

B. F. Keith's Palace Theater in 1930, near the end of its life as a vaudeville house. (*Museum of the City of New York*)

Marion Davies, Justine Johnstone, Vera Maxwell, Peggy Hopkins Joyce, Mae Murray, Barbara Stanwyck, Paulette Goddard, and Irene Dunne. They were talented as well as beautiful young women.

Ziegfeld's unique skill consisted in his ability to present girls attractively. That was what he was primarily interested in. But there was much more than display to the *Follies*. The best composers of their times wrote for Ziegfeld—Rudolf Friml, Victor Herbert, Jerome Kern, Irving Berlin, and others. And some memorable songs were sung in the *Follies*. Ina Claire sang "Hello, Frisco, Hello" to salute the miraculous long-distance telephone. Nora Bayes sang "Shine on, Harvest Moon." Lillian Lorraine sang "By the Light of the Silvery Moon." Berlin's "A Pretty Girl Is Like a Melody" was first sung in a *Follies*.

Although Ziegfeld professed not to be interested in comedians, his shows presented a whole regiment of comic genuises who made enduring reputations under his direction. Bert Williams, W. C. Fields, Ed Wynn, Leon Errol, Eddie Cantor, Fannie Brice, and Will Rogers clowned in various editions of the *Follies*.

Everything Ziegfeld put his name and mind to had style. The New Amsterdam Theater, into which he moved in 1913, had style as long as he used it, and so did the New Amsterdam Roof, where he began to stage smaller shows in 1915. The Ziegfeld Theater, which Joseph Urban designed, was a masterpiece; it had elegance and composure. Ziegfeld also produced many excellent musical dramas, *Show Boat* being the most memorable. He lived and managed his business with the same reckless abandon that he poured into the *Ziegfeld Follies*. To preserve the freshness of Marilyn Miller's dancing in one of his shows, he paid $175 for a new costume for her at every performance. He seldom wrote letters. He telegraphed long messages to people who were on his staff and available in adjoining quarters anytime he wanted to talk to them. He realized that telegrams were theatrical. He had three gold telephones on his desk. He traveled on the railroad in a private car. When he died in 1932, he owed a million dollars—practical though rueful proof of his munificence.

His *Follies* were imitated in *George White's Scandals*, *Earl Carroll's Vanities*, the *Music Box Revues*, the Shubert *Artists and Models* and *Passing Shows*, the *Greenwich Village Follies*, and many other shows. They all had merit and distinction. But none of them could compare with the *Ziegfeld Follies* for taste, abundance, sensuousness, and splendor. They illustrated the showmanship of a man of genius who made a lasting impression on Broadway.

In the meantime, there were two continuing institutions that the whole United States took for granted as it assumed that Niagara Falls would always be there. The Hippodrome and the Palace supplied standard entertainment for everyone without the extravagance of the Broadway musical productions. They were like stores that had entertainment for sale on a familiar schedule. But they were not routine. Although they appealed to mass audiences, each of them had a style that distinguished their product from mass entertainment.

The colossal two-a-day shows at the Hippodrome exactly suited the smalltown audiences of the big town before Broadway became too blasé. The shows were a series of spectacular vaudeville, circus, ballet, and revues, like the first one called *A Yankee Circus on Mars.* But it also produced an occasional smashing historical saga, like a version of the Russo-Japanese War that was better staged than the war on which it was founded.

The Hippodrome was built in 1905 at a cost of $1,500,000. It stretched between two roof minarets from 43rd to 44th Streets on Sixth Avenue, in the shadow of the Sixth Avenue elevated railroad that shattered the calm of the block every time a train rattled by. Everything about the Hippodrome represented a triumph of showmanship. It seated 5,000 people. The immense lobby was decorated with elephant heads, each of which had an electric light bulb at the tip of the trunk. The stage was 116 feet wide. It included a huge tank into which the chorus girls marched out of sight at the end of the performance, giving an illusion of mass drowning. The tank was large enough to float a gunboat during the reprise of the Russo-Japanese War. When the plucky little Japs mounted their powerful counterattack, a troop of Cossacks mounted on reckless horses galloped across the stage and plunged into the tank never to be heard from again —until the next performance. The Hippodrome did nothing by halves. When it staged a portfolio of historical characters, it was lavish, indiscriminate, and omniscient—George Washington, Benjamin Franklin, Buffalo Bill, Pocahontas, Julius Caesar, Mark Antony, Herod, General Pershing, Louis XIV, Duke of Wellington, Admiral Schley, Henry VIII, Helen of Troy, Napoleon—all on friendly terms. With a stage 116 feet wide, the Hippodrome could stage the universe without crowding. The size of the shows is indicated by the fact that, during the actors' strike in 1919, 412 Hippodrome stagehands were out of work, as well as 720 actors, chorus dancers, and swimmers from that tank. *Happy Days* was, ironically, the title of the Hippodrome show closed by the strike.

When the screen began to take over Broadway in the twenties, audiences had new heroes and heroines and the shows at the Hippodrome seemed less amazing. The regular series of shows came to an end in the early thirties. But before the Hippodrome went out of business in 1935, it had one last fling and ended with a memorable joke. Billy Rose, short of stature, long on talent, staged a diffuse circus show called *Jumbo.* As usual, Billy bought the best talent on the market—Ben Hecht and Charles Mac-Arthur to write the book, Richard Rodgers and Lorenz Hart to provide the score, Paul Whiteman and his orchestra to play it, and Jimmy Durante to be funny. Jimmy participated in the final hippodromic jest. According to the book, his role was that of a sneak thief, surreptitiously leading an elephant out of the circus when a peevish sheriff yelled: "Where are you going with that elephant?" Jimmy stopped and looked around with an air of surprise and bewilderment. "What elephant?" he innocently inquired.

When audiences could laugh at an elephant, it was time to close the Hippodrome. Now the site of the old house of amazement is occupied by a hippodromic parking garage.

The Palace Theater also became an institution. It was built in 1913 on Seventh Avenue between 46th and 47th Streets at a cost of more than one million dollars, conveniently next door to a saloon and just across a triangular plaza from Broadway. Built by Martin Beck, head of the Orpheum vaudeville circuit, the Palace was a handsome, beautifully decorated theater that seated 1,800 people in one of the most comfortable auditoriums Broadway has ever had. The top box-office price was $2.00— just twice the top price for vaudeville shows in general. After a monumental campaign of preliminary ballyhoo, it opened on the afternoon of March 24, 1913, with the following bill: The Palace Girls, dance ensemble; Ota Gygi, Spanish court violinist; La Napierkowska, pantomimist and dancer; "Speaking to Father," comedy skit by George Ade, with Milton Pollack; "The Eternal Waltz," flash act based on operetta, with thirty people, including Mabel Berra and Cyril Chadwick; McIntyre & Harty, who were replaced by Taylor Holmes, monologist, after the matinee performance; Four Vanis, wire act; Hy Mayer, cartoonist; Ed Wynn, comedian.

Since the Palace quickly became the most idolized vaudeville house in America, it is interesting to note that the opening bill was a disaster. Before the first week was over, the management—headed by E. F. Albee and B. F. Keith—was wondering what to do with their costly house. All the newspapers agreed that the opening bill was less interesting than the weekly bills of Hammerstein's Victoria Theater at 42nd Street and Seventh Avenue. "The poorest big time vaudeville show New York has ever seen," said a reviewer from Variety, adding, "It is also the worst exhibition of showmanship New York has ever known." Only three rows of seats downstairs were occupied at the Tuesday afternoon performance, and there was only a scattering of theatergoers at the evening performance. Broadway always enjoys disasters. Some sardonic wag sent a telegram of "congratulations on the Palace opening" to Marcus Loew, proprietor of a rival vaudeville theater at 42nd Street and Eighth Avenue. Variety noted with acid satisfaction that "The news of 'the Palace flop' pleased the regulars around Times Square mightily."

But the flop was transitory. The Palace quickly booked Sarah Bernhardt, who received $500 in gold from the management before every performance for a week; and it was not long before the Palace became the vaudeville house every vaudeville actor in America longed to play. No one could hope for any greater distinction. The audiences were alert and shrewd, especially on Monday afternoons, when they gave an informal but final verdict by their enthusiasm or their disdain. Many of the Monday afternoon audiences were professionals. Throughout the week, three-quarters of the Palace audiences took their seats by subscription and were intimately acquainted with the actors and the standards of vaudeville. The pressure of audience opinion was so fierce that some good performers never played the Palace because it did not seem to them an enjoyable establishment.

When talking pictures revolutionized the show business of Broadway, the Palace began to decline. The last full-time vaudeville show at the Palace was performed on July 9, 1932. A new policy of both vaudeville and film lasted, with intermittent variations, until September 20, 1935. For the next fourteen years, the celebrated home of vaudeville became a routine movie house. After that long interlude, vaudeville shows were revived now and then to present famous performers like Judy Garland, Danny Kaye, and Harry Belafonte. Occasionally old favorites, like Smith and Dale in their superb "Dr. Kronkite" sketch, took up briefly where they had left off many years before.

But the sad truth was that vaudeville was over. A brilliant form of stage entertainment that expressed skill, personality, and ideas—and presented some of the most talented actors of all time—disappeared from the Palace and sought refuge in television, night clubs, and motion pictures. The Palace remained one of the most inviting theaters in New York. In its respectable fifties, it booked musical comedies, and it provided a pleasant haven for thousands of theatergoers who were not alive when the Palace became the capitol of American vaudeville in 1913.

DISSENTERS FROM MEDIOCRITY

Not everybody was satisfied with the cheerful, childish, aimless show business of Broadway. With the decline of the stock companies of the nineteenth century, the theater lacked focus. "The theater of today has no standards," said a group of American playwrights in 1903, and they applied the remedy that has always been standard procedure: they proposed a National Theater. It would put on plays that had historical interest. Meeting in a state of constantly rising euphoria, which is the standard mood for all such occasions, they convinced themselves that 3,600 theatergoers would subscribe $40 in advance for ten productions the first year. With the success of the first season, they anticipated a sharp rise in the number of subscribers for the second. Nothing ever came of this familiar fantasy.

But something of considerable significance happened soon afterwards. In 1905, some New Yorkers who were noted for their substance issued a prospectus for a New Theater that would represent the taste of discriminating people. The theater would include thirty boxes; a committee of society women would pass on the eligibility of the applicants. Other committees of eligible citizens were to pass on the scenery, the costumes, the etiquette, and the manners; and, in accordance with the mystique of such projects, all the profits of the operation would be stored in an endowment fund. The president of the society was William K. Vanderbilt, who was both rich and leader of the social élite, and the treasurer was Otto H. Kahn, who was rich but realistic. Among the other founders—John Jacob Astor.

The New Theater was actually built, at 62nd Street and Central Park West. It was a beautifully massive building in the Italian Renaissance style, and it cost three million dollars. It could seat 3,000 people. It was designed on a big scale to accommodate both drama and opera, but the acoustics were poor. On November 6, 1909, it formally opened with a grand production—Sothern and Marlowe in *Antony and Cleopatra*, an ardent, voluptuous play for which neither was suited. The New Theater never recovered from that overblown, injudicious opening production; and, chastened by a painful experience, Sothern and Marlowe never again joined in a movement to uplift the theater.

Money, prestige, and high resolves had brought together some imposing names and skills. The acting company included Louis Calvert, A. E. Anson, Pedro de Cordoba, Rose Coghlan, Beatrice Forbes-Robertson, Olive Wyndham, Edith Wynne Matthison, and others. With the decline of stock companies where actors could get systematic training, English actors were beginning to have a better reputation than Americans; and English actors were reputed to be able to wear evening clothes more competently than American actors. The New Theater, accordingly, felt the need of developing a school of acting. Winthrop Ames, a man of taste and good breeding, was the manager. John Corbin, the drama critic, became play-reader and literary adviser. After opening with *Antony and Cleopatra* and provoking the dismay of critics and friends and the disdain of the public, the New Theater went on to produce Edward Knoblauch's (his spelling of that time) *The Cottage in the Air,* John Galsworthy's *Strife,* a remorseless drama of capital and labor that must have given the rich founders a bad turn, Rudolf Besier's *Don,* René Fauchois' *Beethoven,* Shakespeare's *The Winter's Tale,* H. Wiers-Jenssen's *The Witch,* about the Salem trials, Sheridan's *The School for Scandal,* with Grace George, Pinero's *The Thunderbolt,* Edward Sheldon's *The Nigger,* and Maurice Maeterlinck's *Sister Beatrice.*

Nothing worked. The public was not interested. The New Theater,

The interior of the Century Theater, 1909.
(*The New York Public Library*)

which was fifteen blocks north of the Broadway district, had the reputation of being for millionaires and highbrows but not for people who enjoyed theater. The drama repertory was suspended while the season of opera took over. After the first season, the idea of an operatic season was abandoned, and the auditorium was radically remodeled in the hope of making it less spacious and formidable. The upper gallery was blocked off. The number of boxes was reduced to eighteen, creating serious social and minor financial problems. In October 1910, the New Theater reopened with a glamorous and expansive production of Maurice Maeterlinck's *The Blue Bird*, succeeded by Shakespeare's *The Merry Wives of Windsor*, Josephine Preston Peabody's *The Piper*, Marie Tempest in a dramatization of *Vanity Fair* by Robert Hichens and Cosmo Gordon-Lennox, Mary Austin's *The Arrow Maker*, and Maurice Maeterlinck's *Mary Magdalene*. Before World War I, Becky Sharp, Mary Magdalene, and Sapho were the favorite stage heroines, thus demonstrating the public's concurrent interest in cupidity, religion, and lechery. Olga Nethersole, who had shocked the constabulary with her voluptuous Sapho in 1900, brought some of the same ardor to *Mary Magdalene* at the New Theater in 1910: her Mary had not been sufficiently purified by her encounter with the Nazarene. One reviewer thought that her kisses and embraces were too violent and her undulations too provocative.

Despite Miss Nethersole's exhibition of basic stage technique, the New Theater rapidly fell apart. In March of 1911, the founders leased it to George Tyler, who celebrated his administration by putting on *The Garden of Allah*, which introduced the New Theater to the cultural standards of Broadway. The founders announced that they were going to build a smaller theater between 44th and 45th Streets, just west of the Astor Hotel. But they never did. The idea of a fine theater for people of fine taste was buried under a heap of bills.

For the idea had not come from the theater itself. It came from patrons of art. There may have been an undertone of the sort of anti-Semitism that existed in those days. Although Lee Shubert was one of the officers of the New Theater, some people remarked humorously that one of the functions of the New Theater would be to lead "the children of Israel" out of Broadway and into the promised land. For the founders were rich and complacent members of the establishment. There is a photograph of a banquet of the founders in December 1910, at the time when Olga Nethersole was igniting the stage by doing what came naturally. Judge Gary of the

United States Steel Corporation presided. J. P. Morgan was also at the head table. Henry W. Taft, brother of the President of the United States, was on the dais. Everyone was in full dress and looked fearfully respectable in the flashlight photograph.

But the financial statement when the theater closed was desolate. The surplus fund of $600,000 was gone. Because of the cumbersome and costly repertory schedule, no production could be performed often enough to return the investment (*The Blue Bird* cost $41,000 and earned only $24,-000 in nine performances), and the running expenses were colossal—$1,400 a week for electricity, $700 a month for coal, 384 people on the payroll. The upper classes endorsed the theater with a stupendous deficit.

Under commercial management, the New Theater became the Century Theater and housed musical comedies, a fine production of *The Tempest* for the Shakespearean tricentenary in 1916, a memorable *Hamlet* by Sir John Martin Harvey, Max Reinhardt's stunning production of *The Miracle* (which had more scenery by Norman Bel Geddes than book by Karl Vollmoeller), and magnificent Max Reinhardt productions of *A Midsummer Night's Dream*, *Everyman*, and *Danton's Death*. But the theater building could never overcome the handicap of the cold, solemn pompousness of the original design. It could never surrender to the public. In 1929, the Shuberts tore it down and erected the Century Apartments, where New Yorkers have been living contentedly ever since, unmindful of the Golden Illusion that became the empty Hoax on that fair plot in 1909, 1910, and 1911.

Among those impatient with the tawdriness of the theater was the most modest and lovable little man who ever produced on Broadway. Arthur Hopkins, one of eight sons in an impecunious Ohio family, was an inspired man. A mystic, he was a believer in many intangible things—truth and beauty, of course, but also destiny, fate, spiritualism, or something equally elusive. No one ever really knew the source of his laconic serenity in every situation. In catastrophe, he was as unpretentious and cheerful as he was in time of success. Like Winthrop Ames, whom he liked and respected, he revolutionized Broadway by taking the drama seriously.

His career began as a reporter for the *Cleveland Globe*. In that post, he distinguished himself by quickly tracking down the family and personal history of Leon Czolgocz, the anarchist who shot President McKinley in

1901, and scooping the world on the story. A few years later, he was a vaudeville press agent in New York, and then a booking agent. He booked vaudeville tours for Harry Lauder, the Scottish singer; Bert Williams, the Negro comedian; Will Rogers, the cowboy sage; Vernon and Irene Castle, the "king and queen of ballroom dancing"; and Elbert Hubbard, the philosopher of success. His show-business background included one stunt that astounded New York. He booked a pioneer flight by Roy Knaben-shue, who flew a dirigible from an empty lot on Broadway at 60th Street down Broadway, around the Flatiron Building at 23rd Street, and back to 60th Street. People stopped. Traffic stopped. Streetcars stopped. This quiet man, who believed in philosophy, religion, and other-worldliness, arranged one of New York's most spectacular worldly events.

In 1912, Hopkins began his producing career by putting on Eleanor Gates' *The Poor Little Rich Girl*, which took the Freudian attitude towards character long before Miss Gates or Hopkins had ever heard of Freud. About this time, he went abroad to visit the theaters in England, France, and Germany and thus got an inkling of what theater might be. After his experience in vaudeville—a theater form that has to make its points imme-diately and that is rigidly disciplined—Hopkins disliked the cumbersome and spurious style of the commercial theater: stages crowded with irrele-vant scenery and props, busy actors, turgid speech, lack of interest in minor parts, superficial staging.

After two failures, he bought and, with Sam Harris and George M. Cohan, co-produced Elmer Rice's *On Trial* in 1914—an epochal melo-drama that introduced the technical device of the "flashback." From that time on, Hopkins, the least aggressive of men, transfigured the Broadway theater. He found an equally inspired ally in Robert Edmond Jones, also acquainted with the European theater, who turned scene design from a craft to an art by his use of color, form, and lighting. To him, as to Hop-kins, the theater was a holy place. His favorite quotation, from some Irish theaterman, was: "Keep in your soul some images of magnificence."

Having taste in stage direction as well as in stage literature, Hopkins proceeded to revitalize classics and produce plays that the old Broadway would not know what to do with—John Barrymore in Tolstoy's *The Living Corpse*, Alla Nazimova in Ibsen's *The Wild Duck* (neither of which had ever been done on Broadway in English), John Barrymore in *Richard III* and *Hamlet*, Lionel Barrymore in *Macbeth*, John and Lionel Barrymore in Benelli's *The Jest*, Mrs. Fiske in Philip Moeller's *Madame Sand*, Pauline

Lord and Jacob Ben-Ami in *Samson and Delilah*. He discovered Clare Kummer's unique talent for writing light farce and produced her *Good Gracious, Annabelle* and *A Successful Calamity* (with William Gillette, who was Miss Kummer's cousin). He produced O'Neill's *Anna Christie* with Pauline Lord. He produced the first modern war play, *What Price Glory?* by Laurence Stallings and Maxwell Anderson. Hundreds of people less pure in heart than Hopkins were scandalized by the profanity in that flaring chronicle of the Marines. While one of the earliest performances was going on, police wagons were parked in adjoining streets in case the district attorney decided to raid the performance. He did not give the signal because, at that performance, the actors prudently omitted the profanity.

Hopkins produced Philip Barry's charming *In a Garden*, with the lustrous Laurette Taylor, and Barry's *Paris Bound*, in which a boyish Hope Williams gave her first professional performance. In other plays, Hopkins introduced Katharine Hepburn, Barbara Stanwyck, and Clark Gable.

Among the people Hopkins most believed in was Evangeline Adams, an astrologist. He thought she was a seer, her technique of astrology being incidental. He believed in Miss Adams absolutely. At the time when he was at a peak of success and activity, she told him that he was facing a long period when nothing he would do would be a success. Not being able to be inactive he continued to produce. But his career turned out to be much as Miss Adams had predicted. After 1930 and for more than a decade nearly everything he undertook to do was unsuccessful. There were exceptions. He staged with distinction Robert Sherwood's *The Petrified Forest* for Gilbert Miller in 1935. In 1946, he produced Emmet Lavery's play about Justice Holmes, *The Magnificent Yankee*, and this, too, was a success.

But, for about twenty years, until he died in 1950, this wonderful little man who had had a vision of what modern theater could be and had realized it consistently went silently about his personal affairs with only a flicker of success—never complaining, never commenting. Thanks to the generosity of the Shuberts, he retained rent-free his old offices in the Plymouth Theater where he had done many fresh and magical things. It was an office of long silences. To those who visited him, Hopkins was polite and friendly but uncommunicative. He knew what was happening and offered no resistance. In 1950, when he was in a hospital after a serious heart attack, one of his visitors remarked to him that he seemed to be philosophically able to cope with anything—in this instance, with death. "Yes, I'm lucky," he said with a friendly smile. He died soon afterwards, mourned and loved because, by being selfless, he had given Broadway many things to be proud of.

By the standards of Broadway, Winthrop Ames was more of an immigrant than if he had come from Europe or Asia. He was a New England gentleman and aristocrat—two things seemingly impossible to assimilate into the gaudy community dominated by Klaw and Erlanger and the Shubert brothers. But in a career of a little less than a quarter of a century, this tall, slender Bostonian had a profound and enriching impact on Broadway. He was also the court of last resort on matters involving censorship and the black market in tickets when Broadway needed to put on the appearance of integrity. On these occasions, Ames gave Broadway a good name.

Winthrop Ames was born in 1870 into a wealthy manufacturing family that made plows and shovels. Ames went to Harvard College, which in those days was practically a trade school for sons of the New England rich. Nothing could have been much more alien to his experience than the theater, which at that time and place was thought to be irresponsible and immoral. But the theater fascinated Ames. No dilettante, he learned as much as he could about it. In 1904, he leased the Castle Square Theater in Boston and for three years directed a stock company that put on a new play every week—the most grueling and thorough of apprenticeships. In 1907 and 1908, he went to France and Germany, where the theater was far in advance of anything in America. When he returned, he became general director of the New Theater in New York and, faithful to his commitments, stayed there until the enterprise collapsed. After that traumatic experience he returned to the sort of paternalistic management that was part of his family tradition. Ames was no wheeler-dealer.

He was unique on Broadway. Bewildered by his dignity and reticence, theater people who visited him described him as Roman—a respectful word that also acknowledged his remoteness from huckstering. They had never met anyone like him. But he had not only a great deal of money but a fund of practical experience and a curiosity and interest in the kind of modern drama that the commercial theater automatically rejected. He brought to Broadway some of the enterprise and independence of England and Europe. In 1912, he built a gem of a theater on 44th Street in elegant Georgian taste—the Little Theater, which seated 299 people. It is now a television studio and finds itself conveniently next door to Sardi's restaurant, the center of Broadway's upper-class civilization. Ames' policy, he said, was to produce "the clever, the unusual drama that has a chance of becoming a library classic." He opened the Little Theater with John Galsworthy's *The Pigeon*, a drama about the incongruities of charity administered by the rich.

The next year, Ames built the Booth Theater in 45th Street; it seated 712 people and is still one of New York's finest theaters. He opened it with Edward Knoblock's dramatization of Arnold Bennett's *The Great Adventure*. In building small theaters, Ames was renouncing the trend towards theaters with large capacities—excellent for business, but bad for anything except violent or flamboyant plays. Ames had a suite of comfortable offices upstairs in the Little Theater, where he could be in close touch with his productions downstairs and only a few steps away from the Booth Theater. In the midst of Broadway he had a little enclave of taste, independence, and intelligence.

To discover fresh talent in 1914, he organized a play contest for a prize of $10,000 and received 1,875 scripts. The prize went to Alice Brown for *Children of the Earth*, a study of the New England conscience and a frail piece of theater. Ames produced plays with his own money, as did most of the leading producers at that time. Until 1930, when his health failed, he put on many notable dramas that had ideas and originality—Schnitzler's *The Affairs of Anatol*, with John Barrymore and Doris Keane; *Pierre the Prodigal*, a pantomine acted by Laurette Taylor; *Prunella*, by Laurence Housman and Granville Barker; Shaw's *The Philanderer*, with John Barrymore; a piquant comedy by Cyril Harcourt called *A Pair of Silk Stockings*; *Beggar on Horseback*, a remarkable fantasy by George S. Kaufman and Marc Connelly, still regarded by some people as their best work; *White Wings*, a droll fable by Philip Barry and a cause célèbre because most critics did not like it; Galsworthy's *Old English* and *Escape*; *Minick*, by George S. Kaufman and Edna Ferber; *Will Shakespeare*, by Clemence Dane, in which Katharine Cornell made an unforgettable appearance early in her career; untraditional but gorgeous new productions of *Iolanthe*, *The Pirates of Penzance*, and *The Mikado*. Ames was the finest stage director of the time. He came to rehearsals with the performance blocked; he knew what he was doing, and he treated actors with respect. The scenery and costuming were always fresh and beautiful; his lighting was thought to be better than Belasco's, which was first rate.

He was the pioneer of modern theater, for he had a cosmopolitan point of view and a knowledge of the best work that was being done abroad. During the first years of his experience, the audience of lower-middle-class theatergoers increased four or five times. As a result, he said, the theater was dominated by "a great, new, eager, childlike, tasteless, honest, crude general public." He was not against it. But he helped to create a theater that would better satisfy theatergoers with more exacting standards.

In view of all that he did for Broadway, it would be pleasant to report that he succeeded financially. But he failed. By 1922, he had lost $504,372 at the Little Theater. There were probably other financial troubles that the theater was not responsible for. When Winthrop Ames died in 1937, his total estate was $77,000. His widow had to move out of the family mansion into a cottage on the estate. Like the Broadway that he left, she had to be content with golden memories.

Most of the people who were disenchanted with Broadway were amateurs. They read foreign plays or saw some of them when they went abroad. They knew the plays of Tolstoy, Chekhov, Turgenev, Strindberg, Ibsen, Hauptmann, and Maeterlinck, and were excited by the plays of Shaw and Wilde—and probably thought that Pinero was a major writer. According to the critic Clayton Hamilton, the modern drama sprang fully-armed from the forehead of Arthur Wing Pinero, like Minerva from the forehead of Zeus. American drama was still on the level of slick craftsmanship; it was primarily concerned with plots that worked. When Elmer Rice submitted his first play, *On Trial*, in 1914, Arthur Hopkins liked the craftsmanship but disliked the story. Rice wrote another story for the same plot. Ten years later, when he wrote *The Adding Machine*, Rice was one of the most forceful and individualistic dramatists on Broadway, and Arthur Hopkins was a producer with an almost mystic belief in art, beauty, and integrity. But in 1914, neither one of them thought that there was anything discreditable about jettisoning one story and set of characters and inventing another story and set of characters for the purpose of making a trick of craftsmanship a better box-office attraction. When he blundered onto Broadway after having been a discontented law clerk, Rice put a high value on the mechanics of playwriting and a low value on theme and characters. In his autobiography, which he wrote in 1963, Rice said that he had never been able to reconcile the art of the drama with the realities of show business. Anything that worked was good enough in 1914.

Educated people as a whole were becoming alienated from this kind of theater. This was the period of the little theater, the art theater, the community theater—almost exclusively amateur. All over the country, they represented a revolt against the complacency of Broadway. There were 30,000 members of drama leagues around the country, all of them critical of the commercial theater. The professionals felt insulted by the scornful comments of the amateurs, and the amateurs felt excluded and denigrated. The revolution had very modest beginnings. Between 1912 and 1914, a group of high-minded social workers staged *The Shepherd*, a play about the revolutionary movement in Russia, and John Galsworthy's *The Silver Box* as part of the social service movement of the Henry Street Settlement. In 1914, it became the Neighborhood Playhouse at 466 Grand Street, and eventually it helped to civilize Broadway.

In 1915 a group of restless and scornful young people put on some unpretentious dramas during the summer at Provincetown on Cape Cod. In 1916, they established the Provincetown Playhouse in Macdougal Street in Greenwich Village. Among them was Eugene G. O'Neill, as he was called then, and Floyd Dell, Max Eastman, Louise Bryant, Susan Glaspell, Hutchins Hapgood, John Reed, William Zorach, Wilbur Daniel Steele, Mary Heaton Vorse, all of them scornful of Broadway. Although Broadway was smarter, they were intelligent, and eventually Broadway took lessons from them.

In 1915, the Drama League could recommend only three plays as worth the attention of its subscribers—and two of the plays were of foreign origin. But that was the season when a handful of amateurs laid the foundations for an effective revolution by leasing the Band Box Theater in East 57th Street and producing three one-act plays—*Licensed*, by Lawrence Langner; *Eugenically Speaking*, by Edward Goodman; and *Interior*, by Maurice Maeterlinck. (Robert Edmond Jones, a genius almost unrecognized at the time, helped them to produce the three one-act plays at a cost of $35.) The actors called themselves the Washington Square Players because their cultural center had been the Washington Square Book Shop in the Village. They played on Friday and Saturday evenings in a tiny theater that seated forty people, and they charged 50 cents admission. The total payroll consisted of one stagehand and one office boy.

After some favorable newspaper reviews appeared, the Washington Square Players became an immediate success; they sold out at every performance. During the season, they put on three more bills of one-act plays, by Anton Chekhov, John Reed, Rose Pastor Stokes, Philip Moeller, Alfred de Musset, Lewis Beach, Zoe Akins, and Alice Gerstenberg (author of *Overtones*, which anticipated O'Neill's *Strange Interlude* by dramatizing the interior and exterior personalities of two characters). Chekhov was hardly known in America then. But the Washington Square Players concluded their tenancy of the Band Box Theater by putting on a disastrous performance of *The Sea Gull*. In 1916, they moved to the Comedy Theater in 41st Street just east of Broadway, seating 600 people. Now they charged $1.00 admission, played seven performances, and they received a salary of $25 a week each.

Professional showmen expected them to fail when they challenged the standards of Broadway. But they progressed rapidly. Something quite new was taking root in the professional district. They leased a workshop across the street where they could make costumes and scenery, and they established an acting school. They put on plays with literary values, like Susan Glaspell's *Trifles*, Zona Gale's *Neighbors*, Leonid Andreyev's *The Life of Man*, and Ibsen's *Ghosts*. They gave the first Broadway production to a dramatist who eventually shook up the whole concept of drama in America—Eugene O'Neill. Today, his sea play, *In the Zone*, is a classic. It was unknown then. It is interesting to note that *In the Zone* was well received on its own merits before O'Neill had any professional standing. *The New York Times*—"Of a very high order, both as a thriller and as a document in human character and emotion"; *The New York American*— "The best and the most agreeably acted of the playlets." *The Globe* described it as "the best" and added some appreciative comments about O'Neill's knowledge of life and his talent for writing.

The Washington Square Players also provided a platform for some actors who subsequently had distinguished careers in the theater after World War I—Roland Young, Rollo Peters, José Ruben, Frank Conroy, Glenn Hunter, Helen Westley, and Katharine Cornell. Miss Cornell made her first appearance on Broadway in the Comedy Theater. She played several parts during two seasons and was complimented for her ability to read long speeches in Grace Latimer Wright's *Blind Alleys*. The Washington Square Players disbanded on May 13, 1918, partly because of the war, but largely because they were broke. It is significant that they had been accepted as a fresh and stimulating organization which put on original plays that had to be taken seriously. They were still amateurs, but they were behaving like professionals. In 1919 when the war was over, they became the Theater Guild—the most enlightened and influential theater organization New York has ever had. More than any other group, they led Broadway into the modern world.

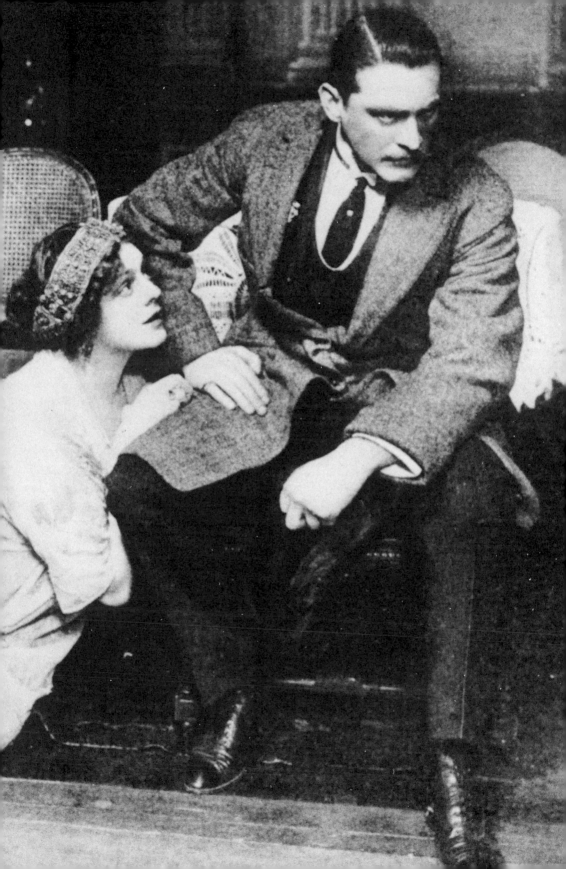

THE
ROYAL FAMILY
OF ACTORS

For more than a half century, "Barrymore" was the most imposing name on Broadway. Maurice Blythe, a witty, handsome, irrepressible Englishman, chose that surname to avoid embarrassing his sedate British parents when he went on the stage. He was no dilettante. Among his most notable achievements was the lightweight boxing championship of England. But he had no training for the stage: to him it was neither a shrine nor a duty, but an easy place in which to earn a living. Being attractive and congenial, he flourished, particularly in America, and he married into a family that regarded the theater as the chief purpose of life.

He married Georgiana Emma Drew, daughter of the senior John Drew, an actor who died when she was a small girl, and Mrs. John Drew, an actress of formidable strength of character. After her husband's death, until 1892, Mrs. Drew managed the Arch Street Theater Stock Company in Philadelphia. She was the mother of John Drew, the most gentlemanly

Ethel and John Barrymore in J. M. Barrie's "advanced drama," A Slice of Life (1912). (The New York Public Library)

actor of his day. (Example of his gallantry: when he was dying, his last words to a member of the family who was sitting with him were: "See that the nurses are taken care of.")

Since Maurice and Georgiana Barrymore, Mrs. Drew's son-in-law and daughter, were generally acting on Broadway or on the road during the season, she brought up their three children—Lionel, Ethel and John—in Philadelphia. She was a loving if domineering grandmother, and she kept the children both orderly and content. Although they saw their parents only between engagements, they were brought up amid the tumult and discipline of the theater. Once when their parents were touring with Helena Modjeska, Lionel and Ethel were taken along and had happy memories of playing with their toys in Madame Modjeska's private railroad car. Modjeska, a splendid human being as well as actress, had one most profound influence on the Barrymore family. Georgiana Barrymore was so deeply impressed by Madame Modjeska's Catholicism that she became a Catholic convert and had Ethel and Lionel rechristened Catholics. Since John was away at school, he was not rechristened. But when Ethel was still in a convent a few years later, she was horrified to realize that John was an infidel. Persuading a boy twelve years old to be John's godfather, she served as his godmother and had him christened a Catholic at St. Patrick's Cathedral. It must have been one of the most precocious christenings in town.

The father, Maurice Barrymore, a cheerful drinker and bon vivant, took little interest in his family; he was a father at several stages remove. His wife's health was frail; and, in 1893, she was sent West for a change of climate. Ethel, thirteen years old, was delegated to accompany her mother by ship to the Isthmus of Panama, across the Isthmus by railroad, and up the West Coast by ship to California. They settled in Santa Barbara. Georgiana was more gravely ill of tuberculosis than anyone had realized. She died in Santa Barbara. Ethel accompanied her mother's coffin across the country on the long railroad journey home. That awful experience must have had a traumatic effect on a girl just reaching adolescence and must have been one of the factors contributing to the indomitable character of her mature years.

Mrs. John Drew lost both the Arch Street Theater and her Philadelphia home in 1893, presumably because her stock company failed. Suddenly the children had to cope with the problem of earning a living. They never knew exactly what had destroyed the security of their childhood and they had not been trained to any career. If the three Barrymores never had a romantic feeling for the theater, it was because they were shoved into it without having a choice. John, the youngest of the three, was still in school at the time. But Ethel, who had had some notion that she might become a concert pianist, accompanied her grandmother to Montreal, where she acted a small part in *The Rivals*—her grandmother's standard play. When the play closed, she was put in care of her aunt and uncle, Mr. and Mrs. Sidney Drew, who were, not surprisingly, actors, and she toured with them. They saw to it that she was fed, housed, and clothed, but they did not pay her anything for the small parts she played or for playing the piano in the orchestra pit on occasion.

Lionel also made his stage debut with his grandmother in *The Rivals* in 1894. He was not a success. In a fond though decisive note, his grandmother dismissed him from the company: "I sincerely wish I did not have to write this letter, for I want to spare your feelings. But, dear boy, I am compelled to inform you of the plain facts concerning your portrayal of Thomas. You were somewhat inadequate, and it is with the deepest regret that I convey the news that it is no longer necessary that you appear in the cast. I shall see you in the morning, dear boy. Until then, good night, and God bless you. Your affectionate grandmother, Mrs. Drew." Lionel was only sixteen, and this dismal episode must have contributed to the sense of insecurity he had about stage acting for the rest of his life.

But Ethel's apprenticeship could not have been without distinction. When William Gillette was about to do *Secret Service* in London, he sent for Ethel to play a small part; and in 1893, Henry Irving engaged her to play in his company in *The Bells* and *Peter the Great*, also in London. She was thus exposed to the rococo acting of the nineteenth century. But it seems not to have affected her. She was always a modern actress.

In 1900, when she was twenty-one, Charles Frohman cast her in the leading part in Clyde Fitch's *Captain Jinks of the Horse Marines*, a society comedy. She did not feel sufficiently professional to carry the responsibility of the leading part, and she was nervous about it. When the comedy opened in Philadelphia, the response was disheartening. One critic wrote: "If the young lady who plays Madame Trentoni had possessed beauty, charm or talent, this play might have been a success." Philadelphia, where she had had an idyllic childhood, rejected her cruelly. Two weeks of one-night stands on the road were equally painful, and Ethel begged Frohman not to bring the play to New York. But Fitch wanted the satisfaction of a New York engagement: "For 2 weeks only— A play by Clyde Fitch called 'Captain Jinks of the Horse Marines,'" the billing read.

The New York opening at the Garrick Theater on February 4, 1901, was a conspicuous success. One newspaper reported the occasion as follows: "Not since John Drew led Ada Rehan before the curtain at Mr. Daly's has there been such cause for hurraying, such kid-glove-bursting applause, such bouquet tossing across the bedazzled footlights, welcoming our newest, our dearest star, Miss Ethel Barrymore." "Dear Miss Ethel Barrymore—Newest Princess of Our Footlit Realm," wrote another. There was more in the same maudlin style. There were also dissenters. *The New York Dramatic Mirror* regarded *Captain Jinks* as a "very bad play" and Ethel Barrymore as a commonplace actress. "Ethel Barrymore, to be perfectly candid," said the perfectly candid *Dramatic Mirror* reviewer, "played Madame Trentoni no better than probably some score of young actresses presently rated as ordinary." But the *Mirror* also employed a lively woman who wrote the weekly column "Matinee Girl." She characterized *Captain Jinks* as "one of the neatest little bits of refined comedy and bright dialogue," and she thought that Ethel Barrymore was "utterly charming. . . . There is no doubt that Miss Barrymore is going to win triumphs of the permanent sort."

After the play had been running for a month (and Ethel was still getting $125 a week), Mr. Frohman put her name up in lights on the marquee as the star. *Captain Jinks* had a long run in New York and on the road. When the actor of one of the small parts was ill, Ethel telegraphed to her brother John at school to substitute. He had not been on the professional stage before, but he played the small part with infectious gaiety. He also demonstrated some of the wayward impulsiveness that was characteristic of him for the rest of his life. Much to everyone's astonishment, he took a solo curtain call at the end of the second act. At the final curtain, he led Ethel onstage, ceremoniously bowed to her and then to the audience as if he were the star. Everyone was thoroughly amused by this impudent prank of a boy of eighteen.

When a New York production of *Alice-Sit-by-the-Fire* was being discussed in London by Frohman and Barrie, Ethel assumed that she would play the part of the daughter. But Barrie insisted that she play the mother: "I can see you playing it and hearing you say those things in the last act," he declared. She did play the mother, and Barrie was right, not only about the part but about Ethel, for she became the mother surrogate of the family. The most stable and professional of the three Barrymores, she consistently promoted the careers of her brothers as soon as she became a star. When she played *Alice-Sit-by-the-Fire*, she persuaded Frohman to give John a small part and to cast both John and Lionel in the curtain-raiser, *Pantaloon*. Lionel played a character part, which was his forte as everyone was to realize later, and he had his first happy experience on Broadway. Ethel took full responsibility for everything. She gave her brothers money when they were in trouble. Although her father had dropped his family and married for the second time without telling his children (they read about it in the newspapers), Ethel paid the bills for his confinement to hospital and nursing homes during the last three years of his life, and saw to it that he was buried with fitting ceremony and attention.

Ethel was a personage first and an actress second. Like her father and her brother John, she was a strikingly handsome person. She had a beautifully proportioned profile. She had a melodious contralto voice— a beguiling part of her stage personality. She had dark vivacious eyes that she inherited from her mother and grandmother. In some elusive way, she had a particular gleam that captivated audiences. It seemed to be compounded of radiance held in reserve, mocking eyes, light and spontaneous movement, and personal grandeur. The stage was the medium in which she earned a rich living and supported family, relatives, and a large entourage.

But it was no obsession, and the fact that she was not a great actress may have been because she never entirely surrendered to it. There was more to her life than the stage. She was a cultivated woman who knew and loved great music and could play it. She read everything from Barrie to Turgenev and from *Alice in Wonderland* to *Daisy Miller* and *The Golden Bowl*. She had broad interests; she took a fanatical interest in baseball and boxing. Particularly in her youth, she was infatuated with society; and, like many American girls of the time, she might have made a glamorous marriage in England. She was once engaged to Laurence Irving, the son of Henry Irving; for a time she considered a marriage proposal from a titled Britisher. Winston Churchill proposed to her. After attending an arranged dinner with him and his colleagues, she concluded that she would not be happy as the wife of a politician.

In 1909, she married Russell Colt, a rich American playboy, with whom she had three children. It was not a happy marriage. He was no more a family man than her father had been, and the marriage was dissolved in 1923. As the years went by, she became progressively queenly. She had supreme self-confidence in her choice of parts and in the staging of the plays. She was complacent enough to play Juliet when she was forty-three years of age, and Ophelia and Portia when she was forty-six. She was not to be trifled with. She slapped Tallulah Bankhead in the face when Tallulah was rash enough to imitate her at a party. She never forgave George S. Kaufman and Edna Ferber for having written a

Fanny Addison Pitt, Sidney Cowell, Ethel Barrymore, and H. Reeves Smith in *Captain Jinks of the Horse Marines* (1900). (*The New York Public Library*)

satirical portrait of a family closely resembling the Barrymores in *The Royal Family*. When Kaufman asked her to appear in a benefit program during World War II she ironically quoted back to him a line from the play more than fifteen years after it had been produced: "But I'm going to have laryngitis that night." She was not amused by humorous comments about the Barrymores, and she was scornful of criticism. In a long, hard-working Broadway career she played more than fifty stage parts and concluded her professional life with some films.

When she was beginning in the days of make-believe theater, she played comedy parts with grace and subtlety, and she became a vogue actress. She could do no wrong; thousands of theatergoers were more interested in her than in the plays she acted. Young girls imitated her dress and manners. Some of the plays, particularly in the early days, were too trivial to be remembered. But in 1908, she played in one of Somerset Maugham's first comedies, *Lady Frederick*. Another Maugham play, *The Constant Wife*, became one of her greatest successes in 1925. The Barrymore gleam and also the haughty style charged these comedies with quicksilver. When she took *Lady Frederick* to Indianapolis, the *Star* said:

> Should men, as in the Pagan Age, adore,
> One goddess would be Ethel Barrymore.

She also gave a winning performance in Edna Ferber's and G. V. Hobart's *Our Mrs. McChesney* in 1915. *The New York Dramatic Mirror* was glad to see her back in a comedy part and thought her acting was breezy and delightful. The *Dramatic Mirror* was also gratified that she had taken off weight. (Critics were always uneasy when she put on weight.)

In 1919, the part of Lady Helen Haden in Zoe Akins' *Déclassée* suited her completely and she had one of her pleasantest experiences in that play. She acted a brilliant Lady Teazle in The Players' revival of *The School for Scandal* in 1925.

Her taste in plays was conservative. Although she acted in *A Doll's House* in her early career, she did not take kindly to advanced playwrights. She regarded Ibsen as "a good technician," but she thought his characters were "perverted and false." She regarded Shaw as brilliant, but trivial;

Richard Waring and Ethel Barrymore in *The Corn Is Green* (1940). (*Museum of the City of New York*)

she said that he had "a small intellect." But she resented being typed as a society actress who dominated her plays by force of personality, and she frequently and defiantly appeared in parts of a different nature. In 1907, in *The Silver Box*, which was John Galsworthy's first play to be done in America, she played a scrubwoman in a bedraggled dress. It was a sharp contrast with the plays her fans were accustomed to. *Theatre Magazine* said that the "part was beyond her," although *The New York Dramatic Mirror* was pleasantly surprised by the emotional force of her acting. Three years later, her portrait of Zoë Blundell in Pinero's lugubrious and portentous *Midchannel* was regarded as creditable, if a little monotonous, and "not limited to the dimensions of personality acting." When she appeared in Hauptmann's *Rose Bernd* in 1922, her acting was dull. "She groaned her lines," said *Theatre Magazine*, and made Rose Bernd "not just dull but lunatic." The poignant characterization of a peasant girl was outside the range of this regal actress.

The dreary conclusion to Ethel Barrymore's marriage and the scope and multitude of the family responsibilities she had assumed must have given her considerable anxiety in the twenties. Perhaps she also feared that the new Broadway with its fresh criticisms of life was not her milieu. With Fitch, Barrier, Maugham, Pinero, and Galsworthy, she was more at home than in a theater dominated by the rude tragedies of O'Neill and the sophistication of the Theater Guild. Whatever the reason, she chose plays to which she was not suited. In some of them, she seemed to be trying to hide behind alien roles. The Shuberts named a beautiful new theater for her in 1928. She opened it as holy Sister Gracia in Martínez Sierra's *The Kingdom of God*. It was nothing more than a tour de force. Two years later, she put on mulatto make-up to appear in a Negro play called *Scarlet Sister Mary*, in which white actors played Negroes in blackface. The result was embarrassing.

The thirties were the low point in Ethel Barrymore's life. After living lavishly for many years, she was in serious financial trouble and was sued by the Federal government for unpaid income taxes. There was a note of desperation about her career. She revived *The School for Scandal*, *The Twelve-Pound Look*, and *The Constant Wife*. In Sidney Howard's *The Ghost of Yankee Doodle*, she ably played a modern part in a poor play. She appeared as an old crone of 93 in *Farm of Three Echoes*, and a woman of 102 in *Whiteoaks*—both of them commonplace plays far below the standards of comedies like *Lady Frederick* and *The Constant Wife*.

While she was appearing in such lackluster plays, she rejected Emlyn Williams' *The Corn Is Green* as being unsuited to her talents. In this rejection, she did not distinguish between what was false and what was genuine. But in 1940, a gifted and imaginative producer of a younger generation, Herman Shumlin, persuaded her that the part of a perceptive and resolute schoolteacher in a grubby Welsh town in *The Corn Is Green* would suit her exactly. He was right. In her early sixties, Ethel Barrymore had the best part she had ever had and proved that she was more than a society actress. She lost herself in the part of Miss Moffat. After a long, anxious, fruitless interlude, she had the satisfaction of being discovered by a generation of theatergoers that was not familiar with her better work.

In the first act, Miss Moffat, the schoolteacher, was aggressive and truculent and scornful of the loutishness of her students. But one of them turned out to be extraordinarily gifted. He awoke a feeling of hope that had long been dormant in Miss Moffat. He reminded her that the most exalting thing in life is the gift of enlightenment by one generation to the next—creation, transfiguration, joy, surrender, victory. Miss Barrymore played the part with selfless delight in the selfless exaltation of an inspired woman. Miss Moffat was her masterpiece; in the few years that remained of her stage career, she never had another part so exhilarating. Since her health had become precarious, she went to Hollywood, where the climate was milder and the pay more secure. In 1950, she briefly returned to Broadway to act *The Twelve-Pound Look* at a benefit performance for the American National Theater and Academy. At the fall of the curtain, she received a thunderous ovation. After taking several curtain calls, she spoke her last sentence on Broadway: "You make it sound inviting," she said. The familiar Barrymore gleam made that sentence sound like both benediction and prologue. She had taken potluck with Broadway for half a century. She died in Hollywood in 1959 at the age of seventy-nine. Neither of her two brothers— one of whom was more gifted—served the theater so long and so admirably. The mother surrogate of the family, she survived both of them.

When Ethel Barrymore persuaded John Barrymore to play Dr. Rank in her production of *A Doll's House* in 1905, she said that although he gave a good performance he needed discipline. That cool observation could be applied to his entire stage career, which had both the brilliance and dark fate of a Greek legend. John Barrymore was Icarus who flew so close to the sun that the wax on his wings melted and he plunged back to the earth—from the peak of classical acting to the banalities of show business.

John was the youngest of the three (Lionel, born 1878; Ethel, 1879;

John, 1882) and the most gifted. A handsome man, he looked like his father; and, like his father, he was restless and witty and a reckless drinker. Steeped in the theater during his childhood, John took it for granted; he had no special liking for it. In his youth, he was a sufficiently talented artist to earn $50 for one drawing a week for the Hearst newspapers. He shared bachelor apartments with Herbert Bayard Swope, a newspaperman who became the powerful editor of *The World* in the twenties.

But to John, the theater was the easiest place to make a good living. The temperamental environment of the theater he found not only familiar but congenial. By 1909, he had become a comedy star in Winchell Smith's *The Fortune Hunter* and a popular matinee idol because of his personal beauty and magnetism, his lean profile, his quick mind, and his gift of gaiety. The next year, Winthrop Ames cast him as Anatol in Schnitzler's *The Affairs of Anatol*. It was practically typecasting; again Barrymore was successful.

Although the theater was a congenial place to make money, he hated the routine of long runs. In 1914, when he was playing with Florence Reed in *The Yellow Ticket*, he once came onstage drunk. Miss Reed had the curtain lowered and resumed the performance with an understudy. It was a sensational and discreditable episode, and John Barrymore was so unnerved by it that he went abroad to recover.

The year 1916, when he was thirty-four, was a crucial one in his career. He played a rash bank clerk in John Galsworthy's *Justice* at the new Candler Theater in 42nd Street. The play was a powerful indictment of the brutishness of prison life. Barrymore acted the part of Falder, a clerk who stole money from the bank to help Ruth Honeywell run away to South America from her cruel husband. Falder's motive was entirely disinterested; Galsworthy went to some pains to explain that Falder and Mrs. Honeywell were not lovers. The crusading intensity of the play stirred theatergoers who were accustomed to theater of the uncommitted. Channing Pollock wrote: "Overnight the theatre has ceased to be a toy, a plaything—and has become a vital part of every day. *Justice* is not a play; it is an emotional experience, a tragedy in which you participate." The last act was overwhelming. As Falder, Barrymore was caged behind bars. The intensity of his performance electrified audiences; the desperation with which he shook the bars illustrated the helplessness of a young man against the implacable impersonality of the law and of prisons. Barrymore shook the bars so vigorously that once they broke in the middle of the performance. In *Justice* a clever actor began to look like an important one.

Edward Sheldon, an old friend and a perceptive theater man, had been urging Barrymore to take himself seriously as an actor. He had written a new play for him, *The Lonely Heart*, and Barrymore had expected to appear in it. But Sheldon withdrew the offer because he thought that a script by John N. Raphael made from George Du Maurier's *Peter Ibbetson* would be a better vehicle. It was characteristic of Sheldon that he not only voluntarily discarded his own play but edited the script of the one he considered better. *Peter Ibbetson*, a play about the occult, opened in 1917 with John Barrymore, Lionel Barrymore, Constance Collier, Laura Hope Crews, and Madge Evans. The performance was sensational. On opening night, it absorbed audiences so completely that, when a piece of scenery fell, no one moved or made any audible remark. (It fell again on the second night, and again the audience sat silent.)

Now John Barrymore had strayed into a part of the theater that he found enormously stimulating. While *Peter Ibbetson* was on the boards, he heard that Arthur Hopkins was planning a production of Tolstoy's *The Living Corpse*. He asked Hopkins to let him play the part of Fadya. When the rehearsals began, he threw himself into preparations with the eagerness of a man who suddenly had a vision of himself as a creative artist. He came to rehearsals thoroughly prepared. He knew his lines. He was always on time. He found plenty of time for fittings. He never felt imposed on when other actors asked him to rehearse individual scenes. He had prepared himself so thoroughly that he came to the first rehearsal with a Russian accent that he had been working on for a long time. (This was a tactical error. Hopkins pointed out that since all the characters were Russian, Barrymore's Russian accent would make all the others seem like foreigners.) Hopkins invited Tolstoy's son to attend the last dress rehearsal. Hopkins was thrilled by the performance. Tolstoy's only comment was dismal as well as laconic: "Where's Fadya's beard?" he asked querulously.

Redemption, as Hopkins called the play, was splendidly performed. At first the public was repelled by the forbidding nature of the story. But Broadway was not populated exclusively by blockheads. When word got around that John Barrymore's acting was brilliant and that the performance and production constituted a work of art, the demand for tickets was greater than the supply. But Hopkins could not waste time on making money, and he closed *Redemption* while it was a smash hit.

In the meantime, Edward Sheldon had discovered Sem Benelli's *The Jest*, which he regarded as suitable for both John and Lionel Barrymore. Technically *The Jest* was in the baleful category of *The Duchess of*

Peter Ibbetson, with Joseph Eagle, John Barrymore, Viva Burkitt, and Lionel Barrymore (1917). (*The New York Public Library*)

Sidney Mather as Laertes and John Barrymore as Hamlet in Barrymore's production of *Hamlet*. (*Museum of the City of New York*)

Malfi and *The White Devil*, but artistically was probably about as immortal as *The Count of Monte Cristo* and *When Knighthood Was in Flower*. Since Sarah Bernhardt played the John Barrymore part in French, and another woman, Mimi Aguglia, in Italian, *The Jest* was obviously not a portrait of life but a piece of theatrical hocus-pocus. But the New York production, which Hopkins staged and Jones set, emerged as a drama of such bold colors and daring contrasts that it seemed to most Broadway theatergoers about the most exciting play they had ever seen. On the opening night, the final curtain did not fall until 11:45. No one moved until it was over. In the next morning's *Times*, John Corbin said that " 'The Jest' fell across the sky of a declining season like a burst of sunset color." He thought Lionel Barrymore "had a touch of genius" and he hoped some day to see Lionel and John play Othello and Iago together.

The Jest was set in the Italy of Lorenzo de Medici. John played a moody artist named Gianette, and Lionel played a roaring mercenary named Neri. The performance was a contrast in styles—John subtle,

Robert Edmond Jones' setting for the burial of Ophelia in John Barrymore's *Hamlet* (1922). (*Jo Mielziner*)

nimble, and evasive; Lionel, booming and busy—the one sensitive and small, the other monstrous and overpowering. Both the brothers were in excellent form, and some theatergoers thought Lionel gave the greater performance. In the course of the run, John and Lionel amused themselves by stealing scenes from each other. There was plenty of hokum in *The Jest*, but the performance had freshness and vitality. John played his part at such a pitch of excitement that he once assaulted and knocked down a spotlight man who had lighted his feet but not his head. This outburst of temperament cost John Barrymore several hundred dollars in reparations.

Several years later, some other actors revived *The Jest*. It was simply hokum. The magic had evaporated.

In 1920, the incomparable trio of John Barrymore, Arthur Hopkins, and Robert Edmond Jones felt that they were on the threshold of great theater, and they took the next step. They prepared a production of Shakespeare's *Richard III*. Barrymore was very modest about his ability to play Shakespeare. Although he was fortunate enough to have a resonant voice with melodious overtones, he had never bothered to train it. It was "furry"—the word Hopkins used about it. But now John Barrymore took lessons from Mrs. Margaret Carrington, a creative voice teacher, who had a vision of the theater as exalted as that of Jones (whom she subsequently married).

Hopkins was as elated by the project as Barrymore and Jones. In order to escape pedantry and the staleness of the past, he eliminated the use of prompt-books at the rehearsals, and distributed the sides to the actors in typewritten form, as if the play were a new one. He staged *Richard III* as a melodrama. The opening was one of Broadway's most tempestuous occasions. Barrymore's Richard was a sardonic, cruel, fiery demon, who radiated a kind of sinister beauty. He was simultaneously winning and repellent. Having eliminated the impurities of his speech and the easygoing mannerisms of his comic acting, Barrymore emerged as an actor of the first rank. Everything in his Richard was subtle, shrewd, agile, and invincible. The production and performance of *Richard III* were recognized as prologues to a new theater that had infinite possibilities. In a flush of great expectations, Hopkins drew up a schedule of two new productions a year that would ultimately compose a repertory for Barrymore to play throughout the United States: *Hamlet, Cyrano de Bergerac, Faust, Peer Gynt, Richard III*, and *Redemption*.

But a program as organized as that assumed more discipline than John Barrymore was capable of. While he was playing *Richard III*, he was also wooing Mrs. Blanche Oelrichs Thomas, a rich society lady who wrote under the pseudonym of Michael Strange. Wooing anybody was a full-time occupation for John Barrymore, who had already wooed one wife. (He wooed two more in later years.) Now his performance in *Richard III* took second place. After acting the part at evening performances, he took a railroad train to Atlantic City, where Michael Strange (now divorced from Leonard Thomas) was living, and stayed there until it was time to catch a return train to New York the next day. This happened two or three times a week, and resulted in a nervous breakdown. *Richard III* had to be closed. Like other wastrels with plenty of money, Barrymore went to William Muldoon's health farm in White Plains to take the standard cure. On August 5, 1920, he married Michael Strange. The next spring, he and his sister Ethel did penance by appearing in a disastrous play, *Claire de Lune*, that his new wife had written.

Icarus had flown so close to the sun that the wax on his wings was getting soft. But there was a final leap into the empyrean. In 1922, at the Sam H. Harris Theater in 42nd Street, John Barrymore played a Hamlet that most people ranked with Edwin Booth's, by tradition considered the greatest. Lean, handsome, moody, sensitive, cultivated, passionate, and manly, he acted a vibrant Hamlet that elated just about everybody. It was no happy accident. He had prepared for it meticulously. His prompt-book—a slender Temple edition of the play—is now in the library of The Players club, and is dedicated to Mrs. Carrington. "This is the copy we worked from. It's a small copy—but good. How we worked!!" the inscription reads. The text is heavily cut. The prompt-book includes specific notes: "He that plays the King" was to be read in "a sort of dreamlike voice." When he read "What a piece of work is man!" he was to "look out" at the audience. Barrymore also enlivened the margins of the prompt-book with thumbnail sketches of, presumably, himself in full face, profile, and in and out of costume, as if he were killing time when he was not onstage during the rehearsals. Today the scribbles in this commonplace-looking book are vivid: we know that they are the personal notes of a great actor at the peak of his career.

The company was a notable one—Blanche Yurka, as the Queen; Tyrone Power, Sr., as the King; Rosalinde Fuller, as Ophelia; Whitford Kane, as the First Gravedigger. Barrymore altered the standard values of the play by the spontaneity of his acting. In the closet scene, his attitude towards the Queen was overtly incestuous—an audacious approach that piqued the interest of audiences who were just beginning to revel in the erotic mysteries of Freud. The reviewers were ecstatic. In *Theatre Maga-*

zine, which had always been a little reluctant about the Barrymores, Arthur Hornblow noted that Barrymore's modern style of acting put a full stop to the "school of recitation" in Shakespearean acting. He described Barrymore's Hamlet as "alive with vitality and genius—a great, beautiful, rare Hamlet—understandable and coherent." (In one respect, Barrymore clung to a custom that has been obsolete for years. He took bows between acts.) Barrymore's Hamlet varied from evening to evening. In his recollections of this event, Arthur Hopkins said he thought Barrymore's best performance was at a rehearsal at which his sister Ethel composed the entire audience. Barrymore could easily be thrown off his stride by extraneous events. He gave an embarrassingly overwrought performance on the evening when Stanislavsky and other actors in the Moscow Art Theater were in the audience. They were shocked and puzzled. Even when his sister and others told him during the intermissions what he was doing, he was unable to regain control.

Since Booth had given *Hamlet* 100 consecutive performances, Barrymore sought to break the record by playing it 101 times, although everyone seemed to have forgotton that an obscure actor, John E. Kellerd, had played it 102 times in 1912. Barrymore took his *Hamlet* to London in 1925. Constance Collier played the Queen, and Fay Compton, Ophelia. The New York success was repeated in London. James Agate called it "nearer to Shakespeare's whole creation than any other I have seen," and Jones' scenery Agate described as "the most beautiful thing I have ever seen on any stage." Bernard Shaw, in his role as devil's advocate, wrote Barrymore a gratuitous and devastating criticism. He accused Barrymore of substituting egotistical acting for Shakespeare's play and urged him to "concentrate on acting rather than authorship, at which, believe me, Shakespeare can write your head off." It was one of the most heartless as well as willful letters Shaw ever wrote. Shaw had seen the play in the company of Barrymore's first wife.

When John Barrymore acted Hamlet, he was forty-three years old—at the peak of his career, at the top of his profession. For nine years, he had striven for perfection in a profession he really did not like. He had had enough. When he finished *Hamlet,* he abdicated from Broadway and devoted the rest of his mercurial life to making films—and huge sums of money. He spent the money recklessly, drank excessively, and destroyed himself wildly. Icarus fell to the earth with a squalid thump. Observing this frenzied conclusion to a great career, Lionel said John was "like some comet tugged by both the earth and the sun. He was a man in flight and in pursuit at the same time." In John Barrymore's own wry phrase, "he applied hot and rebellious liquors to his blood" and indulged in a succession of good-humored binges.

In 1940, when he was fifty-seven years of age, bankrupt, and out of control, he returned to Broadway briefly. He brought to the Belasco Theatre a ramshackle play called *My Dear Children*, which burlesqued his career. On the opening night, the 44th Street block where the Belasco is located was filled with a silent crowd of curiosity-seekers who looked as if they hoped to be present at the final degradation of Icarus. Standing behind police barriers, they looked sinister. The crowds that watched the tumbrils pass in the French Revolution could not have been more pitiless or morbid.

Although *My Dear Children* was a cheap play, Barrymore gave it a first-rate performance in a light key of derision and mockery. His voice was deep and strong. Although he looked ravaged and old, he owned the stage. There was a kind of admirable, if perverse, gallantry about this final fling at the stage and the caricature of his place on it. In his younger years, Barrymore could hardly stand the strain of long runs because he was restless. He could not stand a long run in 1940 for another reason: he didn't have the strength. *My Dear Children* ran four months, and then Barrymore went into a hospital. He died in Hollywood in 1942, having done what he wanted to do.

Of the three Barrymores, Lionel was the one most at odds with the theater. His attitude towards it amounted to a psychosis. He needed it; he had plenty of talent for it. But he was not a public person. He was happier—though less successful—in private occupations like painting, sculpting, etching, composing music, and writing. John Barrymore's conflict was more flamboyant and in the open where everyone could see it. Lionel's conflict was internal—private, wounding, elusive.

His talent as a character actor coincided with his uneasy feeling about the public. In character parts, he could hide behind make-up and costumes, and he began character acting when he was young. When Lionel was still in his twenties, James A. Herne, actor and playwright, saw him act the part of an old man in some forgotten play. When Herne went backstage to compliment him, he was astonished to discover that Lionel Barrymore was in his mid-twenties; his portrait of the old man was a startling and effective tour de force. Herne offered Lionel the part of a young man in his new play, *Sag Harbor*, which opened the new Republic

Theater in 42nd Street in 1900. Acting the part of a young man his own age Lionel was adequate but uninteresting. Herne was surprised and disappointed.

For several years, Lionel played bit parts in productions that starred his uncle, John Drew. In one of the Drew comedies, *The Mummy and the Hummingbird*, Lionel played a colorful Italian organ-grinder with so much skill and flair that he got better notices than his uncle. All that season, John Drew used to complain facetiously: "Every night I have to play second-fiddle to that preposterous nephew of mine."

But Lionel was uncomfortable on the stage. He longed to be an artist. During one period of depression, he had persuaded his uncle to let him enroll in the Art Students League. On another occasion he persuaded his sister to support him for three years in Paris, where he studied art. Not being able to support himself as an artist, he returned to America when his sister was married and it seemed unfair to keep on accepting her bounty. In those days, stage actors looked down on the films. Films were regarded as an inferior form of show business, beneath the dignity of stage actors. But an actor could make a living in the films if nothing else turned up. When Lionel was in serious financial trouble, he could walk from The Players in 20th Street to a film studio managed by D. W. Griffith at 11 East 14th Street. One of the regular actors there was Gladys Smith, who became Mary Pickford later. Lillian and Dorothy Gish also acted there when they had no parts in the theatre. Lionel Barrymore could make $10.00 a day in Griffith's busy studio. In the films, he could also escape the ordeal of having to face an audience.

In the theater of make-believe, there were more character parts than in the more adult theater of the twenties. There were more characters than human beings on the stage; and in the period before the theater began to look at life seriously, Lionel had many motley parts in which he could impersonate characters unlike himself. *Peter Ibbetson* was a play of the supernatural, and Lionel impersonated Colonel Ibbetson effectively. In *The Jest*, Lionel, as the Renaissance bully and braggart, was also conspicuously effective. He let loose one particular scream that paralyzed people in the audience; they wondered if he could scream that loud on matinees as well as in the evenings.

But in Augustus Thomas' *The Copperhead* in 1918, he had a bravura part and a personal success that ought to have reassured anyone. He played the lanky, provincial Milt Shanks who everyone assumed had been a Copperhead but had really been Lincoln's secret agent during the Civil

War. It was a hokum part in a good-natured potboiler, and Lionel was acclaimed as a great star and a patriot.

But he could not take the next step when Arthur Hopkins produced *Macbeth*. It was a disaster. Recalling that performance, Hopkins said Lionel was hypnotized by the part. Interpreting Macbeth as he would interpret a character part, he imprisoned himself in it; he was so involved in the evil of Macbeth that his performance was unbearable. "His eyes were those of a stricken madman," Hopkins wrote. "His voice was a cry of pain." The pace of the performance was also intolerably sluggish. Robert Edmond Jones had provided abstract settings in brooding, malignant colors and shapes that might have suited a more intellectual performance. But, in Kenneth Macgowan's phrase, Lionel's performance was "absolutely tedious and unimaginative." It was another version of the bombastic Neri he had played to everyone's delight in *The Jest*, but it was totally alien to *Macbeth*.

The failure of his *Macbeth* must have been a painful experience for Lionel. Afterwards he played in Henry Bernstein's violent *The Claw* with considerable success. But in 1925, he departed for Hollywood for the rest of his life. It must have been a comfortable retreat from Broadway. He played many good parts in the films. He had a charming home life with his second wife, Irene Fenwick. He wrote an autobiography. He wrote a novel. He took part in radio dramas. He was honored by everyone. The entire country was entranced with his radio portrait of Scrooge in Dickens' *A Christmas Carol* each year on Christmas Eve. Begun in 1936, his sonorous reading became an annual rite. Lionel Barrymore died in 1954—a splendid, modest actor who could not make peace with Broadway.

TWO
BROADWAY
PROMENADERS

When Marc Klaw declared in 1914 that four of the newspaper drama critics were dishonest, a reporter from *The New York Herald* attempted to interview the whole corps of theater writers. Unless or until Mr. Klaw named their four dishonest brothers, the drama critics (called dramatic critics in those days) refused to make any comment. The reporter had to be content with observing that the critics looked like well-to-do members of the middle class; he noted with approval that they did not wear jewelry, excepting cuff links. *The New York Herald* management, professing to have several critics, could not designate one person as its official representative. The recognized newspaper critics were as follows: Alan Dale, *The American*; Charles Darnton, *The Evening World*; Acton Davies, *The Evening Sun*; Louis de Foe, *The Morning World*; Adolf Klauber, *The New York Times*; Burns Mantle, *The Evening Mail*; Lawrence Reamer. *The Morning Sun*; Arthur Ruhl, *New York Tribune*;

Alexander Woollcott. (*Vandamm*)

Louis Sherwin, *The Globe*; J. Ranken Towse, *The Evening Post*; Carl Van Vechten, the *New York Press*; Robert Welch, *The Evening Telegram*; Rennold Wolf, *The Morning Telegraph.*

Mr. Klaw's undocumented charge of dishonesty provoked an argument. In subsequent statements, he retreated a bit. He said that drama critics could have been bought for cash twenty years previously, but no longer, and he pointed out that he did not mean that any of the contemporary critics would "steal your watch." But he did not back away from his basic statement. Referring to the "moral degeneracy into which dramatic criticism in this town has fallen," he said that four of the critics had a habit of meeting at a café after opening performances and deciding what to say, and he considered them to be dishonest because they did not believe what they wrote. He further contended that no critic could give unbiased opinions about plays if he submitted a script of his own to producers of these plays, if he rewrote plays to their order, if he attended dress rehearsals and made suggestions about the performance, or if he had social relations with managers. He was particularly irritated with "one moose-headed fellow who usually brings a woman to the theater with him, has lately been sitting in judgment on dressing and who knows as much about good taste in clothes, if his own apparel is an example, as a pig does about algebra." As a partner in the crude firm of Klaw and Erlanger, Mr. Klaw was especially sensitive about good taste.

The Billboard could not have agreed with Mr. Klaw more completely. Representing the management of show business, it pointed out that the "dramatic critic does not belong in the twentieth century. He has about as much place in the modern theater as the town crier or the night watchman who told the public the news of the day or the hour of the night." Ninety percent of the dramatic critics, it said, were discreditable; no good journalist would accept such an ignominious post, wrote the journalist who was responsible for the editorial in *The Billboard*. He went on to say that drama critics were smart, flippant, narrowminded and egotistical, and refused to report the judgment of audiences. *The Billboard* believed that no other business took from the newspapers what the theater did: "Theaters should deal with newspapers as do other trades and callings—so much for so much," *The Billboard* believed.

Most publishers did not like drama critics who made trouble by having the effrontery to have personal opinions. But there were some magazine critics who were professional and had a broad enough background in the theater to know that show business on Broadway was generally shallow, mean, and petty. Huneker and Eaton knew more about the art of the theater than most playwrights, actors, and producers. The most flamboyant and the most reckless critic was George Jean Nathan, who wrote drama criticism from 1905 to 1958 and a library of more than forty books that memorialize his attitude. Having been liberally educated abroad as well as at home, Nathan knew that the theater of Broadway was worthless during the first twelve or thirteen years of the twentieth century, and he said so in a clowning style that was both popular and abusive. He called Belasco "the Broadway Rasputin" at a time when most people were taking him seriously. He vigorously and rudely dissented from the belief that Mrs. Fiske was intellectual. He lay about him with meat-axes and billy clubs. For Nathan was conducting a revolution against the stupidity of Broadway, and in time he won.

He was a showman who competed with Broadway by writing audaciously. He dramatized himself. Although he wrote like a low comedian with a slapstick and frightwig, he was personally a fastidious gentleman. There was considerable panache about his manners and personal appearance—tailored suits with the breast pockets on the right side of the jackets, modish overcoats in a variety of styles (once he owned eighteen overcoats, one of which was made of Siberian dog) long cigarette holders that could be flicked daintily, a patrician walk, and a formidable manner. His digs were less elegant than his manners. Until he married Julie Haydon, when he was in his seventies, he ostentatiously lived the life of a bachelor in two dark rooms in the Royalton Hotel in 44th Street, a block and a half from Broadway. Since he refused to be inconvenienced by having his rooms redecorated and since he resisted normal schedules for routine cleaning, the rooms became dingier and more cluttered year by year. In the last decade of his life, there were so many piles of books on the floor that a visitor was hard put to find a place to sit. This domestic squalor was part of the attitude he assiduously cultivated: it proved that a gentleman who dressed beautifully and dined in the finest restaurants and drank only the most select European wines could live frowsily without losing dignity.

Nathan was a romantic. He took special pride in his disdain for the rest of the world: "Among the many millions of persons in this fair land, there are not more than a dozen at the very outside who, known to me personally, interest me personally in the slightest," he said. He declared that his motto was "Be indifferent." In time of peace, this was an entertaining pose. But it shocked people during the period of World War II, when Nathan issued this personal caveat: "When I read some enlightened yogi's indignation over the slaughter of eight thousand Polish

George Jean Nathan. (*Culver Pictures, Inc.*)

Jews, or over the corrupt administration in this or that country, state or city, or over the Klu Klux Klan, the absence of true culture in Kansas, the riots in Dublin, or the political machinations of the American Legion, I only smile and wonder."

He took sardonic delight in writing highbrow criticism for such disparate magazines as *Outing*, *The Bohemian* magazine, *Puck*, and *Smart Set*, where he and his colleague, Henry L. Mencken, deliberately startled respectable people by poking fun at eminent leaders of culture. When Mencken and Nathan were writing uproarious comments in *Smart Set*, and later in *The American Mercury*, the life of the mind in America was unpredictable and exciting.

Nathan was such a disarming poseur that his critical attitude might have been dismissed as boyish mischief except for one important thing. He instantly recognized the ability of the first American dramatist to redeem Broadway from futility. In 1917, Eugene O'Neill, at that time known only to a few people in Provincetown, Massachusetts, and Greenwich Village, submitted the manuscript of an early sea play, *The Long Voyage Home* to the *Smart Set*. Nathan, as co-editor with Mencken, accepted and printed it, and later printed *Ile* and *The Moon of the Caribbees*, thus giving O'Neill his first recognition from a cosmopolitan institution. From that time on, Nathan was one of O'Neill's intimate friends. As a critic, Nathan subsequently took issue with many of O'Neill's plays, but he had understood O'Neill's stature at once and always gave him the inestimable support of belicf. In the thirties, Nathan stated his conviction that O'Neill "alone and single-handed waded through the dismal swamp lands of American drama, bleak, squashy and oozing sticky goo, and alone and single-handed bore out of them the water lily that no American had found before him."

In the mid-twenties, Nathan performed the same service for Sean O'Casey, with whom he was in constant correspondence for the rest of his life, commenting on plays and giving friendly advice. On these two most important events in his career, Nathan was ready and willing.

But Nathan was most influential in the period when he was denouncing Broadway and its idols. When Broadway became adult in the twenties and when the best of its work had to be taken seriously, Nathan was less influential; and jeering and the long lists of recondite allusions to foreign drama looked more and more like a pose. There was a good reason: the abusive style became him; and he had less facility for adulation. In the early days of the twentieth century, his iconoclasm had moral force. Nathan always believed that criticism was either destructive or it was nothing. His destructive criticism was a constructive influence on the American theater in the first part of his career.

Among Nathan's most celebrated articles was a guffawing blast against the "Seidlitz powder of Broadway." He did not mention the name of Alexander Woollcott in that jeremiad. But everyone knew whom he meant. For Woollcott, who had succeeded to the post of drama critic of *The New York Times* in 1914, brought something fresh into theater journalism and became the foremost critic on Broadway until he retired in 1928.

Woollcott was a roly-poly newspaperman with a warm and expansive literary style in the Dickensian manner—humorous, witty, romantic, sentimental, excitable, and effusive. He was so temperamental that his personality evoked such acid descriptions as "God's big brother" and "a butterfly in heat." Like Nathan, he was a highly personal critic, but he was more positive than negative. He was famous for his enthusiasms. "Dancing in the streets" was one of his phrases to express his delight with a new hit. He doted on the theater. He admired Mrs. Fiske in particular— no doubt estranging Nathan for that reason alone. Woollcott was fond of theater people and was on friendly terms with many of them. Ultimately he became the center of a cult.

But his good nature had limitations. After writing what now looks like a mildly negative notice of a French farce called *Taking Chances*, on March 17, 1915, he became the central figure in a series of legal moves that had a crucial and lasting effect on a critic's right to express an opinion in public. Woollcott had said that, despite Lou Telegan's competence as a sex symbol in the leading part, he thought *Taking Chances* was "not vastly amusing." The English adaptation to suit American tastes he characterized as "quite absurd," and took issue with "other moments when a puzzled audience wonders what it is all about." "The complaint here," he said in conclusion, "is not that it is vulgar but that it is quite tedious."

Taking Chances was a Shubert production. Having destroyed the power of Klaw and Erlanger, the Shuberts were proceeding to establish their own. They promptly barred Woollcott from their theaters. They mailed the tickets to their next production directly to Carr Van Anda, managing editor of *The New York Times*, and advised him that any staff member except Woollcott would be welcome. Mr. Van Anda instantly returned the tickets by messenger and instructed Woollcott to buy tickets at the box office of Maxine Elliott's Theater for the next Shubert production. But Woollcott was not admitted. The doorman and Jake Shubert turned him back.

Newspapers on the whole were inclined to solve situations like that by appointing another critic—as in the case of Walter Prichard Eaton, who had been discharged by *The Sun* when Klaw and Erlanger complained of his work. But Adolph Ochs, publisher of *The New York Times*, and Mr. Van Anda had more character. They brought an injunction to restrain the Shuberts from excluding Woollcott. *The Times* also refused to publish any Shubert advertising. In those days, bylines were seldom used in the *Times*, but Woollcott's name was printed over the next review he wrote of a Shubert production. It was *Trilby*; Woollcott liked it and said so with his customary elation. The byline was the *Times'* gesture of support and defiance.

Subsequently the Shuberts won a release from the injunction. The appellate division of the state court ruled that a manager could not exclude anyone because of his race, religion, or social status, but could exclude any individual it did not like. Woollcott banned became more famous than Woollcott welcomed. He was given four columns for his "Second Thoughts" in the Sunday paper, and he printed many letters about the case. The *Times* raised his weekly pay to $100—($25 less than *The Sun* paid Huneker in 1902). He was conspicuously quoted on billboards and in theater advertising. By losing the court case, *The New York Times* and Woollcott had won a large following.

After about a year, the Shuberts found that they were losing business by having won the case. They needed reviews of their production in *The*

New York Times; they also needed to advertise in the *Times,* but Mr. Ochs and Mr. Van Anda were intractable. In those days, Mr. Ochs also published the Philadelphia *Public Ledger.* It was his custom to go to Philadelphia on the same train one afternoon each week and take a seat on the parlor car. When he took his seat one day, he found that one of the Shubert brothers had the seat adjoining. Mr. Ochs was by instinct a cordial and kindly man; and, by the time the train pulled into Philadelphia, *The New York Times* and the Shuberts had settled their differences. The Shuberts agreed to seat any critic *The New York Times* sent, and Woollcott returned to the Shubert theaters triumphantly. Not being a modest man, he did not conceal his feeling of victory. The next Christmas, the Shuberts sent him a box of cigars, giving Woollcott the occasion to make a wisecrack about the celebrated ruckus: "The whole thing went up in smoke," he said. Years afterwards, the law was rewritten to deny a theater owner the right to exclude people he didn't like. But to this day, the producer retains his immutable right to punish drama critics by producing intolerable dramas.

BROADWAY WINS
WORLD WAR I

Before the United States declared war on Germany in the spring of 1917, Broadway—like the rest of America—was not seriously concerned. It did not want to be bored with reality. It knew very little about reality. In November of 1915, George Tyler had produced a grim war play called *Moloch*, by Beulah Marie Dix. It dramatized distasteful topics like suffering, injustice, and brutality. Although Holbrook Blinn and Mrs. Whiffen were in it, the public went to more cheerful plays. Some people thought that the portrayal of war as cruel and ugly was, in fact, unpatriotic.

Frances Starr was more fortunate the next year, when she played the part of a convent novice in Edward Knoblock's *Marie-Odile*. Amid the trappings of a religious institution, the naïve novice was seduced by a German soldier. Since the play was produced by Belasco, it was gravely garnished with ritual prayer, church bells, holy processionals, and unctuous songs, as well as banks of flowers benignly attended by an elderly gardener.

"Columbia Stands by the President"—tableau from the *Follies of 1917*, with Allyn King as Miss Columbia and Walter L. Catlett as Woodrow Wilson. (*The New York Public Library*)

Marie-Odile was successful. It gave the audience the privilege of being up-lifted and titillated at the same time. Although war was not a popular subject, the betrayal of an innocent maiden was.

When America became one of the fighting allies, Broadway supported the war in the only way it knew—as a carnival. Actresses did their bit in ravishing costumes. Hazel Dawn appeared on the cover of *Theatre Magazine* wrapped in a flag and looking very patriotic indeed, and Laurette Taylor combined beauty and mercy in the chaste though disarming costume of a Red Cross nurse. There was a rash of tableaux—Ethel Barrymore as "Unconditional Surrender," pointing vaguely at the horizon; Ina Claire in a coat of mail, mounted on a horse, carrying a huge sword as St. Joan, suggesting uplift in general. In the *Follies of 1917*, Allyn King, in a net gown with spangles, stared into space in a patriotic trance. She seemed to be avoiding a direct confrontation with Walter L. Catlett, who was usually a comedian but now wore pince-nez and carried a silk hat in the style of Woodrow Wilson. Miss King contrived to cover Mr. Catlett with an American flag. In the *Passing Show of 1917*, one girl, crowned with a golden helmet, looked very much like the Statue of Liberty; she was flanked by six unsmiling girls who were wrapped in the stars and stripes and sacrificed their all for their country.

Actresses also did their bit offstage. Julia Marlowe made recruiting speeches from an open automobile that was surrounded by sheepish men in civilian clothes. Recruiting was reported to be brisk after the beautiful Miss Marlowe appealed to the better natures of male New Yorkers. The chorus girls of *Cohan's Revue of 1918* slipped into loose overalls and studied the craft of driving trucks in case all the men were called overseas. Peggy Wood and Mary Boland knitted sweaters between acts in their dressing rooms. Many actresses joined the Women's War Relief, and put on demure robes and nurses' caps that would distinguish them from unglamorous housewives. They folded bandages and made clothing for European refugees, under the supervision of Minnie Dupree, who had taken a course in bandage folding.

Actresses volunteered to relieve the threatened shortage of food. Virginia Harned (E. H. Sothern's cashiered wife) planted one and a half acres of potatoes in Harriman, upriver. Other actresses pledged crops: Margaret Wycherley, turnips; Elsie Janis, stringbeans; Billie Burke, strawberries; Frances Starr, radishes; Viola Allen, onions; Marie Doro, asparagus. A Broadway restaurant offered to buy all the vegetables raised by Broadway's instant farmers.

There were other services more to the point. E. H. Sothern and Winthrop Ames, looking very civilian in full army uniform, toured the front for the Y.M.C.A., and made plans for entertaining the troops. This was a new departure for show business—the genesis of the USO, which has never forgotten the American Armed Forces. Many actors volunteered for this unfamiliar and sometimes dangerous mission in 1917 and brought songs, sketches, and vaudeville turns to American soldiers overseas. Jettisoning her crop of stringbeans, Elsie Janis won the devotion of the entire overseas army by the enthusiasm, variety, and personal warmth of the shows she took abroad. Americans overseas, and many who never went overseas, always remembered the good fellowship of her war shows.

When America became part of the war, some of the businessmen of Broadway had natural misgivings and succeeded in overlooking freedom and democracy. *Theatre Magazine* declared that the war must not be permitted to disturb business; it viewed with alarm the talk of taxing theater tickets. It said that rich people should quit hoarding their fortunes—that they should open their strongboxes and put their money into circulation for the benefit of everybody. Dr. Frank Crane, the guru of 1917, pointed out that amusement was an essential part of the efficiency of the people and should not be curtailed: "The stage is not a nation's weakness, extravagance or undoing, but it is a nation's deep refreshment that gives to the hearts and minds of a great people that spirit of courage and light and adventure that is needed to achieve success in the arena of world conflict." Marc Klaw complained about the discrimination of taxing theater tickets ten percent and taxing movies nothing. Noting that theater business had fallen off, he feared that the theaters might be closed by January of 1918. In order to reduce the ruinous costs of production, he thought that the salaries of the actors might have to be reduced—always a popular Klaw and Erlanger remedy.

But the theater survived. The abundance of entertainment is illustrated by the fact that a couple from Iowa visiting New York managed to see twenty-nine shows, including vaudeville, in a space of ten days. George M. Cohan, the song-and-dance man who for years had had the first call on the American flag, used the theme of three bugle notes to write "Over There" to lighten the hearts of the Allies and scare the Germans. By 1918, Broadway was inundated with war plays; most actors wore uniforms behind the footlights. In *Friendly Enemies,* Sam Shipman and Aaron Hoffman showed the homely truths that persuaded a German-American to renounce his loyalty to Germany and support the doughboys of the United States.

Three Faces East alerted the naïve Americans to the insidious skills of the German spies, and so did *Watch Your Neighbors* and *Allegiance*. Nor were the playwrights alone in their suspicions. A. Mitchell Palmer, attorney general of the United States, investigated the Broadway theater. He was determined that German writers should not slip propaganda into Broadway plays or get an income from Broadway through indirect channels.

The Prince of Pilsen, which had roistered in the beer halls of Germany for fifteen years, suddenly became all French. In a war play with spiritual overtones by Henry Bernstein, Lionel Atwill, wounded and lying in a hospital bed, swore that he never knew what love was until he was in the trenches; and although Billie Burke in the play was married to another man, she candidly said that she loved him. *The Better 'Ole* was redeemed by a sense of humor. Based on a familiar cartoon and written by Captain Bruce Bairnsfather and Captain Arthur Elliot, it told a ludicrous story about the experience of enlisted men and it gave Mr. and Mrs. Charles Coburn, normally classical actors, the most winning parts they ever had.

But the climax of Broadway's participation in the war was a 1918 musical production called *Yip, Yip, Yaphank* at the imposing Century Theater. A skinny Broadway songwriter in tight leggings and a huge campaign hat that threatened to unbalance him sang "Oh, How I Hate to Get Up in the Morning" in a weak, wavering voice and conquered New York without having to fire a shot. He was Irving Berlin, then thirty years of age. Temporarily evicted from Broadway, he was a sergeant stationed at Camp Upton on Long Island. On the assumption that he had more skill in music than with weapons, he had been commissioned to write a show for his mates. It was so effective that it was permitted to visit New York to raise money for war relief. In form it was a conventional Broadway musical show, but equipped with soldiers who impersonated chorus girls. It included a minstrel show and a "Darktown wedding." But some of the songs Berlin had written were assimilated permanently into the American vernacular. Anheuser-Busch had already given him $10,000 for a song that ridiculed non-alcholic suds—"You Can't Stay Up All Night on Bevo." (Berlin turned the $10,000 to war relief.) But his cartoon of kitchen police, called "Safe for Democracy," aroused the enthusiasm of thousands of Americans who would rather have fought than wash a dish; and the ballad "Oh, How I Hate to Get Up in the Morning" transformed the crushing boredom of Army life into humor.

Overseas, the citizens of Broadway supported their country admirably. Some of them stayed permanently in the fields of France where they had died. But Broadway adapted itself to the war as if it were only a new form of show business. The armistice came before all the war plays could be staged; and some of them had the misfortune to open after the boys had come home and did not want to be brave anymore. But perhaps the war had been more of a traumatic experience than those who had stayed home realized. The next generation of theater people had some disturbing doubts about the Broadway theater and the quality of life in America.

1918–1939

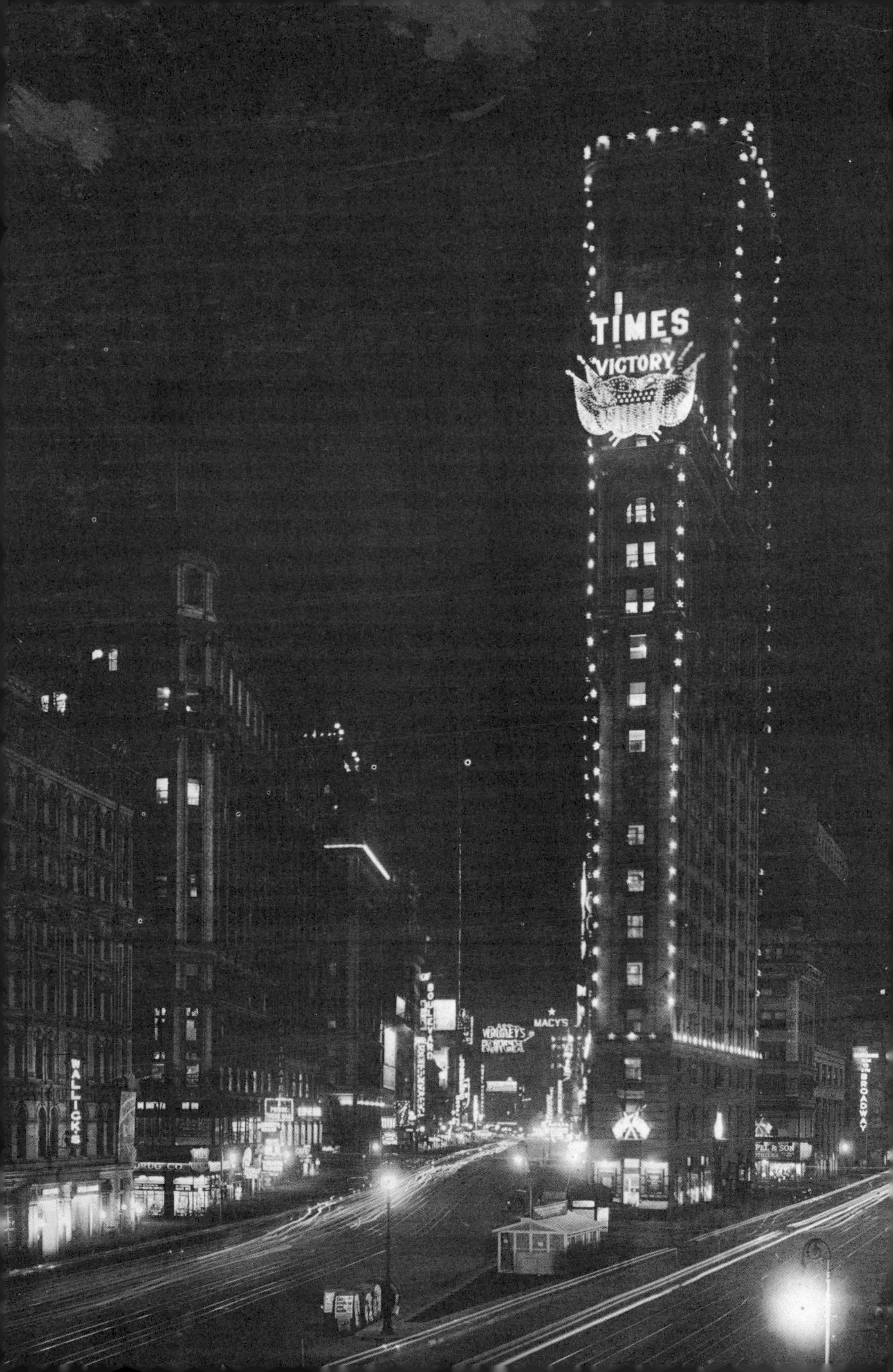
TIMES
VICTORY
MACY'S
WALLICK'S
BROADWAY

BROADWAY
AFTER THE WAR
WAS OVER

All through the war, Broadway had been full of servicemen wandering around aimlessly in search of a good time. There was an information center for soldiers and sailors on Seventh Avenue near Pennsylvania Station, where the attendants prudently recommended refined shows for homeless heroes. When the armistice was signed, Times Square was choked with a stupendous mob of exuberant citizens who carried small flags, pounded one another on the back, and made joyful noises. *The New York Times* took official notice of the occasion by stringing electric lights around the contours of the Times Tower and displaying an illuminated national shield and the happy word "Victory." On great occasions—New Year's Eve, Election Night, and victory celebrations—Times Square has always been the gathering place for the entire city. It is not the most central place, nor is it the most significant. City Hall Park would be the logical place. But for many years, New Yorkers have instinctively headed for Times Square

imes Square—1918. (*Culver Pictures, Inc.*)

when they feel like rejoicing. The giddy environment is especially congenial.

After World War I, Broadway looked very exciting indeed. The era of the spectacular signs was at its prime. Broadway was a mammoth billboard of flashing slogans, bright colors, and competitive designs. Many of the old buildings were no longer maintained for tenants, but became the backgrounds of display signs. All the old buildings between 45th and 46th Streets on the west side of Broadway were faced with a long, massive billboard that covered all the windows. The rooms facing Broadway were dark and airless, and the obscure businesses conducted there looked ephemeral and furtive.

The small building on 47th Street that covers the block between Broadway and Seventh Avenue has always been the focal point of the extravaganza of Times Square. The signs on three levels above the roof of that building usually consist of two declamatory words—"Lucky Strike," "Four Roses," "Canadian Club," "Pepsi Cola," "Rupert's Beer"—all of which are the ingredients of a good time. During the dismal years of Prohibition, "Squibb's Dental Cream" was the most intoxicating product recommended there. Fortunately there were any number of speakeasies close by. Some of the signs along the perimeter of Times Square were particularly delightful in the postwar era. "Wrigley's Gum" was impish. The sign stretched the full block between 43rd and 44th Streets above the old building where the Paramount Building now stands. On either side of the Wrigley's trademark, three marionettes went flawlessly through the manual of arms and saluted the public briskly. The sign was innocent and charming. On another sign nearby, the modest White Rock maiden peered into the fairy-story pool of luminous water. She and the six marionettes were sociable and respectable.

The most endearing sign stood at the top of the most eccentric building in the area. It consisted of a playful kitten toying year after year with a spool of Corticelli Silk. "Too Strong to Break" the sign asserted. If you were walking south on Broadway or Seventh Avenue, you had to look at the sign askance because it was partially obscured by the taller Times Tower. This impediment to total visibility was all the more remarkable because the nineteen-story Heidelberg Tower, on which the Corticelli sign was situated, had been built for the sole purpose of supporting advertising spectaculars, and the Times Tower, which obstructs the view north, had stood there five years before the Heidelberg Tower was built. The Heidelberg Tower cost $400,000 in 1910. It was—and is—lean and rectangular. To provide the perfect background for signs, it has no windows. For many years, a seven-story office building with a restaurant on the ground floor has enveloped three sides of the base of the Heidelberg Tower. But the upper levels remain as useless now as they were when they were built. The Corticelli sign was the first and the last that was displayed there. The Heidelberg Tower is blank and impracticable. For more than half a century, it has been the most irrelevant building in the theater district where real estate values are high. It is a tall, lonely monument to absurdity.

In the decades between the two world wars, most people would probably have described Broadway as garish. It had the reputation of being cheap and tawdry. But foreigners who came to Broadway with a fresh mind were much impressed by its light, color, and magic. Stephen Graham, an English writer, declared that "there is no garishness" in it. It might not be real, he went on, but it looked to him like a "transfiguration": "humanity is also shedding light," he continued, "and it wells upward into that artificial light which is greater than the day." Paul Morand, the French novelist, was lyrical: "In Forty-second Street," he wrote, "it is a glowing Summer afternoon all night: one might almost wear white trousers and a straw hat. Theaters, night clubs, movie palaces, restaurants are all lighted at every porthole. Undiscovered prisms, rainbows squared."

Broadway was the carnival spirit fantastically commercialized. During the depression, one public relations sign announced disingenuously: "Forward America. Business Is Good. Keep It Good. Nothing Can Stop Us." In point of fact, everything stopped us throughout the grisly thirties until the evil prosperity of preparations for war got America started again. No one on Broadway could have been naïve enough to believe a pompous sign like that.

Despite its size and worldliness the Broadway community looked local and familiar. Streetcars clattered through the Square. At 45th Street, the Broadway and Seventh Avenue tracks crossed, presenting a dangerous problem in logistics that seemed always to have been solved because no cars ever collided there. The ornate grillwork that supported the sidewalk canopy of the Knickerbocker Hotel looked homey. In 42nd Street, just west of Seventh Avenue, the Times Square Theater gleamed like a Greek temple, and that whole block of theaters looked clean, as if the owners took pride in what they were doing. A man with advertising boards over his shoulders walked through the Times Square throngs on stilts. Another man in full evening dress strolled amiably through the crowds like a member of the aristocracy. He was actually a sandwich-board man; a cigar advertisement in electric lights flashed on and off on his starched shirt front. A bogus gypsy girl carried a sign that advertised tea-reading service for people uncertain about the future.

At theater time, when many of the theatergoers were wearing evening dress, the combination of streetcars and taxis made the traffic sluggish. Most people walked. Theaters were built close together because pedestrians were accustomed to shop from theater to theater. Out for a good time, they provided some sort of audience for the plays that were not hits. So did Joe Leblang's cut-price ticket office in the basement of Gray's Drugstore in the Broadway block between 42nd and 43rd Streets. Theaters that had not sold out by six o'clock sent bunches of their tickets to Joe Leblang's shop to be sold at half-price. To theatergoers who were not committed to attending only the hits, Joe's shop was a bonanza. Joe was a nice guy, and so was his wife, which made their shop all the more inviting. There were 123 ticket brokers in the theater district and in hotels and clubs. (There were seventy-eight in 1967.) McBride's, at the corner of 43rd Street and Seventh Avenue, was the honest one. Among the other conveniences was an unroofed out-of-town newspaper stand on the sidewalk on the north side of the Times Building. It was a miraculous institution. Not only newspapers from all the big cities but newspapers from many small communities—like Catskill—were on sale there. The attendants knew where every newspaper was located and waited on the trade with an expert dispatch that seemed to raise the tempo of Times Square. Visitors from out of town were known as "farmers." Broadway people thought their manners were good but their tips ludicrous.

In the suffocating heat of summer, Times Square was oblivious to anything except itself. In the stinging cold of winter, wind swept boisterously around the streetcorners, picking up torn newspapers and gritty dust and spiraling loose handbills twenty or twenty-five stories in the air. Rain, snow, and cloud were natural elements that did not recognize the autonomy of Broadway. The gleam of wet pavements, tinged with color, flashing and shimmering under the animated signs; the sparkle of the snow as

Whether Broadway was beautiful or ugly was beside the point. Broadway was never intended to be beautiful. All Broadway had ever hoped for was that people should feel livelier when they plunged into its "tonic light-bath," as Stephen Graham called it. Night was its natural hour. By day, many of the lights were turned on impatiently as if the proprietors could not wait for the sun to get out of the way. Nature was in large part eliminated from this vast, clangorous bazaar. Even on clear nights, the stars were outdazzled by the great flare of light that leaped from Broadway, as if a supernatural furnace door had been opened. If you hunted long enough over the building tops, sometimes you could see a pale moon moving through its lonely orbit in the sky. Like a discarded mistress, it kept its distance. It looked reproachful and humiliated.

it fell out of the darkness and the silent white drifts in the deserted door-
ways overwhelmed Broadway with natural beauty that somehow did not
seem alien. When the clouds were low and the pavements wet and the
atmosphere saturated, the magic of Broadway looked more like necro-
mancy. In foul weather, the crowds were smaller than normal. But
Broadway people regarded weather as an impertinence. They refused to
recognize it. They were always on parade. The sidewalks were always full
of sightseers, peddlers, beggars, horseplayers, cops, and prostitutes. Nineteen stories in the air, the dainty little kitten chased the spool of Corticelli
silk. On the street level, Broadway was brash and cosmopolitan.

In the twenties some instant statisticians said that the New York
theaters numbered eighty; some said, seventy. No two people agreed, and
perhaps no one really counted. But particularly in the summer and early
autumn, everyone agreed that there were not enough for all the productions
looking for houses. During those booming years, the annual number of
productions increased from 126 in 1917 to 208 in 1927 and to 264 in 1928
—the all-time peak of production. There were never that many productions
again.

The figures of seventy or eighty theaters included some that would
have been classified as Off Broadway when that term came into use in the
late forties, and among them were a few small theaters in Greenwich
Village and on the East Side, where plays were produced on a less ruthlessly commercial basis. Whatever the total number may have been, the
theaters available for professional productions in the midtown area were
not less than sixty. They included a few miniature houses like the Belmont
in 48th Street, the Princess (which seated 299) in 49th Street, the Punch
and Judy (which seated 300) in 49th Street, and the Little (299 seats) in
44th Street. Since the cost of putting on a production was moderate, it
was possible to keep solvent in theaters that seated fewer than 500 people.

A Broadway drama could be put on for $2,000, although $10,000 was
the more familiar figure. In small theaters, the relation between the audience and the stage was sociable. Something of inestimable value was lost in
later years when audiences of fewer than 1,000 or 1,200 people were not
large enough to pay the bills. Small, elusive, fanciful plays evaporated in
big houses. In the big houses, the relationship between audiences and
actors was—and is—defiant; the audience defies the actors to entertain
them. Large theaters put a premium on violence and scandal—on themes
and performances that startle the audience.

In the twenties, twelve of the Broadway theaters were actually on

Broadway—the Empire, Knickerbocker, and Casino below 42nd Street, the George M. Cohan, Criterion, Globe, Central, Gaiety, Astor, Broadway, Manhattan, and Winter Garden above 42nd Street. (In 1950, only three were left—the Empire, Winter Garden, and Broadway. In 1970, two.)

During World War I, and through the next decade, there were not enough theaters to go around. Some excellent theaters were built at that time—the Plymouth, Morosco, Broadhurst, and Bijou, all in 1917, when the war was going on; and Henry Miller's Theater in 1918, when the war was over. They all became permanent parts of the legitimate theater and have been continuously used and well maintained ever since. In the twenties, two brothers in the construction business suddenly became infatuated with the theater and built six theaters in five years. Irwin S. and Henry I. Chanin built the 46th Street Theater in 1925 and the Majestic in 1927—two very large and very attractive musical theaters with excellent public accommodations—and the Biltmore in 1925, the Mansfield (now named for some former drama critic) in 1926, and the Royale and Masque (now the Golden) in 1927. The Majestic, Royale, and Masque opened within a period of only a few weeks in the winter and early spring of 1927. In 1929, the Chanin Brothers built their fifty-six-story Chanin Building in 42nd Street and Lexington Avenue—a reputable office building then and now. They were still so infatuated with show business that they put a small theater close under the roof.

Although the Chanin Brothers were influential businessmen who made a significant contribution to the theater in the bountiful twenties, they were personally modest and lacked the panache or bounce of theater people in general. To introduce a little variety into the routine of show business they put metal nameplates on the backs of the seats where the critics sat on opening nights (a form of name dropping), and they labeled two pairs of seats for themselves. When they attended first nights in their own theaters, they were shy and diffident; they took no part in the brassy diabolism of opening-night performances. But they were a business factor to be reckoned with as long as show business was good business and theaters could be managed as pieces of real estate and not as institutions reflecting the personal tastes of the owners.

Most of the Chanin theaters have attractive façades in a modern Spanish style; they have balconies overlooking the street, and they have ornamental fenestration and cornices. Since the lobbies of the drama houses occupy space that does not show a profit, they are tight. At curtain-time or between acts, the audience is either squeezed into a wriggling, choked, panicky solid or else detonated into the street. The social graces are deleted. But real-estate operators have not been the only builders to reduce public space to a minimum. The Belasco has a tiny lobby; so has the Booth, which was built by Winthrop Ames, and the Plymouth, the headquarters of Arthur Hopkins. The old Empire had lavish public space. So has the Hudson, which ceased being a profitable theater long ago, the Guild Theater, which was always an economic liability, and the Craig (now the George Abbott) which has never been prosperous and is scheduled for the services of the wrecker. The rule is that when a Broadway theater builder deals in real estate the public always loses.

During the period of acute theater shortage, the most preposterous house was the tiny Mayfair Theater on the south side of 44th Street, east of Broadway. It had been a cheap restaurant. In 1926, it was improvised into a theater. The building was long but it was so narrow that there was no room for side exits for the actors, and there was no backstage space. The dressing rooms were in the basement. The actors had to make awkward entrances and exits through a tiny hutch at the rear and on one side of the stage. The Mayfair opened in the winter of 1926 and was immediately recognized as ludicrously inadequate. The first New York production of O'Casey's *Juno and the Paycock* opened at the Mayfair on March 15, 1926, with a cast that included Augustin Duncan, Claude Cooper, Ralph Cullinan, and Barry Macollum. Squeezed on a tiny stage that kept Captain Boyle, Joxer, and Juno within upper-cut or left-hook distance of one another, the production was hamstrung and immobile, although it lasted seventy-four performances. The Mayfair returned to reality after one year of masquerading as a theater; it closed. Lope de Vega said that all you need for a theater is four planks, four trestles, two actors and a passion. The Mayfair proved that, even if the passion is hot, the planks do need air.

The end of theater building came in 1928. On December 20 of that year, Ethel Barrymore opened the Ethel Barrymore Theater as a holy mother in a dull play called *The Kingdom of God*, by the Sierra brothers; and four days later, the Craig opened with a memorably idiotic play called *Potiphar's Wife*. (The Countess of Aylesbrough lusted after her chauffeur. He did not lust back. The Countess had to engage another chauffeur.) That was the last new Broadway theater, although the Vivian Beaumont in Lincoln Center regards itself as a Broadway house, and the Center Theater might be regarded as a pretender. The Rockefellers built it in 1932 as a film house with a capacity of 3,700 people. When the owners concluded that it could not succeed as a film house they equipped it with a huge stage in 1934 and opened it as a musical theater with *The Great*

Waltz—a fabulous musical circus that canonized "The Beautiful Blue Danube," by Johann Strauss the Younger, and anesthetized the public for 289 performances. But the Center could never be made to look like a genuine theater, and the Rockefellers regretfully destroyed it in 1954. The Craig and the Ethel Barrymore were the last strictly Broadway theaters built to house spoken drama. Contrary to accepted doctrine, the Craig—and not the Ethel Barrymore—was actually the last. Gradually the shortage of theaters ended in a surplus. In 1950, thirty-six theaters were enough to keep the legitimate drama under cover. One-third of the theaters available in 1928 were more than enough forty-two years later.

During the explosion of the building period, the custodians of the theater were oblivious to one important fact that ultimately changed the nature of Broadway. But businessmen with a practical sense of values were already building some excellent theaters for silent films. The Strand was built in 1914; the Rivoli in 1917, early enough to show Charlie Chaplin in *Shoulder Arms* while the war was still going on. No citizen unhappily drafted into a democratic army thought he was losing dignity when he stepped into the Rivoli to see that immortal cartoon of Armageddon. By the time the businessmen got around to building the Capitol Theater in 1919, the Paramount in 1926, and Roxy's in 1927, the cultural standards of the film theaters had become imposing at box-office tariffs of 25¢ to 75¢. S. L. Rothafel, generally known as Roxy, was a humorless showman with the vision of a demented prophet and supreme self-confidence. He turned the Capitol Theater into a cultural orgy. There were not enough filmgoers coming there to pay the bills, but Roxy discovered the way to bring them in. He installed a 110-piece symphony orchestra that played classical music under good direction. He put on stage-shows that included cameo versions of grand opera, Gilbert and Sullivan, and ballet. When the orchestra players filed out for a drink, a smoke, or a bite, a mammoth Wurlitzer organ took over with roaring harmonies played by virtuosos who pummeled the keyboard in the round halo of the spotlight. The Capitol had another asset. The seats in the loges were so soft that amorous couples were able to do what came naturally without being distracted by the films.

When Roxy opened the Roxy Theater in 1927, he inflated his personal formula of size, wealth, and luxury—everything in excess, everything and everyone suffocated in magnificence. The theater (constructed by the Chanin Brothers, incidentally) could seat 6,200 sybarites. It was drenched in décor. It was swarming with marble statuary and French rock crystal chandeliers. The public rooms were spacious and gorgeous. The washrooms were lined with marble, and the plumbing was immaculate and costly. The stairways, inundated in deep carpets, were grand enough for a royal procession. There were two Kimball pipe-organs in the auditorium and one in the lobby. On great occasions, two athletic organists, seated at two consoles in line, played the same piece of music simultaneously with such ferocity that it seemed as if the Apocalypse were descending. Fourteen Steinway concert pianos were strewn around the house. On the day the Roxy opened, some unhinged actor loosened the following invocation: "Ye portals bright, high and majestic, open to our gaze the path to the wonderland, and show us realms where fantasy reigns, where romance, where adventures flourish. Let Ev'ryday's toil be forgotten under thy sheltering roof, oh glorious, mighty hall—thy magic charm unite us all to worship at beauty's throne."

As the result of a dream he had one morning when he was watching the sun rise out of the Atlantic Ocean from the deck of some incredible liner, Roxy designed his next cathedral—the Radio City Music Hall, and he opened it as a vaudeville house in 1932. The opening performance lasted from 8:30 until 2:30 the next morning, and neither Roxy nor vaudeville ever recovered from that brutal avalanche of fun. The Radio City Music Hall soon became a film house and continues to be the one theater in New York that millions of people throughout the nation trust completely.

In his own theater, Roxy hired, tamed, and drilled a battalion of uniformed ushers who wore starched collars, white gloves, gold braid, tassels, ribbons, and the facial expression of well-trained morticians. Men in uniform gave all the film houses authority and class. The doorman at the Paramount was the most stately human being on Broadway. The individual doormen there changed according to the lamentable vicissitudes of human nature: some were weak enough to get sick, and had to be replaced by sturdier people; some graduated from college and looked for less conspicuous employment. But whoever the doorman might be, he stood over six feet in Adolph Zukor's socks, wore a stunning uniform, and was the envy of every man and the illicit dream of every woman who walked up Broadway.

By contrast, the Broadway dramatic theaters were hardly more than meeting places. In 1927, Al Jolson permanently changed the nature of show business on Broadway and throughout the nation by appearing in the first talking film. After *The Jazz Singer*, there was no need for more legitimate theaters. In 1927, the only distinction the Broadway theater had to offer was O'Neill's *Strange Interlude*, the Heywards' *Porgy*, Philip Barry's *Paris Bound*, Jerome Kern's *Show Boat*, John Galsworthy's *Escape*, and O'Casey's *The Plough and the Stars*. The theater's only luxury was not in the washrooms but on the stage.

"WE WON'T COME BACK
'TIL THE MANAGERS
ARE FAIR"

The actors' strike in 1919 was not only significant but gay. There can
never have been another strike that entertained the public so exuberantly.
Certainly the time had come for some sort of change. Since the decline
of actor–managers, like Augustin Daly and Dan Frohman, the ordinary
actor had become the retainer of commercial managers, like Klaw and
Erlanger and the Shubert Brothers. His social standing had declined to
the level of actors during the Elizabethan days—"Rogues, vagabonds,
sturdy beggars, and vagrants." Before the strike, commercial managers
exploited the actors callously or perhaps only thoughtlessly—requiring long
periods of rehearsal without pay, closing plays during rehearsals without
compensating the actors for the work they had done, closing plays on the
road without paying return fares, obliging the actor to pay for part or all
of his costume, requiring extra matinees without extra compensation.

In 1916, Milton Sills told an early meeting of Actors' Equity that "the actor is the one and only class that is bullied, belittled, despised, cheated and enslaved." The stagehands and musicians had already organized and were members of the American Federation of Labor and had rights that the managers were obliged to recognize. The disparity in the relative positions of the actors and the musicians is illustrated in an order that one producer gave his stage manager: "Tell the actors there is to be an extra matinee tomorrow and ask the orchestra leader how much he is going to charge for it." He was right in assuming that the actors would do their work free. Keeping actors from working free has always been one of the biggest responsibilities of Actors' Equity Association.

Actors' Equity was organized in 1913 for the express purpose of getting the producers to sign a standard contract with minimum pay and basic safeguards against exploitation of actors. Although in the beginning the managers adopted a benevolent attitude, the actors had no real power to bargain. Some actors thought that Equity should join the A.F.L., but this proposal shocked others. They thought membership in a labor federation was beneath their dignity as artists. In his 1916 address, Mr. Sills tried to reassure the uneasy members by promising them that "the plumber and the engineer would not slap you on the back and call you brother." The producing managers agreed to a contract in 1917 that limited unpaid rehearsals for plays to four weeks, with a guarantee of two weeks' pay, no matter how short the run might be. Producers of musical shows were permitted under the contract to demand six weeks of free rehearsals.

When the standard contract came up for revision and renewal in the spring of 1919, the managers amiably agreed to everything except the one issue that seems most indefensible now: they would not agree to pay the actors for extra matinees on legal holidays and other special occasions. They would not limit the number of paid performances to eight a week. Since Equity was not asking for more money and was, in fact, very modest in what it asked in general, the refusal of the managers to agree to the most reasonable item in the contract would seem unbelievable except for one thing: they really did not want to recognize Equity as the sole bargaining agent for the actors because Equity was considering joining the A.F.L., and they thought that the backing of the A.F.L. would be a threat to the autonomy of the producers.

Since actors were thought to be living in a world of fantasy, the notion of an actors' strike was unbelievable. But it happened. On August 6, 1919, Actors' Equity voted to go on strike; and within five minutes to a half hour of curtain time, one hundred actors closed twelve productions. Neither the managers nor the public could believe it. Most productions accepted the situation silently and spent most of the evening refunding the

e actors march through lumbus Circle during the 19 strike. (*United Press International Photo*)

cost of the tickets to the theatergoers. (Those who had bought their tickets from speculators have never yet succeeded in getting a return of the premiums.) At the Cohan and Harris Theater, where *The Royal Vagabond* was playing, Sam Forrest offered mild opposition. He raised the curtain on a stage full of chorus people in street attire. He told the audience that all the actors who were striking were being paid $200 to $300 a week, and were shockingly indifferent to the welfare of the lower-paid chorus. Of the principals he declared: "They have no grievance against the management. We have played fair." Turning to the chorus people, he asked if they had any grievance. "No," they shouted. "Have you not always been treated fairly by the management?" "Yes," they cried. If the strike was not immoral, it was at least unreasonable, the Cohan and Harris management seemed to think.

Since the *Follies* had not been struck, many of the theatergoers who had been turned out of other shows were able to buy standing-room and have a jolly evening. All the productions that had not been struck did capacity business that evening. George M. Cohan and William Brady reorganized their productions—*The Royal Vagabond* and *At 9:45*, respectively —and prepared to reopen with understudies and with themselves in the star roles. But then the stagehands and the musicians walked out, and the strike was complete, except for *John Ferguson*, a Theater Guild production not allied with the producing managers.

The strike quickly spread to other cities. The stagehands, who believed in meeting force with force, denounced 193 houses owned or leased by the Shuberts throughout the country as "unfair," and called out all their members everywhere. In New York, Equity closed twenty-one theaters and blocked six openings.

If the producers were indignant, so were a few actors. E. H. Sothern addressed an Equity meeting on behalf of the managers and was coldly received. George M. Cohan pledged $100,000 to a rival union, called the Actors' Fidelity League ("Fido," the Equity members called it contemptuously) and became its president, although he was still one of the producing managers. He resigned from the Lambs and the Friars with a loud report, and so did David Belasco and his son-in-law, Morris Gest. In resigning from the Lambs, Morris Gest said: "Any club which permits its members to indulge in personal abuse and vilification of such an eminent member and great man as David Belasco, the lifelong friend of the actor and the dean of the entire profession, can no longer have my sympathy and respect." Among the actors who opposed Equity by joining Fidelity were E. H. Sothern and Julia Marlowe, Mrs. Fiske, Margaret Anglin, Otis Skinner, and David Warfield. The Shuberts sued Equity for $500,000. The Producing Managers Association sued individual members of Equity under the primitive Danbury-hat ruling, in which individual members of a union were held financially responsible for the actions of the whole.

Process servers were soon skipping around Broadway in an attempt to identify individual actors and serve papers on them. Arthur Hopkins made two uncharacteristic statements: "If we give way to Equity we will be ruined; and if we are going to be exposed to other calls, now is the time to be ruined, not then." He was one of the first American businessmen to invoke the awful menace of Soviet Russia. Referring to the actors he said: "What they have done is in complete defiance of property and contract rights; and that in my understanding is Bolshevism." Most of the contacts between the opposing sides were bitter and abusive. But people in the theater always have difficulty in being unfriendly. When Al Woods, producer of cheap melodramas and co-producer of musical shows, saw some chorus girls picketing in the rain, he asked them why they were not wearing raincoats. Since they didn't have any or had left them at home, Al Woods told them to buy raincoats in a neighboring store and charge them to him. "I don't want you to get pneumonia because when this is all over I'm going to need you again," he said.

For the actors, the strike turned into a bravura show. Instead of giving performances in the theater, they gave them in the streets to explain the strike to the public. Ed Wynn gave such an emotional speech on one street that some of the bystanders picked him up and carried him up the street on their shoulders. Ethel Barrymore and Marie Dressler—two stars who could not have been more unalike—were everywhere—smiling, cheering, and giving impromptu talks. Ten chorus girls in an open car solemnly invaded Wall Street displaying an Equity sign. Douglas Fairbanks, Dustin Farnum, and Francis X. Bushman, formidable film stars, joined in the display of force. Partisanship was fierce and flamboyant. If Owen Davis had written the script the emotion could not have been gaudier.

On a rainy day in the middle of August, two thousand actors, stage-hands, and musicians paraded from Columbus Circle down Broadway, led by Francis Wilson, Frank Gilmore, John Cope, and Grant Stewart, the prime movers of Equity. Actors who had served overseas wore their uniforms and carried American flags. Despite the rain, there were big crowds on the sidewalks. Actresses and actors enthusiastically beamed at them and they cheered in return. "No More Pay. Just Fair Play," one of the signs read. Actors carried signs bearing the names of their productions, and Florence Edney found herself carrying a disingenuous sign that delighted people on the sidewalks. *Too Many Husbands,* the sign read. Everyone thought Frank Bacon was particularly gallant in being one of the leaders. After a long, undistinguished career, he had suddenly found himself the star of an especially successful play called *Lightnin';* but he joined the strike and instantly closed the play just as he was reaping the reward of many dull years in the theater. Lillian Russell, Josephine Hull, Florence Reed, and George Arliss enthusiastically supported the strike.

When the strike began, there was only $13,500 in the Equity treasury. To raise money, the actors staged a series of benefits at the Lexington Avenue Opera House—big, exuberant shows that provided lavish entertainment and were naturally very popular. Among the stars who appeared were W. C. Fields, Joseph Santley, Blanche Ring, Charles Winninger, Eddie Foy, Ethel and Lionel Barrymore, Conway Tearle, Doris Rankin, Van & Schenk, John Charles Thomas, Pearl White, Frank Tinney, Eddie Cantor, Brandon Tynan, and Hassard Short. In normal times, the public would have had to visit twenty or twenty-five shows to see as many stars as that.

At the opening performance, Marie Dressler put on one demonstration calculated to rebut the producers' assertion that they needed six to sixteen weeks of rehearsal to perfect the chorus dancing in musical shows. She said she could teach two hundred chorus men and women a new set of steps in six to sixteen minutes. And she did. Ed Wynn contributed an uproariously droll sketch. When his turn came, he was found in an orchestra seat and climbed up on the stage. He said that Judge Lydon had served him with an injunction that ordered him not to appear in the show.

In the circumstances, he said he would not be able to perform his act, which would have consisted of—whereupon he performed the whole act. The audience loved it, and Ed Wynn never went to jail.

Among the songs written for Equity was a parody of George M. Cohan's "Over There." The Equity version was as follows:

> Over fair, over fair,
> We have been, we have been over fair.
>   But now things are humming
>   And the time is coming
>   When with Labor we'll be chumming
> Everywhere.
> So beware, have a care,
> Just be fair, on the square, everywhere,
>   For we are striking, yes, we are striking,
>   And we won't come back 'til the managers are fair.

All through the strike, George M. Cohan was the favorite butt of all the strikers. They felt that he was selling out his own kind.

The gala performances at the Lexington Avenue Opera House raised several thousand dollars every night. There was a rumor that the Producing Managers Association might apply for a writ to impound the show's bank account. George Christie, manager of the Lexington Avenue Opera House, found an ingenious way to evade that contingency. The title of the account he opened at the Harriman National Bank was "Isaiah 59:14." By consulting the King James Bible, unmarred by literary revisions, the producers could find a timely though galling analogy between the strike and holy writ: "And judgment is turned away backward, and justice standeth afar off: for truth is fallen in the street, and equity cannot enter."

On August 26, Samuel Gompers, head of the American Federation of Labor, returned to New York from the Versailles Peace Conference in the U.S.S. *George Washington*. The producers sent a delegation by tug to Quarantine to put their case to Mr. Gompers while his ship was coming up the Bay. But as soon as his ship docked, Mr. Gompers went directly to an Equity meeting, advised the actors to continue the strike and pledged the Federation's full support, which included the nice sum of one million dollars.

During the strike, the producers were as temperamental as the strikers, though not so gay. The strike might have been settled earlier except for a clash of temperament between Francis Wilson, president of Equity, and David Belasco. A committee of producers—Arthur Hopkins, Winthrop

Ames, Henry W. Savage, Sam H. Harris, and Alf Hayman—had drawn up a contract they thought Equity might accept. To put the meeting on a social basis, they arranged a luncheon at the Claridge Hotel. When the business session opened, Francis Wilson began dramatically: "This is a new day for the actor. After standing for years, with hat in hand, outside the manager's office, he is invited . . . ," whereupon Mr. Belasco stood up, pounded the table so vigorously that he smashed a glass and cut his hand, hissed "Fransssis Wilssson" contemptuously, and the meeting broke up in disorder. (This is Arthur Hopkins' recollection of the affair.)

The producers were intransigent throughout the strike. Ultimately they agreed among themselves to new terms they thought Equity might accept and called a joint meeting at the St. Regis Hotel. Before the meeting, Arthur Hopkins told Belasco: "The important thing is that we show no anger. It has to be settled, so we may as well be friendly about it. If Francis Wilson is there, give him a little kiss." Much to everyone's astonishment, Belasco did exactly that. He took Wilson's hand and kissed it. Wilson looked stunned. But the strike was over on September 6, exactly a month after it had begun.

By winning the strike, Equity was recognized as the legal bargaining agency for stage people. Members of the chorus were to be paid half salary immediately after rehearsing free for four weeks and they were to be paid a minimum of $30 a week for performing in town and $35 on the road. It now seems strange that Equity made no financial demands for actors except for the right to be paid for extra matinees. It was not until 1933 that minimum pay for actors was written into the contract—$40 for actors who had been members of Equity for two years, and $25 for all others; and it was not until 1935 that rehearsal pay was written into the contract—$20 a week for senior members and $15 for all others. Since actors in 1919 regarded themselves not as laborers but as artists, they tended to think that bargaining for money was beneath their dignity.

The membership increased from 2,700 to 14,000 and the treasury rose from $13,500 to $120,000. People who had nothing had won, not only because their demands were valid, but also because they had enthusiasm, energy, charm, humor, and loyalty. The impending advance in the cultural and artistic state of the Broadway theater thus rested on the sound foundation of an enlightened union of actors. Everyone knew that the old days were over.

EARL CARROLL THEATRE

EARL CARROLL THEATRE

EUGENE O'NEILL'S
DESIRE
UNDER THE ELMS
WITH WALTER HUSTON

HAIR GOODS
MASSAGE

CULTURE

SYSTEM

WILFRED
COSMETICS

WILFRED
SYSTEM

MARCEL WAVING

WILFRED
SYSTEM

SALE of DRESSES - DIRECT FROM
MANF'R to WEARER

TAXICAB
BONDS
AND
INSURANCE

TAXICAB
INSURANCE
AND
BONDS

EUGENE O'NEILL'S
DESIRE UNDER THE ELMS
EARL CARROLL THEATRE

SALE!
PRICES BEYOND COMPARE

HABERDASHER

THEATER
FOR ADULTS

After World War I, and during the next twenty years or so, Broadway was in top form as an art and as show business. The momentum was forward. The theater was revitalized. Everything seemed new; the future looked glorious.

It would be gratifying to be able to account intelligibly for this sudden transformation of adolescence into maturity and provinciality into a cosmopolitan point of view. But the national experience had had a paradoxical influence on the mood of the country. The war had been won. Thousands of young men and women had returned from Europe victoriously after succeeding in what they regarded as a moral crusade. This gratified most of them. It especially gratified the political leaders who had led the nation into war and the industrialists who had supported it and profited by it. They had the comfortable feeling that they had been right.

But many of the returned soldiers had bitter feelings about the generation in control of national life. A large part of the younger generation was alienated from the establishment. The brutal war experience had convinced them that the traditional standards of American morality and authority were either inadequate or evil and certainly unrealistic. They did not believe that the death of 116,516 Americans on European battlefields was necessary to the security of American life or was the right way to conduct foreign policy. They were not nihilists. They were not withdrawing from American life in protest. They were patriotic young men in search of a fresher and more humane code of values.

Having gone abroad for the first time in their lives, they had encountered economic, social, and moral standards unlike their own. American provinciality came to an end, although many older Americans, like Henry Cabot Lodge and William Borah, did not know it and were still tied to yesterday. Since any new experience is an aspect of enlightenment, the impact of World War I on the American consciousness was constructive. If one crusade for freedom succeeded, it was logical to assume that other crusades might also succeed, and that it was therefore worthwhile to take moral stands, fight for good causes, and help create a better world. To many of the new generation, reform seemed possible; and the leading new playwrights expected to change not only the theater but life. They were basically believers—believers in social justice and in the worth of human beings.

But the external life of the nation—the political, social, and commercial life—was mindless and sordid. The best period in the Broadway theater coincided with one of the low periods in the surfaces of life. Since the politicians had given nothing to the nation and had learned nothing, Congress rejected the League of Nations and Americans joyfully voted for mediocrity—or "normalcy," in the ripe vocabulary of Warren Gamaliel Harding.

Terrified by the revolution in Russia, United States Attorney General A. Mitchell Palmer, led the nation into one of the most hysterical witch-hunts in modern history. Later generations would find it difficult to believe that, in the twenties, thousands of blameless Americans were thrown into jail without charges because someone suspected they were Russian spies. The crusade lost contact with reality. On May 1, 1920, the entire police force of New York was ordered to remain on the alert for twenty-four hours—on Broadway as well as Fifth Avenue—to forestall a diabolical Communist takeover that the alert attorney general had predicted for that day. Nothing happened except that the police got terribly

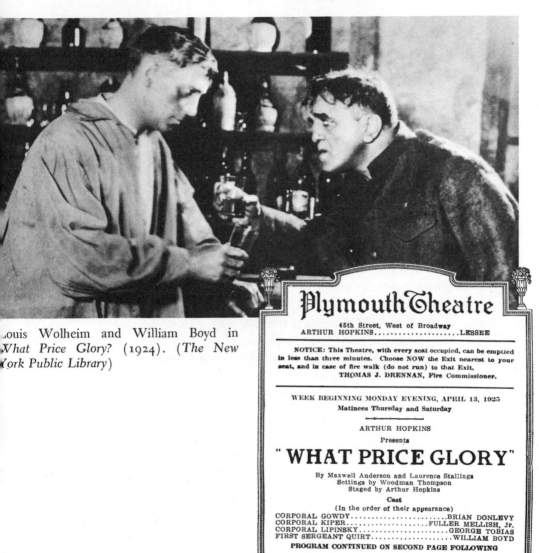

Louis Wolheim and William Boyd in
What Price Glory? (1924). (*The New
York Public Library*)

Plymouth Theatre

45th Street, West of Broadway
ARTHUR HOPKINS....................LESSEE

NOTICE: This Theatre, with every seat occupied, can be emptied
in less than three minutes. Choose NOW the Exit nearest to your
seat, and in case of fire walk (do not run) to that Exit.
THOMAS J. DRENNAN, Fire Commissioner.

WEEK BEGINNING MONDAY EVENING, APRIL 13, 1925
Matinees Thursday and Saturday

ARTHUR HOPKINS
Presents

"WHAT PRICE GLORY"

By Maxwell Anderson and Laurence Stallings
Settings by Woodman Thompson
Staged by Arthur Hopkins

Cast
(In the order of their appearance)

CORPORAL GOWDY........................BRIAN DONLEVY
CORPORAL KIPER.....................FULLER MELLISH, Jr.
CORPORAL LIPINSKY....................GEORGE TOBIAS
FIRST SERGEANT QUIRT...................WILLIAM BOYD

PROGRAM CONTINUED ON SECOND PAGE FOLLOWING

sleepy and the citizens accumulated more than their normal share of
boredom.

The sanctimonious uplift of the Prohibition Amendment made boot
leggers out of many enterprising Americans and lawbreakers out of the
rest. It was a decade of stupefying materialism. Seduced by schemes for
easy installment buying, millions of citizens went cheerfully into debt to

buy automobiles, which were the instruments of mobility and freedom, and many kinds of household appliance—including radios, which were just beginning to blanket the nation with standardized thought and entertainment. At the end of the decade, thirteen million radios were squawking in thirteen million living-rooms and offices. The population had become restless. Uprooted by the war, Americans were breaking with the past and moving from one part of the country to another—principally into the cities, where they became social émigrés. It was the day of the flapper—the girl with the bobbed hair, short skirts, and casual promiscuity. Her counterpart was the predatory youth with the raccoon coat, sports car, and hip flask. By traditional standards, the decade of the twenties was reckless, irresponsible, self-centered, giddy, vulgar, and destructive. Although America had not come of age it seemed to have reached puberty.

But the arts were stimulating: the collapse of standards was liberating. H. L. Mencken and G. J. Nathan, then in their prime, convinced delighted readers everywhere that old-fashioned dignity and respectability were frauds. In *Main Street*, Sinclair Lewis ridiculed the myth of the righteous small town. Scott Fitzgerald told fascinating truths about the depravity of sophisticated society. William Faulkner dug into the primitive evils of life in the small towns of the South. Theodore Dreiser undermined the doctrines of purity and optimism. Ernest Hemingway, his pride wounded by indifference at home, emigrated to Europe in search of a romantic code of honor worthy of his ego. Poets like Robert Frost, Carl Sandburg, Edwin Arlington Robinson, and Robinson Jeffers left the sanctuary of polite letters and made poems out of reality. From overseas came the unsettling influence of Sigmund Freud: he put erudite names to pleasantly lascivious aberrations of human behavior and terminated the calvinist doctrine of free will. Suddenly it appeared that there was a streak of bestiality in the best of men.

In the raucous twenties, nothing turned out to have been as simple and sublime as Americans had assumed. The truth was less uplifting than the realities. Since the truth rejected traditionalists, it liberated young people who were sick of cant. "Bunk" was the freshest word in the vocabulary. The most enterprising of the new plays dispensed with the old canons. In *What Price Glory?*, war turned out to be not noble but irrelevant. *They Knew What They Wanted* reduced the ecstasy of romance to pity and kindness. The house-proud *Craig's Wife* was a monster. In *The Silver Cord*, mother love became malevolent and destructive. In *Desire Under the Elms*, the idyll of life on the farm degenerated into incest and greed.

The collapse of traditions had at least one positive result: it turned the best drama into a sharp criticism of life. Paradoxical as it may be, the best period in the Broadway drama corresponded to a debased period in the life of the nation.

In 1918, the first Pulitzer Prize was given to Jesse Lynch Williams' *Why Marry?*—a forgotten comedy in a style of sterile craftmanship that had satisfied Broadway for years. In 1920, the second Pulitzer Prize was given to Eugene O'Neill's *Beyond the Horizon*, and Broadway has never been the same since. A romantic tragedy about two brothers trapped by fate, *Beyond the Horizon* became the great divide between the provincial theater of ready-made plays and the modern American drama concerned directly with human life. After O'Neill's first full-length play was cautiously produced at special matinees at the Morosco Theater on February 3, 1920, hokum dramas like *The Easiest Way, Salvation Nell*, and *The Witching Hour* became impossible.

Eugene O'Neill, the handsome, tormented son of James O'Neill, a swashbuckling actor of the old school, not only began the modern American drama; to a large extent he sustained it by writing powerful plays in several styles. He wrote forty-five plays, excluding several early one-act plays that he discarded from his collected works. All through his career, he was concerned not with provocative topics, surfaces of character, or ingenuities of craftsmanship, but with the basic elements of life—"Fate, God, our biological past creating our present, whatever one calls it," in his words; and the Broadway theater began to have cultural significance when he became part of it.

Although O'Neill deliberately avoided Broadway during most of his mature years, he was born on Broadway, on the third floor of the Barrett House at 43rd Street, on October 16, 1888. He used to like to point out the room to his friends. The Barrett House was pulled down in 1940, and was succeeded by a smaller building that contains a shoe store on the ground level. Admirers of O'Neill once persuaded the proprietor of the shoe store to let them post a bronze tablet to O'Neill on the store front where passersby could see it. But it was an incongruous item in the debased, heedless Broadway of the second half of our century. Ultimately the tablet was removed and stored away on a shelf inside the shop. In 1970 the shoe shop was scheduled to be pulled down, and eventually the birthplace of the nation's foremost dramatist will be entombed inside an office building.

If the American theater was a decisive influence on his personality, it was because he had no home life. Son of an actor who trouped in *The*

Count of Monte Cristo for many years, he went on tour with his mother and father when he was a baby. During his school years he was separated from his parents. No doubt temperament as well as experience made him a natural rebel. He was instinctively against everything his father stood for and contemptuous of everything that was conventional in American life. He was a belligerent, romantic, and merciless egotist—ruthlessly self-centered. His youthful reading consisted of romantic misanthropes or iconoclasts like Byron, Jack London, Nietzsche, and Schopenhauer.

Under the influence of Conrad's *The Nigger of the Narcissus*, O'Neill shipped out as a paid passenger in a Norwegian bark in 1910, and sailed to South America and England in various vessels during the next two years —beachcombing in Buenos Aires, carousing in Jimmy-the-Priest's Fulton Street saloon in New York between voyages. Twice he toured with his father—once as assistant stage manager for *The White Sister*, in which Viola Allen was co-starred, and once as a bit player in a vaudeville version of *The Count of Monte Cristo*. In 1912, he became a reporter on the New London, Connecticut, *Telegraph*. At the end of that year, he was ill with tuberculosis and went to a sanatorium in Connecticut, where he remained for six months.

These details are significant because O'Neill was a completely self-centered person, and the great bulk of his drama derived from these three years—the moody sea plays, *The Hairy Ape, Anna Christie, The Straw, Beyond the Horizon, The Emperor Jones, Ah, Wilderness!, The Iceman Cometh, Long Day's Journey into Night*, and perhaps some of the others or some parts of the others. His experience of life outside the theater was limited. But he had a great reservoir of temperament, dissatisfaction, hatred, moodiness, cynicism, scorn. Out of tiny experience and abundant emotion, he wrote some of America's most powerful dramas.

For many years, he was a heavy drinker—a Greenwich Village bohemian, the equivalent of the beatniks and hippies of later years. When he was sober, he was a soft, shy, silent, attractive young man with black hair, black eyes, a black moustache and a general impression of melancholy and frustration. His humor was mild and rueful. But there was nothing soft about the conduct of his life. His denials were ruthless. He eliminated everyone and everything that he regarded as irrelevant to his work. He left his first two wives. He exiled his children. He walked away from every home he had because he found fault with all of them. Strongly influenced by Strindberg's *The Dance of Death* and Dostoevsky's *The Idiot*, he found the tragic view of life consoling and congenial; and, unconsciously no doubt, he set about the mission of making his own life tragic. He was his own best theme. He proved his thesis by the loneliness he imposed on his life and by the cruel scope of his rejection. If the furies had not lived in his bloodstream, he could have been as happy as anyone.

Before the Broadway production of *Beyond the Horizon*, O'Neill was admired for his one-act plays about the sea—*Bound East for Cardiff*, *In the Zone*, *The Long Voyage Home*, *The Moon of the Caribbees*—put on in 1916 and 1917 at the Wharf Theater in Provincetown, Massachusetts, and at the Provincetown Playhouse in Macdougal Street in Greenwich Village. John D. Williams, a Broadway producer with better taste than most, bought an option on *Beyond the Horizon* in 1918 but never came to the point of producing it. While acting in Williams' production of Elmer Rice's *For the Defense* in December 1919, Richard Bennett read the script of *Beyond the Horizon* in Williams' office. He found it so stimulating that he persuaded Williams to put it on at special matinees at the Morosco Theater when *For the Defense* was not being performed. In addition to himself, Bennett assembled a cast that included Louise Closser Hale, Mary Jeffrey, George Riddell, Edward Arnold, and Helen MacKellar.

When *Beyond the Horizon* opened, it was received with enthusiasm by press and public. Alexander Woollcott wrote in *The New York Times*: "The play has greatness in it and marks O'Neill as one of our foremost playwrights." After praising it, Heywood Broun said in the *New York Tribune*: "I am no longer drawn to the play 'with a big idea,' or the comedy constructed for the sake of a single telling scene"—thus recognizing the nature of the organic style of theater O'Neill had introduced to Broadway. Rice's *For the Defense* had a short run, but *Beyond the Horizon* ran for 111 performances. O'Neill did not have to wait for recognition on Broadway. For the most part unconsciously, but consciously in the cases of many people, Broadway was waiting for something genuine, independent, and imaginative. O'Neill brought it, and the handwriting was on the wall of the Morosco Theater. The old Broadway was finished.

O'Neill never wrote a play based on a plausible topic torn out of the context of contemporary life. He was no journalist. He got the idea of *Beyond the Horizon* from a Norwegian sailor in a vessel sailing from New York to Buenos Aires. The seaman was convinced that he had made a tragic mistake when he went to sea; he believed that he should have stayed on the family farm in Norway. O'Neill suspected that the seaman's longing for the farm was an illusion—which became one of O'Neill's basic themes. In *Beyond the Horizon*, he dramatized the story of two brothers who were in love with the same girl but made the wrong choices of career. The unromantic one who might have made the farm pay and might have provided a satisfactory life for the girl went to sea. The romantic one married the girl, stayed on the farm and failed and also lost his wife's devotion. Both husband and wife dreamed of the wonderful life the other brother was having all over the world. When he returned, however, it appeared that he was no poet or adventurer but a very commonplace moneygrubber who had seen nothing that had interested him. The dreamer failed; the materialist succeeded.

By the standards that O'Neill ultimately helped to establish, *Beyond the Horizon* was a sophomoric tragedy, limited by the author's romantic self-pity and literary pessimism. But it attracted a public that was unused to indigenous tragedy of that kind, and it stimulated O'Neill enormously. He flourished; he was full of projects. While *Beyond the Horizon* was on the stage, he revised the script of another full-length play, *Chris Christo-pherson* (in which young, unknown Lynn Fontanne appeared); he worked on the script of *Gold*, planned a production of *The Straw* and cooperated on the Provincetown Playhouse's production of his one-act *Exorcism*, which was a rationalization of his attempt to commit suicide in 1919. In the same year, he worked on the scripts of *The Emperor Jones* and *Diff'rent*. *Chris Christopherson* failed in Atlantic City that year, but it succeeded brilliantly in 1921 as *Anna Christie* with the elusive, tremulous, infinitely gifted Pauline Lord in the leading part.

The scope of O'Neill's capacity for work and the eagerness of Broadway's interest in him is indicated by the fact that between 1920 and 1923 he completed seven long plays and helped in the production of five of them. Between March 1924 and January 1926, five of his plays were produced on and off Broadway—*Welded, All God's Chillun Got Wings, Desire Under the Elms, The Fountain,* and *The Great God Brown.* Some of them failed. Some people complained that in America life was not tragic and that O'Neill was slandering his country. George C. D. Odell, a professor of English at Columbia University, declared that O'Neill was debasing the stage and was personally responsible for the increasing use of profanity on the stage and for portraits of insanity. Some theatergoers denounced *The Hairy Ape* as socialist propaganda and therefore subversive and un-American. The mother of a Provincetown Theater actress swore that she would kill O'Neill because he had introduced her daughter to the works of Nietzsche.

The law felt uneasy about O'Neill. Startled by a rumor that a Negro would kiss a white woman in *All God's Chillun Got Wings,* the license commissioner threatened to close the theater if the drama was produced; and just before the first performance, the police gave the management an injunction forbidding the use of child actors. The management evaded the injunction by reading the manuscript of the first act from the stage, and improvising the rest of the performance without child actors. District Attorney Jacob H. Banton, who had the mind of a reformer, threatened to "get" O'Neill for this evasion of the law and did bring charges of obscenity against *Desire Under the Elms*. A jury of citizens did not agree with Banton, and the charge was dropped, although from that time on *Desire Under the Elms* had the reputation of being an obscene work— and drew big audiences on Broadway. Scandal is usually good box office.

The new drama alienated some people. But the record of O'Neill's first period on Broadway, between 1920 and 1934, is one of unique activity, bountifulness, and versatility—nineteen new plays of which at least two, *Desire Under the Elms* and *Mourning Becomes Electra*, were masterpieces, and four (all of them successful) were written in new forms —*Emperor Jones, The Hairy Ape, All God's Chillun Got Wings*, and *Strange Interlude*; and it is impossible to be any the less enthusiastic about more conventional plays like *Anna Christie, Marco Millions*, and *Ah, Wilderness!*

One mark of a genius is an abundance of work representing talent and fresh ideas, whatever its quality may be. O'Neill fits that category. Once the doors to the new drama were opened, he came in with innumerable manuscripts and many scornful ideas about the artistic capacities of Broadway, as well as the social and political conventions of American life. An obsessive writer, he broke formulas repeatedly; he defied audiences. *Strange Interlude* and *Mourning Becomes Electra* were each five hours long; audiences had to go to the theater in the late afternoon, take dinner during an intermission, and then return to the theater for a full evening of drama. Both plays were so absorbing that the dinner-break seemed like an unwelcome return to the slovenly prosiness of Broadway. No one could ignore O'Neill, including the Nobel Prize Committee, which gave him the Nobel Prize for Literature in 1936.

O'Neill not only wrote dramatically; he also lived dramatically. At the height of his career, he disappeared from Broadway and proposed to write an American saga of eight plays, none of which was to be produced until all were written. He never completed the cycle, but two unfinished sections of it—*A Touch of the Poet* and *More Stately Mansions* —were acted after his death. Doubtless he would have forbidden the productions if he had been alive.

Dudley Digges in *The Iceman Cometh* (1946). (*Vandamm*)

MARTIN BECK THEATRE

OPERATED BY MARTIN BECK THEATRE CORP.　　　LOUIS A. LOTITO, MANAGING DIRECTOR
302 WEST FORTY-FIFTH STREET

FIRE NOTICE: The exit indicated by a red light and sign nearest to the seat you occupy is the shortest route to the street. In the event of fire please do not run—WALK TO THAT EXIT.
　　　　　　　　Frank J. Quayle,
　　　　　　　　FIRE COMMISSIONER

Thoughtless persons annoy patrons and distract actors and endanger the safety of others by lighting matches during the performance-and intermissions. This violates a city ordinance and renders the offender liable to a summons from the fireman on duty. It is urged that all patrons refrain from lighting matches in the auditorium of this theatre.

THE · PLAYBILL · A · WEEKLY · PUBLICATION · OF · PLAYBILL · INCORPORATED

Week beginning Monday, December 23, 1946

THE THEATRE GUILD

presents

EUGENE O'NEILL'S
THE ICEMAN COMETH

with

JAMES BARTON　　　　　　DUDLEY DIGGES
CARL BENTON REID　　　　NICHOLAS JOY

Directed by Eddie Dowling

Production designed and lighted by Robert Edmond Jones

Production under the supervision of
THERESA HELBURN and LAWRENCE LANGNER

Associate producer,
Armina Marshall

CAST

HARRY HOPE .... DUDLEY DIGGES
　　proprietor of a saloon and rooming house
ED MOSHER .... MORTON L. STEVENS
　　Hope's brother in law, one-time circus man

One masterly play that was not a part of the cycle—*The Iceman Cometh*—was put on in 1946 at the Martin Beck Theater. It was another one of the works Broadway referred to as "marathon plays." Returning to the vein of autobiography, going back again to those few formative years when he developed his tragic philosophy, he set *The Iceman Cometh* in Jimmy-the-Priest's waterfront saloon, where he had loafed between voyages or touring jogs with his father. Again he dramatized his theme of illusion; this time he argued that illusions were necessary if life was to be tolerable. Another family play involving illusions and called *A Moon for the Misbegotten* was put on in the miniature Bijou Theater in 1951—unsuccessfully. After his death, a masterly play based on the New London home life of the O'Neills and called *Long Day's Journey into Night* was acted at the Helen Hayes Theater in 1956. Since it was highly personal and had an element of family scandal in it, he had specified that it was not to be produced until twenty-five years after his death and presumably after the deaths of any people who might have been personally concerned. But Mrs. Carlotta O'Neill released the play for publication in 1956. The few people who did know the facts of the O'Neill family life were distressed and felt that Eugene had brutally misstated them.

For a slight man with insecure health, and for many years with an addiction to alcohol, O'Neill overwhelmed Broadway with a prodigious body of work that could not be ignored, even when parts of it were inferior. He disliked Broadway. He seldom had a good word to say for Broadway productions. He grumbled about casting and staging. In his later years, he seldom went to the Broadway theater. But from the very first time one of his plays appeared there, Broadway recognized his worth and supported and valued him for the rest of his career. The consistent trash produced on Broadway during the first twenty years of the century had not ruined the taste of many theater people and most theatergoers. When Broadway matured, the public was ready for it.

O'Neill regarded himself as a dramatic poet confronting the furies. "I am always acutely conscious of the one eternal tragedy of Man in his glorious self-destructive struggle," he said. The use of the word "glorious" to describe man's universal fate shows how far removed O'Neill was from the austere discipline of the Greeks. His Irish temperament was hot and personal. Always self-conscious about his work, usually disgruntled by the comments on it, he complained that the public did not credit him with having evolved "original rhythms of beauty where beauty apparently isn't —'Jones,' 'Desire,' 'Ape,' 'All God's Chillun,' etc." He regretted that the public did not see in his plays "the transfiguring nobility of tragedy in as near the Greek sense as one can grasp it, in seemingly the most ignoble, debased lives."

The characters did not control his plays. He put them in situations that illustrated his philosophy, and he wrote universal concepts—hatred, greed, lust, death, the illusions that mask the truth of life and, at the same time, make living possible. He was not a clever intellectual, but he did have a philosophical view of life. In *Dynamo*, he consciously dramatized "the death of an old god and the failure of science and materialism to give any satisfactory new one for the surviving primitive religious instinct to find a meaning for life." (He could write clumsy sentences now and then.) A lapsed Roman Catholic, he frequently tried to rationalize, on the one hand, his repudiation of dogmatic religion and, on the other, his need for it. *Days Without End*, produced in 1934, was his attempt to make some personal adjustment to his spiritual dilemma. Hardly anyone thought he had succeeded.

Since he did not write with the grace of a poet there is something paradoxical in the fact that, although he had the temperament of a poet, his literary style was flat. He never wrote a quotable line. In the middle of his career, he made this comment about *Mourning Becomes Electra* in a letter to Arthur Hobson Quinn: "It needed great language to lift itself beyond itself. I haven't got that. And, by way of consolation, I don't think . . . that great language is possible for anyone living in the discordant, broken, faithless rhythm of our time."

But his literary style—flat on paper—had great power on the stage. The last line in *Desire Under the Elms* is hardly inspired. Looking around him the sheriff says, "It's a jim-dandy farm, no denying. Wished I owned it." But the line reverberates in the theater, because it makes a vivid dramatic contrast with the preceding events of the play. After the fierce struggle between hostile ambitions, after the agony of a hopeless love affair, after the baby has been smothered, the sheriff makes a commonplace remark that becomes eloquent in the theater. In *The Iceman Cometh*, the reiterated phrase, "pipe dreams" (a slang way of saying "illusions") seems sophomoric in print. But in the context of the drama, "pipe dreams" sounds like a requiem for hope. Nothing said in *Mourning Becomes Electra* is memorable. But the long series of short plays about a doomed family that has been rejected by God is overwhelmingly powerful; and in the last scene, Lavinia's retreat into the family mansion while the hired man is closing the shutters has the ruthless impact of divine judgment: "It takes the Mannons to punish themselves for being born," Lavinia says.

Eugene O'Neill in 1946, just after *The Iceman Cometh* had opened. (*F. Roy Kemp*)

The prose has none of the incantation of poetry. But it comes alive in the theater because in that Broadway hotel room O'Neill was born a congenital theater man. He despised bravura romances like *The Count of Monte Cristo*, on which his father had squandered a fine career, but he had the spaciousness and the melodrama of that kind of play in his bones. That accounts for the romantic flair in his tragedies. The irony of O'Neill is that the swashbuckling theater he repudiated was the basis of his dramatic style. He spent more of his life in the theater than he did in the world of men. He never forgot the men; in fact, he wrote about the same men repeatedly. But he expressed them in terms of the theater.

The last years of his personal life were harshly theatrical and confirmed his tragic view of life. They were as pitiless, overwrought, and demonic as *The Great God Brown* and *Desire Under the Elms*. In the early 1940s, O'Neill began to develop a degenerative form of paralysis—superficially like Parkinson's disease—that impaired his speech and afflicted his hands with a tremor. Gradually he lost the capacity to write in the small, neat, clear style that makes all his letters and manuscripts beautiful. For he was a composer as much as a writer: he could not write plays on the typewriter or dictate them. The tremor marked the beginning of the end of his life as a dramatist. The curse of the gods was beginning as in the case of Hickey in *The Iceman Cometh* or Brutus Jones in *The Emperor Jones*.

In 1948, he and his third wife, Carlotta Monterey, also a very theatrical person, moved into an isolated house on a cliff overlooking the sea in Marblehead, Massachussetts. For years they had lived alone as much as possible. Now they isolated themselves almost completely. Both of them were ill. Tormented by disease, cut off from the rest of the world, frustrated, always facing "dat ole davil, sea" that Chris cursed in *Anna Christie*, they lived together with a neurotic intensity that might have come straight out of any one of several O'Neill dramas.

There was a bad accident one freezing night. O'Neill slipped on the ice and broke a leg. A short time after he had been taken to a hospital, Mrs. O'Neill was taken there because the doctor thought she was irrational. Some of the doctors who attended them thought both of the O'Neills were insane. But they were not; they were merely theatrical—two big temperaments clashing and building scenes. For a while, they were separated— he in a hospital in New York, and she in a hospital near Boston—and they fought each other with legal moves and countermoves. But O'Neill's marriage to Carlotta Monterey was the only stable relationship in his whole life. In the end he gratefully returned to her and they lived in the Shelton Hotel in Boston.

For the next year and a half Mrs. O'Neill, with the assistance of one nurse, took charge of a helpless invalid. "Born in a hotel room and—God damn it—died in a hotel room," he groaned a few days before his death on November 27, 1953. He was still thinking in terms of the theater. The last slow movement of his life was, not only a recapitulation of his own dramas, but like a scene from Strindberg's *The Dance of Death*, which had stimulated his interest in drama when he was a young man.

During forty enormously prolific years, O'Neill had transformed the backward American drama into a form of literature and art. In the end, the fates made him their most tortured victim. Nothing he wrote was more terrible than what he endured at the end.

THEATRE
· GUILD ·
PROGRAM

AH, WILDERNESS!
BY EUGENE O'NEILL
WITH GEO. M. COHAN
at the
GUILD THEATRE

THE
THEATER GUILD

During the 1920s—and to a lesser extent, during the 1930s—the most dynamic and the most creative organization on Broadway was the Theater Guild. The Guild annihilated provinciality in the American theater. Once it was established, Broadway became an active part of the theater of the world.

Lawrence Langner was the catalyst. A Welshman who had come to New York at the age of seventeen to join a patent attorney's office, he was a restless, alert extrovert who was stagestruck and who was always over-flowing with ideas. He looked like a slender Spaniard; he had an oval face, black eyes, black hair, and a thin black moustache. He was one of the most articulate men alive. He lived in Greenwich Village. Being by nature convivial, he participated in the ritualistic activities of Village life before World War I. He was an active member of the Liberal Club, which intended to reform America in any number of ways, particularly

he directors of the Theater Guild: Lee Simonson,
elen Westley, Philip Moeller, Theresa Helburn,
aurice Wertheim, and Lawrence Langner. (*The
ew York Public Library*)

in the arena of sex. He was a partner in the Washington Square Book Shop, which was the intellectual center of the Village. When he was not attending to the patent law business, he wrote plays, most of which had an iconoclastic strain, and all of which were undistinguished.

In 1915, he was one of the Villagers who founded the Washington Square Players. One of his one-act plays, *Licensed*, was acted in the first bill of plays. It took a few liberties with the doctrine of birth control at a time when respectable people practiced it but did not mention it. In May of 1918, the Washington Square Players reluctantly acknowledged that World War I was taking precedence over the amateur theater. Too many of its people were being drawn off into the irrelevant occupation of fighting for their country.

Always a man to keep everything in proportion so long as the theater was on top, Mr. Langner remarked after the armistice that he was glad the war was over because he wanted to organize another theater. The war had inconvenienced a lot of theater idealists. By chance, he met two of his old comrades, Helen Westley and Philip Moeller, in the basement buffet of the old Brevoort Hotel, where many implausible schemes were constantly discussed. He lost no time—Mr. Langner never lost time in getting things started—in calling a preliminary meeting on December 19, 1918, at the home of Mrs. Josephine Meyer, who had been one of the best friends of the Washington Square Players. Mr. Langner noted that Miss Westley and Mr. Moeller "had the kind of impractical imagination that makes impractical ventures possible." Although Mr. Moeller and Miss Westley had had some academic training in the theater, they were, like Mr. Langner, not professionals yet. Mr. Langner tracked down Lee Simonson, an artist of formidable energy and terrifying self-confidence, who was impatiently awaiting discharge in an Army camp. His ardor was always easily aroused, whether pro or con. At a later date, Maurice Wertheim, a banker who had inadvertently studied drama in G. P. Baker's famous 47 Workshop at Harvard, joined the board of managers, bringing one more amateur into the organization. Another amateur, Theresa Helburn, who had also studied with Professor Baker, joined the organization and soon became a member of the board.

Since they were all amateurs, they naturally decided to found a professional theater. Other amateurs and a handful of professionals began to come to the board meetings—Rollo Peters, a California painter; Dudley Digges and Augustin Duncan, actors; Edna St. Vincent Millay, who liked anything that was impractical; Helen Freeman, an actress with a strong mind and a sharp tongue; Justus Sheffield, a lawyer whose hobby was the theater.

Utopians, they were not interested in making money. They were interested in establishing an art theater with modern standards. Since their budget was practically invisible, they started looking around for a small theater that would not be prohibitively expensive. It turned out to be an intimate house called the Garrick Theater, which had been built a half-century earlier by the comedy team of Harrigan and Hart. The Garrick Theater, east of Broadway in 35th Street, seated about 600 people. In 1919, it was under lease to Otto H. Kahn, the elegantly groomed investment banker who was quite as knowledgeable about the theater as the amateurs who visited him in his Wall Street office. He was not only rich but he had better taste than most theater people at that time and a greater sense of civic responsibility than most people at any time. He had just become the chairman of the board of the Metropolitan Opera Company, and by all odds, he was the most progressive the Met ever had. After discussing the Garrick Theater situation with the managers of the proposed Theater Guild, Mr. Kahn made a civilized and totally acceptable business arrangement: "When you make the rent you pay the rent," he said. "When you don't make it you need not pay it."

When the Guild was ready to start work on its first production the next spring, it had a capital of $2,160, of which Mr. Langner had contributed $1,610. It had sold subscriptions amounting to $474—a good augury for the future, because the subscription audiences turned out to be almost as creative as the board of managers. For the first production, the board chose Jacinto Benavente's *The Bonds of Interest*—staged by Philip Moeller and designed by Rollo Peters, who also played the leading part. Other actors in the first production were Augustin Duncan, Helen Westley, Edna St. Vincent Millay, Mary Blair, Dudley Digges, Amelia Somerville, and Helen Freeman.

In designing the production, Mr. Peters spent money frugally but effectively. He used odds and ends of the scenery left by the last tenant, who was Jacques Copeau. The most gorgeous item in the production was an elaborate hooped gown of cloth of gold, which Mr. Peters had made for $30 by spreading gilt radiator paint on oilcloth. It looked magnificent. In the course of the opening performance, Miss Somerville had to sit for a long period on a chair which she could not help warming. When she rose to make her exit, the chair rose with her. Inside the opaque oilcloth, she had generated enough body heat to bond the radiator paint. Dudley

Digges succeeded in pulling the chair away, but it left a huge white patch in the oilcloth. The audience cheered. That was the only gauche episode in the evening. Although the first night seemed to be a success, *The Bonds of Interest* failed. When the curtain had gone up, the Guild's total assets had been $19.50 in the cash box. First-night receipts were $403.35; the second-night receipts were $281.45. The production proceeded to lose about $500 a week, which Mr. Langner paid until Maurice Wertheim, now a reckless convert, offered to share the losses equally.

While *The Bonds of Interest* was failing, Mr. Langner happened to find a copy of St. John Ervine's *John Ferguson* in the downtown Brentano's near Madison Square. Ervine in London gave the company permission to put on his play with no advance payment. *John Ferguson* was a tragedy set in Ireland, portraying a simple farmer who had exalted standards of conscience. Augustin Duncan staged it. Rollo Peters designed it. It opened on May 12, 1919, with nine of the actors who had appeared in the Benavente play. *John Ferguson* was an instant success. There was a line at the box office the next morning. In August, Actors' Equity Association went on strike and closed every other play on Broadway. It did not close *John Ferguson* because the profit-sharing arrangement the Guild had with its actors suited Equity's aims exactly. Until the strike was settled on September 6, *John Ferguson* was the only play open for business on Broadway. It moved uptown to the Fulton Theater in 46th street where the receipts were larger, and the Garrick was available for the next production.

Since the Guild became the most civilizing producing organization that Broadway has ever had, its obscure and chancy beginning is interesting. A handful of amateurs who were trying to behave like professionals might have gone out of existence in April or May of their first year. As a play, *The Bonds of Interest* ranks on the same level with *John Ferguson*, but it was *John Ferguson* that stirred the interest of the audience. A caprice of public taste saved the Guild. Fundamentally, the board of managers had little to offer except belief in a better theater than Broadway was offering. In lieu of money, they endowed the Guild with passionate dedication and personal force of character. Most theaters are the expression of one dominating person, like Henry Irving, Konstantin Stanislavsky, Jacques Copeau, or Max Reinhardt. A good theater is usually a dictatorship. But the Guild was founded and administered by six people of fiery temperament. They not only chose the plays but participated in the direction of the productions.

No one expected them to succeed. None of them ever expected to succeed on the scale they did. But in the next ten or twenty years they added a strong infusion of art to show business, and they brought thousands of intelligent people into the theater. In May 1919, they had put on one small production that earned enough money to stage the next, John Masefield's *The Faithful,* which was a pious failure. But that hand-to-mouth existence was temporary. Only ten years later, the Guild had four productions simultaneously on view in four theaters on Broadway and seven companies traveling in other parts of America. That is the measure of the Theater Guild's success. That also measures the enthusiasm the public had for art in the theater. Art had become vastly more successful than commerce.

Most of the Guild's early plays came from abroad. Although Broadway had lived off the English and European theaters for years, the taste of the Guild managers was sharper, fresher, and more perceptive than the other Broadway managers. They had a bad failure with Lillian Sabine's version of William Dean Howell's *The Rise of Silas Lapham,* largely because they violated their own principle by hiring a star actor for the leading role. James K. Hackett played the chief part in the expansive, egotistical style that represented the old theater. That dismal experience may have prejudiced the Guild managers against American plays in general.

Like Winthrop Ames and Arthur Hopkins, the Guild put stage direction on the same level as playwriting. There was nothing routine about the productions. The Guild gave very original productions to very original plays, most of which were designed by Lee Simonson, who became one of the leading modern stage designers. In its early years, the Guild produced Tolstoy's *The Power of Darkness* (1920), staged by Emmanuel Reicher, whose enterprising direction of the Volksbühne Theater in Germany had influenced the managers of the Guild; St. John Ervine's *Jane Clegg,* (1920) which, like Ervine's *John Ferguson,* rescued the Guild from bankruptcy; Emmanuel Reicher's production of Strindberg's *The Dance of Death* (1920), which made heavy demands on the imagination of the theatergoer; and David Pinski's *The Treasure* (1920), a formidable play in its day. Only one of these productions, *Jane Clegg,* was a financial success. But they all illustrated the alert taste and the daring of the managers, and also the principle that failure is as creative as success. *The Power of Darkness* is a superb play. It was splendidly acted by Helen Westley, Frank Reicher, Ida Rauh, Henry Travers, and

Erskine Sanford—all first-rate people. Despite this wealth of talent, the public could not be roused out of its customary lethargy. *The Power of Darkness* failed.

A particular sign of the Guild's independent taste was the interest it took in Bernard Shaw, who was in disgrace in 1920. He had opposed World War I and angered Americans as well as English. In England, he was treated by some people like a traitor. In 1914, he had published a provocative and derisive pamphlet called "Common Sense About the War," which made him look like a saboteur to people unaccustomed to his intellectual agility and his jeering style. Henry Arthur Jones, the British playwright, was particularly bitter. He attacked Shaw in a ferocious polemic that had wide newspaper circulation. Shaw resigned from the Dramatists' Club in London after Jones had persuaded his fellow members to tell Shaw that he was no longer welcome at club meetings. During the war, Shaw wrote one of his finest plays, *Heartbreak House*, which expressed a sad farewell to England's moral greatness. When he published it with a scornful preface after the war, he further wounded the feelings of men who had fought in France and the parents, wives, and friends of men who had died there.

But the managers of the Guild were as unintimidated by public opinion as Shaw was. On November 10, 1920, just after the United States had jubilantly elected a nonentity (Harding) as president of the nation, the Guild put on *Heartbreak House* in an incandescent production staged by Dudley Digges, designed by Lee Simonson, and acted by Lucile Watson, Effie Shannon, Helen Westley, Elizabeth Risdon, Dudley Digges, Erskine Sanford, Ralph Roeder, Henry Travers, and others. It had a long and prosperous run. After the Guild had broken the taboo, *Heartbreak House* was put on in London, though without success. At the beginning of its third season, an embryo theater organization, founded by amateurs, had given the world première of an audacious play by the world's greatest contemporary dramatist.

As proof of its growing virtuosity, the Guild went on to give a delightful performance of A. A. Milne's droll *Mr. Pim Passes By*, with Erskine Sanford, Dudley Digges, Phyllis Povah, Laura Hope Crews, and Helen Westley. And it captured the enthusiasm of thousands of theatergoers with a colorful production of Ferenc Molnar's wistful romance, *Liliom*, acted in contrasting styles by Eva Le Gallienne and Joseph Schildkraut. Then Leonid Andreyev's lyric *He Who Gets Slapped*, a circus allegory that no one understood but everyone loved. Like elusive figures in a haunting dream, Margalo Gillmore and Richard Bennett gave stirring performances.

But the triumph that established the Guild solidly was the world première of Shaw's interminable *Back to Methusaleh*, the first part of which opened on February 27, 1922. It took enthusiasm, skill, self-confidence, and a broad streak of sound theatrical madness to stage that play. Shaw had been writing it during World War I, possibly to keep himself occupied during the interlude when he was excommunicated from normal society. If it is not the longest play in the drama of the West, it is one of the longest, for it begins with Adam and looks into a remote and singularly unattractive future when human beings will apparently live forever. This was before the day of the population explosion. The play is dogmatic, ponderously jocose, prolix, and on the whole intolerably boring. When the indomitable Lawrence Langner asked for a contract, Shaw replied: "Don't bother about a contract. It isn't likely that any other lunatic will want to produce *Back to Methusalah*."

The Guild divided the manuscript into three sections, each of which was to be played a week before the next one was put on. Two directors collaborated on staging the section for the first week, and two others staged the second and third sections respectively. Lee Simonson designed a bold, colorful unit-set on which images could be thrown from a projector. No one had expected the play to be a public success, if only because the theatergoer had to go to the theater one night a week for three weeks to see the whole play. Only Shaw could be so presumptuous as to put such a strain on the theatergoer. When one of the managers asked the doorman at the Garrick how the play was going, he replied: "Fine. Less and less people walk out on it every night."

Back to Methusaleh was played twenty-five times, that is, each part was played twenty-five times, for a total of seventy-five performances. When the Guild undertook to produce it, the managers had expected to lose $30,000. They lost $20,000, prompting Shaw to assert that they had really made $10,000. This protean labor proved that the Guild did have a real talent for the impossible. In later years, Shaw gave the Guild the rights to produce *Saint Joan* (world première), *The Devil's Disciple, Caesar and Cleopatra, Arms and the Man, Androcles and the Lion, Pygmalion, The Doctor's Dilemma, Major Barbara, The Apple Cart, Getting Married, Too True to Be Good, The Simpleton of the Unexpected Isles* (world première), and *You Never Can Tell*. The Guild performed many services for Shaw, but he performed many services for the

Guild. He rescued the Guild from bankruptcy more than once. "When in doubt play Shaw," the board of managers used to say.

It seemed to many people at the time that the Guild was operating on such a rarefied level that it was defying the public to enjoy the theater. It put on Georg Kaiser's expressionistic *From Morn to Midnight*, which was an original play that was hard to understand and impossible to love. But it was so successful that the managers moved it from the Garrick to the Frazee Theater for forty-eight performances. In 1923, the Guild produced Ibsen's most unactable drama, *Peer Gynt*, and was enterprising enough to import Theodore Komisarjevsky from Russia to stage it. The production was not very good, but it ran for 121 performances. Broadway as a whole was interested in foreign drama at this period. If the cosmopolitan and independent taste of the Guild managers was not responsible for Broadway's increasingly civilized taste, it was certainly very influential.

When an organization like the Guild becomes firmly established on Broadway, the standards go up. More is expected of anyone who succeeds; repetition is never sufficient. There is, in fact, an element of jealousy involved. Broadway is so used to failure that it is by nature a negative community. It resents sustained success, particularly, as in the case of the Guild, when the literary taste is above the average; producers and playgoers with ordinary taste feel insulted. Broadway's vindictive attitude illustrates Rochefoucauld's maxim that a man can hardly avoid taking satisfaction in the failures of his friends. Since the Guild had become almost sensationally successful and was admired by many people not only for its successes but also for the challenge and daring of its failures, it was frequently accused of being either a fraud or dilettante. It was particularly vulnerable to the charge of ignoring American playwrights. For instance, it did not produce a single American play in the 1925–26 season. All the plays came from abroad: Shaw's *Arms and the Man*, brilliantly acted by the Lunts; Molnar's *The Glass Slipper*, with a vivacious cast that included June Walker, Helen Westley, and Armina Marshall; Shaw's *Androcles and the Lion*, played with great humor by Romney Brent, Henry Travers, Reginald Owen, Tom Powers, Clare Eames, and Edward G. Robinson; *Merchants of Glory*, an antiwar play by Marcel Pagnol and Paul Nivoix, with many of the same actors, and also Betty Linley, Lee Baker, Augustin Duncan, George Nash, Philip Loeb, Charles Halton and José Ruben; Franz Werfel's puzzling and portentous *Goat Song*, played in a flaring style by the Lunts, Zita Johann, Blanche Yurka, Dwight Frye, Albert Bruning, Harold Clurman, and Bela Blau; Nicholas

Evreinoff's sophomorically cosmic *The Chief Thing,* which was acted by a long cast that included some actors who were less familiar to Guild audiences, such as McKay Morris, Edith Meiser, Estelle Winwood, C. Stafford Dickens, Alice Belmore Cliffe, Peggy Conway, and Ernest Cossart; and finally, a lighthearted comedy from England—C. K. Munro's *At Mrs. Beam's,* with the Lunts and with Jean Cadell from England. Good and bad, it was a season that bored no one, although it provoked considerable discussion, and the absence of anything by an American was indignantly noted. The Guild "is not an essentially American institution," Lawrence Langner told a London reporter who was querying him on this most vulnerable point. "Half the actors are English and up to now English plays have dominated in the productions. We are an English-speaking theater," he added, ignoring the fact that many Russian, French, German, Belgian and Hungarian plays were also on the schedules. There had, in fact, been so many Hungarian plays that the Guild was sometimes called "the Budapest House." In the first four seasons, the only American plays put on by the Guild were Lillian Sabine's version of *The Rise of Silas Lapham* and Arthur Richman's *Ambush,* both far below the standards of the foreign plays. When it was criticized for being anti-American, the Guild retorted that Americans were not writing plays of equivalent merit. The retort was true with a few exceptions—chiefly Eugene O'Neill's devastating *The Hairy Ape.*

After begining its fifth season with more foreign plays (one of which was Karel Capek's now famous satire on the machine age, *R.U.R.*), the Guild in 1923 produced the most original and brilliant play any American had written up to that time—Elmer Rice's *The Adding Machine.* During the previous nine years, Mr. Rice had been writing in the traditional formulas, without much success except for his first play, *On Trial.* But in *The Adding Machine,* which portrayed the trauma of an obscure book-keeper, he made a vivid criticism of American civilization and began to express his lifetime concern for social justice and the quality of life in America. *The Adding Machine* was written in an expressionistic style that might have bewildered most Broadway producers. But the Guild had had abundant experience in this genre. Directed by Philip Moeller, designed by Lee Simonson, *The Adding Machine* was the harshest, most provocative and illuminating play about modern society that any American had written; and the Guild gave it a stunning performance with a cast that included Dudley Digges, Helen Westley, Margaret Wycherly and Edward G. Robinson, who was just beginning a career that soon became illustrious. When an American submitted an explosive manuscript, the

Guild had the good sense to accept it and had the artistic experience needed to produce it.

This was one of the happiest periods in the Guild's history. To open the seventh season in October 1924, the Guild took the manuscript of an old Molnar play that had failed and gave it a droll, subtle performance that was brilliantly successful. In essence, *The Guardsman* was the familiar story of the jealous and suspicious husband. But Molnar had told it allusively. And something of first importance happened that evening. Alfred Lunt and Lynn Fontanne played the husband and wife in a tandem performance that had the lightness of a dance and the virtuosity of a serenade. It was the beginning of a joint career that became matchless in America and perhaps throughout the world. It was just the thing to distinguish the Guild from the commercial theater. Star actresses had invariably turned the play down because they thought the male part was the better. Male stars turned it down because they thought the female part was the real lead. To the Lunts, it was an ideal vehicle because they could act it together with the brio and counterpoint of two perfectly matched geniuses. In this case, the Lunts and the Guild produced high comedy with a sophistication that no other Broadway organization could equal. In *The Guardsman*, everything was in high fettle—the skimming direction by Philip Moeller, frolicsome settings by Jo Mielziner, at the beginning of his career, and supporting performances by established Guild actors like Dudley Digges, Helen Westley, Edith Meiser, Philip Loeb, and Kathryn Wilson. Hungary had given the Guild another plum.

In the middle twenties, the tyranny of the foreign theater was weakening, or perhaps the level of American playwriting was rising. In 1924, the Guild opened its door to another admirable American and talented writer, Sidney Howard. It produced *They Knew What They Wanted*, a folkplay of enduring beauty and compassion, played with a kind of wistful romance by Pauline Lord, Richard Bennett, and Glenn Anders. Another venturesome American play came in 1925: John Howard Lawson's *Processional*, a socially aware, politically motivated jazz symphony of American life. Philip Moeller, who had staged *The Adding Machine* with so much ingenuity, found the right idiom for this bizarre drama and assembled a cast of players, most of whom were to have notable theatrical careers as time went on—George Abbott, June Walker, who had already made her mark in run-of-the-mill Broadway plays, Lee Strasberg, Philip Loeb, Ben Grauer, Donald Macdonald, and Charles Halton.

Having succeeded with one Sidney Howard play, the Guild produced two of his plays in succession in the 1926–1927 season: *Ned McCobb's*

Daughter and *The Silver Cord,* which was an early excursion into Freudian philosophy. And then came an early play by a gifted writer who was to become one of the Guild's most adored authors—*The Second Man,* by S. N. Behrman, played by another lustrous cast that included the Lunts, Margalo Gillmore and Earle Larimore.

The season of 1927–1928 was overwhelmingly American, with plays that have become part of the permanent American heritage—Dorothy and Du Bose Heyward's *Porgy,* which Rouben Mamoulian staged with a great theatrical flourish, and two plays in succession by Eugene O'Neill— *Marco Millions* and *Strange Interlude. Strange Interlude* eventually had 432 performances on Broadway, in addition to many more in the rest of America. By this time the Guild, which had been accused of a snobbish disdain of native drama, had become a genuinely cosmopolitan theater. It put on plays of merit from all parts of the world. It also had 30,000 subscribers in New York—a quarrelsome body of theatergoers who nevertheless took the drama seriously and were receptive to all kinds of ideas, particularly if they were startling. Without the support of the subscribers, the Guild would never have been able to transform Broadway so rapidly and so completely.

Having become the leading producing organization, the Guild naturally decided to build a theater of its own. There were 12,000 subscribers in 1923, when the plan was first discussed. Since the subscribers had supported the Guild so loyally, the managers decided to try to make the new building a joint venture by selling them $600,000 in bonds, most of which were to be in denominations of $100. The sale of bonds was a gratifying success. The beautiful Guild Theater in 52nd Street west of Broadway was ready to open in 1925. It was one of the finest New York theaters— hospitable, comfortable, daintily though modestly designed in an Italian style; and, thanks to Lee Simonson's untiring foresight and ingenuity, it was equipped with a deep stage behind an unframed proscenium—a departure from the trite picture-frame stage. It could be adapted to a variety of imaginative styles of production. The new theater seated about 1,000 people, with more leg-room than most Broadway theaters; and it cost more than one million dollars. On April 13, 1925, it opened with one of its most mediocre productions—Helen Hayes, at the beginning of her starring career, and Lionel Atwill, towards the end of his, in Shaw's *Caesar and Cleopatra,* regarded as an iconoclastic play at the time. The performance did not convey the crackle of Shaw's writing. In the course of his review of the opening night performance, Alexander Woollcott also reviewed the new theater. The walls of the theater were covered with

Architect's sketch of the Guild Theater, built in 1925. It is now the ANTA Theater. (*The New York Public Library*)

expensive Gobelin tapestries, purchased incidentally with the proceeds from the first edition of the *Garrick Gaieties*. "The Gobelins will get you if you don't watch out," said Mr. Woollcott.

The wisecrack turned out to be prophetic. Beautiful and useful though the new theater was, it turned out to be a financial burden because taxes and interest on the bonds were so high. Although it was ideal for theater-goers, it could not seat enough of them to earn a profit. It provided generous room for putting on unusual plays with dash and splendor but a full house was still too small to pay the bills. The Guild Theater earned a profit in only two years. As the Guild grew in size and put on plays that had long runs, it had to lease other theaters. In one season, it had plays in its own theater and also in the Empire, the Alvin, Henry Miller's, the Royale, and the Ethel Barrymore.

Ultimately, the Guild had to relinquish the Guild Theater, which finally became the ANTA Theater, managed by a nonprofit organization that was exempt from some of the tax burdens the Guild had to carry. Despite the able business minds of Lawrence Langner and Maurice Wertheim, the Guild was more successful with art, which it could fling around impulsively, than with business, which has always been the weakest factor in the theater.

In the middle twenties, the Guild was always expanding. In 1926, it went on to the next step in the ritual of founding an art theater. It undertook to establish a repertory system. In Europe, and especially in France, Germany, and Russia, the word "theater" signified a permanent company of actors who appeared in several productions performed on an alternating schedule. Actors have broader experience in repertory and, accordingly, grow in range and stature. There is no doubt that the actors in the Moscow Art Theater, the Comédie-française, the Volksbühne, and Max Reinhardt's Deutsches Theater flourished on the repertory system. The managers of the Guild were conscious of the fact that, although they had accomplished much in the widened scope of their choice of plays, they had done nothing for the actor. On Broadway, people used to say sardonically that the Guild permanent company consisted of Helen Westley.

But repertory is expensive, as the managers of the Metropolitan Opera Company know. It costs money to shift productions after each perform-ance; it costs money to provide room enough to store several productions. In the case of the Guild, there was another negative factor: the public did not like repertory. Between 1926 and 1933, Eva Le Gallienne managed repertory in her theater in 14th Street. But she had to abandon it when, during the depression, her sponsors were no longer able to meet the annual deficits. A valiant theater institution that provided the public with a series of classics was too expensive to operate after seven admirable seasons. The Broadway public has always been interested in plays, but it is less interested in acting. It takes acting for granted.

Not being able to afford the expense of shifting every production three or four times a week, the Guild proposed to organize an approximate repertory by shifting productions once a week. On November 15, 1926, for example, it produced Shaw's *Pygmalion* at the Guild Theater, with a cast that included Lynn Fontanne, Helen Westley, Henry Travers, Reginald Mason, Beryl Mercer, and others. Seven days later the Guild produced Sidney Howard's *Ned McCobb's Daughter*, with a cast that included Alfred Lunt, Dudley Digges, Earle Larimore, Edward G. Robinson, Morris Carnovsky, Philip Loeb, Clare Eames, most of whom were already Guild actors. A month later, the Guild produced Sidney Howard's *The Silver Cord* at the John Golden Theater, with a cast that included Laura Hope Crews, Margalo Gillmore, Earle Larimore, Elizabeth Risdon, and Elliot Cabot. Three weeks later, the Guild completed the repertory with a production of *The Brothers Karamazov* at the John Golden Theater, with Alfred Lunt and Lynn Fontanne, now reunited in one production, and with many of the same actors who had appeared in the previous productions. After two months, the Guild cast the actors from other productions in Pirandello's *Right You Are If You Think You Are*, a gay and ironic comedy. When the public began to tire of *The Brothers Karamazov*, the Guild staged S. N. Behrman's *The Second Man*, with a cast of five sparkling actors—the Lunts, Earle Larimore, Margalo Gillmore, and Edward Hartford. To keep Laura Hope Crews busy every week instead of every other week, the Guild revived *Mr. Pim Passes By* and thus had six plays running in three theaters. All seemed for the best in the best of all possible worlds.

It should be noted here that between April 1926 and October 1928, the Guild may have set some sort of record by producing fourteen plays, most of which were excellent and some of which permanently enlarged the cultural life of New York. The plays of these two and one-half memorable years: *Juarez and Maximilian, Pygmalion, Ned McCobb's Daughter, The Silver Cord, The Brothers Karamazov, Right You Are If You Think You Are, The Second Man, Porgy, The Doctor's Dilemma, Marco Millions, Strange Interlude, Volpone,* and the revival of *Mr. Pim Passes By.*

These were the Guild's golden years. Broadway as a whole was in top form, for the period was an exultant one. But the Guild led the procession. The board's investment of taste, knowledge, and enthusiasm in an inexperienced theater in 1919 had earned big dividends in artistic achievement. The Guild dominated not only Broadway but many cities in other parts of the country, where it had another 30,000 subscribers.

But things were happening that began to impair the repertory system. Two of its finest productions—*Porgy* and *Strange Interlude*—could not be fitted into the schedule. There was no second play in which the Negro actors of *Porgy* could act in alternate weeks; and there was no way of balancing *Strange Interlude*, which took five hours of playing and occupied the John Golden Theater from late afternoon until late evening. The sensational box-office success of *Strange Interlude* was also a factor in eliminating it from the repertory schedule. On Broadway, the public jams the most glamorous successes, but neglects or ignores successful plays that are not sensations. In any series of plays, the most celebrated productions are packed. Audiences are composed largely of brainwashed egotists who cannot be bothered with anything that is not fashionable. The Guild repertory scheme was quietly jettisoned.

There were many factors working against the pre-eminence of the Guild at the time. Several other first-rate producers were active—Brock Pemberton, Max Gordon, Guthrie McClintic, Walter Hampden, Kenneth Macgowan, and Morris Gest, in addition to Arthur Hopkins and Winthrop Ames. Thus, for the first time, there was serious competition in art theater. Also, in 1927, the era of talking pictures began with Al Jolson in Samson Raphaelson's *The Jazz Singer,* and it was obvious that Broadway was no longer going to dominate the entertainment industry. Hollywood suddenly needed writers and directors experienced in the spoken drama, and it offered more security than Broadway. In the late twenties, radio was beginning to give the public free entertainment at home. Thousands of New Yorkers followed the dialect adventures of Amos and Andy every night. In October of 1929, the stupefying collapse in the stock market led into the depression. Audiences declined in numbers and it was difficult to find people rich enough to invest in theater productions.

Nor was everyone satisfied with the cosmopolitan flavor of the Guild. John Corbin made some bitter comments about the Guild in an article about "Drama and the Jews" in *Scribner's Magazine* for May 1933. He said that on Broadway the Jews were animated by the spirit of a separate minority; he specifically objected that "the bent of the Guild is corrosive, vitriolic—the bent of a critic detached and uprooted. No such things exist as faith, hope and charity. . . . For years now," he continued, "Jewish playwrights have repeatedly attempted the thing Edmund Burke declared impossible, the indictment of the American people entire." The result, he declared, was that "Americans of elder stock have suffered an eclipse of what is best in their dramatic heritage."

In that peevish article, John Corbin, a reputable critic, joined the Americans of elder stock who had suffered an eclipse of intelligence and understanding. Anti-Semitism was the last gasp of a dying theater generation. In his discussion of the old theater of the East Side, Corbin wrote: "These yids wrote plays first hand out of their daily experience." He found himself alienated from Broadway by what he called the "acrid intelligence of our new Jewry." It was more progressive and illuminating than the acrid intelligence of an aging goy.

There was something else that would eventually hurt the Theater Guild seriously. The board of managers were beginning to get on one another's nerves. In 1919, they had begun as a handful of vigorous individualists who had little talent for compromise; and the more successful the Guild became, the fiercer the differences of opinion became. Lee Simonson was not only relentless but voluble; he could keep an argument at the peak of fervor all night. Lawrence Langner was also a man of strong convictions and restless imagination, and he, too, could talk interminably. None of the managers was a nonentity, like Mr. Zero in *The Adding Machine*. The board meetings were degenerating into dogfights. There was no longer much pleasure in presiding over the most dynamic theater on Broadway.

Philip Moeller and Theresa Helburn took leaves of absence to work in Hollywood. Helen Westley went to Hollywood permanently. During the rehearsals of productions, the conferences between the managers and the directors were becoming intolerable. A Guild rehearsal was something to fear. Ultimately the Lunts left the Guild for the comparative peace of straight commercial management, although they later returned on a more independent arrangement. Five of the Guild's finest playwrights—Maxwell Anderson, Elmer Rice, Sidney Howard, S. N. Behrman, and Robert Sherwood—founded their own organization in which the mood was less savage. Some of the young people whom the Guild had trained—Harold Clurman, Cheryl Crawford, Lee Strasberg, and others—seceded from the Guild and founded their own Group Theater to carry on a program similar to the Guild's original program.

Always generous with its young people, the Guild gave the Group

Theater the rights to Paul Green's *The House of Connelly*, with which the Group Theater successfully began its notable though brief career. Through these young people, all of whom had extraordinary talent, the original spirit and principles of the Guild have permeated the theater and, in a minor way, Hollywood.

Most of these changes in and outside the Guild organization took place gradually in the next decade after the triumphant seasons of 1926 to 1928. But the disintegration had begun. Temperament had created the Guild; temperament was destroying it.

The subscribers hardly knew that anything serious was happening, for the Guild continued to make vivid productions of some original plays—Philip Barry's mystic and puzzling parable called *Hotel Universe*, which Ruth Gordon acted vividly; Maxwell Anderson's beautiful *Elizabeth the Queen*, in which the Lunts were magnificent; Lynn Riggs' joyous folk play called *Green Grow the Lilacs*, which became the Rodgers and Hammerstein *Oklahoma!* a decade later; O'Neill's masterly *Mourning Becomes Electra*, which was perfectly acted in a gloriously dramatic production, for the pairing of Alice Brady and Alla Nazimova was an inspired bit of casting; Robert E. Sherwood's sophisticated, hilarious *Reunion in Vienna*, in which the Lunts gave one of their most festive performances; *Ah, Wilderness!*, O'Neill's charming, nostalgic comedy with George M. Cohan and Gene Lockhart in the leading roles; Maxwell Anderson's *Mary of Scotland*, with Helen Hayes at the peak of her abilities; *Porgy and Bess*, with George Gershwin's unforgettable score and Ira Gershwin's idiomatic lyrics; the long series of S. N. Behrman comedies with their humorous radiance and skillful performances—*Meteor, Biography, Rain from Heaven, End of Summer, Wine of Choice, Amphitryon 38*, from the French of Jean Giradoux, innumerable plays by Shaw, including three new ones; Sherwood's playfully highminded antiwar comedy, scornfully entitled *Idiot's Delight*; and Anderson's exalting play about George Washington, *Valley Forge* ("This liberty will look easy by and by when no one dies to get it," Washington said in the last scene).

These productions were so tonic that it was difficult to believe they were the work of a declining organization that was full of rancor and approaching bankruptcy. It was $60,000 in debt in 1939. About that time, Lee Simonson, Philip Moeller, and Helen Westley resigned, leaving responsibility for the Guild to Lawrence Langner, Theresa Helburn, and Maurice Wertheim. Wertheim resigned later. There was talk of dissolving the Guild. In 1939, Mr. Langner and Miss Helburn saved it from complete disaster by producing Katharine Hepburn in Philip Barry's *The Philadelphia*

Story. The comedy was one of Mr. Barry's best. Miss Hepburn's acting was her best. Fortunately, she was also a national celebrity of the first rank. At the moment, her films were introducing the nation to a new star, and the audiences she attracted everywhere were large, voracious, and profitable.

There was one more great occasion that revealed the Guild in its top form. In 1940, after World War II had broken out in Europe, the Guild produced Robert Sherwood's *There Shall Be No Night,* a thoughtful, deeply moving tribute to the heroism of the Finns. Although the Lunts were just finishing a long and exhausting schedule and wanted to go home to rest, they regarded *There Shall Be No Night* as a public duty as well as a personal opportunity, and they gave a subdued, earnest performance that made an enormous impression on audiences. Confronted with the realities of a war for freedom against tyranny, Mr. Sherwood had reversed the boyish and amiable irresponsibility of his *Idiot's Delight*. In the circumstances of 1940, when Americans were trying to find out what to think, the Guild production of *There Shall Be No Night* expressed a sense of public concern that was wholly admirable and used all the Guild's best talents of acting and staging.

But from that time forward, the Guild tended to become a producing organization that was difficult to distinguish from other commercial organizations. The confidence had weakened, the momentum was lost, and the choice of plays less enterprising. In 1943, the Guild did raise the level of the musical theater by producing *Oklahoma!* Making a musical play out of *Green Grow the Lilacs* had been Miss Helburn's idea for a long time. It turned out to be one of her best ideas, because she knew who could write it and how it could be staged. The fabulous success of *Oklahoma!* gave the Guild the privilege in 1945 of producing the Rodgers and Hammerstein masterpiece, *Carousel,* made from *Liliom,* which the Guild had produced in 1921. Those were happy occasions for everybody. The next season, the Guild gave O'Neill's *The Iceman Cometh* a production worthy of a superb drama, and the best of the actors was Dudley Digges, who had been one of the best of the Guild actors in *John Ferguson* in 1919.

But the general level of the Guild was below the standards of its best days. Many of the plays were commonplace—John Patrick's inept play about insane people, *The Curious Savage,* for example, or Jean–Pierre Aumont's *My Name Is Aquilon,* a sentimental comedy without distinction. In 1947, the Guild had a deserved success with Terence Rattigan's *The Winslow Boy,* but Mr. Rattigan's craftsmanship was a throwback to the kind of playwriting the Guild had revolted against twenty years before. It was like a recrudescence of Pinero and H. A. Jones.

About this time, the management was strengthened by the increased responsibilities of Armina Marshall, a handsome energetic woman who had been born in the Oklahoma Cherokee Strip, had studied acting at the American Academy of Dramatic Arts, had acted in many of the Guild productions; and—on her own time and his—married Lawrence Langner. She brought stability, good judgment, and confidence into the management. Miss Helburn, Mr. Langner, and she gallantly struggled against a general decline in Broadway producing, the deterioration and polarization of public taste, and the scarcity of American scripts. Costs of production had become perilously high. The Guild could no longer substitute enthusiasm for capital, as it formerly had been able to do. And the independent point of view that the Guild had brought to Broadway in the twenties was better represented in the many off-Broadway theaters, where the financial investment was less rapacious.

The Guild continued as a commercial producer and as a business organization. But by 1950, Broadway was no longer much interested in art. Brought up on movies and television, the public was getting to be more and more bored and supercilious. It did not have either the resilience or the voracity of the theatergoers of the twenties.

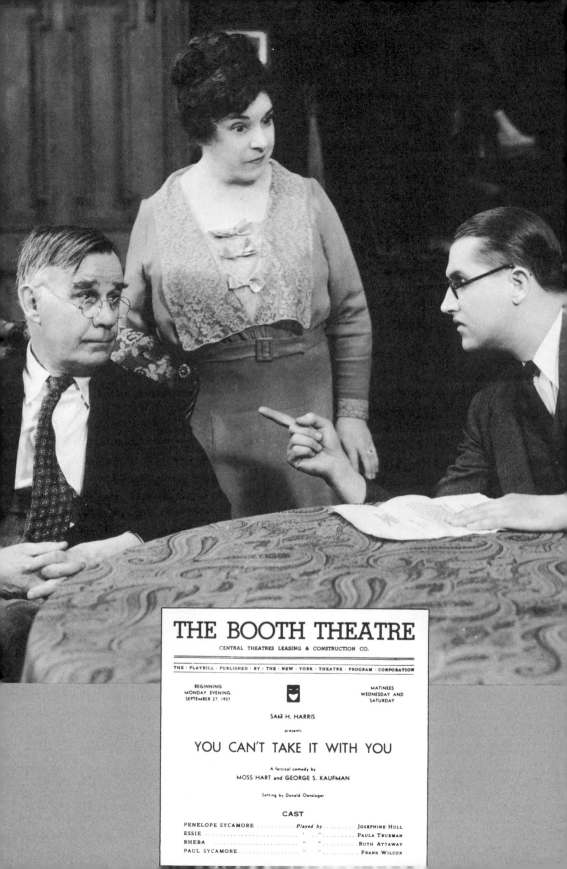

THE BOOTH THEATRE

CENTRAL THEATRES LEASING & CONSTRUCTION CO.

THE · PLAYBILL · PUBLISHED · BY · THE · NEW · YORK · THEATRE · PROGRAM · CORPORATION

BEGINNING
MONDAY EVENING,
SEPTEMBER 27, 1937

MATINEES
WEDNESDAY AND
SATURDAY

SAM H. HARRIS

presents

YOU CAN'T TAKE IT WITH YOU

A farcical comedy by

MOSS HART and GEORGE S. KAUFMAN

Setting by Donald Oenslager

CAST

PENELOPE SYCAMORE .... *Played by* .... JOSEPHINE HULL
ESSIE .... " " .... PAULA TRUEMAN
RHEBA .... " " .... RUTH ATTAWAY
PAUL SYCAMORE .... " " .... FRANK WILCOX

THE

GIDDY TIMES

Perhaps it was because Broadway was working from strength. The significant dramas—all of them by new playwrights—expressed youthful exuberance and confidence. They were varied in form, theme, and point of view. They also had lavish scenarios; many of them had long casts of characters because they were primarily concerned with the externals of human beings—the social not the psychiatric elements in human nature—and they enjoyed company. There were fifty-eight characters in Marc Connelly's *The Green Pastures* and fifty-six in Paul Green's *Johnny Johnson*. Broadway was not practicing false economy. It was a lavish interlude. When Morris Gest imported Max Reinhardt's version of Karl Vollmoeller's *The Miracle* in 1924, Norman Bel Geddes transformed the inside of the Century Theater into a Gothic cathedral—not only the stage but also the walls of the auditorium. Nothing about the production was as miraculous as the scenery. Since there was no dialogue and the performance consisted

Henry Travers, Josephine Hull, and Hugh Rennie
in *You Can't Take It with You* (1936). (*Vandamm*)

of dumbshow, no one liked *The Miracle* as passionately as Gest, Reinhardt, and Geddes; they had produced it for themselves. Lady Diana Manners, who impersonated the Madonna, was no actress. But she was beautiful and had high social standing, and it would have been in bad taste to speak ill of a member of the upper classes. *The Miracle* was art, which was commendable; it also had a religious theme, which placed it among the untouchables; but it was also big, which was show business. Losing a vast sum of money on such a holy enterprise was regarded as righteous. A profit would have been degrading.

Broadway was hospitable to everything from abroad. It was excited by the Abbey Theater performances of *Juno and the Paycock* and *The Plough and the Stars*, by a roaring new Irish writer named Sean O'Casey. It was interested in conventional dramas like John Galsworthy's *The Skin Game*, *Loyalties*, and *Old English*, and Somerset Maugham's *The Circle*, in which John Drew and Mrs. Leslie Carter acted; but it was also impressed with such exotic dramas as Pirandello's *Six Characters in Search of an Author* —in which Moffat Johnson, Margaret Wycherly, and Florence Eldridge appeared—and Karel Capek's belittling "insect comedy," known formally as *The World We Live In*. These European plays challenged the complacent minds accustomed to conventional dramas. The theme of Sven Lange's *Samson and Delilah* was difficult to define, but it was impossible not to admire the mystical acting of Pauline Lord and Ben Ami and the reality of Edward G. Robinson; and it was also impossible not to surrender to the vagrant, sinister romanticism of Ferenc Molnar's *Liliom*, in which Eva Le Gallienne, Joseph Schildkraut, Helen Westley, and Dudley Digges acted enchantingly. Audiences were eager and receptive to iconoclastic ideas from abroad. Basil Sydney played *Hamlet* in modern dress—a daring, scandalous idea he lifted from London.

Broadway contentedly listened to many dramas in foreign languages. Duse was paid $2,500 a performance for acting repertory plays in Italian. Other foreign troupes included Firmin Gemier of the Odéon, and Cécile Sorel with a troupe of Comédie-française actors; the Habimah actors playing *The Dybbuk* in Hebrew; the rotund, beaming Nikita Balieff with his amusing *Chauve-Souris* in Russian; the Moscow Art Theater, led by Konstantin Stanislavsky, in a superb repertory of Chekhov, Gorky, and other Russian dramatists. The Art Theater was regarded as a little old-fashioned in Russia and Europe; realism, which had been a sensation in the time of Ibsen, had degenerated into sterotype by the time of Ernst Toller and Georg Kaiser. Stark Young, critic for *The New Republic*, thought Pauline Lord, David Warfield, and Laurette Taylor were as brilliant as anybody in the Russian company, and he regarded Robert Edmond Jones as a finer designer than any of the visiting Russians. Young also thought that Chekhov was in the same tradition as Clyde Fitch. But Broadway as a whole had a more abject attitude towards the Moscow Art Theater, perhaps partly because Morris Gest, with his black fedora and black string tie, was a born promoter, and believed he had brought salvation to Broadway.

In 1927, Reinhardt enthralled serious theatergoers with colossal productions in German of A *Midsummer Night's Dream, Danton's Death,* and *Everyman* at the Century Theater. They were superb: organized and played with an easy versatility beyond anything comparable in America at the time. Since thousands of Americans had gone abroad during the war and all of America was involved in European affairs, Americans had been exposed to European art and understood some of the deficiencies of the theater at home. In the twenties and thirties, Broadway became for the first time an integral part of the theater of the world. Chekhov and Ibsen were acted in English by Nazimova, Eva Le Gallienne, and Blanche Yurka. Chekhov was a new discovery on Broadway.

Not that it was turning into an academy of art. Entertainment was then—as it always is—the theater's chief occupation. Nonsense from abroad delighted everybody, particularly if it seemed risqué. Noel Coward's decadent first play, *The Vortex,* was so successful when it opened at Henry Miller's genteel theater in September 1925 that two other plays by him, *Hay Fever* and *Easy Virtue,* were produced the same season. Coward's lean, taut reports of depravity in England (including drug addiction) appealed very much to theatergoers accustomed to simpler sins.

Coward was an electrifying personal success. In *The Vortex,* he played the dissipated son of a shameless wanton whose current lover was making unethical advances to the son's susceptible fiancée. The situation was claustrophobic. In his swift-paced acting of the dissipated youth, Coward became increasingly vexed and neurotic; he spoke rapidly in the glib manner of a dissolute man about town, and he played the piano vehemently to relieve his nerves.

In Somerset Maugham's *Our Betters,* which had been advertised as "the most shocking comedy in New York," and also in his *The Circle,* the characters had more poise; they sinned with the elegance of people bred to vice and ease. Coward's high-strung egotists were less stable, representing a new trend in British society.

Most of the American comedies on Broadway in the early twenties were little interludes about love or human eccentricities, based on mechanical situations, and they were inclined to be folksy and uplifting. A homespun

Gertrude Lawrence and Noel Coward in *Private Lives* (1931). (*Vandamm*)

comedy called *Lightnin'*, by Winchell Smith and Frank Bacon, suited the public so exactly that it had 1,291 performances. Lightnin' Bill Jones was a landlord who ran a hotel on the boundary line between Nevada and California; he jumped from one state to the other when their respective constables threatened him with the law. He was also lovable; and although he was mischievous, he never did anything bad. When *Lightnin'* moved to Chicago after three years on Broadway, Frank Bacon, the star as well as the co-author, marched to the railroad station behind a brass band, and Mayor John F. Hylan, Commissioner Grover Whalen, Winchell Smith, and producer John Golden grandly marched beside him. "So long, Frank. Bring home the Bacon," some sidewalk punster cried. After three years, *Lightnin'* had become part of the ethos of Broadway.

But in the same year, when it moved on to Chicago (where, unfortunately, Frank Bacon died), another comedy in a wholly different vein reversed the tradition and introduced two young writers who had a fresh point of view. They were representative of the postwar theater they helped create. They were both satirists—George S. Kaufman and Marc Connelly, newspapermen with an interest and some unhappy experience in the theater. Their comedy was called *Dulcy*. In the leading part, Lynn Fontanne was immediately recognized as a comedienne of the first rank. Among the other actors in this landmark play were Gregory Kelly, a talented comic actor who died before he could achieve all that he was capable of; Elliott Nugent, who went on to a brilliant career as writer, actor, and director; and Howard Lindsay, a virtuoso theater man who in 1939 collaborated with Russel Crouse on *Life with Father*, which had an even longer run than *Lightnin'*. The success of *Dulcy* was the beginning of a new era of comedy.

Dulcy was the familiar name for Dulcinea, a character whom Franklin P. Adams had created in his humorous column, "The Conning Tower," in the *New York Tribune*. She spoke in bromides (the in-word for clichés then) that would have been maddening if she had not been such an attractive young woman. She made cheerful yet crushingly banal statements like "When I want a policeman I can never find one," or "It never rains if I am carrying my umbrella."

Adams, Kaufman, and Connelly were members of an informal group of congenial writers and theater people who came to be known as the "Algonquin Wits" because they lunched at the fabulous Round Table of the Algonquin Hotel. They were all young. They were all lively. They all had fresh and skeptical attitudes about the theater, writing, and culture in America. By force of character, they changed the nature of American comedy and very largely established the tastes of a new period in the arts and theater. In addition to Kaufman, Connelly, and Adams, the principal lunchers were Robert Benchley, Robert E. Sherwood, Herman Mankiewicz, Ring Lardner, Dorothy Parker, Heywood Broun, Edna Ferber, Alice Duer Miller, Harold Ross, Jane Grant, Frank Sullivan, Alexander Woollcott, Neysa McMein, Tallulah Bankhead, Margalo Gillmore, Peggy Wood, John V. A. Weaver, and Brock and Murdoch Pemberton. In 1922, they wrote, staged, and acted in a humorous revue called *No, Sirree!* for one Sunday night at the Ambassador Theater. (That was the origin of Benchley's famous "Treasurer's Report," a burlesque of the bourgeoisie that he repeated in *Music Box Revue*.) *No, Sirree!* was their only group enterprise. They were talented individualists, all working at their professions. Although they took no formal action and made no group decisions, they did change the public taste. What they thought had considerable influence because some of them were newspaper writers or theater people to whom Broadway listened.

In the opinion of Woollcott, Kaufman was "the first wit of his time." His one-line gags were legendary, corrosive, and devastating—"I saw the show under unfortunate circumstances: the curtain was up"; "business was

Don Freeman's lithograph of show-break time in the 45th Street block in 1932, when the Ed Wynn *Laugh-In* was at the Imperial, the George Gershwin–George Kaufman–Morrie Ryskind *Of Thee I Sing* was at the Music Box, and Katharine Hepburn was having her first stage success in *The Warrior's Husband* at the Morosco. (*Don Freeman*)

so bad they were shooting deer in the balcony." Of an actor with a vulnerable name: "Guido Nadzo was nadzo guido." Although Kaufman's wisecracks were destructive, hc was humane in his dealings with people. He was scrupulously honest. He and Max Gordon, one of his producers, never signed contracts, for it never occurred to either of them to doubt the other. Kaufman also had a quixotic sense of responsibility for his friends when they were in trouble. Although his manner was austere and his personality reserved, his ethical instincts were irreproachable.

He was a tall, lean, melancholy man with a thick crop of bushy black hair, and he wore rimless glasses. He was one of the most disciplined men on Broadway. He turned out a prodigious amount of work, because he was thoroughly organized. Despite his fabulous success, he lacked self-confidence. Long after he had come to occupy a conspicuous and envied place in the Broadway hierarchy, he clung to his eighty-dollar-a-week job as drama editor of *The New York Times* (and conscientiously performed its duties), because he trusted the stability of the *Times* but not that of his career in the theater. A skeptic by nature, he needed to be surrounded by things he trusted. Although the theater is basically an emotional medium, he lacked personal warmth; and that may be why he wrote only one script without a collaborator. Although he was uneasy about it, *The Butter and Egg Man* was one of his best. In writing a play, he could supply the discipline—the organization of the script, the dramatic situations, and the wording of the dialogue—but he felt insecure in the elements that involved emotion. He was so famous and his laconic style was so familiar that he was generally credited with anything particularly brilliant in the dialogue of the plays of which he was co-author. Kaufman was constantly embarrassed by this inequality of recognition; he was forever trying to set the record straight to the advantage of his collaborators.

Since Marc Connelly was a humorist, he admirably supplemented Kaufman's more astringent wit, as the plays he later wrote himself suggest. *The Wisdom Tooth, The Green Pastures,* and *The Farmer Takes a Wife*

Van Heflin, Shirley Booth, and Katharine Hepburn in *The Philadelphia Story* (1939). (*Vandamm*)

have a charm and good nature alien to Kaufman's personal style. The Kaufman–Connelly collaborations were good-natured—not only *Dulcy*, which treated a boring woman with a certain degree of amused tolerance, but also *To the Ladies* and *Merton of the Movies*, in 1922, and their most uncharacteristic collaboration, *Beggar on Horseback*, an early expressionistic drama about materialistic success that Kaufman and Connelly composed out of a German play by Paul Apel. Written in terms of fantasy, directed by the gentlemanly Winthrop Ames, with an evocative score by Deems Taylor and some pantomine by Grethe Rutz-Nissen and with Roland Young and Osgood Perkins in the leading parts, *Beggar on Horseback* illustrated Kaufman's and Connelly's ability on at least one occasion to write with scope and imagination. It was not the most successful of Kaufman's collaborations, but it was the most beguiling.

In the course of more than thirty active years in the theater, Kaufman collaborated with several other people—notably Edna Ferber, Ring Lardner, and Alexander Woollcott. With Morrie Ryskind, he wrote, among other productions, the script of *Of Thee I Sing*—a musical cartoon about the Presidency and Vice Presidency, for which George Gershwin wrote a memorably sardonic score ("Wintergreen for President," "Of Thee I Sing, Baby"). *Of Thee I Sing* won the Pulitzer Prize in 1932—the same season in which Eugene O'Neill's *Mourning Becomes Electra* was produced. In the comic character of Alexander Throttlebottom, which was acted with disarming pathos by Victor Moore, *Of Thee I Sing* recognized in public the empty ambiguity of the office of Vice President. Now every Vice President is recognized as Throttlebottom.

In 1930, when he was forty-one years of age, Kaufman collaborated with an unknown man of twenty-six who turned out to be the most generally congenial of all the writers he worked with. Moss Hart, an ambitious Bronx boy who had been writing and directing on the fringes of the theater and had long been infatuated with Broadway, submitted a promising script that eventually became *Once in a Lifetime*, a hard, swift, devastating caricature of Hollywood, with a wild plot and hilariously improbable characters. Neither Kaufman nor Hart had visited Hollywood at the time; they composed their comic extravaganza out of the legends about Hollywood and out of the staples of farce theater.

It is impossible to separate the individual contributions each writer made to the final script. By age and experience, Kaufman was no doubt the dominant figure in the final preparation of the script. But Hart's style resembled Kaufman's; the play represented each of them fairly, and they went on to collaborate on other comedies. *You Can't Take It with You,* a charming portrait of an amiable, chaotic family, which won the Pulitzer Prize in 1937, and *The Man Who Came to Dinner,* in 1939, a caustic lampoon of their friend, Alexander Woollcott, were the most characteristic and successful.

Being mortal, Kaufman and Hart wrote a few plays that lacked distinction, like *The Fabulous Invalid,* a mechanically contrived affirmation of faith in the theater; *The American Way,* a well-meant though commonplace uplift drama about America at the time when another war seemed imminent; *George Washington Slept Here,* a piece of hackwork. In 1934, they wrote a morality play about corruption in the theater. *Merrily We Roll Along* began with a picture of a fabulously successful playwright who had reached the summit of a dazzling career. The authors told the story backwards. Reversing the order of time, the next two acts recorded the disarming beginning of his career, when he was an idealist. In clawing his way to the top, the idealist became a moral leper. It took fifty-eight characters, as well as large anonymous crowds, to keep pace with the disintegration of a high-minded apprentice into a degenerate millionaire. Although *Merrily We Roll Along* ran for 155 performances, it was not a contribution to thought or literature, and it came with ill-grace from two of Broadway's most successful playwrights. It is best remembered by an ironic comment Herman Mankiewicz, one of their friends, made after the opening performance: "Here's this wealthy playwright who has had repeated successes and earned enormous sums of money, has mistresses as well as a family, an expensive town house, a luxurious beach house and a yacht. The problem is: How did the son of a bitch get into this jam?"

Although their attitudes towards the theater were much alike, they differed personally. Hart was gregarious and overflowing with enthusiasm. His enjoyment of success was like a volcanic eruption. When it was obvious that *Once in a Lifetime* was going to be enormously profitable, he snatched his mother, father, and brother out of a dreary Brooklyn apartment and settled them in New York permanently. The move was made on the spur of the moment. Jettisoning their furniture and other properties, the Harts simply moved out and away in a taxicab and began a new life, as in a fairy tale. Although Hart was a modest person, he lived as extravagantly as a movie star. Whatever could be bought, he bought on impulse. After a few years of enormous success, he bought a country estate in Bucks County, Pennsylvania, near the estate that the Kaufmans had had for several years. Since the grounds looked bare, he had some towering elms transplanted in the dooryard. Looking over the new park, Kaufman observed that "it showed what God could do if he had the money." Hart married a beautiful singing actress, Kitty Carlisle, who was as gregarious as he was and who presided over a hospitable social life that delighted him.

Although Hart collaborated with Kaufman on eight plays, he wrote several good ones alone—the librettos for *Face the Music* (1933), *As Thousands Cheer* (1933), and *Jubilee* (1935). In 1941, he transmuted a long, agonizing experience under psychoanalysis into a kind of spectral fantasy, *Lady in the Dark*, which had a very modern score by Kurt Weill, pithy lyrics by Ira Gershwin, and two brilliant performances by Gertrude Lawrence, an established star who was all theater, and Danny Kaye, making his first success on Broadway. Among other accomplishments, he sang a mad song that Ira Gershwin had made out of the names of Russian composers:

> There's Malichevsky, Rubinstein, Arensky and Tchaikovsky,
> Sapelnikoff, Dimitrieff, Tscherepnin, Kryjanovsky—

to quote the first two of fifteen rattlebrained lines. It could not be sung, but Kaye sang it. Everything about *Lady in the Dark* was professional and enchanting. It was also the biggest therapeutic factor in Hart's own psychoanalysis. He wrote *Winged Victory* in 1943 as a salute to the Air Force. It conveyed his natural respect and enthusiasm for good causes and gallant people.

After collaborating on several plays, both Kaufman and Hart wrote less but worked more consistently as directors of plays by other people. For they were total theater people, and a large part of the success of their plays derived from their instinctive knowledge of stage direction. Kaufman's masterpiece in direction was the dryly comic performance of *Guys and Dolls*, which Jo Swerling and Abe Burrows had made from Damon Runyan's stories of Broadway characters, with a gaudy score by Frank Loesser. It was the quintessence of Broadway—naïve, impulsive, self-centered, and lively. Kaufman's discipline and skeptical intelligence brought this wry portrait of Broadway into focus. Hart's finest stage direction was for *My Fair Lady*, the musical play that Alan Jay Lerner, librettist, and Frederick Loewe, composer, made from Bernard Shaw's *Pygmalion*. Hart's instinct for the stage, casting, and performing—and his respect for Shaw, whom he venerated and hoped to emulate—made the difference between a splendid musical play and a classic. The clarity of the performance derived from Hart.

Both Kaufman and Hart gave Broadway not only wit and skill but also integrity. They were not greedy. It was typical of both of them that they did not demand fees for their direction, but took their money from the box office after the show opened. They did not expect to be protected against failure. Broadway was the center of their lives; they loved its absurdities and ludicrous pretensions as well as its professionalism. They presided over an era and pioneered the darting, withering, iconoclastic play that made routine comedy obsolete.

George Kelly, a slender and agreeable young man, belonged to the same unbelieving generation. He had learned his craft as a vaudeville actor and sketch writer. The vaudeville discipline was formidable; every line and situation had to be in exactly the right place, and the parts had to be cast precisely. With vaudeville as background, he was acutely aware of the sprawling incompetence of amateur acting; and his first Broadway comedy, *The Torchbearers* (1924), satirized the bungling and vanity of the Little Theater movement. As a professional, he was not about to be patronized by the Little Theater amateurs. Two years later, he expanded a vaudeville sketch called *Poor Aubrey* into *The Show-Off*, a richly comic caricature of the bluff and bragging of American business life. When it opened on February 5, 1924, everybody recognized in this expertly written comedy a common frailty in the American character, and it ran for 575 performances. Kelly cast the leading part so perfectly that Louis John Bartels, who had a dazzling success as the show-off, never found another part in which to continue his career. There was no more glory for Bartels after *The Show-Off* finished its long run.

The Pulitzer Prize advisory board scandalized the public that year. Instead of giving the prize to Kelly's lively criticism of the American character, they gave it to a second-rate folk drama, *Hell Bent for Heaven*, by one of their colleagues, Hatcher Hughes. Perhaps they had not realized the national significance of the prize that they were expected to administer impartially. Two years later, they provided some sort of compensation by giving the prize for 1925–1926 to Kelly's *Craig's Wife*—a withering portrait of a housewife whose neurosis about her home gradually drove her neighbors and her husband away and left her aghast and alone at the final curtain. This sketch of a coldly malevolent home was the handiwork of a bachelor writer. The performance of *Craig's Wife* was another example of Kelly's insight into casting. The part of Mrs. Craig was played with controlled hatred and general perfection by Chrystal Herne, daughter of James A. Herne, pioneer of realism in the American theater in the 1890s. The cast also included Josephine Hull, dumpy and delightful, Anne Sutherland, and Charles Trowbridge, and the play ran for 289 performances.

After the glamorous successes of *The Torchbearers*, *The Show-Off*, and

Craig's Wife, all within a space of three years, Kelly wrote *Daisy Mayme*, *Maggie the Magnificent*, *Philip Goes Forth*, *Behold the Bridegroom*, *Reflected Glory*, *The Deep Mrs. Sykes*, and *The Fatal Weakness*—all of which had character, but none of which repeated the freshness and perception of his early plays. Kelly was a favored son of the incredulous twenties.

After his several collaborations with Kaufman, Connelly had a distinguished career of his own. A jovial man who was as bald in the twenties as he is today, he wrote one popular comedy in an affectionate mode, *The Wisdom Tooth*, in 1926, and then a masterpiece, *The Green Pastures*, produced in 1930. With its huge cast and chorus, and its masterly suite of fantastic settings by Robert Edmond Jones, it amply illustrated the sweep, abundance, and assurance of the Broadway theater of the late twenties and early thirties before the public's self-confidence was shattered by the depression.

There must have been rejoicing in heaven, as well the more familiar jubilation in the theater, on the evening of February 26, 1930, because Broadway got religion instantly. Using some of Roark Bradford's stories in *Ol' Man Adam an' His Chillun* as his sourcebook—a very rich sourcebook, too—Connelly told the fable of the Bible as a Negro Sunday schoolteacher might imagine it. When the curtain rose, the quiet scene laid in a Negro Sunday school was tender and disarming; and while the scene was being changed, the Hall Johnson choir sang "Rise, Shine, Give God the Glory." The next scene, representing a festival of people and angels in heaven, was both humorous and ingratiating.

Then came the most famous entrance cue in modern drama. "Gangway!" the Angel Gabriel called, "Gangway for de Lawd God Jehovah!" Onto the stage walked a kindly, broad-shouldered man of many years in a parson's coat, and *The Green Pastures* straightway became a classic. The man was Richard B. Harrison, grandson of fugitive slaves, sixty-two years old, a reader, lecturer, and teacher, who had never been on the stage before. A genuinely religious man, he had hesitated to take the part because he feared that *The Green Pastures* might be irreverent or sacrilegious. Herbert Shipman, suffragan bishop of New York, spent one evening persuading him that, on the contrary, it was a religious play; and that is the way things turned out, partly because of Mr. Harrison's playing. He was a spiritual man. After he had been playing the part a few weeks, it was hard not to believe that a special divinity surrounded him. He was treated with great respect backstage. Many people in his home neighborhood stood in awe of him. He was constantly being asked to baptize children in Harlem churches. It was thought to be a healing thing to touch him. Harrison was a thoughtful conversationalist, slow and sincere, anxious not to give any false impressions. He believed that playing the Lord had a profound effect on his personality. He said it had increased his patience; he found himself being more tolerant at home; he said his landlady told him his temper had improved. When he died about five years after the play opened, it became impossible to keep *The Green Pastures* on the stage. For those who had seen Harrison, no substitution was possible.

Although simple Southern Negroes were the characters in *The Green Pastures,* the story they told and their responses to it became universal. Their willingness to believe made them the perfect instruments through which a glorious story was spoken. And *The Green Pastures* contributed one exalting idea to the Bible legend. It showed the Lord—the mighty man with awful powers—learning something humbling from his children on earth. He learned that mercy comes from suffering. In the last scene of the play, the Lord was quiet and pensive and Gabriel was disturbed:

> *Gabriel:* Lawd, is de time come for me to blow?
> *God:* Not yet, Gabriel. I'm just thinkin'.
> *Gabriel:* What about, Lawd?
> *God:* About somethin' de boy tol' me. Somethin' 'bout Hosea, and himself. How dey foun' somethin'.
> *Gabriel:* What, Lawd?
> *God:* Mercy. Through sufferin', he said.
> *Gabriel:* Yes, Lawd.
> *God:* I'm tryin' to find it, too. It's awful impo'tant. It's awful impo'tant to all de people on my earth. Did he mean dat even God must suffer?

In the early thirties, before the freezing realities of the Great Depression had hardened the minds of the public, it was possible to write and act an unworldly drama of faith in the most skeptical corner of New York City. *The Green Pastures* had 640 performances in New York and five national tours. Harrison gave 1,659 consecutive performances of his part before he went to his own green pasture on March 14, 1935.

Although Philip Barry could write fashionable comedies, he was not really a man of the twenties. He had a religious conscience. He wrote many light, silken comedies about the foibles and inadequacies of the rich— notably in the cases of *Paris Bound,* in which Hope Williams and Madge Kennedy subdued Broadway in 1927, and *The Philadelphia Story,* in 1939, in which Katharine Hepburn gave her most triumphant Broadway performance. The arrogance of the rich, their hardness and insularity and

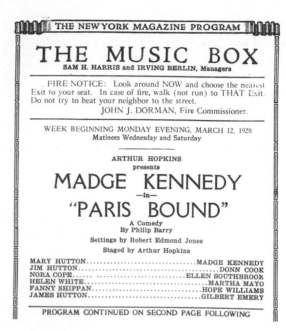

PROGRAM CONTINUED ON SECOND PAGE FOLLOWING

pettiness, also their easy manners and clever conversation appealed to Barry. In *Paris Bound*, he proved that a husband's adultery with one woman of taste and breeding need not make divorce inevitable if his wife was a good family woman. "You haven't forgotten anything, have you," the husband inquired of his wife in the last scene. "Not a thing. Just my dignity," she answered. "That's not serious," he said as they resumed domestic bliss. In *The Philadelphia Story*—his best play—Barry saved a haughty woman from making a disastrous second marriage, by undermining her complacence about herself. As the rich lady brought to her senses just before the last curtain, Miss Hepburn convinced audiences of the essential humility of a fashionable snob for 417 consecutive performances.

But Barry would have liked to write uplifting plays about the human dilemma in a materialistic world. He liked the role of prophet; he was attracted to moralistic themes about mankind. He was a complex man who disliked Broadway, but needed it, and who distrusted the rich, but lived according to the formula of the rich in Park Avenue, Hobe Sound, Cannes, and other fashionable gathering places. After graduating from Yale in 1919, he studied playwriting with Professor G. P. Baker in the famous 47 Workshop course at Harvard.*

* Baker's students at Harvard, and later at Yale, included many who had Broadway careers: Eugene O'Neill, John Mason Brown, Donald Oenslager, George Abbott, Philip

His first Broadway success was a play that had won a prize in Baker's workshop, where it was known as *The Jilts*. It was called *You and I* when it opened in the cordial little Belmont Theater in New York on February 19, 1923, and it paid the impecunious Barry about $700 a week for quite a long time. (On Broadway, the difference between failure and success is unbelievable and destroys the financial acumen of nearly everyone who has anything to do with it.)

In *You and I*, Barry told the story of a successful businessman who had given up a career in art in order to earn enough money to marry. He was determined that his son should not make the same mistake. In the early twenties, the theme of the businessman whose dazzling mercantile success masked the broken heart of a frustrated artist was accepted as progressive. If it did not make Barry exactly a revolutionary, it made him a dissenter from the materialistic mythology of America.

You and I put Broadway on notice that a fresh talent (generally called "literate") had arrived and had to be taken seriously. The next play the next season was less engaging. *The Youngest*, in 1924, discussed the severity with which a rich, established, provincial family persecuted their youngest member for being unconventional. In 1925, *In a Garden* renewed interest in Barry's literary talent and sensitivity. It was a paradox— a penetrating, somewhat fanciful comedy about the tragedy of trying to be omniscient about human character. It was gallant, charming, and rueful, and Laurette Taylor gave a soft and shining performance as a woman married to the dramatist who arrogantly misunderstood her. Arthur Hopkins staged and produced *In a Garden*, which failed although it was loved for its literary grace and tenderness. In a curtain speech after the final performance, Laurette Taylor made a remark that startled Broadway for its effrontery. "Perhaps our playwright isn't ready yet," she said in a condescending tone. "Perhaps we did a disservice to his brilliant talent by producing him too soon." Both Barry and Hopkins were furious.

Through the rest of his career, Barry succeeded brilliantly with his comedies about the rich. In addition to *Paris Bound*, there were *Holiday*, in which Miss Williams was starred; *Tomorrow and Tomorrow*, in which Osgood Perkins and Zita Johann appeared; and *The Animal Kingdom*, with Leslie Howard as a rich young man who disliked rich people. Barry's amusing dialogue, his witty comments, the luxurious environments, and the parts he wrote for stars were irresistible.

Barry, Maurice Wertheim, Sidney Howard, Lee Simonson, Edward Sheldon, S. N. Behrman, Lewis Beach, Edward Goodnow, James Seymour, Maurine Watkins, George Haight, Elia Kazan, Stewart Chaney, George Sklar, Albert Maltz, and Theresa Helburn.

But he still yearned for the prophet's role. He wrote several futile plays, not about characters, but about the human race, and he handed down some cosmic judgments in terms of symbolism. *White Wings*, in 1926, was a lark about an old, established family of streetcleaners who lost their social distinction when the automobile supplanted the horse. *Hotel Universe*, in 1930, psychoanalyzed a group of unhappy people whose lives had been saddened by crucial episodes in their past. In 1938, *Here Come the Clowns* improvised some vaudeville actors into representative prophets. *Liberty Jones* was a musical allegory about the sickness of liberty in the United States. An active member of the Catholic Church, Barry had a fondness for religious themes. *John*, which he wrote in 1937 (the same year in which *Paris Bound* was produced), portrayed John the Baptist in Jericho at the time when Jesus was preaching more successfully in Jerusalem. *The Joyous Season*, in 1934, showed how a nun sweetened the dreary home-life of her family by paying them a radiant visit.

But Barry was at his best when glamorous actresses like Hope Williams and Katharine Hepburn were illustrating the emptiness of the affluent life or making witty, belittling remarks about it. His mind was not sharp, lucid, and angry enough, and his invention was not spontaneous enough, for moral allegories. He died in 1949 at the age of fifty-three. It was his misfortune to be at the peak of his powers during a skeptical age that resisted moral instruction. "If you have a message send for Western Union," Kaufman said—cruel but realistic. Although Barry's literary style was modern, his mind was closer to Langdon Mitchell than to S. N. Behrman. It may be significant that in *The Animal Kingdom* in 1932 the wife locked her bedroom door against her unloved husband just as the wife had in George Broadhurst's *Bought and Paid For* in 1911. The differences between the two plays were primarily literary.

It was a wonderful time for exuberant melodramas that did not have to be taken seriously because they did not proselytize for virtue. They reveled in the diabolism of the underworld. They seemed to come all at the same time, as if the same virus were appearing everywhere. Three of the best of them appeared in the 1926–1927 season—*Broadway*, by George Abbott and Philip Dunning; *Chicago*, by Maurine Watkins; and *The Barker*, by Kenyon Nicholson. Two similar plays—*Burlesque*, by George Manker Watters and Arthur Hopkins, and *The Racket*, by Bartlett Cormack—appeared the next season. The similarities of style reflected the giddy mood of the time. *Broadway* had the form of a merry-go-round. It consisted of actors and bootleggers conducting their personal affairs on the wing as if their personal lives were afterthoughts. The climactic murder was incidental to a triangular affair among a bootlegger, a hoofer, and an actress. *Broadway* was vivid theater that did not teach a moral lesson. "Pull yourself together, kid," the detective whispered to the murderess when he had decided to protect her by reporting the murder as a suicide. Sentimentality was shifted into reverse so that crookedness emerged as virtue.

In *The Barker*, the ballyhoo man for a tent show (played by Walter Huston) tried to bring his son up as a respectable lawyer. But the son fell in love with an amorous snake-charmer (played by Claudette Colbert). Respectability succumbed to passion, as in real life. *Chicago* was a shrill, breezy cartoon about the travesty of justice. A murderess won the sympathies of a male jury by pretending to be an expectant mother. *Burlesque* was a backstage drama in which scenes between the characters alternated with scenes onstage, as they had in *Broadway*. Barbara Stanwyck and Hal Skelly acted in it for 332 performances.

The Racket was another centrifugal tale about the corruption of justice in Chicago, written by an informed newspaper reporter. Apart from its violent story, it was distinguished by the fact that Hugh O'Connell, playing a reporter, carried in his pocket a copy of *The American Mercury*, which was a handsomely printed magazine edited by H. L. Mencken and G. J. Nathan and regarded at the time as an essential part of the equipment of every intellectual. One character listed in the program as "An Unidentified Man" was played by Edward G. Robinson.

Two former newspapermen concluded the cycle of derisive melodramas about Chicago justice by writing the best of the lot. Charles MacArthur and Ben Hecht wrote *The Front Page* in 1928; George S. Kaufman staged it with a gusto that startled every respectable newspaper publisher. Osgood Perkins and Lee Tracy played the principal parts furiously; and Dorothy Stickney, who had played a hussy in *Chicago*, played another in *The Front Page*. To complete the cast of similarities, Jed Harris, who had staged and produced *Broadway*, produced *The Front Page*. Hecht and MacArthur were a reckless pair of practical jokers with an instinct for good craftsmanship—also, a creative vocabulary. "H. Sebastian God! I'm trying to concentrate!" shouted one of their more impatient characters. (Seven years later, Hecht and MacArthur would become the prototypes of two knockabout scriptwriters in a loud farce called *Boy Meets Girl*, in which Bella and Samuel Spewack offered their impressions of Hecht and MacArthur in Hollywood).

The Front Page was set in the reporters' room of the Chicago police headquarters on the day when a man suspected of being a Communist was about to be hanged for political purposes. "Reform the Red with a Rope" was one of the most gruesome slogans. *The Front Page* showed an aggressive managing editor trying to blackmail the sheriff into hanging the prisoner at 5:00 A.M., in time for a scoop in the last edition of his newspaper. The tag-line was as memorable as the tag-line for *What Price Glory?* Just before the last curtain in *The Front Page*, the managing editor screamed into the telephone, "Arrest Hildy Johnson and bring him back here. The son of a bitch stole my watch!"—a fraudulent accusation, as the audience knew. For hooliganism, impudence, callousness, and speed, there has never been such an entertaining melodrama.

Some newspapermen and publishers took exception to *The Front Page* because it portrayed reporters as hoodlums and newspapers as dictatorial and unprincipled. The public took no exception whatsoever. *The Front Page* ran for 276 performances. Hecht and MacArthur, dubbed the Katzenjammer Twins, had skill as well as gusto and exactly represented the gay irresponsibility of the era.

Note that three of these explosive melodramas—*The Front Page, The Racket,* and *Chicago*—were concerned with the malfeasance of justice in Chicago. But they were not realistic, they were not iconoclastic, they were not polemical: they were romantic in the happy mood of the twenties. Their motive was no more serious than a conspiracy between the authors and the audience to have a good time.

The Pulitzer Prize in 1927 caught just about everyone napping. It went to an episodic Negro tragedy that had had several weeks of poverty-stricken performances at the Provincetown Playhouse in the Village and then at the Garrick Theater uptown. Paul Green's *In Abraham's Bosom* was produced in the same season in which *The Silver Cord, Broadway, Saturday's Children,* and *The Road to Rome* were box-office and critical successes. Amid the razzle-dazzle of Broadway, Green's soft, knowledgeable, merciful, loosely organized play was almost invisible. Until the Pulitzer Prize choice was announced, hardly anyone knew that a talented young man with poetry in his head and principles in his heart had been in the neighborhood. He was thirty-two years of age at the time.

Paul Green was born on a farm in Lillington, North Carolina and worked at farming until he entered the University of North Carolina. Despite military service in combat overseas during World War I and a year of graduate study at Cornell, he remained a Southerner in temperament and fact. Everything he wrote—poetry and stories as well as plays—came out of his own experience in North Carolina. When he was a small boy, he went to an adjoining town, Angier, for a load of fertilizer and hung around the railroad station to see a train arrive. The woodburning locomotive thrilled him, and he looked at the passengers enviously. When the train came to a stop, a very sullen engineer jumped down to tinker with some of the machinery. A neatly dressed and happy Negro school-teacher strolled down the station platform, greeting everyone cordially. For no reason except bad temper, the engineer snatched a cane from an old man on the platform and struck the Negro in the face. The act was totally barbaric. Green never forgot the bewilderment of the Negro, his shocking loss of dignity as well as the bloody wound on the face. That was the genesis of *In Abraham's Bosom*. Seven scenes long, it was the biography of a Negro illegitimate son of a white planter. His attempt to rise from the ranks of field hand to the ranks of schoolteaching alienated him from both blacks and whites and turned him into a blundering fanatic. *In Abraham's Bosom* was the first play on Broadway that told the harsh story of Negro life without any of the usual clichés, sentimentalities, or melodramatics. The cast included some particularly gifted Negro actors —Rose McClendon, whose delicacy of style and beauty always made her a poignant figure on any stage, Julius Bledsoe, L. Rufus Hill, and Frank Wilson, a letter-carrier who got leaves of absence whenever Broadway had a part for him. The life of the Negro actor was particularly grim at that time. There were many good Negro actors but very few Negro parts; and except for a few music-hall stars, like Bill Robinson, the dancer, and Bert Williams, the comedian, they could not make a living in the theater. They lived lives of total frustration.

Green could have had a lively career on Broadway if he had wanted it. He was much respected. He was known to be a poet at a time when many serious thinkers believed that poetry would redeem the theater from cultural squalor. He wrote folkplays, which were thought to be somehow purer than ordinary plays. He also knew things about human beings that no one on Broadway had dreamed of. But Green did not like Broadway. He thought that it cheapened serious drama and that in subtle ways it destroyed the integrity of his work. He did not believe that success on Broadway was equivalent to salvation.

The Group Theater began its career in 1931 with Green's moody Chekhovian *The House of Connelly* (1934) about the decadence of the Old South. When Kurt Weill, the German composer of *The Threepenny Opera*, came as a refugee to America, he was received as a hero, and the Group Theater asked Green to write the text for a comedy based on *The Good Soldier Schweik* with songs by Weill. *Johnny Johnson*, as the play was called, was a jeering antiwar play, by an American who had been in combat in Europe during World War I, and by a refugee from the Nazis. It was not very well acted by the Group Theater, which seemed unable to master the form. Admired without being liked, it had sixty-eight performances.

The compact, highly charged, one-act form suited Green best; and his one-act play about chain-gangs, *Hymn to the Rising Sun*, left a deep impression on everyone who saw it when a politically motivated theater called the New Theater acted it in 1936. It was virtually a case history in the brutality of penal discipline, based on an episode Green had witnessed. When a Negro group of the Federal Theater proposed to act it in Chicago, the state WPA administrator stopped it just before the curtain was to go up. He told some newspapermen in the lobby that it was a play "of such moral character that I can't even discuss it with a member of the press." The moral character of *Hymn to the Rising Sun* reflected the humanism of an enlightened citizen. The truth upset the Chicago Federal Theater, as usual.

It is doubtful that any of these plays by Green were box-office successes. Broadway could have taught Green something about the art of communication, for it is still true that the theater's laws the theater's patrons give. Broadway has no patience with craftsmen who do not observe the elementary facts of stage life. But it is also true that Broadway had nothing to give a man of independence and convictions who was more interested in stating his truth than in succeeding commercially. In 1937, after a discontented and spasmodic experience with Broadway, Green created a form of outdoor play with music that could dramatize the human facts and patriotic truths of American life for large outdoor crowds. *The Lost Colony* on Roanoke Island, North Carolina, was the first of a series of ritualistic dramas; and, through the years, it has become part of the regional heritage. Since Green had both the literary style and the intellectual riches of a successful writer, he could have become a working dramatist like Maxwell Anderson and Robert E. Sherwood if he had wanted to. He didn't. He believed in being a citizen of North Carolina where he began.

Another memorable Negro play, *Porgy*, appeared the next autumn after *In Abraham's Bosom* had won the Pulitzer Prize. Both plays showed how far Brodway had come from the theatrical hocus-pocus of Edward Sheldon's *The Nigger*. Like Paul Green, the authors wrote out of rich personal experience. Dorothy and Du Bose Heyward were natives of

South Carolina. Observers rather than polemicists, they were not arguing points but composing a lightly stated, free-hand sketch of Catfish Alley. The Heywards were sympathetically looking on from a white man's distance. Occasionally white men intruded on Catfish Row and, by their presence, alarmed the community and put it on the defensive. The white and Negro worlds touched but never mingled. *Porgy* included songs and folk celebrations as well as a disarming story. It was brilliantly staged for the Theater Guild by Rouben Mamoulian and acted by a long cast that included some talented people—Rose McClendon and Frank Wilson, again, and also Jack Carter, Georgette Harvey, Wesley Hill, and Leigh Whipper. Original in theme, steeped in native lore, detached in style, *Porgy* won the admiration of Broadway, where it had 367 performances. Eight years later, in 1935, George Gershwin's opera, *Porgy and Bess*, with lyrics by Ira Gershwin, overwhelmed the Heyward drama on which it was based by the eloquence of the music. "I Got Plenty o' Nuttin'," "Bess, You Is My Woman Now," and "Summertime" added glory to Catfish Row and vitality to the American language.

While dramas of all kinds were flourishing, the city elders were becoming progressively uneasy about the loose behavior of some of the Broadway people. District Attorney Jacob H. Banton, legal arm of a municipal government that was addicted to thievery, rounded up a panel of three hundred citizens to pass on the moral content of theater productions. A citizens' jury of twelve denounced an insignificant revue that was candidly entitled *Bunk of 1926*. But instead of closing it, as the district attorney advised, the management applied for a court injunction, which it got, and the revue kept on playing until the public stopped coming. Since Broadway continued to be unchaste and lustful, Mayor James J. Walker (who was both of those things) threatened the Broadway managers with punitive action unless they cleaned up the merchandise. The district attorney handed them a list of shows he regarded as morally unacceptable: Edouard Bourdet's *The Captive*; *Sex*, by Mae West and Jane Mast; Philip Kearney's dramatization of Dreiser's *An American Tragedy*; *Lulu Belle*, by Edward Sheldon and Charles MacArthur; William Francis Dugan's *The Virgin Man*; and Roland Oliver's *Night Hawk*, which told the familiar tale of a noble prostitute.

When the managers continued to take no action, the impatient district attorney raided three of the shows he regarded as socially degrading—*The Captive*, *Sex*, and *The Virgin Man*. Mae West spent ten days in the workhouse and paid a fine of $500. The author and producer of

The Virgin Man paid fines of $250 each and loitered in jail briefly. *The Captive* was the only one of the plays that had literary merit. It was Arthur Hornblow, Jr.'s adaptation of Bourdet's *La Prisonnière*. Written with taste, acted with style and reticence, it was the story of a French diplomat's daughter who was seduced by another woman and finally involved in a permanent lesbian relationship. There was nothing overt in the play. A jury of citizens had exonerated it by a vote of seven to five before the district attorney sounded his alarm. *The Captive* had 160 performances at the Empire Theater before the police wagons backed up to the stage door and carted off the actors and management. It was a carnival for photographers, reporters, assistant district attorneys, policemen, and citizens who liked scandal. Rather than fight the case in the courts, Gilbert Miller, the producer, closed *The Captive* and broke up an excellent production. As usual, the district attorney could not tell the difference between literature and hokum.

In 1927, the New York legislature passed a censorship act popularly known as the Wales Padlock Law, which empowered the police to arrest the producers, authors, and actors of plays that the police disapproved of, and to padlock the theater for a year if the courts brought in a verdict of guilty. The district attorney promptly closed *Maya*, a philosophical drama about the various dreams a French prostitute induced in her clients. The chief part was played by Aline MacMahon, an inspired woman and actress. Rather than run the risk of losing their theater for a year, the producers accepted the district attorney's action. The Shuberts celebrated the Wales Padlock Law by producing a revue called *Padlocks of 1927*, in which Texas Guinan, the symbol of revelry during the prohibition era, made her entrance on a white horse, sang some songs, and browbeat the audience with insulting remarks that everyone adored. The more Texas upbraided an audience, the more passionately they loved her. Custodians of public virtue urged the district attorney to padlock Ben Jonson's *Volpone* and Eugene O'Neill's *Strange Interlude*. He virtuously abstained. In 1928, the police closed Mae West's *Pleasure Man* after two performances. She subsequently became a national goddess. Jimmy Walker's record was less sublime. In 1932, he resigned as mayor and skipped to Europe to avoid facing charges of excessive larceny.

Although the twenties were rich years in the drama, the 200 or 250 productions a season inevitably included a great many bad plays, known as turkeys. (Originally a "turkey" was a weak show that was deliberately opened on Thanksgiving Day in the hope of making a little undeserved money during the holiday season.) The proportion of mature drama to trash was ten to one hundred, which is a fairly standard formula even today. While a few playwrights were making history by writing intelligent dramas, the hacks kept on turning out illiterate rubbish that somehow got produced and left the first-night audiences stunned. There was a famous one in 1925 called *Love's Call*. In the first scene, a tall actor in a wide hat, white pants, and Western shirt strolled in from the wings and pompously announced "I am Clyde Wilson Harrison." While visiting a Mexican village, he met a handsome firebrand called Pequita. "Although you are a wanton, you fire my senses," he grandiloquently confessed to her. Even when her lover held a pistol to his head, Clyde Wilson Harrison did not flinch: "The thrill of passion I have just felt is worth it," he announced. In the end, the lover shot Pequita by accident and Clyde Wilson Harrison strolled on into some dubious immortality.

And this was the period in which one of the most naïve plays in history ran for 2,327 performances. *Abie's Irish Rose* was a mechanical little piece of buncombe that Ann Nichols wrote in 1922 about an Irish girl who married a Jewish boy. Their respective families were estranged until, in the last act, the married couple produced twins—one named Rebecca, the other Patrick Joseph. The comedy bored all the critics except one (William Chase, of *The New York Times*) when it opened, and infuriated them when it settled down to an epochal run. Ultimately *Life with Father*, with 3,224 performances, and *Tobacco Road*, with 3,182, outran *Abie's Irish Rose*. Moreover, both of these were plays of genuine quality.

When *Abie's Irish Rose* opened, Robert Benchley was drama critic of the old *Life* and had to compose a new descriptive line every week for *Abie's Irish Rose* in the weekly summary of current plays. His first lines were severe, like "Something awful." But then his congenital sense of humor began to repossess him: "People laugh at this every night, which explains why democracy can never be a success." "Where do the people come from who keep this going? You don't see them out in the daytime." "An interesting revival of one of America's old favorites." "We understand that a performance of this play in modern dress is now under way." "Closing soon. (Only fooling.)" To use another Broadway euphemism, *Abie's Irish Rose* did not go out of the ticket-selling business for four years.

When Broadway was at its best, the awful plays were still in the majority. But they seemed more ridiculous in comparison with the best. After *Desire Under the Elms*, it was impossible to sit through three acts of *Abie's Irish Rose* or keep from groaning at *Love's Call*. The twenties proved that the theater could be art, if it was not controlled by show business. In the twenties, O'Neill made more money than Cohan.

The New York Drama Critics Circle in 1936 when it gave its first award to Maxwell Anderson for *Winterset*. (*The New York Public Library*) Front row, left to right: George Jean Nathan, Burns Mantle, Robert Garland, Kelcey Allen, Brooks Atkinson. Second row, left to right: Percy Hammond, Richard Lockridge, Gilbert Gabriel, John Anderson, Whitney Bolton, Rowland Field, John Mason Brown, Arthur Pollock.

THE
NIGHT WATCH

Since there were fifteen daily newspapers in Manhattan and Brooklyn in the twenties, there were fifteen daily critics (as in 1900), and it did not particularly matter what any one of them said. Everything was so abundant that nothing was crucial. There were more than two hundred productions a season. Eleven new plays opened on the fabulous December 26 in 1927; five more opened during the next three evenings. Nor were all of them trivial. They included some notable items: George Kelley's *Behold the Bridegroom*; *Show Boat*, by Oscar Hammerstein II and Jerome Kern; Philip Barry's *Paris Bound*; and *The Royal Family*, by George S. Kaufman and Edna Ferber.

Costs were moderate by the standards of ten or fifteen years later. A first-rate drama production could be put on for $10,000 or $20,000, depending upon the size and the cast. The best seats cost $3.00. What the critics wrote did not seem to be decisive. Critics were generally taken for granted as necessary irritants or occasional benefactors. Every now and then, the Shuberts (it was an article of faith to hate the Shuberts) barred a critic when he did not praise their productions sufficiently. It was widely believed that the Shuberts subsidized two critics who might otherwise have had difficulty in writing constructive criticism of Shubert productions. If so, no one was scandalized. It was a benign period on the whole. George M. Cohan thought that "a pleasant evening in the theater" was a good quote in an advertisement. It was not necessary to panic the public in order to get people into the theater.

The leading critics were Alexander Woollcott, Percy Hammond, and Burns Mantle. Woollcott, obese and prolix, was the most celebrated. His mercurial enthusiasms and his rhapsodic literary style suborned more readers than any other critic of his time. After serving in the Army during World War I, he returned to his old post on *The New York Times*, whence his pinwheels of prose again lighted the sky over Broadway. In 1922, Frank Munsey, a grocer who believed in buying whatever he wanted (including women and newspapers), offered Woollcott the staggering salary of $15,000 a year to join *The New York Herald*, and Woollcott did. When *The New York Herald* was combined with the *New York Tribune*, Woollcott was invited to join the brilliant "opposite editorial page" of *The World*, where he kept company with Heywood Broun, Deems Taylor, and Laurence Stallings. It was the most popular cultural newspaper department New York had ever had. For three years, Woollcott continued his buoyant theater reviewing. He wrote his impetuous notices immediately after the performances in a Times Square telegraph office, whence they were sent by wire to the newsroom of *The World* downtown, near City Hall.

But in 1928, Woollcott carried the responsibilities of criticism one step too far; he was a shade too enterprising. He denounced a play before it opened. The play was O'Neill's *Strange Interlude*, which had been a conversation-piece long before the curtain went up on the first performance. For several years, Woollcott had been increasingly bored with O'Neill's artistic intransigence. While *Strange Interlude* was in rehearsal, Woollcott acquired a script and wrote an article eviscerating it in *Vanity Fair*. Because of a change in the theater schedule, *Vanity Fair* appeared before *Strange Interlude* opened, and Woollcott's attack on the play became a recognized peccadillo. Herbert Bayard Swope, the dashing managing editor of *The World*, thereupon impounded Woollcott and assigned Dudley Nichols to write the review. Nichols' review was so fresh, lyrical, and exciting that soon afterwards he advanced to Hollywood where he had a broader field. If Woollcott's review in *Vanity Fair* had praised *Strange Interlude*, would he have been restrained from reviewing the opening performance in *The World?* It is an interesting speculation.

Woollcott left *The World*—and daily journalism—at the end of the season. He wrote a page called "Shouts and Murmurs" in *The New Yorker.* At the time when radio had little cultural standing, he gave it style with a regular radio feature he called the "Town Crier," in which he insulted his friends (he said that Heywood Broun looked like an unmade bed) and praised the plays and books he liked. Having been a frustrated actor for years, be became a sort of virtuoso fat man. He gave colorless amateur performances as a fat man in two of S. N. Behrman's plays—*Brief Moment* and *Wine of Choice.* George S. Kaufman and Moss Hart wrote a hilarious lampoon of him in *The Man Who Came to Dinner*—another fat part, which Woollcott acted on the road. Beneath the storminess of his public career, he was a man of generosity and loyalty, and he was particularly depressed because, on account of age and a damaged heart, he was not able to participate in World War II, which he believed in and supported. He died in 1943, in the broadcast studio.

Percy Hammond was also a portly man, with a round, red face and a boyish manner. His style was the opposite of Woollcott's—concise, polished, deftly malicious, a blend of Mark Twain and Anatole France. His phrases were famous: of a Shakespearean actor, "He wore his tights competently"; of an amorous actor, "bulging with lust"; of a vaudeville team in an old act: "They've played it so often that they can play it in their sleep, which they did yesterday." "Never praise an actress," he wrote waspishly, "because it will bite you." Having been a Chicago newspaperman since 1898, and a critic since early in the century, and having seen Booth, Mansfield, Modjeska, Jefferson, Bernhardt, Duse, and all the great stars in whatever plays they acted in, he knew more about the theater than any of his colleagues. For many years, he was famous in Chicago; his witticisms were admired and repeated, and some of them became the kind of scandal that people dote on. In 1920, the *New York Tribune* offered him $25,000 a year to leave Chicago and join the staff. He did.

During the twenties, Hammond bought a charming, old house in Hither Lane, East Hampton, where his wife Florence and he lived on weekends and whenever he did not have to review a play. After her health failed in the thirties, the East Hampton house, its gardens and lawn, and the affable neighborhood became the center of their lives. He returned to New York by railroad whenever a play opened. After an opening-night performance, the appearance of a *New York Herald Tribune* office boy in the Type and Print Club in 40th Street to buy a can of gin was the signal that Hammond was at work in his cubicle in the composing room. When he was a youth, he had set type in the Government Printing Office in Washington; and, for the rest of his life, he felt at home in composing rooms.

There were two celebrated crises in his cubicle. Once the door stuck. He pounded on it desperately but there was so much noise in the composing room that no one heard him. He called his wife in East Hampton on the long-distance telephone. "What shall I do, Florence?" he asked. She telephoned to the desk in the newsroom and someone went to the composing room and got his door open. On another occasion, the lights went out. Again, Hammond telephoned to his wife for instructions. "Just sit there and the lights will come on again," she said, and that turned out to be true. It amused Broadway that a man who wrote such sophisticated reviews was so helpless in practical situations.

Towards the end of his career, Hammond complained that he was tired of the theater and would like to quit. He refused to sign another contract, although he continued to write reviews because Ogden Reid, the amiable publisher, begged him to. But he was more and more contented with life in East Hampton and more and more dependent upon the advice and care his wife gave him. When she died in the autumn of 1955, Hammond had no more interest in living. He died in April 1956, after having occupied a conspicuous place in the theater for nearly half a century.

Burns Mantle had begun his newspaper career by setting type in Denver. His career and Hammond's overlapped not only in time but in space. Mantle was drama critic of the *Denver Times* and later the *Denver Republican* from 1898 to 1901. He moved to Chicago at the time when Hammond was subjugating the city. Mantle was successively on the staffs of the Chicago *Inter-Ocean* and the Chicago *Tribune* from 1901 to 1910. Then the most conspicuous part of his career began. Coming to New York in 1910, he was critic of *The Mail* from 1910 to 1922, when he went to the *Daily News*, which was published by the same organization that published the Chicago *Tribune*. Mantle became the critic of New York's tabloid newspaper, and served it until he retired in 1943.

A small, modest, sociable, quietly humorous man with a predisposition to say "yes" when possible, he wrote reviews that derived from long experience and humane attitudes about people. In general, his comments expressed the pleasure he took in going to the theater. Even when his opinions were negative, he was never devastating. Since the *Daily News* had a prodigious circulation, and since Mantle gave it conscientious service for many years, he had formidable influence.

He also made a permanent contribution to Broadway. In 1920, he edited the first volume of *The Best Plays*, which was—and still is—the "Year Book of the Drama in America," the most reliable and comprehensive sourcebook of the productions in New York. Mantle chose what he regarded as the ten best plays of the season and synopsized them in versions that retained most of the text. He completed the volume with the vital statistics of the season, including the casts of every production. *The Best Plays* soon became the essential reference book of Broadway. After Mantle died in 1948, it was continued, first by his assistant, John Chapman, then by Louis Kronenberger, Henry Hewes, and Otis Guernsey in succession. Without *The Best Plays*, Broadway would disappear at the end of every season.

With Mantle, *The Best Plays* was a family project, because he was a family man. He lived in Forest Hills, in a house run by four women who adored him. He was married to a witty and congenial woman who went to the theater skeptically but was not skeptical about her home. Her two sisters were widows and lived with the Mantles. Since the Mantles had no children, they adopted a girl who was the idol of the family. Mantle had a study upstairs, where he could work in seclusion; and he needed to, because, in addition to his daily reviews and the annual book, he wrote a weekly syndicate article and an article for the *Sunday News*. One of his sisters-in-law faithfully performed the terrible chore of keeping the statistical records of the season in order. If Mantle was a friendly critic, it may have been because he had a happy home life among four women who regarded him as the center of their lives. After so many years in the theater, he was naturally sophisticated, but he was never egotistical, condescending, or pretentious. He respected the theater as an institution. Among his many virtues was a congenital fondness for the people he knew and dealt with and an impish sense of humor.

In addition to the newspaper critics, there were excellent critics on weekly or monthly magazines—Stark Young, on *The New Republic* (he was critic for *The New York Times* during the season of 1924–1925); Joseph Wood Krutch, on the *Nation;* George Jean Nathan, on *The American Mercury;* R. Dana Skinner, on *Commonweal;* and Kenneth Macgowan, Edith Isaacs, and Rosamond Gilder on *Theatre Arts,* which was frugal with money but not with people.

The male newspaper critics were individualists. They looked imposing. Most of them carried canes. Some of them wore black felt hats with broad brims and looked vaguely like recognized personages—part gangster, part dilettante. In the urbane vocabulary of Hammond, the reviews they wrote were "venom from contented rattlesnakes." A well-turned phrase was rather to be chosen than thought or judgment.

The situation began to change towards the end of the twenties, when the era of revelry and plenty was crumbling. During the thirties, critics began to acquire the reputation of butchers; their influence was regarded as mischievous and lethal. In the first place, the number of newspapers was declining. The number of critics declined accordingly, and the importance of individual opinions increased in reverse proportion to the numerical decline. In the second place, criticism became more serious. John Mason Brown of *The Evening Post* had specifically educated himself for a career of criticism by theatergoing as a youth in Louisville, Kentucky, and by writing comments in the *Courier-Journal;* also, by studying drama with G. P. Baker at Harvard and acting in Harvard Dramatic Club plays. Theater was the obsession of this very cultivated young man. He was better prepared to be a serious critic than any of his predecessors, and he raised the level of criticism perceptibly. Gilbert Gabriel of *The Evening Sun,* and later of *The American,* was another positive influence. He had a genius for art; he was saturated in music and literature as well as drama; he had the insight into drama of a participant. John Anderson, first of *The Evening Post* and then of *The Evening Journal,* was also a man of insight. Although he wrote in a humorous style, after the manner of Woollcott, he had a serious mind. He had high critical standards and a thorough understanding of the theater. What these men had to say influenced the public because they took the theater and criticism seriously.

In the third place, the mood of Broadway was less prodigal. The number of productions declined from a high of 264 in 1927–1928 to 149 in 1934–1935 and fewer than one hundred towards the end of the decade. Attendance was falling off rapidly, due partly to the depression but largely to the increasing popularity of the talking pictures. The screen was the more popular entertainment medium, and it was cheaper.

Theater people, accordingly, began to regard the critics as a barrier they had to penetrate before they could reach their public. Elmer Rice was particularly bitter. After two failures, in 1933 and 1934, he made some withering remarks about critics before a class of students at Columbia. He said that "for the most part they are men without intellect, perception, sensitivity or background. They pander to the tastes of the empty-headed, the bored, the insensitive and the complacent." He described one of the critics as "a senile alcoholic." He added that he intended to give up writing plays for the commercial theater. Rice had not realized that the Columbia class included at least one student newspaper correspondent, and he was surprised to find his remarks prominently displayed in *The Sun* that evening. When he appeared at an opening performance that night, his presence was more dramatic than the play. The play failed. But Rice continued to write plays and produced one of his worst, *American Landscape*, four years later.

Being egotists, the critics avoided social relations as a group. There was too much difference of opinion for good fellowship. But there was one critic who never got over his conviction that Broadway was an enchanted land and that critics were illustrious people. Although he had never been on a stage, he was stagestruck in his youth. He was born Eugene Kuttner but he called himself Kelcey Allen because Herbert Kelcey and Viola Allen were the two actors he most admired. When he was eighteen, he joined the staff of the *New York Clipper*—a theater sheet. In the twenties, he was critic for the *Women's Wear Daily*. He was reputed to have attended more than 6,500 opening-night performances, which is possible, because going to the theater had been his business about forty years. (It turned out to be fifty-eight years at his death in 1951.)

What Allen wrote about the theater was negligible; the opinions were routine and the prose elementary. But Broadway was his whole life. He was married to a shy, dainty, soft-spoken Irish woman who attended the theater with him regularly but never participated in the first-night rites. She did not offer devastating remarks. She ruefully remarked that "Kelcey would rather saunter around Broadway in the hope of seeing someone famous and have a hot dog and a glass of orange juice at a Nedick's stand than come home for a fine steak dinner." None of his colleagues knew exactly what Allen wrote about the shows, for they did not read

Women's Wear Daily. But in the days when McBride's was the best known ticket agency, he made a famous remark. When Lionel Barrymore as Macbeth came to the familiar line, "Lay on, Macduff" and declaimed it valiantly, Allen whispered to his neighbor, "Lay off, McBride." That entitled him to a line in the scrapbook of immortality.

Since Allen doted on critics, he dreamed of a happy club of critics where they could exchange witticisms and calumny and entertain the stars. There might even be money in it. He envisioned an annual dinner where stars would be guests and the public would happily pay large sums to be in such resplendent company. No one agreed with Allen, but he was such an ingratiating person that it was difficult to dispel his dream. Eventually he wheedled a free meeting-place out of the management of the Astor Hotel (the meeting-place was a basement room adjacent to the heating plant) and beguiled several of the critics into coming there one afternoon. It was a solemn occasion. As chairman, the critics elected James S. Metcalf, the elderly critic of *The Wall Street Journal*, best known for his work on the old *Life* weekly before Robert Sherwood and Robert Benchley captured it. The critics then addressed themselves to business worthy of their eminence: they voted to have some official stationery printed. They voted to require press agents to assign individual critics the same seats in the various theaters for every opening. That was the first and last meeting. Since Woollcott and Hammond did not appear, the organization had no validity.

The definitive and continuing New York Drama Critics Circle was founded in 1935, because a press agent supplied the enterprise. She was Helen Deutsch, at that time press representative of Maxwell Anderson's *Winterset*. She was a dynamic and personable young lady who did not stand in awe of egotists or custom. She shared a general dissatisfaction with the Pulitzer Prizes, some of which had no theater significance. The Pulitzer Prize for the previous season was a case in point. The significant plays of that season were Lillian Hellman's *The Children's Hour*, Robert E. Sherwood's *The Petrified Forest*, Maxwell Anderson's *Valley Forge*, and Clifford Odets' *Awake and Sing*. But the Pulitzer Prize went to Zoe Akins' sentimental dramatization of Edith Wharton's *The Old Maid*.

After listening to the grumbling about this inept award, Miss Deutsch decided to do something positive about it. She telephoned to the critics of *The New York Times* and the *Daily News* and asked them if they would attend a meeting to discuss a Critics Circle with a mission. No one was in the habit of refusing Miss Deutsch anything; she had style. Having got the consent of two critics, she wrote letters on her own authority to other critics whom she regarded as qualified and urged them to attend a preliminary meeting at the Algonquin Hotel. They all came. Frank Case, the affable manager of the Algonquin, provided a room, a long table, liquor, and a waiter—all free, in keeping with the recognized policy of dealing with critics.

During the preliminary discussion of giving an annual critics' prize, it appeared that the dissenters would have to share responsibility for a choice they had not made. The critics decided on a compromise: that there would be no award unless at least three-quarters of the members endorsed it. Having made that agreement, the critics voted to organize and tipped the waiter for Frank Case's free drinks—a spontaneous, quixotic gesture that became settled policy.

Miss Deutsch lived in New City in Rockland County, where Maxwell Anderson also lived. Among their neighbors was an uncommonly talented artist, Henry Varnum Poor. He offered to design a plaque that the critics could give to the author of the "best play." Since he offered to design the plaque free, the critics accepted; and he designed a beautiful, bold relief of the John Street Theater of the eighteenth century. Some of the critics, who were not afraid to look a gift-horse in the mouth, thought that the plaque lacked refinement; they would have preferred something more banal. But the majority were pleased and appreciative and realized that the Circle had acquired a genuine work of art. A magazine publisher magnanimously offered to pay the cost of having the plaque rendered into silver. But the critics established some sort of independence by deciding to pay for it themselves—$300 as it turned out. After the plaque had been awarded several times, the Circle lost the mold and substituted a scroll, which was cheaper. No one knows what became of the superb design Poor gave to the Circle.

Having supplied the initial impulse for the organization, Miss Deutsch continued to oversee it by serving as its unpaid secretary. The critics of *The New York Times* and *The Morning Telegraph* wrote a constitution. The preamble announced: the "purpose of the Circle is the fostering and rewarding of merit in the American theater, and the awarding of a prize, to be known as the Drama Critics Prize, for the best new play by an American playwright produced in New York during the theatrical season."

The charter members of the Circle, when the minutes opened on October 22, 1935, were: Kelcey Allen of *Women's Wear Daily*, John

Anderson of *The Evening Journal*, Brooks Atkinson of *The New York Times*, Robert Benchley of *The New Yorker*, Whitney Bolton of *The Morning Telegraph*, John Mason Brown of *The Evening Post*, Rowland Field of the *Brooklyn Times-Union*, Gilbert Gabriel of *The American*, Robert Garland of the *New York World-Telegram*, Percy Hammond of the *New York Herald Tribune*, Joseph Wood Krutch of the *Nation*, Richard Lockridge of *The Evening Sun*, Burns Mantle of the *Daily News*, George Jean Nathan of *Vanity Fair* and *Life*, Arthur Pollock of the *Brooklyn Eagle*, Walter Winchell of the *Daily Mirror*, and Stark Young of *The New Republic*.

In April of 1936, the Circle met to ballot on the best new American play of the season. In the course of five ballots, six plays were considered: Maxwell Anderson's *Winterset*, Robert E. Sherwood's *Idiot's Delight* (which won the Pulitzer Prize that season), S. N. Behrman's *End of Summer*, George S. Kaufman's and Katharine Dayton's *First Lady*, Sidney Kingsley's *Dead End*, and Owen and Donald Davis' dramatization of Edith Wharton's *Ethan Frome*. On the fifth ballot, *Winterset* won the necessary fourteen votes and became the first award of the Critics Circle. A motion was made to declare the choice unanimous. The inherent separatist nature of the Circle came to the surface on that motion. It was voted down. Three critics refused to join in the folly of fourteen, and formally dissented. On Broadway, the Circle award to the play that Miss Deutsch represented made the judicious grin. Cynical people regarded the Circle as an Anderson lobby. (In 1937, the second award went to Anderson's *High Tor*. It took eleven ballots to make a choice that year.)

The formal *Winterset* award was made to Mr. Anderson at dinner at the Algonquin, all the critics being smartly attired in their evening suits but the guest appearing in mufti. There was a radio broadcast after the dinner. Since the Circle had agreed not to impose a group choice on the members who objected to it, the dissenters were represented in the broadcast, and Hammond spoke for them sardonically and bluntly. Acting, he said, as the death's head at the feast, he described *Winterset* as "spinach and I say to hell with it." As an aid to decorum, the dissenters' speech was omitted from subsequent exercises.

After the novelty of the first season had worn off, the critics settled down to the normal practices of a theatrical organization: they were suspicious, crotchety, and negative. They met once every autumn to choose officers and to race impatiently through any business the president had the temerity to bring up. They were happiest when they voted "no." They met once in the spring to choose the best new American play of the season and, ultimately, the best new foreign play and the best new musical production. That was all. A romantic idea that a Christmas party might be festive was dismissed after two or three unsuccessful attempts to make the critics jolly.

There were occasional outbursts of temperament. In 1943, George Jean Nathan resigned ostentatiously without giving any specific reason, although he did say that he preferred to remain outside the Circle until it returned to some sort of sanity and good manners. Burton Rascoe, substituting for John Mason Brown during wartime on the *New York World-Telegram*, formally moved that the Circle dissolve because it served no useful purpose. When the other members declined to dissolve, Mr. Rascoe dissolved himself by resigning instantly and departing with dignity. Once John Chapman resigned to protest a "no award" decision at the end of the season. He returned when the Circle revised the voting rules to permit a choice by simple majority; and Nathan also returned, refreshed by a two-year absence. During these years of incipient insurgency, the Circle elected Brown president four years in succession, because no one else had the good humor, tolerance, and prestige to preside over so many insurgents.

The existence of the Circle did not improve the relations between the critics and the theater. Late one night in 1938 at the Artists' and Writers' saloon, Jack Kirkland, who had dramatized *Tobacco Road* in 1933, took a looping punch at Richard Watts, who had not appreciated Kirkland's dramatization of *Tortilla Flat*. Watts went down for the count. Friends of both parties separated them, and then everyone resumed discussion as usual. The episode was irregular but not serious. In 1946, Maxwell Anderson was so enraged by the reviews of his *Truckline Café* that he bought an advertisement in *The New York Times* to stigmatize the critics as the "Jukes family of journalism." Using boldface type to express the violent state of his emotions, Anderson said: "The public is far better qualified to judge plays than the men who write reviews for our dailies. It is an insult to our theater that there should be so many incompetents and irresponsibles among them. There are still a few critics who know their job and respect it, but of late years all plays are passed on largely by a sort of Jukes family of journalism who bring to the theater nothing but their own hopelessness, recklessness and despair." *Truckline Café* closed after thirteen performances.

In the same year, the Dramatists' Guild presented the Circle with a social dilemma. In a formal letter signed by Richard Rodgers and endorsed by other eminent writers, the Guild complained that "a small number of your members come to opening nights (*a*) in a physical condition that precludes the capacity to appraise a play intelligently, (*b*) after curtain time, and (*c*) carry on audible conversation with their companions during the performance." The Dramatists' Guild was courteously implying that some critics came to the theater drunk. But who? No one dared say. After an embarrassed discussion, the Circle replied that it lacked jurisdiction over the personal habits of the members. Any member had the right to come to the theater sober if he wished to.

Although the members of the Circle were closer to the theater than the judges who awarded the Pulitzer Prize, the Circle awards were just as capricious. In 1938, the Circle selected John Steinbeck's lean, taut *Of Mice and Men*, when the Pulitzer Prize went to Thornton Wilder's *Our Town*. *Of Mice and Men* became a statistic; *Our Town* became a classic. In 1939, the Circle could not muster enough votes to select any play, although Lillian Hellman's *The Little Foxes* and Robert Sherwood's *Abe Lincoln in Illinois* were available. In 1942, the Circle patriotically chose Sidney Kingsley's competent *The Patriots*; the Pulitzer Prize went to Wilder's *The Skin of Our Teeth*, another classic. Although Thornton Wilder is one of the eminent writers of the world, the Circle has never recognized him. In 1944, the Circle made no award, although Lillian Hellman's *The Searching Wind*, Moss Hart's *Winged Victory*, Ruth Gordon's *Over 21*, and John van Druten's *The Voice of the Turtle* were available. To avoid so many "no award" seasons, the Circle changed the voting rules to permit a choice by simple majority. But again in 1946, the members could not agree on an award. The Pulitzer Prize that season went to *State of the Union*, by Howard Lindsay and Russel Crouse, which some members of the Circle favored. Other plays the Circle members voted on without a majority agreement were Garson Kanin's *Born Yesterday*, Elmer Rice's *Dream Girl*, Arthur Laurents' *Home of the Brave*, and Arnaud d'Usseau's and James Gow's *Deep Are the Roots*. In 1946, the Circle chose Arthur Miller's *All My Sons* over O'Neill's *The Iceman Cometh*. The Pulitzer Prize judges made no award that year. The Circle had the good taste to choose Tennessee Williams' *The Glass Menagerie* in 1945, when the Pulitzer Prize went to Mary Coyle Chase's whimsical *Harvey*. The Circle made unexceptionable awards to Tennessee Williams' *A Streetcar Named Desire* in 1948, Arthur Miller's *Death of a Salesman* in 1949, and Carson McCuller's lyrical *The Member of the Wedding* in 1950.

Since the taste of human beings is fallible, it is better to have two major theater awards than one. But committees frequently go to pieces

The Drama Critics Circle in 1956, caught in a relaxed moment. Clockwise from lower left: John McLain, Brooks Atkinson, Tom Dash, John Chapman, Frank Aston, Rowland Field, Jack Gaver, Robert Coleman, Louis Calta, Mark Barron, Ward Morehouse, Tom Wenning, Henry Hewes, Ethel Colby, Walter Kerr, Emory Lewis. The waiter is also at ease. (*Paul Berg*)

when they make art awards, and many of the Circle and Pulitzer awards look hackneyed in retrospect. In 1935, it seemed likely that professional theatergoers would be more discerning than the Pulitzer newspapermen, but it has not turned out that way. The average taste of the Critics Circle is no more discerning than the average taste of the Pulitzer judges. Neither the Circle nor the Pulitzer prizes can be intimidated by genius; both of them have on occasion preferred commonplace plays to classics.

In 1950, there were only seven daily newspapers—less than half the number in 1920. (In 1970, three). Since costs of production had risen alarmingly, it was no longer possible to regard the critics as of negligible importance. The reviews had an immediate impact on the box office; and since operating costs were high, a play that did not pay its way in its first two weeks was almost certain to be a financial failure. The trade maxim was that favorable notices in *The New York Times*, *New York Herald Tribune*, and *Daily News* indicated success; that favorable reviews in two of the three newspapers indicated a possible success, but that one favorable review out of three was not enough to save a production. What the other four critics wrote was not regarded as of much importance. The trade believed that theatergoers read *The New York Times*, *New York Herald Tribune*, and *Daily News*. If Broadway did not dote on myths, the exceptions to this formula would have been enough to discredit it. Plays went on succeeding and failing as if the three leading critics had no influence. But it is easier to believe in a myth than in nothing.

In 1950, the newspaper critics were Richard Watts of the *New York Post*, Robert Coleman of the *Daily Mirror*, Brooks Atkinson of *The New York Times*, John Chapman of the *Daily News*, Howard Barnes of the *New York Herald Tribune*, John McClain of the *New York Journal American*, and William Hawkins of the *New York World-Telegram* and *The Sun*. What they wrote had the appearance of a verdict, but it was really a public-opinion poll. The seven men were so unalike that they inadvertently represented seven different segments of the theatergoing public. Somebody agreed with somebody sometime; and over a period of weeks, the seven reviews constituted a fair sample of public response.

By 1950, all the newspapers had outgrown the old notion that a critic agreed with somebody sometime; and over a period of weeks, the seven papers expected their critics to give disinterested opinions, and managers had outgrown the habit of withdrawing their advertising from newspapers that commented unfavorably on their productions. The reviews expressed independent opinion and were seriously intended. None of the reviewers was as bigoted as William Winter in the first decade of the century had been.

Although an alert press agent founded the Critics Circle, she never tried to influence its decisions, and no press agent or producer has ever had or tried to have the slightest influence on the annual awards. The collective taste of the Circle is no better or worse than that of the members who compose it, but its integrity is unimpeachable. In 1950, the wits said that the initials of the Circle—D.C.C.—stood for Damned Cranky Cobras.

For the public, as well as the theater as an institution, is always thrilled by mayhem and slaughter: in the mythology of Broadway, "critic" stands for assassin. Praise is maudlin; homicide is popular and thrilling. On Broadway, people do not quote extravagantly enthusiastic things critics have said about a play. The enthusiastic lines are reserved for the advertisements. The lines that are repeated are the malicious ones. "Gives obscenity a bad name" is more quotable than "masterpiece." Broadway deplores critics who make wisecracks, but it is only the wisecracks that Broadway repeats.

THE
BIG FIVE

After attending a Dramatists' Guild meeting in November 1937, Elmer Rice, Maxwell Anderson, and Robert E. Sherwood dropped into the Whaler's Bar in the Midston Hotel in Madison Avenue for a drink and conversation. A couple of hours later, they emerged with a scheme that startled everyone on Broadway. They proposed to organize a producing company to put on their own plays. Sidney Howard joined them when he heard about it. At a second meeting in the Oak Room of the Plaza Hotel, they invited S. N. Behrman to become the fifth member of an organization to be known as the Playwrights' Company. They were leading dramatists; they had already set the cultural tone for the postwar theater. All of them were individualistic theater writers. But all of them were also responsible citizens very much interested in the political and social welfare of America. They were, in fact, more interested in the world outside the theater than in the current affairs of Broadway.

Katharine Cornell and Laurence Olivier in No Time
or Comedy (1939). (Vandamm)

To raise enough capital to start producing, the five playwrights contributed $10,000 each and had no difficulty in raising another $50,000 from other sources. Sherwood raised most of it at a weekend party on Long Island the next week. The playwrights were sagacious enough to select as their adviser an alert, knowledgeable and stagestruck lawyer— John Wharton, who has always represented good sense in the theater.

When the news got around that five influential playwrights were renouncing commercial management, Broadway was not altogether pleased. Broadway invariably sees disaster in anything new. Some managers believed that the Playwrights' Company foreshadowed the end of the commercial manager. It seemed to them like further proof that the dramatists, who had already imposed stiff terms in their play contracts, were going to become the dictators of the Broadway theater. The Theater Guild, which lost five of its best dramatists to the company, was particularly distressed. "There's no money in producing any more," Theresa Helburn gloomily remarked. "The money's in authorship."

The first season of the Playwrights' Company seemed to confirm the producers' worst misgivings; it was sensationally successful. Sherwood's *Abe Lincoln in Illinois*, directed by Elmer Rice and produced on October 15, 1938, was an enormous success and won the Pulitzer Prize the next spring. Four days later, Maxwell Anderson's *Knickerbocker Holiday*, with a score by Kurt Weill (who became a member of the company the next season), was also a great success. (It gave "September Song" to a nation that has never forgotten it.) The third play, Elmer Rice's *American Landscape*, staged by Mr. Rice six weeks later, was not a success; but Mr. Behrman's *No Time for Comedy*, which Guthrie McClintic staged the next April, was. Three out of four productions were hits. Twelve years later, the treasury of the Playwrights' Company would be down to $10,000, and the situation would be desperate. But the first season seemed to prove that the Playwrights' Company could do no wrong. In 1938 and 1939 the Playwrights' Company and the Theater Guild dominated the cultural aspects of Broadway.

One of their ablest members never had a play produced by the Playwrights' Company. Sidney Howard, who won the Pulitzer Prize in 1925 with *They Knew What They Wanted*, died in 1939, and the only completed script he left, *Madam, Will You Walk*, closed on the road the next autumn. (It later became the first production of the Phoenix Theater off Broadway and was well received.) Since Howard was a citizen in a valiant tradition that goes back to the founding fathers, Broadway and the Playwrights' Company lost one of its most admirable people when he died at the age of forty-eight in the midst of an active career and full of ideas for more plays.

Like all the members of the Playwrights' Company, he already had a distinguished record when they organized, and he represented the point of view they all believed in. A tall, vigorous man with the determined jaw of an athlete, he was a humanist all his life. He grew up in California, where he knew the exuberant characters who delighted New Yorkers in *They Knew What They Wanted*. Emotionally involved in the European war, he joined the ambulance corps before the United States joined the Allies, and afterwards he enlisted in the United States Air Force and earned the rank of captain. His first civilian jobs were concerned with public affairs. He wrote a notable series of articles about labor for *The New Republic*. He wrote for *Hearst's International* magazine. He was literary editor of the old *Life*. His first play, *Swords*, was typical of the idealists of that time. It told a medieval story in the period of the Guelphs and Ghibellines, it had a gorgeous setting by Robert Edmond Jones, it was written in verse, and it failed—standard practice for the liberal intellectual in the early twenties.

Three years later, with the superb Theater Guild production of *They Knew What They Wanted*, Howard enriched the lives of thousands of Broadway theatergoers with a tender, original, merciful drama, in which Pauline Lord gave a memorable performance. Mr. Howard had special talent for endowing reality with glamour. From that time on, he wrote copiously about the life of America—*Lucky Sam McCarver*, which dramatized an alliance between a shifty nightclub operator and a reckless society lady; the pathological side of mother-love in *The Silver Cord*, which shocked some people and titillated others; the innocence of a Middle-Western businessman in a dramatization of Sinclair Lewis' *Dodsworth*; the heroism of the research into the cause of yellow fever, told in a reticent abstract play called *Yellow Jack*.

Many of Howard's plays were failures, including *The Ghost of Yankee Doodle*, in which Ethel Barrymore appeared in 1937; it discussed the conflict between business and patriotism in terms of a second world war, which had begun to cloud the American horizon. Problem plays like that seemed plausible at the time; there was a streak of George Broadhurst, Eugene Walter, and Charles Klein in Howard's routine work: he could argue a moral point in the melodramatic style of the first decade of the century. Since Katharine Cornell appeared in Howard's *Alien Corn*, the meretri-

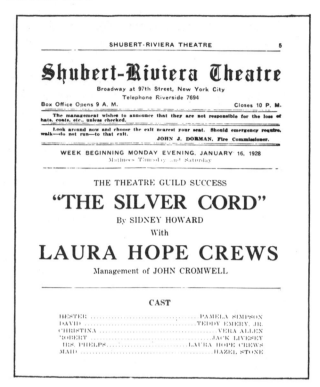

SHUBERT-RIVIERA THEATRE   5

Shubert-Riviera Theatre
Broadway at 97th Street, New York City
Telephone Riverside 7694

Box Office Opens 9 A. M.   Closes 10 P. M.

The management wishes to announce that they are not responsible for the loss of
hats, coats, etc., unless checked.

Look around now and choose the exit nearest your seat. Should emergency require,
walk—do not run—to that exit.
JOHN J. DORMAN, Fire Commissioner.

WEEK BEGINNING MONDAY EVENING, JANUARY 16, 1928
Matinees Thursday and Saturday

THE THEATRE GUILD SUCCESS

"THE SILVER CORD"
By SIDNEY HOWARD
With

LAURA HOPE CREWS
Management of JOHN CROMWELL

CAST

HESTER	PAMELA SIMPSON
DAVID	TEDDY EMERY, JR.
CHRISTINA	VERA ALLEN
ROBERT	JACK LIVESEY
MRS. PHELPS	LAURA HOPE CREWS
MAID	HAZEL STONE

ciousness of his script was not a matter of much concern, but it was hardly more than mediocre uplift drama.

In his thinking, Mr. Howard was very much a man of his time. He was a Wilsonian; he brooded on the tragedy of the League of Nations. He intended to write an ironic tragedy on the theme of the destruction of such a league that would be devoted to the service rather than the conquest of humanity. He intended to write it in the impersonal, pseudo-Chinese technique that made *Yellow Jack* such a forceful drama.

Ever since his youth in California, Howard had been an outdoorsman. He owned and managed a 700-acre cattle farm in Tyringham, Massachusetts, in the Berkshires. One afternoon in the summer of 1939, he went to the shed to get a tractor stored there. Whoever had used it before had left it in gear. When Howard cranked the engine the tractor leaped at him and crushed him to death against the wall of the shed. His death was a Broadway calamity. When he died, he was beginning to dramatize Carl Van Doren's biography of Benjamin Franklin—an American whose vigor, independence, and devotion to his country were qualities that Howard understood because he shared them.

Since S. N. Behrman wrote in the comic vein, his ethical and political principles have never been appreciated. It is an ancient rule that prizes are not given to comic plays about serious subjects. The court jester invariably ranks with dilettantes and flâneurs. Mr. Behrman is a short, rounded, merry, owlish-looking man who is marvelously erudite and civilized and has an enchanting personality. Although he writes with remarkable facility about the rich, the idle, and the genteel, he was born in a tenement at 31 Providence Street in Worcester, Massachusetts, son of immigrants who spoke little English. His father was an impecunious Talmudist—"a kenner," as he was known—who did not have the rank of rabbi but was qualified by the breadth and depth of his learning to advise the community on religious matters. When he was a boy Behrman saw all the famous plays and players of the first decade as an usher in a Worcester theater. What he did not understand in the theater, he dug out of the public library. He was always in search of anything that would clarify the paradoxes and dilemmas of human beings, including his own. Friends and relatives helped to get him educated at Clark and Harvard universities and at Columbia, where he received an M.A. When he was at Harvard, he studied with G. P. Baker in the 47 Workshop. When he was finished with his schooling, he supported himself in an unheated room in 23rd Street in New York as a book reviewer and press agent. He also wrote fiction, some of it for *Smart Set*, when Mencken and Nathan were editing that ebullient magazine. He collaborated with Owen Davis and Kenyon Nicholson on a few undistinguished plays.

In the middle twenties, he dramatized a short story he had written for *Smart Set*. Suggested by a statement Lord Leighton had made about the duality of his own nature ("For, together with, and as it were behind, so much pleasurable emotion, there is always that other strange second man in me, calm, critical, observant, unmoved, blasé, odious") the play was entitled *The Second Man*. It was played in 1927 by the Theater Guild with Lynn Fontanne, Alfred Lunt, Margalo Gillmore and Earle Larimore. This quartet of comedians made a gay dance out of a tenuous plot. From that time on, Mr. Behrman was recognized as a master of comedy of manners about rich people, as a rule, who lived a life of pleasure and spoke not hard, witty lines, but humorous lines that had grace and elegance.

Like his colleagues, Behrman began his career by writing copiously. There was usually a new Behrman play every season. The plots were, on the whole, unsteady; Clyde Fitch and Langdon Mitchell would have complained that the stories lacked tension. But they gave Broadway a whole series of light and refreshing evenings—*Brief Moment, Biography, Rain from Heaven, End of Summer, No Time for Comedy,* and *The Talley Method* being the best known of his plays. His collaborations or adaptations of *Serena Blandish, Amphitryon 38,* and *Jacobowsky and the Colonel* were equally deft and amusing.

The transition of Behrman from a tenement in Worcester to the milieu of luxurious estates in the United States and England might have been egregious except for one thing: Behrman was always primarily concerned with the human condition. Like the other members of the Playwrights' Company, he has always been more engrossed in the state of the nation than in the hubbub of Broadway. The Behrman characters were bright figures on a human screen. The most he expected of them was that they keep in their minds "a little clearing in the jungle of life." "Is it more profound," Linda Esterbrook inquired of Gaylord Esterbrook in *No Time for Comedy,* "to write of death of which we know nothing than of life of which we may learn something, which we can illuminate, if only briefly, with gaiety, with understanding?"

In 1939, when *No Time for Comedy* was produced (Katharine Cornell, Laurence Olivier, Margalo Gillmore, John Williams, and Robert Fleming were members of a brilliant cast), the civilized world was falling apart, and Behrman's theme asked a very formidable question: Should one live gaily and irresponsibly as if life were for individuals but not societies? Six years earlier, in *Rain from Heaven,* he had grappled with an early problem of Nazi brutality. It had been epitomized for him in the viciousness with which Gerhart Hauptmann, the leading German playwright, had repudiated Alfred Kerr, Berlin's finest critic, a long-time champion of Hauptmann, and a Jew. As a Jew, Behrman no doubt had a particular interest in this instance of the perfidity of Nazism. But any theater person would be shocked by such an annihilation of ethical values. Theater people as a whole do not betray one another in the vicious world of politics. Behrman's quick response to this example of treason by writing *Rain from Heaven* proved that the Playwrights' Company had been right in inviting him to be one of the members. For the gaiety and charm of his comedies are only the polished surfaces of a concerned American whose heart has never been as light, sophisticated, and good-humored as his literary style. He is a skeptic; he does not believe the slogans; he believes in a civilized behavior.

Elmer Rice was the most aggressive member of the Playwrights' Company. Essentially, he was an advocate of good causes—rational behavior, a more humane society. He professed not to like the theater. He thought that art and show business were irreconcilable. When he received the Pulitzer Prize for *Street Scene* in 1929, he chilled the atmosphere by declaring: "I do not enjoy playgoing." Rice was the only native New Yorker in the Playwrights' Company. Born Elmer Leopold Reizenstein in a dreary 90th Street apartment in 1892, he became somewhat of a loner—detached, critical, discontented. While he was working as a clerk in a relative's law office, he took the two-year law course at the New York Law School and got his LL.B. degree in 1912. It was typical of his independence that he quit his job in the law firm as soon as he was admitted to the bar of New York State. He was bored by law-office routine.

Being then without any recognized vocation, he experimented with writing. By chance, he read an article Clayton Hamilton had written in *The Bookman*. The article suggested that an interesting play might be written if it presented background events by reversing the order of the narrative—stepping back in time to illuminate the present. That was the origin of a play that Rice originally called *According to the Evidence*, but which was called *On Trial* when it was produced in 1914. It dramatized a murder trial, but the evidence was not told in the form of a consecutive narrative; it was illustrated by scenes that stepped back to previous time —a technique later known as the flashback.

At that time, Rice was totally ignorant of the theater. The rewrites, the rehearsals, the road tour, the Broadway opening of his first play were a total surprise to this thin, bespectacled, somewhat gauche youth who masked his ignorance of the medium behind a façade of contrived dignity and indifference. His first play was a purely commercial transaction. Eventually he earned about $100,000 from it—more money than he could have imagined before. He was too dazed by the whole thing to realize that he had stumbled onto a way of life that could be fantastically profitable when it was not a shattering disaster.

Although the theater paid him handsomely over a period of many years and also gave him a public forum, he was primarily a political person. He was a socialist who believed that socialism would bring freedom to everybody. Even World War I, he said, did not destroy his belief in the purposefulness of life and the eventual triumph of good over evil. His most powerful plays had social or political points of view—*The Adding Machine; Street Scene; We, the People; Counsellor-at-Law; Judgment Day; Flight to the West.* Even *The Left Bank,* a pungent comedy about émigrés in Paris in 1931, had serious social overtones. It expressed his hatred of intellectual insincerity.

It was characteristic of him that he took an active part in the Civil Liberties Union, Authors League, the Dramatists' Guild, and the P.E.N. Club, and he was the first New York director of the Federal Theater. It was also characteristic of him that he left the Federal Theater with a blast of scorn when government policy restricted freedom of speech. He was a plain, rather sober man with a reticent, unyielding personality. He was a socialist who distrusted crowds. He regarded himself as a minority person. But when a social principle was at stake, he was more clearheaded than most people, and he was quietly invincible. Once he drew up his personal decalogue, which documents his personality:

> It is better to live than to die;
> to love than to hate;
> to create than to destroy;
> to do something than to do nothing;
> to be truthful than to lie;

        to question than to accept;
        to be strong than to be weak;
        to hope than to despair;
        to venture than to fear;
        to be free than to be bound.

Street Scene was his most famous play. It was a casual sketch of neighborhood life on a frowzy New York block on a summer day when everyone knew everyone else's business. With fifty characters casually strolling through it, it looked like an improvisation. The setting by Jo Mielziner was especially dramatic. Based on the façade of a house at 25 West 65th Street, which Rice selected as typical, the tall massive setting caught the tone and humanity of a decaying brownstone and contributed a feeling of unworldly compassion to a worldly theme. Most people who had seen the script rejected it as untheatrical. It was difficult to get a director. When George Cukor abandoned it as hopeless two days after he had started rehearsals (he blandly moved further down 48th Street to direct Maxwell Anderson's *Gypsy*), Rice undertook the direction himself, although he had never staged a play before. He gave the ephemeral groupings and conversations of fifty characters the ordered look of human life; and a script that many theater people dismissed as gibberish emerged as an organic picture of life. Originally Rice had called it *Landscape with Figures*—a trifle self-conscious as a title, but one that did indicate the detachment and respect with which he portrayed a company of obscure citizens who were going through the motions of existence.

Most of Rice's plays stayed well inside the framework of observable life; they were realistic. But his finest play was his most uncharacteristic— *The Adding Machine*, which was acted in 1923. It was not a play that he had planned. While he was laboring over another script one summer, the whole scheme of *The Adding Machine* popped into his mind—story, characters, and setting. He dropped everything else and wrote *The Adding Machine*, in something of a fury, in seventeen days. It had an imaginative flair unlike anything else he had written or ever wrote, and it had an undercurrent of sardonic humor. It took a caustic look at the inhumanity of big business. Everything fell neatly in place during the rehearsals, under the sensitive direction of Philip Moeller. Deems Taylor wrote some bizarre incidental music. Lee Simonson provided a brilliant, mad setting that filled the theater with the inhuman hostility of the world of commerce; and the cast included some vigorous and accomplished actors—Dudley Digges,

Edward G. Robinson, in his apprentice years, Helen Westley, Margaret Wycherly, and Louis Calvert, an actor of the old school with a sweeping style. *The Adding Machine* was—and is—Rice's masterpiece. His socialism and his dramatic skills abetted and supported each other and gave Broadway one of its finest plays.

Although Rice was the most practical member of the Playwrights' Company, he contributed only one success—*Dream Girl,* in which Betty Field gave a shining performance in 1945. Some of the plays he wrote were never produced; most of those that were produced failed—*American Landscape. Two on an Island, Flight to the West, Not for Children, The Grand Tour,* and a beautiful musical version of *Street Scene* with a penetrating city score by Kurt Weill and poignant lyrics by Langston Hughes. Although the musical version of *Street Scene* had 148 performances, it failed financially. Rice was not a moneymaker for the Playwrights' Company, but he was professional and versatile, and he epitomized the social responsibility that distinguished the Playwrights' Company. He was one of Broadway's most eminent citizens.

Maxwell Anderson was the most consistently successful member of the Playwrights' Company, and he had the most sublime intentions. He consciously tried to write on a high artistic and ethical plane, and he was prolific. Broadway could hardly keep up with his busy pen. Over a period of thirty years, he wrote an average of one play a season, and sometimes more than one. Two of his plays were produced in 1925—*Outside Looking In,* in which James Cagney gave one of his earliest performances, and *First Flight,* a play about Andrew Jackson, which Mr. Anderson wrote in collaboration with Laurence Stallings. Two of his finest plays were produced in 1933— *Mary of Scotland,* a highly emotional historical play, in which Helen Hayes and Helen Menken appeared, and *Both Your Houses,* a trenchant indictment of dishonesty in politics, which won the Pulitzer Prize. During the 1936–1937 season three Anderson scripts were produced—*Wingless Victory,* a romantic play in which Katharine Cornell took the liberty of playing a Malay Princess, who looked and behaved like a cultivated American; *High Tor,* a humorous fantasy set on a mountaintop near New City, where Anderson lived; and *The Masque of Kings,* a flamboyant costume drama set in the Vienna of Emperor Franz Joseph. (None of these plays was produced by the Playwrights' Company, which actually did not start producing until the next year.) Writing all his plays and many of his letters in a clear, orderly hand, Mr. Anderson was a prodigious workman.

He came by his code of principles naturally. He was the son of a Baptist clergyman. During World War I, and afterwards, he was a pacifist. His pacifism got him into trouble during his brief career as a teacher. One result of his religious background was his predisposition towards good and evil as subjects. His heroes and heroines included a number of martyrs. After his abortive career as a teacher in the West, Anderson became an editorial writer for *The New Republic* and then for *The World*. He was not infatuated with the theater, but he was attracted to it when a man of his acquaintance made a lot of money out of a play that was not very good. Broadway looked like a plausible marketplace to him.

After writing a bleak North Dakota tragedy in verse, *The White Desert*, which failed, Anderson collaborated with a colleague on *The World*—Laurence Stallings, who had lost one leg but not his patriotism when he was fighting in the Marine Corps overseas. The pacifist and the war hero at a table in the New York Public Library composed a war play. They ironically called it *What Price Glory?* In 1924, it was joyfully received by audiences that admired it for what they regarded as its realism, which they heralded as a welcome departure from the romantic mythology of the conventional war drama.

It had a headlong performance. Louis Wolheim, a liberated college professor with a flat face that seemed to have been beaten and broken, played Captain Flagg with a ferocity that provoked an equally fierce performance by William Boyd as First Sergeant Quirt. The minister's son and the war veteran startled Broadway by writing a lot of words that the stage usually avoided: "this Goddam army," "toot Goddam sweet," "your tongue is as thick as your Goddam head," "I ain't no Goddam college boy," "Christ, but this war is shore a great relief to me."

Admiral Plunkett, commander of the Brooklyn Navy Yard, was outraged; he considered *What Price Glory?* a libel on the decorum and politesse of the armed forces, and he urged the license commissioner of New York City to close it. Broadway was so excited by the rude vitality of the play and by its slambang speech that a lot of funny stories were soon going the rounds, like the one about a stern dowager who looked at the play in silence during the first act and accidentally dropped something during the intermission. "I seem to have dropped my Goddam program," she remarked to her escort.

Although *What Price Glory?* was praised for its pitiless realism, it is really the most romantic of plays. Its sense of proportion is romantic— the war being actually only the background of a highly personal feud over a trollop between the captain and the sergeant. In the last act, it invokes the obligatory military staples of loyalty, gallantry, comradeship, and bravery. The last line puts the values in romantic proportion: when the company starts back to the trenches Sergeant Quirt, who has been wounded, makes his heroic decision, "Hey, Flagg, wait for baby!" he yells. *What Price Glory?* was one of the most exciting and provocative plays ever produced on Broadway. It scrapped old manners for new ones. So did Anderson. He scrapped journalism and embraced the theater.

Stallings collaborated with him on two more plays, although both failed. Stallings also wrote the libretto and lyrics for a beautiful opera, *Deep River,* which expired after thirty-two performances, leaving a particular memory of a tender and elegant performance by Rose McClendon. Then he set out for Hollywood, where he wrote *The Big Parade, Old Ironsides,* and *The First World War.* Stallings never got clear of the trenches, but Anderson settled down to a theatrical career that was busy, productive and now and then exalting.

He was a serious man. Stocky, severe in appearance, he seemed to suggest that life was not to be taken frivolously. He believed in the possible perfectibility of man. "I am not a defeatist," he said in one of his essays. "My hope for the human race is that it will so far improve in mentality and magnanimity, over a period of millenniums, that it will be able to govern itself without recourse to violence." Or again: "The dream of the race is that it may make itself better and wiser than it is, and every great philosopher or artist who has ever appeared among us has turned his face away from what man is towards whatever seems most godlike that man may become." Anderson was an old-fashioned liberal: he believed that personal freedom would not come from a powerful government; he believed the less government, the better.

Especially in his early days in the theater, he crusaded for good causes. *Both Your Houses,* in 1933, was an angry attack on political corruption in Washington. *Gods of the Lightning,* which he wrote with Harold Hickerson in 1928, was such a harrowing play about the Sacco–Vanzetti case that some people were afraid it was subversive; such vigorous opposition to legal justice made them feel uneasy. The play had a tumultuous performance by Leo Bulgakov, Sylvia Sidney, and Charles Bickford. *Winterset,* in 1935, was a fiery and graphic recapitulation of the same theme, written in dark, passionate poetry on a lofty artistic plane, and played against a masterly Jo Mielziner setting by Burgess Meredith, Margo, and Eduardo Ciannelli—a memorable night in the theater when high purpose and artistic skills blended. In 1949, Anderson returned to the theater of exhortation in a musical play he and his neighbor Kurt Weill made out of Alan Paton's superb novel about African race relations, *Cry, the Beloved Country*. The musical play, filled with wildness and anguish, was called *Lost in the Stars*.

Mr. Anderson was the most expert craftsman in the Playwrights' Company. After more than a decade of playwriting, he devised a formula for tragedy: "A play should lead up to and away from a central crisis, and the crisis should consist in a discovery by the leading character which has an indelible effect on his thought and emotion and completely alters his course of action." Mr. Anderson acknowledged that his formula owed something to Aristotle, but it also derived from his study of Shakespeare and his own experience. In those formative years, roughly from 1924 to 1938, he wrote some soaring plays that made Broadway glow—*Elizabeth the Queen*, in which Lynn Fontanne and Alfred Lunt gave an ardent, glorious performance; *Valley Forge*, which dramatized the lonely passion of George Washington; *Joan of Lorraine*, in which Ingrid Bergman gave her grandest performance; *Anne of the Thousand Days*, in which Anne Boleyn, acted by Joyce Redman, and Henry VIII, acted by Rex Harrison, ruefully submitted to destiny.

No one else wrote on that plane; no one else was influenced so profoundly by Shakespeare. But once the formula was devised, Anderson tended to write glibly. *The Masque of Kings, Journey to Jerusalem*, and *Candle in the Wind* were ornate potboilers; and in 1946, he struck his low point with a maudlin, routine melodrama called *Truckline Café*. Although he wrote the most vigorous prose of any dramatist, and also some of the most exalting verse, he also wrote poetry that was hardly more than a mannerism, because it did not express a deeply felt conviction. Mr. Anderson was a complex man. He could not control his career as ably as he controlled the themes of *What Price Glory?, Elizabeth the Queen, Mary of Scotland, Winterset, Knickerbocker Holiday*, and other notable plays. The quality of his work deteriorated in his last years, although he never lost his commitment to freedom and to America.

The member of the Playwrights' Company who cast the longest shadow was Robert Emmet Sherwood. That was partly because he stood 6 feet, 6½ inches. A tall, lean, somewhat haunted-looking man, he spoke with a disconcerting deliberation as if it took a long time for conversation to rise to his towering height. Mr. Sherwood was conspicuous wherever he went; he couldn't help dominating any crowd he joined. But he cast a long shadow also because he touched life in many places. He practiced what he preached. He concluded his career by serving as a speechwriter for Franklin D. Roosevelt, just before and during World War II, and by directing the overseas staff of the Office of War Information. Since he never wrote a successful play after the war, it could be said that he gave his career to his country, as he very nearly gave his life for the Allies in World War I.

The tradition of service to the country—noblesse oblige, really—came naturally to him. Educated at Milton Academy, where young gentlemen learned the rules of life, and at Harvard, where young men could loiter pleasantly, he volunteered for military service early in the war. He joined the Canadian Black Watch, which admitted many non-standard people, and served overseas in the ranks. He was gassed and spent the last months of the war in hospitals overseas. He came out of the war full of contempt for the governments responsible for it. He cast his first vote for Warren Gamaliel Harding, a nonentity he could not possibly have taken seriously. He opposed the League of Nations because he had no faith in world statesmanship. He generally adhered to the pacifist philosophy until 1940 when, as a dedicated American, he soberly accepted the realities of another world war. Like all his colleagues, he believed that "the world is populated largely by decent people"—a generous statement that argued his own decency.

But he was no prig. He never quite shook off the college student's propensity for revelry. He enjoyed eating and drinking and parties and a good time. After World War I, he became the first systematic critic of motion pictures, on the staff of the old *Life* magazine. He became editor of *Life* but was eventually fired because he could never seem to get down to the office by 11:00 A.M. Like all the members of the Playwrights' Company, he started to write plays to earn easy money. They were droll, boyish plays with an iconoclastic touch, which seemed very worldly and sophisticated on Broadway at the time. The first one, *The Road to Rome* in 1926—with Jane Cowl, as wife to a Roman senator, and Philip Merivale, as Hannibal—poked fun at the solemnity of history; and *The Queen's Husband*, two years later, poked fun at the solemnity of royalty. It was easy tomfoolery in a style that Broadway found much to its taste.

Sherwood had a fundamentally editorial mind. The distinguished part of his professional career began in 1931, when the Lunts gave sparkling

Alfred Lunt and Lynn Fontanne in *Reunion in Vienna* (1931). (*Vandamm*)

performances in his *Reunion in Vienna,* a harum-scarum comedy that depicted the dull boorishness of a totalitarian regime. His chief characters —dowdy relics of the old regime—recreated, in his words, "the semblance of gaiety in the face of lamentably inappropriate circumstances." He frequently expressed his editorial ideas in serious prefaces to plays that could never quite keep their faces straight. In the preface to *Reunion in Vienna,* during the depression, when some Americans were beginning to think wistfully of the Soviet Russian system, Sherwood called Marxism "the ultimate ant-hill," and said that many men rebelled against Marxism by "being unruly—drunk and disorderly." *Reunion in Vienna* was an explosion of good humor against a sullen background.

With that play, Sherwood began to write in his top form—a grave man of grave ideas who created vivacious plays to illustrate what he believed. His best plays came quickly: *The Petrified Forest,* in 1935, a breezy modern Western that mocked the ineffectuality of the intellectual (Leslie Howard was the intellectual, and Humphrey Bogart began his fabulous strongman career as a gunman); *Idiot's Delight,* in 1936, a roistering play with an antiwar last act (again the Lunts gave the play humor and scope); *Abe Lincoln in Illinois,* in 1938, a deeply moving primer of democracy, with Raymond Massey at the peak of his career as Lincoln; and *There Shall Be No Night,* in 1940, a poignant, brooding, valiant acceptance of war by a democracy defending itself against a totalitarian nation, with the Lunts standing for principle as earnestly as the author. These were all powerful plays. *Idiot's Delight, Abe Lincoln in Illinois,* and *There Shall Be No Night* all won Pulitzer Prizes. These plays form the biography of a noble mind—personally disinterested, courageous, humane.

When Sherwood left government service towards the end of the war to return to the theater, no one could believe that his career as a dramatist was over, but it was. In 1945, *The Rugged Path* seemed trite and diffuse. A musical play, *Miss Liberty,* which he wrote with Irving Berlin and Moss Hart in 1949, was banal. He won a fourth Pulitzer Prize that year for a book he had written about *Roosevelt and Hopkins.* But a great American friend and patriot was worn out. He had given the best he had to the things he believed in. Only Maxwell Anderson and Elmer Rice were left to carry on the active career of the Playwrights' Company. Sidney Howard had died. S. N. Behrman had resigned. Robert Sherwood had lost the touch. Two members were not enough, and the Playwrights'

Company became a commercial producing organization, saved from bankruptcy only by the success of an amusing trifle written by a Dutch journeyman, Jan de Hartog, called *The Fourposter*. The Playwrights' Company stumbled along for one more decade. But that was the wrong world for believers. The Korean war and McCarthyism destroyed it.

THE BOOTH THEATRE

CENTRAL THEATRES LEASING & CONSTRUCTION CO

FIRE NOTICE: The exit, indicated by a red light and sign, nearest to the seat you occupy, is the shortest route to the street.

In the event of fire or other emergency please do not run—WALK TO THAT EXIT

JOHN J. McELLIGOTT, Fire Chief and Commissioner

THE · PLAYBILL · PUBLISHED · BY · THE · NEW · YORK · THEATRE · PROGRAM · CORPORATION

BEGINNING MONDAY EVENING, DECEMBER 25, 1939	It is urged for the comfort and safety of all, that theatre patrons refrain from lighting matches in this theatre.	MATINEES THURSDAY AND SATURDAY

First production of the Twenty-second Subscription Season

THE THEATRE GUILD, INC.
in association with
EDDIE DOWLING

presents

THE TIME OF YOUR LIFE

a New Play by
WILLIAM SAROYAN

Directed by EDDIE DOWLING and WILLIAM SAROYAN

Settings by WATSON BARRATT

Production under the supervision of THERESA HELBURN and LAWRENCE LANGNER

CAST

(In the order of their speaking)

NEWSBOY	*Played by*	BLACKIE SHACKNER
DRUNK	"	JOHN FARRELL
WILLIE, a marble maniac	"	WILL LEE
JOE	*Played by*	EDDIE DOWLING
NICK, owner of Nick's Pacific Street Saloon, Restaurant and Entertainment Palace	"	CHARLES DE SHEIM
TOM, Joe's admirer, stooge and friend	"	EDWARD ANDREWS
KITTY DUVAL	"	JULIE HAYDON
DUDLEY, a young man in love	"	CURT CONWAY
HARRY, a natural born hoofer	"	GENE KELLY
WESLEY, a colored boy who plays the piano	"	REGINALD BEANE
LORENE, an unattractive woman	"	NENE VIBBER
BLICK	"	GROVER BURGESS
ARAB, an Eastern philosopher and harmonica player	"	HOUSELEY STEVENS, SR.
MARY L	"	CELESTE HOLM
KRUPP, a waterfront cop	"	WILLIAM BENDIX
McCARTHY, a longshoreman	"	JACK HARTLEY
KIT CARSON, an old Indian fighter	"	LEN DOYLE
NICK'S MA	"	MICHELETTE BURANI
SAILOR	"	JACK ARNOLD
ELSIE	"	CATHIE BAILEY
A KILLER	"	EVELYN GELLER
HER SIDE KICK	"	MARY CHEFFEY
A SOCIETY LADY	"	EVA LEONARD BOYNE
A SOCIETY GENTLEMAN	"	AINSWORTH ARNOLD
FIRST COP	"	JACK ARNOLD
SECOND COP	"	JOHN FARRELL

PARADOX
OF THE
THIRTIES

After the devastating stock-market crash in October 1929 and during the next decade, America endured a traumatic experience that raised serious doubts about the validity of the American political and economic system. It permanently changed the values of national life and the happy folklore about a rosy future. The depression affected Broadway profoundly; the number of productions declined from 239 in 1929–1930 to 187 in 1930–1931, 100 in 1938–1939, and 72 in 1940–1941. In the theater, anxiety was universal; privation was common. Many theater people, including five thousand actors, were out of work on Broadway, and audiences declined not only in numbers but in affluence. It was an ominous period, and it seemed to be so interminable that artists and intellectuals began to question the legitimacy of American institutions.

By some inscrutable paradox, it was also a creative period in the theater. Perhaps the depression had a ghastly dramatic undertone; perhaps it

ılie Haydon and Eddie Dowling in *The Time of*
our Life (1939). (*Vandamm*)

sharpened the minds, broadened the range of interests, and excited the emotions of theater people. Perhaps it drew them closer together. Whatever the reason, it was one of Broadway's most stimulating times. Established writers like Eugene O'Neill, George Kaufman, Marc Connelly, and the five who organized themselves into the Playwrights' Company continued to write interesting plays, some of which were more concerned with the state of the union than their previous work had been. In addition to the dramas already noted, the eleven years from 1928 to the outbreak of World War II included many unique and memorable occasions charged with unforgettable personalities: Katharine Cornell's glowing portrait of Elizabeth Browning in Rudolf Besier's romantic *The Barretts of Wimpole Street*, with piquant intimations of incest; Helen Hayes' enchanting portrait of a gallant Queen Victoria in Laurence Housman's *Victoria Regina*; Lynn Riggs' hearty cowboy idyll, *Green Grow the Lilacs*, with Franchot Tone, Helen Westley, June Walker, and Lee Strasberg in a fresh and lyrical performance; Thornton Wilder's *Our Town*, which became a permanent part of the American mythology; William Saroyan's genial *The Time of Your Life*, in which Eddie Dowling, Julie Haydon, Will Bendix, and Celeste Holm loitered around a cheerful saloon; Dorothy Stickney and Howard Lindsay in a perfect American comedy called *Life with Father*, which ultimately had 3,224 performances, the longest run of any play ever produced on Broadway; and Jack Kirkland's *Tobacco Road*, which had 3,182 performances, second only to *Life with Father*.

Max Gordon, the bustling producer, thought that the 1933–1934 season—in the depths of the depression—was the most thrilling in the history of the New York theater. To suggest its vitality, a list of the best productions is appended here:

O'Neill's *Ah, Wilderness!* with George M. Cohan and Gene Lockhart.

Sidney Kingsley's *Men in White*, vividly acted by the Group Theater.

John Wexley's polemical *They Shall Not Die*, with Ruth Gordon and Claude Rains.

Maxwell Anderson's *Mary of Scotland*, with Helen Hayes and Helen Menken.

Mordaunt Shairp's *The Green Bay Tree*, with Laurence Olivier at an early stage of his magnificent career.

Clare Kummer's droll *Her Master's Voice*, in which Roland Young and Laura Hope Crews appeared.

Jack Kirkland's *Tobacco Road*, with Henry Hull as Jeeter Lester.

Sidney Howard's dramatization of Sinclair Lewis' *Dodsworth,* with Walter Huston in the leading part.

Sidney Howard's *Yellow Jack.*

Stevedore, by Paul Peters and George Sklar.

Let 'Em Eat Cake, with a score by George Gershwin and a book by George Kaufman and Morrie Ryskind.

Jerome Kern's *Roberta.*

Although the nation seemed to be falling apart and money was scarce on Broadway, the theater was in top form. No wonder John Mason Brown referred to that perplexing period as "these full lean years."

During the flush years of the twenties, Broadway had tolerated revolution. It was rich enough to listen to radical ideas with equanimity. While the stock market was joyfully leaping upward in 1924, the Theater Guild's subscribers had politely sat through a lively performance of *Man and the Masses,* by Ernst Toller, a Communist. For a brief time, Toller had led the Bavarian Soviet Republic—an honor for which he spent five years in jail when the bourgeois government of Bavaria got back in power. His drama was overtly revolutionary.

The next season, the Guild produced John Howard Lawson's "jazz symphony of American life," which he called *Processional.* In a succession of flamboyant styles, it portrayed the American citizen as the victim of capitalists, the Ku Klux Klan, and other organizations and conventions. Heyward Broun, who admired it, described it as the "scratch paper of a great American play." Gilbert Gabriel, who also admired it, dubbed it "a rhapsody in red." Among the capitalists who appeared in it and got good notices for good acting were Ben Grauer, later an opulent television star, and George Abbott, later one of the wealthiest of all stage directors. Abbott played the savage part of Dynamite Jones, who confronted capital belligerently. The Guild audiences were for the most part puzzled and annoyed; some of them were enraged. But enough of them were sufficiently impressed to give *Processional* a permanent reputation for skill and imagination in the free use of theater.

That was also the period when a group of left-wing writers—John Dos Passos, Emjo Basshe, John Howard Lawson, and Mike Gold—(whom Woollcott dubbed the "Revolting Playwrights") proceeded to undermine the capitalistic system with a series of incompetent dramas in Greenwich Village. They were supported by one of the richest and most cultivated New York capitalists—Otto Kahn of Kuhn, Loeb & Company. Rich people felt secure enough to patronize their class enemies in the manner of indulgent parents towards unruly children. It was fun.

In the 1930s, Otto Kahn was no longer financially able to support the follies of the young. And the political bent of many young theater people was no longer amusing. Since the American system seemed to have failed, since the Soviet system had not yet begun to assassinate dissenters and had made no pact with Hitler, and since it also subsidized its own theaters, some Broadway actors and theater people joined the Communist party, and many who didn't join were interested. In Moscow, thirty-five or forty theaters were packed every night, and the actors not only had parts but knew where their next meal was coming from. In New York during the depression, that sounded like a corner of Paradise. After the closing performance of a harrowing Broadway drama about the depression, 1931, someone in the gallery cried, "Long live Soviet Russia." That was not what the producers had in mind; Franchot Tone, one of the actors who was taking a curtain call, shouted back, "Hurrah for America."

Most of the local dramas of social protest ("Theater as a Weapon" was the belligerent slogan) took place off Broadway where the New Theater League and the Theater Union produced passionate dramas to indoctrinate "the working class"—a mythical stereotype of the American intellectual. But Broadway gave houseroom to plays of social protest in the hope that theatergoers would pay top box-office prices to undermine

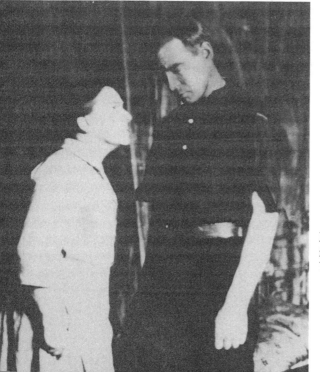

Blanche Frederici and George Abbott in *Processional* (1925). (*The New York Public Library*)

ORREST THEATRE

ECTION . . . . KIRKLAND AND GRISMAN

FIRE NOTICE: The exit, indicated by a red light and sign, nearest to the seat
you occupy, is the shortest route to the street.
In the event of fire or other emergency please do not run—WALK TO THAT EXIT.
JOHN J. McELLIGOTT, Fire Chief and Commissioner

· PLAYBILL · PUBLISHED · BY · THE · NEW · YORK · THEATRE · PROGRAM · CORPORATION

BEGINNING
MONDAY EVENING.
AUGUST 23, 1937

MATINEES
WEDNESDAY AND
SATURDAY

ANTHONY BROWN

PRESENTS

JAMES BARTON

IN

TOBACCO ROAD

A PLAY IN THREE ACTS
BY
JACK KIRKLAND

Based on the Novel
by
ERSKINE CALDWELL

Directed by Mr. Brown

Settings by Robert Redington Sharpe

Henry Hull and Ruth Hunter in
Tobacco Road (1933).
(*Vandamm*)

the system that supported them. Left-wing productions were fashionable.
To the surprise of the disgruntled subscribers, the respectably bourgeois
Theater Guild hired Paul Peters, George Sklar, and other social reformers
to write a left-wing review, *Parade*, which Philip Loeb staged. Jimmy
Savo, a lovable pantomimist in the tradition of Charlie Chaplin, did a
few innocent tricks that captivated the audience, but nothing else entertained anybody. After 40 performances, *Parade* broke up. The public was
more contented at *The Great Waltz*, which had a Strauss score, including
"The Beautiful Blue Danube," and 347 performances.

There was some left-wing drama on a professional level. John Wexley's
explosive *Steel* gave fourteen performances at the Times Square Theater.
It portrayed a vigorous young man who not only seduced his sister-in-law
but led a strike against a steel company—a man of admirable vitality in

both instances. The play was full of sound and fury, signifying an obtuse playwright. But Wexley's *They Shall Not Die,* produced by the Theater Guild in 1934, blasted public complacency with a savage attack on the police, attorneys, and judges responsible for locking up the nine Negroes in Scottsboro in 1934, who had been falsely charged with having raped two white girls. The cast of the play called for sixty-four actors, not including the lynching mob, white hobos, soldiers, and court guards. Among the actors were many professionals with no particular political commitment— Ruth Gordon, Claude Rains, Tom Ewell, Dean Jagger, Linda Watkins, Hugh Rennie, Helen Westley. Although this incendiary drama had sixty-two performances, it cost the Guild a lot of money and did not add to the social security of the actors. But it struck a hard blow for freedom and very likely represented the prevailing opinion of Broadway.

The mood was fiercely antiwar. In Irwin Shaw's *Bury the Dead,* which played ninety-seven performances in 1936, six dead soldiers rose from the trenches and refused to be buried, because they said they had a message for the world. They had been killed in the second year of "the war that is to begin tomorrow," as Irwin Shaw ominously phrased it. Climbing out of the trench where they had died, they began to march grimly across the world to warn people against a new holocaust (which indeed exploded a few years later).

Theatergoers took a new interest in minority groups. John Steinbeck's terse drama of "bindlestiffs" on a California ranch, *Of Mice and Men,* was fresh and engrossing, particularly in the lean performance that George S. Kaufman staged. The immediate success of *Tobacco Road* probably derived from the scandal value of its foul language and its reputation for obscenity—both in short supply in 1933. During the course of Jack Kirkland's rambling narrative about the poverty and degradation of the backroads of the South, Jeeter Lester and his harelipped daughter, Ellie May, gaped through the open windows of their shack while Jeeter's son, Dude, and his lecherous bride, Bessie Rice, consummated the lawful rites of matrimony on a bed inside. Voyeurism of that kind shocked critics and community in the thirties. But the theatergoers who kept *Tobacco Road* on the stage for eight years must also have been startled by the bleakness, ignorance, and shiftlessness of a part of Georgia they hardly knew about. *Tobacco Road* was a genuine folkplay that substituted brutal truth for the bucolic charm of the genre. During the eight years when it kept a theater lighted (it opened at the Mansfield), some first-rate actors shuffled through it night after night until they could stand it no longer.

Among the successive Jeeters were Henry Hull, James Barton, James Bell, Eddie Garr, and Will Geer. The original cast included Margaret Wycherly, originally from the Abbey Theater, Sam Byrd, Ruth Hunter, and Dean Jagger. The actors did not have to make-up for the performance. They had to make-down. They acted in rags amid dirt, squalor, and degeneracy.

Of the several theater organizations formed during the depression, the most effective, the most genuine, and the one that left a permanent mark was the Group Theater. It had a program, talent, and unbelievable tenacity. During the last half of the twenties, Harold Clurman, Lee Strasberg, and Cheryl Crawford had been in the lower echelons of the Theater Guild—eager, observant, but dissatisfied. They regarded the Guild as a dilettante organization that survived on nothing more substantial than glamour. They were all fanatics—an essential ingredient of any theater career.

Clurman, one of the most articulate men in America, was highly educated and had studied abroad. He had the best mind of anyone in the organization and one of the best on Broadway. Strasberg was consumed with passion for the theater. Nothing else mattered. He was an actor of minor roles (he had acted in *Processional*), but he squandered most of his energy on directing amateur groups. Cheryl Crawford was "assistant to the Board of Managers" of the Theater Guild—an efficient administrator and a practical idealist. They were all dreaming of a theater that would be an institution with a permanent company, an artistic policy and a point of view. After innumerable preliminary talks at parties over a period of many months, Clurman, Strasberg, and Miss Crawford seceded from the Guild and appointed themselves managers of a new theater. As a farewell present, the Guild gave them the rights to Paul Green's *The House of Connelly*, a check for $1,000, and two excellent young Guild actors— Franchot Tone and Morris Carnovsky.

On June 8, 1931, when the economic state of the United States was shaky and the future looked bleak, three managers, twenty-eight actors, a few wives, two children, and some friends left in an assortment of cars from the front of the Guild Theater in 52nd Street for Brookfield Center, Connecticut. Escaping the distractions and corruptions of Broadway, they were to spend the summer studying, experimenting, listening to interminable discussions, and becoming—if possible—an artistic organization. It was a period of indoctrination and work.

On September 28, 1931, they opened in *The House of Connelly* at the

Martin Beck Theater under the auspices of the Theater Guild. Lee Strasberg and Cheryl Crawford had directed the performance. Cleon Throckmorton had designed the production. Since the cast included many actors who later became influential on Broadway and in Hollywood, it may be useful to print the names of all of them: Fanny De Knight, Rose McClendon, Margaret Barker, Franchot Tone, Art Smith, Stella Adler, Eunice Stoddard, Morris Carnovsky, Mary Morris, J. Edward Bromberg, Dorothy Patten, Ruth Nelson, Walter Coy, William Challee, Clement Wilenchick, Philip Robinson, Clifford Odets, Friendly Ford, Gerrit Kraber, and Herbert Ratner. The reviews the next day were uniformly enthusiastic. The critics and the public cordially welcomed a new idea and a fresh band of actors. A passionate dream had become a reality. Nothing else in those dreary years seemed to be so creative and jubilant.

That was one of the two or three high points in the bizarre tale of the Group Theater. During the rest of the decade, it was rarely successful by Broadway standards. It always spoke scornfully of money, which was fortunate, for the Group was nearly always short of money; occasionally it was destitute. On special occasions, a few actors got $300 a week. But $30 to $140 was the more usual salary; the three directors paid themselves $50 a week, although they did divide in three equal parts a $1,500 fee for staging productions. There was one bitter time when there was no money for anyone and no income except gifts. During the period of the Group Theater's personal depression, most of the actors lived in a ten-room tenement in West 57th Street, for which they paid $50 a month. Meals came out of a common fund; two of the actresses did the marketing, and a few of the men did the cooking. It was like a metropolitan kibbutz.

In the beginning, the Group took no interest in politics. Temperamentally, it eliminated all the world except the theater. But after a year or two of listening to the ordinary conversation of the time and after sharing the common privations, the Group did take an interest in politics, and some of the members joined the Communist party—in most cases, briefly. Since they were argumentative people, their politics were as much a social diversion as a political conviction. Talk was the lifeblood of the Group. They were serious people; they had little humor and no gaiety. They were evangelists who had little capacity for fun, and that was their only weakness on the stage. In an art form that tries to give pleasure, they worked too hard and too rigidly. Stella Adler complained that they had "pathological manners"—the result of feverish psychological education.

After a decade, it was clear that an art theater could not exist as show business; the box office could not suport an institution dedicated to an unworldly ideal. But the Group Theater trained some notable people who continued to deepen the art and content of the theater—not only Harold Clurman, Lee Strasberg, and Cheryl Crawford, but Elia Kazan and Bob Lewis, directors; Lee J. Cobb, Morris Carnovsky, John Garfield, J. Edward Bromberg, Sanford Meisner, Frances Farmer, Luther Adler, and Stella Adler, actors and, in some cases, teachers of acting. Although the Group Theater failed, the members never lost their independence and vision; they drew strength from their exciting though harsh experience.

And the scripts they acted had original style and remarkable pertinence to the life of America—Irwin Shaw's *The Gentle People*, John Howard Lawson's *Success Story* and *Gentlewoman*, Sidney Kingsley's *Men in White*, Robert Ardrey's *Thunder Rock*, William Saroyan's first and most endearing play, *My Heart's in the Highlands*. Most of them failed, but none of them was hackneyed, and all of them disclosed an intelligent concern for the human condition. The Group did make the theater a vital form of life.

During the season when the Group Theater was incarcerated in the 57th Street tenement ("the Group's poorhouse," Clurman called it), one of the minor actors lived in a cold room that was too tiny for a desk or table. Sitting on his camp bed with a typewriter in his lap, Clifford Odets was writing a play he called *I Got the Blues*—a pertinent title. Since he was one of the most compulsive talkers on grandiose topics, no one took either him or the play seriously. In December of 1934, he was invited to write a short, provocative play for a Sunday night benefit for the *New Theatre Magazine*. He wrote *Waiting For Lefty* in three nights; form and content fell into place perfectly.

On Sunday night, January 5, 1935, it was given a rousing performance in the crumbling Civic Repertory Theater in 14th Street. First the audience, then gradually theatergoers all over the city, exploded with enthusiasm. Everyone knew at once that *Waiting for Lefty* was the best revolutionary play written by an American. It faced and addressed the audience as if they were attending a union meeting. On a bare stage, a conniving union leader and some labor racketeers were trying to persuade the members of a taxicab union not to strike. As successive workers addressed the delegates from the platform, the meeting got out of hand. "Hello America! We're stormbirds of the working class," shouted the chief rabble-rouser (played by Elia Kazan) in the last scene. After word came that Lefty, the hero of the workers, had been murdered, everybody

Morris Carnovsky, J. E. Bromberg, Stella Adler, Luther Adler, Sanford Meisner, and Art Smith in *Awake and Sing* (1935). (*Vandamm*)

BELASCO THEATRE

(OWNERSHIP AND MANAGEMENT OF HAZEL L. RICE, INC.)

115 W. 44th St.

FIRE NOTICE: The exit indicated by a red light and sign, nearest to the seat you occupy, is the shortest route to the street.
In the event of fire or other emergency please do not run—WALK TO THAT EXIT
JOHN J. McELLIGOTT, Fire Chief and Commissioner

THE · PLAYBILL · PUBLISHED · BY · THE · NEW · YORK · THEATRE · PROGRAM · CORPORATION

BEGINNING
TUESDAY EVENING
FEBRUARY 19 1935

MATINEES
THURSDAY AND
SATURDAY

THE GROUP THEATRE INC
presents
THE GROUP THEATRE ACTING COMPANY
in

"AWAKE AND SING!"

By CLIFFORD ODETS

"Awake and sing ye that dwell in dust"—Isaiah 26:19

Production directed by HAROLD CLURMAN
Setting by BORIS ARONSON

CAST

(In the order of appearance)

MYRON BERGER	*Played by*	ART SMITH
BESSIE BERGER		STELLA ADLER
JACOB		MORRIS CARNOVSKY

in the cast, onstage or in the aisles, simultaneously cried, "Strike! Strike! Strike!" The audience felt as if it were participating in a revolutionary occasion. *Waiting for Lefty* was an agit-prop play—a glib term derived from Russia where the workers never struck. In addition to Kazan, the cast included Bob Lewis, Russell Collins, George Heller, and Clifford Odets. Among the anonymous "voices"—Lee J. Cobb. *Waiting for Lefty* was so successful in its special performances that the Group Theater formally produced it two months later at the Longacre Theater with another short Odets play called *Till the Day I Die*, concerned with a German Communist who was tortured to the point of suicide by the police. *Waiting for Lefty* had 168 performances on Broadway.

Everything had changed for Odets by that time. His *I Got the Blues* had become *Awake and Sing* and was produced at the Belasco Theater on February 19, 1935, staged by Harold Clurman, with an ingenious, moody setting by Boris Aronson, and acted with emotional electricity by the Group's leading actors—Art Smith, Stella Adler, Morris Carnovsky, Phoebe Brand, Jules (John) Garfield, Roman Bohnen, Luther Adler, J. Edward Bromberg, and Sanford Meisner.

In its fourth season, the Group Theater had found its best playwright in its own ranks, and Broadway had found its most eloquent spokesman against the depression. *Waiting for Lefty* was acted all over the country by special groups, some of whom were carted off to jail as subversives. Odets, a minor actor with no money but romantically exciting ideas, instantly moved into a good apartment, bought a huge record-player and hundreds of records of classical music, treated his friends generously, and made imposing statements to the press. "Just once before I die," he declared, "I want to write a fine revolutionary play." He became the favorite leader of political causes. He led a delegation of fifteen members

Lucile Watson and Paul Lukas in *Watch on the Rhine* (1941). (*Vandamm*)

of the American League Against War and Fascism to Cuba to investigate the political situation under its current tyrant. The delegation was expelled before it landed and returned to New York in the ship that had brought it.

In addition to being the darling of the Left, he was the most stimulating dramatist on Broadway. His knowledge of middle-class life, his allusive, spinning dialogue that glanced off subjects and revealed the loneliness of individual people, and the instinctive tensions of his style of stage expression moved the American drama one step further from the old stereotypes and closer to the human being. In 1935, *Awake and Sing* had 209 performances and the Group revived it more than once when its affairs looked desolate.

Although political dissidents assumed that Odets was a revolutionary playwright with a firm knowledge of Marxian dialectics and a rational political program, he was actually the most unworldly of men. He took to success like the traditional bourgeois apprentice who had made good. Like Aubrey Piper in *The Show-Off*, he played the role of universal genius. Incapable of orderly work schedules, he squandered much of his time on pleasant distractions. He saturated himself in classical music. Although he could not read a musical score, he played chords on a small organ until his associates went mad. He became an art expert. He bought paintings lavishly, specializing in Klee. He became a painter. In 1947 he put thirty-three of his paintings in an art exhibition. It was noted at the time that they were not the work of an angry young man; they were cheerful and full of love. Boris Aronson, the artist and scene designer, took a poor view of Odets' painting and sardonically told Odets that he would promise never to write a play if Odets would promise never to make another painting. There was one period when Odets was obsessed with stamp collecting. He could be frequently observed in an upstairs window of a stamp emporium in 43rd Street peering at rare stamps through an enlarging glass. Whatever Odets did—including being generous and thoughtful with friends—he did with passion and singleness of purpose.

At heart he was not a revolutionary but a romantic reformer. "Hugo inspired me," he once said in a humorously reminiscent mood. "I wanted to be a good and noble man, longed to do heroic deeds with my bare hands, thirsted to be kind to people, particularly the meek and humble and oppressed." As a dramatist, he said he wanted to talk about "the fulfillment of each individual human being—about what develops all of the inherent possibilities of each man and woman and what holds them back, what stymies them."

Although he was not the organized leader that many people imagined, he was the best dramatist the Group Theater had and an important figure on Broadway. In the few years after *Waiting for Lefty* and *Awake and Sing* had taken Broadway by storm, he wrote several plays of uneven quality but with missionary zeal. *Paradise Lost* followed *Awake and Sing* in December 1935. It contrasted a conservative, gentle-mannered business-man with his radical partner. Although the business collapsed—as did the family life—and the children went astray, the play ended on an optimistic note because, Odets pointed out, people learn through suffering. In the future, the leading character said, men "will sing at their work," and "no man fights alone." *Paradise Lost* had seventy-three performances.

In 1937, Odets wrote his most successful play—*Golden Boy*, a metaphor of cultural corruption in a materialistic society. A young Italian boy who had a talent for playing the violin chose the alternate career of prize-fighting, because he was a good fighter and could make vast quantities of money in the ring. The play had 250 tumultuous performances in New York and was acted successfully in other American cities and in London; and it was sold to the movies. It made Odets richer than a radical had any right to be, and it temporarily relieved the Group of its financial misery.

The next year, *Rocket to the Moon*, which had 131 performances, discussed the baneful influence of money on love. It was full of cosmic epigrams, which always gave the Odets plays the sound of universal wisdom. "Looking at this newspaper," said the girl who wanted to marry well, "makes me think the world must be run by a committee; one man couldn't be so stupid." *Night Music* had only twenty performances when it was produced in 1940. Undisciplined, composed of self-conscious phrases, it was soap opera about the rescue of a nice young man from the iniquities of Hollywood by the love of a New York actress. Odets had been dabbling with art and money in Hollywood. The next year, his *Clash by Night*, in which Tallulah Bankhead appeared, was produced, not by the Group Theater, but by Billy Rose. It was the Staten Island version of the familiar triangle; a wife left her husband to live with one of his best friends. Despite Odets' savory dialogue, it had only forty-nine performances, and it was clear that Tallulah Bankhead did not have the true spirit of Staten Island in her heart.

By this time, Odets was no longer a leader of the Left. Nor was he a box-office success. He went to Hollywood to earn money and to put his life in order. In 1949, he returned to New York with an overwrought drama about the evil of Hollywood called *The Big Knife*. Although the

Group Theater was no longer in existence, John Garfield, one of the Group Theater actors, played the part of the persecuted star and J. Edward Bromberg, also once of the Group Theater, played an infamous Hollywood businessman. The vivid setting was by Boris Aronson, the most gifted of the Group Theater's designers. The play tried to make a moral dilemma out of a familiar business situation and did not come with much grace from the pen of a man who had fled to Hollywood when he thought Broadway had let him down. *The Big Knife* had 108 performances. In 1950, Odets absented himself from the cosmos, where he had been making big noises and using oversized gestures, and wrote a touching sentimental drama, *The Country Girl*, about an old actor rescued from alcoholism with the help of his wife and a stage director. Boris Aronson, who had designed the sets for *Awake and Sing*, designed the battered backstage sets for *The Country Girl*. That was all that remained from the Group Theater, which had discovered Odets' genius and had depended on him for its well-being. *The Country Girl* had 235 performances; it was a commercial Broadway hit.

Many people felt bitter about Odets. They charged him with having betrayed the revolution and having betrayed the art of the theater by escaping to Hollywood. But they misunderstood him. He was too unworldly to put his life in order. He could not cope with realities. He was a generous, talented man, full of ideas and flashing phrases, but diffuse. When he was at the peak of his career, he said he wanted to discover how in a materialistic world a man could retain "the conviction of innocence." Although he never knew it, he was his own best exhibit. He never lost his innocence about the world. Contrary to the exultant philosophy of *Paradise Lost*, he fought alone. No one could help him.

Of the many writers opposed to the status quo in American society, the most clearheaded and the best organized was Lillian Hellman. Male critics took pleasure in assuring one another that she had a masculine mind. After an apprenticeship as a press agent, play reader, and book reviewer, she burst onto Broadway in 1934 with a trenchant drama ironically called *The Children's Hour*. She was in complete possession of the forms of the theater, as if she had been writing plays for years. Suggested by a famous Scottish court-case, *The Children's Hour* dramatized a disastrous episode in a girls' school. A spiteful pupil precipitated a painful scandal by fraudulently implying that two of her teachers were involved in a lesbian relationship. Lesbianism was a prurient subject then, as the producers of *The Captive* had discovered in 1926. But the drive of Miss Hellman's writing, and the momentum of the performance that Herman Shumlin had staged, turned *The Children's Hour* into an indictment of smalltown malice. It had 691 performances.

Miss Hellman's *The Little Foxes* appeared in 1939, in another taut performance directed by Herman Shumlin. The title came from the Song of Solomon: "Take us the foxes, the little foxes, that spoil the vines: for our vines have tender grapes." Melodramatic in style, *The Little Foxes* was a merciless portrait of a rapacious Southern family that devoured its own people to appease its hunger for wealth. The play made a genuine star out of Tallulah Bankhead, after she had been behaving like a star for six years. Since 1933, she had been frittering away her talents on worthless plays or injuring good plays by self-conscious performing. But Shumlin gave Bankhead back the talent she had been dissipating foolishly. She acted the part of a ladylike Southern monster with subtlety and power.

Like just about everybody on Broadway and probably in America, Miss Hellman was horrified by the spread of Nazism in Europe. Unlike other people, she was able to do something about it. She wrote *Watch on the Rhine* in April 1941, seven months before Pearl Harbor. It was Miss Hellman's commitment; it told everyone where she stood. As an anti-Nazi drama it was original, if only because there were no uniforms in it, no rhetorical speeches or Nazi salutes, and none of the mumbo-jumbo of war dramas. In the livingroom of a genteel, wealthy Washington family, the play brought into confrontation a blackmailing Roumanian count and a freedom-loving German who belonged to the anti-Hitler underground. Apart from Miss Hellman's convictions, the play had grace and humor—witty dialogue, a tender feeling for the children, respect for character, and an undertone of good-natured family banter. Under Shumlin's direction, the performance was as fresh as the script. Lucile Watson, who had a special gift for bringing a crackle of mischief to the parts of ladies, played a dowager with witty arrogance. Mady Christian's tired loyalty to a cause, George Coulouris' bitter doubledealing, and Paul Lukas' quiet resolution translated *Watch on the Rhine* into a powerful statement of faith in people and principles. The play had 378 performances. What Sherwood and the Lunts had begun the year before, Miss Hellman continued with an exhilarating play that consolidated public opinion because her drama was unanswerable.

In her next play, *Another Part of the Forest*, in 1946, Miss Hellman returned to the Hubbards of *The Little Foxes,* but she went one generation deeper into their story. The older people were more malevolent than the Hubbards of *The Little Foxes;* they practiced blackmail, theft, torture, and a little incest. *Another Part of the Forest* was a demoniac play in the traditional melodramatic style by a skillful craftsman with a modern mind. Having written the play with passion, Miss Hellman personally staged it with a notable cast that included Patricia Neal, Mildred Dunnock, Margaret Phillips, Paul Ford, Percy Waram, and Leo Genn. They managed to terrify Broadway for 182 performances. *The Little Foxes* indicted the Hubbards. *Another Part of the Forest* clobbered them. They became unbearable in the theater, or perhaps they only seemed so because the mood of 1946 was less rancorous than the mood of 1939.

Watch on the Rhine received the Critics Circle award for 1940–1941. But the Pulitzer committee made no award that year; it pretended not to have heard Miss Hellman's voice. In 1935, when her *The Children's Hour* was available, the Pulitzer Prize went to a commonplace dramatization of Edith Wharton's genteel *The Old Maid.* Twice the Pulitzer committee passed Miss Hellman by. But neither was the Critics Circle guiltless. In 1939, when the Pulitzer Prize went to *Abe Lincoln in Illinois,* the Critics Circle made no award. It could not make up its mind between *The Little Foxes* and *Abe Lincoln in Illinois. The Little Foxes* led in the last of ten ballots, but it lacked the necessary three-quarters vote. In the valiant person of Miss Hellman, the depression and the brutal conquests by Hitler and Mussolini produced a major dramatist. She had the hatred and fearlessness, the clarity and independence, to deal with the major evils.

In 1935, theater people achieved equality with mechanics and laborers. The Works Progress Administration founded the Federal Theater to provide useful employment for theater people in need of it. Hallie Flanagan, director of the Vassar Experimental Theater, accepted appointment as national director. On August 27, 1935, she took the oath of office to protect and defend the Constitution of the United States of America against all enemies, foreign or domestic. The terms of the oath turned out to have particular relevance. Mrs. Flanagan was a slender lady of formidable courage and energy who thoroughly believed in the American system and had complete faith in the WPA program and the theater. In a burst of Washington euphoria, Harry Hopkins, the President's personal assistant, said: "What we want is free, adult, uncensored theater." Everything began in a cloud of love.

Since the Federal Theater was a national institution, it must not be discussed as if it were a Broadway episode. Even the New York branch of the Federal Theater was not exclusively Broadway. It had an active Harlem unit; it served the whole city. But the New York branch was the biggest in the nation, and the busiest part of the New York branch was Broadway. In May of 1936, the New York branch employed 5,385 people. Qualified professionals were paid $103.40 a month in New York. During the three-year period from 1936 to 1939, 12,500,000 people attended the New York productions and paid $681,914 admission fees. Some Broadway producers (not Lee Shubert, however) objected to the competition of a government-supported theater; and, following standard practice, they wrote to their congressmen to express alarm. But the Federal Theater did not compete with Broadway, it supplemented Broadway; and there was no likelihood of its becoming permanent. Suspicion of the theater is an essential ingredient of congressmen.

In Washington, the WPA administrators probably assumed that the Federal Theater would provide pleasant entertainment for docile masses, by actors grateful to a benevolent government. But in the middle of a calamitous depression, and during the barbaric days when Hitler and Mussolini were striding through Europe and Africa, it was naïve to assume that any form of public expression would be innocuous. Particularly in the case of unemployed citizens: they could not be neutral about a world that seemed to have rejected them. The Federal Theater had hardly got into production before it was in trouble.

Elmer Rice, a passionate advocate of freedom of speech, had accepted Mrs. Flanagan's invitation to administer the New York branch from an abandoned bank building on Eighth Avenue. His first production was to be the first edition of a new theatrical form called the Living Newspaper, which was in essence a staged documentary. The topic was to be Ethiopia, which Mussolini had cynically invaded, with contempt for the opinion of the free world; and the script included excerpts from published speeches by Roosevelt and Mussolini. But the restrictions on freedom of speech for a government-supported theater were immediately apparent. The State Department protested that *Ethiopia* might offend Mussolini, who had blatantly offended the rest of the world; and the Federal Theater administration in Washington put a stop order on the play. Rice invited the press to the final dress-rehearsal of *Ethiopia*. In the context of censorship of ideas, the press instinctively cheered the play and excoriated the government. Rice then resigned with the appropriate flourishes.

But the Federal Theater continued. Among all its productions for all

Orson Welles and Muriel Brassler in Welles' modern-dress production of *Julius Caesar* (1937). (*The New York Public Library*)

One Third of a Nation (1938). (*The New York Public Library*)

Frank Craven, Martha Scott, and John Craven in *Our Town* (1937). (*Vandamm*)

Florence Eldridge, Frances Heflin, Fredric March, and Tallulah Bankhead in *The Skin of Our Teeth* (1942). (*Museum of the City of New York*)

kinds of people—children, adults, foreign-language citizens, random people on the streets—it put on a number of excellent dramas: T. S. Eliot's *Murder in the Cathedral* and Bernard Shaw's *On the Rocks*, neither of which had ever been done in America; E. P. Conkle's idyllic *Prologue to Glory*, which dramatized the boyhood of Lincoln; Shakespeare's *Coriolanus*, which was a new play to most New Yorkers; William Du Bois' brightly colored history of *Haiti;* Marlowe's *Dr. Faustus*, which few people had ever seen; Sinclair Lewis' *It Can't Happen Here*, an anti-Fascist play that the government meekly consented to. Thousands of New Yorkers who had never been able to afford the theater paid 50¢ or $1.00 to see these plays.

The Living Newspapers improvised a technique that made efficient use of the Federal Theater's most conspicuous asset—manpower. The information on which the various Newspapers were based was assembled by a staff of seventy or one hundred reporters, and the raw material was then composed in stage form by Arthur Arent and several other dramatists. The Living Newspapers had long casts, and the Federal Theater had a limitless supply of bit actors. Since the Living Newspapers provided abundant employment, they helped solve the Federal Theater's fundamental problem.

Theoretically, the Living Newspapers were objective. They were "learning plays"; they presented information in brief capsule form—terse, trenchant, stimulating. But it was impossible for anyone to have objective opinions about the topics the editors selected. Ethiopia was not a subject any American could feel dispassionate about in 1936. And the farm program, which was the topic of *Triple-A Ploughed Under*, was a partisan issue. It argued that farmers and consumers were victims of capitalistic speculators. Earl Browder, chairman of the American branch of the Communist party, was one of the characters included in the production; Thomas Jefferson, also an American, was another. When *Triple-A Ploughed Under* opened on March 14, 1936, at the Biltmore Theater, uniformed police were in attendance. They were instructed to break up any riots that might occur. But there were no riots. *Triple-A Ploughed Under* was inevitably partisan, as was *Injunction Granted*, which explored the subject of labor relations in the United States.

The career of the Living Newspapers closed with a masterpiece. It was an exposition of the housing problem entitled *One Third of a Nation*, written by Arthur Arent, vividly staged by Lem Ward, and played with conviction and virtuosity. In his second inaugural address, Roosevelt had said that as he looked about him he saw one third of a nation ill-housed, ill-clad, and ill-nourished; that was the source of the title. Howard Bay designed an ominous, spectral set that represented a crumbling tenement house that blighted the lives of the people who lived there. In the master production, which had been staged the previous summer in Poughkeepsie, Abe Feder designed a dramatic lighting plot that culminated in a simulated tenement fire. The performance represented a practical synthesis of all the theater arts, including choreography—to give continuity and significance to the movement of the actors—and music—to arouse the emotions of the audience. *One Third of a Nation* was a sensational success at the Adelphi Theater where it opened on January 17, 1938; it had 237 performances, No one who saw it had a disinterested opinion about it. No one who read about it was neutral.

The increasing expertness of the Living Newspapers decreed the end. By this time, the enemies of the New Deal were looking for an emotional issue, and the Living Newspapers were vulnerable. They were essentially New Deal plays or New Deal "propaganda," as the opposition asserted. And what Roosevelt supporters regarded as New Deal, his opponents denounced as Communist. Many Congressmen thought of the Federal Theater as part of some monstrous Communist conspiracy. "You are quoting from this [Christopher] Marlowe," Congressman Joseph Starnes said to Mrs. Flanagan at a Washington hearing. "Is he a Communist?" She did not join in the laughter that greeted this eruption of ignorance. She knew the enemy; ignorance was the enemy. In 1939, Congress dismantled the Federal Theater by not voting an appropriation for it. The next season, two Broadway producers tried a Living Newspaper, *Medicine Show*, which pleaded for socialized medicine. But it didn't work. The passion was out of it.

Among the Federal Theater's many assets were two talented young directors who thought that the theater should be an exciting place— Orson Welles, a round-faced child prodigy who had almost reached voting age in 1936, and John Houseman, about the same age and equally gifted though more rational when possible. After serving his apprenticeship at the Gate Theater in Dublin, after editing three Shakespeare plays, after making his Broadway debut as Tybalt in Katharine Cornell's *Romeo and Juliet* in 1934, Welles was ready to shake the living daylights out of the journeyman theater and recreate it in his own image. In the spring of 1936, he transposed *Macbeth* from Scotland to Haiti—which Shakespearc had overlooked because of his limited knowledge of geography. With Mr. Houseman's assistance ("supervision" the program rather pompously declared), Welles staged an original, lively, flaring voodoo show that delighted everyone and gave the Negro unit of the Federal Theater remarkable prestige. Then Welles and Houseman moved down to Maxine Elliott's Theater in the winter of 1937 and staged a starkly modern version of Marlowe's *Dr. Faustus* on a bare stage and with bizarre lighting effects. It would have surprised Marlowe; it fascinated Broadway and ran for six happy months.

In the spring, Welles surpassed himself. He put the Federal Theater and Actors' Equity in their places by producing a play they had both excommunicated. It was Marc Blitzstein's *The Cradle Will Rock*, a militant, proletarian drama with music—part opera, perhaps, or oratorio—which Welles had been directing for several weeks. At Maxine Elliott's, it had a full suit of scenery and an orchestra which Lehman Engel conducted. The advance ticket sale numbered fourteen thousand. The final dress rehearsal was scheduled for June 15, 1937, before an audience. But two hours before the curtain was to go up, the Washington administration of the Federal Theater closed all Federal Theater performances pending reorganization of the entire project. No one doubted that the Federal Theater administration was, in Aesopian language, banning a partisan play that might embarrass the government.

Welles was as good a showman offstage as on. He and Houseman improvised a dramatic coup that humbled the bureaucrats. When the audience started to collect outside Maxine Elliott's Theater, the actors entertained them on the sidewalk by singing songs from the show. In the meantime, Houseman, working on the telephone, made an impromptu booking at the Venice Theater (originally Al Jolson's) at Seventh Avenue and 59th Street, paying $100 down. Actors and audience then proceeded uptown in buses and taxis—in a gratifying mutinous mood. Since the scenery had to be left at Maxine Elliott's, the stage at the Venice was bare; the props consisted of a borrowed piano, on which Blitzstein played the score, and a chair, where Welles sat as master of ceremonies. To circumvent the orders from Equity, the actors bought tickets and attended as members of the audience, sitting in the audience instead of on the stage. At 9:45, the performance began. Blitzstein sang some of the songs. Welles supplied the continuity. Actors popped up from various parts of the auditorium to sing or act their scenes, and orchestral instruments tooted and squealed wherever the players happened to be seated.

The performance was a rousing success—partly because of the scandalous circumstances but, as later productions indicated, basically because of the astringent score, the biting lyrics and the graphic simplicity of the production. It ran ten nights at the Venice Theater at a $1.00 top. In December, it had three Sunday-night performances at the Mercury Theater with the actors in street dress seated in three rows of chairs onstage. Beginning the next January, it had a run of 108 performances at the Windsor Theater in 48th Street. It was again presented at the City Center on November 24, 1947, in a theater sponsored by the City of New York. A month later, it was put on at the Mansfield Theater on the night of the heaviest snowfall of the century, with a notable cast that included Alfred Drake, Will Geer, Vivian Vance, Dennis King, Jr., and Muriel Smith. *The Cradle Will Rock* is the classic proletarian musical drama. Since a proletariat does not exist either on Broadway or in America, the play has never reached the masses. But it is cherished by music lovers and by playgoers who admire the theater arts.

Having taught the United States government a lesson, Welles and Houseman proceeded to establish a theater of their own on Broadway. They leased the little Comedy Theater in 41st Street between Broadway and Sixth Avenue, where the Washington Square Players had once appeared, and renamed it the Mercury Theater. On November 11, 1937, Welles and Houseman opened with a modern-dress production of *Julius Caesar*, set against the brick back wall of the theater and with wooden steps and a wooden platform. The play was offered as an anti-Fascist tract, but since Julius Caesar was presented as the Fascist, many people were confused. To them it seemed like a pro-Fascist play, but Welles contended that Brutus—the part he played—was the crucial character; Brutus, according to Welles, represented the fatuous, stupid, weary liberal who did not realize that something hideous was absorbing him. The Mercury *Julius Caesar*, which had 157 performances, urged liberals to stop Hitler and Mussolini at once. No one questioned the plain vitality of the production, but many people were confused by its ideology.

Everything about the Mercury Theater was novel and daring; it was excellent theater even when it failed at the box office. In the winter of 1938, it put on Thomas Dekker's droll and bawdy *The Shoemaker's Holiday*, just 338 years after its première in London. It was hilarious, with a sparkling cast that included George Coulouris, Frederic Tozere, Joseph Cotten, Vincent Price, Whitford Kane, Norman Lloyd, Hiram Sherman, Elliott Reid, Edith Barrett, Marian Warring-Manley, and Ruth Ford. The finest actors were willing to work with Welles. There were two more Mercury productions—Shaw's *Heartbreak House*, in which Welles played Captain Shotover and thrilled everyone—including himself—with awful prophecies of doom, and *Danton's Death*, in which he played St. Just, an inhuman demagogue. Since the background consisted of hundreds of evil little faces painted on a drop, the production looked macabre and ominous. But the acting lacked movement, and *Danton's Death* lasted only twenty-one performances—an anticlimax for a theater that had begun with a whoop of exhilarating ideas. After *Danton's Death*, the Mercury Theater closed its doors permanently.

When the Mercury succumbed to reality, Welles took himself and some of his fellow Mercurians to Hollywood, where he simultaneously made *Citizen Kane*, a profit, and an uproar—all essentials of good showmanship. But success did not corrupt Welles. Back on Broadway in 1945, he staged a gigantic musical drama based on Jules Verne's *Around the World in Eighty Days*, with music and lyrics by Cole Porter, carloads of scenery, and the signature of "a Mercury Production." It was a disaster. When he compiled his next tax return, Welles claimed a deduction of $350,000 for his personal losses in the show. When the government auditors disallowed it, Welles recognized an old conspiracy. After trying to deprive him of *The Cradle Will Rock* nine years earlier, the government now proposed to deprive him of his debts. Welles renounced the United States and took his genius abroad. Subsequently, the government, which knew its place, made more civil arrangements. It could not bear the thought of being cut off from Welles entirely. It let him return to America occasionally to make films and television appearances.

Having less money to lose, Houseman remained in America, made an excellent film of *Julius Caesar*, redeemed the Stratford, Connecticut, Shakespeare Festival from chronic provinciality, and directed an enlightened professional theater program on the Los Angeles campus of the University of California. Orphans of the depression, Welles and Houseman came to Broadway emptyhanded and endowed the American theater handsomely. They gave it talent and imagination at a time when the nation needed both.

Amid the encircling gloom of the depression and preparations for war, a quiet man with an enormous fund of knowledge spoke some inspired words about the human race. He was Thornton Wilder, scholar, teacher, novelist, author of several disarming little plays, and a conversationalist who instructed and delighted his friends. In 1928, he had received the Pulitzer Prize for an exotic novel called *The Bridge of San Luis Rey*. The plays he had written were like fables—*The Happy Journey to Trenton and Camden, The Long Christmas Dinner, Pullman Car Hiawatha*. Except for the shy wisdom that irradiated them, they seemed naïve and childlike.

Although Wilder had always enjoyed going to the theater, he felt that something fundamental was lacking in the drama. Its truth did not seem to him to be the truth he knew. He believed that the theater should awaken not superficial sentiments but the inner truths of the universe that every human being inherits and carries around in the recesses of his mind —not factual truth, but truth of human experience; mythology, perhaps. His phrase for it was "the recollection within us." As a student and man of letters, Wilder had accumulated more philosophical wisdom than any other person writing for Broadway. He was in the tradition of Plato, Goethe, Santayana, W. H. Auden. Success was not his motive. He was concerned with destiny.

In 1938, he wrote a play of childlike simplicity that took a mature view of mankind. To avoid the appearance of realism in *Our Town*, Wilder dispensed with the proscenium curtain and scenery. There were a few props—chairs mostly, two ladders, two incidental arched trellises with vines and flowers. But there was no scenery that defined a place. The stage manager, who performed the function of master of ceremonies, described the scenery in his introductory remarks, and the audience constructed the scenery in its head.

The program asserted that *Our Town* portrayed Grover's Corners, New Hampshire, from 1901 to 1913. But the universe was the real setting. "This is the way we were in the provinces north of New York at the beginning of the twentieth century. This is the way we were: in our growing up and in our marrying and in our living and in our dying," the stage manager observed. During the first two acts, which were concerned with the casual life of a small community, *Our Town* was tender, humorous, and beguiling. Evil was not part of Wilder's mythology; the native impulses of his characters were good. In the last act, set in the local cemetery and suggested by Dante's *Purgatory*, *Our Town* became an almost unbearable elegy on the loneliness of the dead. With all its compassion and faith, *Our Town* gave its audiences a moving experience. Jed Harris, who had staged the raucous *Broadway* twelve years earlier, staged *Our Town* with a soft beauty that looked less like a Broadway play than a tone poem. The acting was sensitive and unassuming. As the stage manager, Frank Craven was a sublimation of the smalltown sage—artless, familiar, colloquial. The young neighbors who married in the second act were acted with unsophisticated modesty by Martha Scott and John Craven. The parents were played with warmth and pride by Evelyn Varden, Jay Fasset, Helen Carew, and Thomas Ross.

Our Town was not received with much enthusiasm at first. During the Boston tryout, the theater was so empty that the producer canceled the

rest of the booking. In New York, where it opened at Henry Miller's
Theater, the press notices were divided. Audiences did not come in numbers until the play received the Pulitzer Prize. (The Critics Circle award
that season was for John Steinbeck's *Of Mice and Men*.) But after Broadway had adjusted to the purity of Wilder's vision of life, the play ran for
336 performances and became a classic, played somewhere in the world
every night of the week. At a bleak moment in Broadway history, an unassuming writer with mind and spirit expressed confidence in the human
race.

Four years later, the public mood was worse. The nation was at war.
The armies of the world had assembled at Armageddon, and some of the
cities of the nations had fallen. But Wilder, who joined the Air Force the
same year, was not despondent. Looking back on the long history of the
human race and noting what it had accomplished by applying intelligence
to its problems, he retained his belief in the future. *The Skin of Our Teeth*,
which opened in November of 1942, was a cartoon of the story of mankind.
It was a bit too clever and facetious. Some of the jokes it played on itself
and on the audience were self-conscious. But it made an optimistic statement about mankind's stubborn ability to pick itself up after disaster and
blunder forward. After the end of a war unidentified in the play, Sabina,
the legendary courtesan, grumbled: "That's all we do—always beginning
again! Over and over again. Always beginning again. How do we know that
it'll be any better than before? Why do we go on pretending? Some day
the whole earth's going to have to turn cold anyway, and until that time
all these other things'll be happening again: it will be more wars and more
walls of ice and floods and earthquakes." Wilder had no grandiose an-
swers. But Mrs. Antrobus, the representative housewife in the play, made
this homely rejoinder: "Now, Sabina, I've let you talk long enough. I
don't want to hear any more of it. . . . I could live for seventy years in a
cellar and make soup out of grass and bark, without ever doubting that this
world has a work to do and will do it. . . . So we'll start putting this house
to rights. Now, Sabina, go and see what you can do in the kitchen."

Not everyone liked *The Skin of Our Teeth*. Some disliked it so heartily
that they walked out during the intermission, fuming and groaning. The
bizarre form was difficult. Wilder said that his play was indebted to
Joyce's *Finnegans Wake*—never the most lucid of books. But *The Skin of
Our Teeth* was one of the first dramas that Elia Kazan directed, and the
performance had the bold form and resounding impact of his personal
style. It was acted with comic extravagance by a notable company that included Tallulah Bankhead, Florence Eldridge, Florence Reed, Fredric

March, E. G. Marshall, and Montgomery Clift. It had 359 performances. In a frightened world that lived from day to day, Wilder instinctively took the long view.

In the autumn of 1938, when *Our Town* had only recently closed, Wilder's second play, *The Merchant of Yonkers,* was produced under the inept staging of Max Reinhardt. It had only thirty-nine performances before it succumbed to the boredom of Broadway. *The Merchant of Yonkers* was restaged in 1955 as *The Matchmaker,* under Tyrone Guthrie's direction with Ruth Gordon and Eileen Herlie in the principal parts. It succeeded very well indeed and later became the book for an interminable song-and-dance show called *Hello, Dolly!.* It was ironic that Wilder's biggest hit had none of his personal quality. He was best when New York was lowest in mind.

ALL THE SOUNDS
ON THE STAGE
ARE LIKE MUSIC

From a scholarly point of view, the musical show may be more legitimate then the spoken drama. If the art of theater began with tribal festivals, with singing, dancing, pantomine, mummery, and celebration in primitive times, the musical show retains more of the original ingredients and spirit than the spoken drama. What the spoken drama has gained in form and mind, it has lost in scope and variety.

After *Show Boat* in 1927 had demonstrated the value of integrating music with characters and story, the standard musical comedy began to look blowzy. It had an increasingly hackneyed appearance after *Of Thee I Sing* and *Porgy and Bess* used music to express ideas or points of view about human beings. It was no longer exciting to see a squad of chorus girls prancing in front-dress formation at curtain-rise or to hear them screaming an unintelligible song while the audience was getting settled. On the traditional stage, no smart songwriter wasted his talent on an

ary Martin in *South Pacific* (1949).
he New York Public Library)

opening number or on an "ice-breaker" song, which came a few minutes later and tried to reduce the audience to sobriety. The songwriter husbanded his genius for the songs that could be hummed by the departing audience and sung in restaurants. The score did not have to have continuity or momentum.

The chorus girls who began the show and kept sweeping through it were likely to be attractive young women, but few of them knew anything about dancing or singing. They were aspects of carnival—young, healthy, and lively, and for the most part, commonplace. In the first decade of the century, they were paid an average of $20 a week and were required to provide their own shoes and stockings. They were also required to work without pay during the rehearsal period, which might be eight weeks long. At the beginning of the actors' strike in 1919, Frank Gillmore had promised that if the strike was won they would no longer have to provide their own shoes and stockings. That turned out to be the truth. When the strike was settled, the minimum pay for chorus girls was $30 a week in New York and $35 out of town. They were to rehearse free for four weeks, draw half pay the next two weeks, and full pay thereafter. By 1930, chorus girls of any distinction were being paid from $50 to $75 a week. Ziegfeld and his competitors paid an average of $100 a week, and as much as $200 a week to the dazzlers. If any chorus girl had talent, she soon became a specialist or an actress. Elsie Ferguson, Jeanne Eagels, Fannie Brice, and Helen Broderick graduated from the chorus line to stage-center. They began their stage careers in shows saturated in mediocrity.

The standard musical show lingered for more than a decade for two reasons. First, some gifted composers wrote some memorable songs for shows that had no other distinction. *No, No, Nanette* was almost unbearably "charming" in 1923, but one of the songs Vincent Youmans wrote for it, "Tea for Two," captivated New York and eventually the nation. That was all the success a songwriter hoped for. Rudolf Friml's *Rose Marie* in 1924 was hokum, but his "Indian Love Call" drenched the town in banal musical mystery. The written material for *Lady Be Good* in 1924 was worthless, but George Gershwin's title song, with its descending refrain, delighted everybody, and his "Fascinating Rhythm" has outlived the show and him. In 1929, the book for *Spring Is Here* was claptrap, but Richard Rodgers' glowing "With a Song in My Heart" was irresistible. Nobody can remember the theme of *Gay Divorce* in 1932, but no one can forget Cole Porter's rueful melody he called "Night and Day." Jerome Kern had invented the modern musical drama in *Show Boat*, but as late as 1931, he was squandering the melody of "The Night Was Made for

Love" on the old-fashioned hocus-pocus of *The Cat and the Fiddle*. And as late as 1939, he was imposing a lovely song called "All the Things You Are" on the humbug of *Very Warm for May*. The revolution on the musical stage was torpid. Even after the modern musical drama had demonstrated its superiority and inevitability, the standard musical comedy or revue satisfied songwriters who had no real understanding of theater. It also satisfied the great masses of theatergoers.

The second reason the standard musical show lingered was more positive. Since the books consisted of contrived stage situations, the standard musical shows provided the perfect platforms for superb comedians and entertainers. W. C. Fields, Bobby Clark and Paul McCullough, Fannie Brice, Al Jolson, Eddie Cantor, Ed Wynn, Bert Lahr, the Marx Brothers, Joe Cook, Willie Howard, Jimmy Durante had energy, skill, and a wild streak of humor that convulsed and delighted the public. They were more theatrical than Sothern and Marlowe or Ethel Barrymore, for the musical show was more theatrical than the spoken drama. A *Ziegfeld Follies* without W. C. Fields, Bert Williams, Ed Wynn, or Will Rogers was unthinkable. The standard musical comedy, *Sinbad*, which ran for two years, was written expressly to display the brashness and clamor of Al Jolson. "You ain't heard nothin' yet," he would tell the audience after bellowing a song that deafened them. Without Bobby Clark and Fannie Brice running, shouting, and leering as Adam and Eve, there would have been no *Music Box Revue of 1928*. All these mountebanks or minstrels were the quintessence of theater, because they had been born with magnetism, humor, and enthusiasm. They learned their craft, but they had been born with the essentials.

W. C. Fields was the most formidable. A portly figure with grayish blond hair, a scraggly black mustache, small vulpine eyes, and a reedy voice, he was always in earnest. As a juggler, a pool-table wizard, or a petty crook, he was deliberate and serious; what he did was wild, but he did it with sobriety. He had a splendid sense of propriety. As a dentist in a *Vanities*, he once leaned down over the chair to perform some act of merciful surgery when a bird flew out of his patient's beard. Fields knew the etiquette for that situation. Clapping a hunter's cap on his head, he snatched up a rifle and shot the bird. Also, he always said the right thing. As a woodsman coming into a log cabin out of a furious snowstorm, he observed: "It ain't a fit night out for man or beast," contributing a phrase to the American language. As a smalltown thief, he was about to rob a sleeping cowboy. He changed his mind when he discovered that the cowboy was wearing a revolver. "It would be dishonest," he virtuously remarked as he tiptoed away. Everything Fields did was logical. The premises of the action might be absurd; the action was that of a man of intellect and probity.

Since Clark and McCullough came from the circus, they were running clowns; they were always in motion even when they were standing still. Bobby Clark, a thin short man, wore a flat hat and a cavernous topcoat, and he carried a cane and a cigar that he popped in and out of his mouth with superhuman dexterity. He painted the rims of absurdly big glasses around his eyes, and he exuded mischief. Paul McCullough, the taller of the two, was the stooge. He wore a raccoon coat, a flat straw hat, and a toothbrush moustache; and his function was to point with pride and incredulity at his mobile partner. Clark and McCullough were boyhood chums who had taken lessons in tumbling in a local Y.M.C.A. and learned how to play the bugle, which became part of their act. They were uproarious low comedians. When they thought the lion in the cage with them was a prop lion they tormented him with great bravado, winking at the audience roguishly. When the lion turned out to be real, they ran around the cage at terrible speed, desperately looking for an exit.

But it was not all fun and games for McCullough. In 1936, he shocked Broadway by taking his own life. Most people assumed it would be the end of the fabulous act. But Clark continued by himself for another twenty years. Offstage he was a serious man with very little personal humor and a businesslike attitude towards the stage. He longed to play in the classics. At various stages of his career, he played Ben in Congreve's *Love for Love*, Bob Acres in Sheridan's *The Rivals*, and M. Jourdain in an English version of Molière's *Le Bourgeois Gentilhomme*. Clark was so exuberantly comic that he blew the plays off the stage. It was impossible for him to play with discretion. He was the king of the running fools, and the musical stage of the twenties and thirties was just right for him.

When Ed Wynn became celebrated enough to have his own show, he dubbed himself "the perfect fool." He dressed in extravagant costumes, with hats that were either too big or too small. He wore large tortoise-shell glasses under eyebrows that were highly arched in a state of constant surprise. He lisped. He was not a wit but a storyteller. Blundering around the stage with a piece of rope in his hand, he confided to the audience that he must either have found some rope or lost a horse. He had foolish tantrums. When the prop man could not understand what Wynn meant by the term "egg-wiped," Wynn obligingly spelled it for him—"e–g–y–p–t."

He invented an eye shield on a typewriter carriage that made eating grape-fruit safe. He giggled at the audience in embarrassment. When he talked, he used his hands eloquently to point up the earnestness of his intentions. By 1930, he had achieved the peak of his Broadway career—*Simple Simon*, with a score by Rodgers and Hart, fifty-three other actors, and a production staged by Ziegfeld. There was a winning purity about Ed Wynn—purity of method as well as material. He made a point of innocence, and won his audiences with beguiling nonsense; he did not try to conquer them with wit.

In 1924, a great comedy team appeared in an awful musical comedy. The Four Marx Brothers opened in a ramshackle musical called, for no discernible reason, *I'll Say She Is*, which contained most of the horseplay they had invented during eight lean years on the vaudeville circuits. They were anarchists; they destroyed everything they did with a wisecrack or a slap. They were uproarious in person. For a few merry years, until Hollywood absorbed them, the rickety structure of the old-fashioned musical comedy sustained their mutinous behavior, in *The Cocoanuts*, by George S. Kaufman, with music and lyrics by Irving Berlin, in 1925, and *Animal Crackers*, by Kaufman and Morrie Ryskind, lyrics and music by Bert Kalmar and Harry Ruby, in 1928. The writers provided a rough working formula that served the Marx Brothers for years. It included the society lady whose dignity the comedians outraged. The songwriters provided the customary musical interludes. But neither the plot nor the music was important. When *The Cocoanuts* was being beaten into shape on the road, Berlin unwillingly agreed to cut some of his songs, one of which was "Always," one of the best ballads he ever wrote. Nothing could withstand these free-wheeling zanies. The writers complained that the Marxes paid less and less attention to the lines as the show went on. "I may be wrong," Kaufman said acidly when he once revisited *The Cocoanuts*, "but I think I just heard one of the original lines."

Groucho was the most articulate of the four brothers. Slightly stooped, clad in a swallowtailed coat with a cigar and a painted moustache, he looked at the audience in astonishment and dismay and tossed puns over the footlights contemptuously. Harpo was the maniac mime with the carrot-colored wig, a stick with a rubber-bulb horn that he squeezed when he was feeling high and a series of tortured facial expressions that carried him out of this world. He never spoke, but he played the harp with lyricism, if not according to the rules. Chico was the little guy with a fake Italian accent and a style of piano playing that was syncopated but unorthodox. His left hand was functional, but his right hand could play not only music but piano tricks that were bright and flippant. Zeppo, the straight man, obligingly plodded his way through the tornado that his three brothers blew up. His common sense and good manners looked so pale by contrast that he finally stepped out of the act and devoted himself to a quiet life and rational business.

After *The Cocoanuts*, the Marx Brothers moved to Hollywood, where their working schedule was less merciless than it had been on Broadway. They made money and a world-wide reputation. But they lost the ecstasy of their performances on Broadway. The limitless spaces of the screen and the realism of the screen settings made something mechanical out of something that originally had been spontaneous and inspired. Inside the boxlike structure of Broadway stages, the buffoonery of the Marx Brothers was explosive. The standard musical show gave them a perfect setting. It was the right atmosphere for fantasy, and on Broadway they were fantastic.

The last of the great clowns assaulted Broadway in 1928. *Hold Everything*, by B. G. DeSylva and John McGowan (songs and lyrics by Lew Brown, DeSylva, and Ray Henderson), was not written: it was assembled from a shed of spare parts. And so was *Flying High*, two years later. But both of these routine shows served their purpose by giving Bert Lahr a public platform for his bulbous nose, his crossed eyes, his bellows of anguish and his groaning capers around the stage. God must have laughed when Lahr was born. In *Hold Everything*, he was a prizefighter who was easily floored. In *Flying High*, he was an airplane pilot who had never learned how to bring a plane down for a landing. (Among his colleagues in that show, the most boisterous singer was Kate Smith of the grand manner and the hearty voice. She hated being stooge for a clown. To compound the indignity, he called her Etna in reference to her size.) During the performance of *Hold Everything*, Bert Lahr was discovered with his clown's head poked out of a steambath that was parboiling him. A roar of laughter filled the Broadhurst Theater. It was obvious at that moment that Broadway had acquired a great mountebank. Lahr regarded himself as a comic actor. Eventually, he played Bottom in Shakespeare's *A Midsummer Night's Dream*, the cowardly lion in the screen version of *The Wizard of Oz*, and Estragon in *Waiting for Godot*. As the musical drama superseded the standard musical comedy and revue, the last of the great clowns found fewer and less glamorous places in which he could play the fool. "Gnong, gnong, gnong" was the throttled sound he made for the doom he was always seeing over his shoulder in musical comedies. Since he was a bundle of neuroses and apprehension, he was not surprised when Broadway drifted away from him.

There were other memorable comics. In 1928, the team of Clayton, Jackson, and Durante hustled out of the nightclubs into the Ziegfeld *Show Girl,* and in 1930 into *The New Yorkers,* which had a smart score by Cole Porter. Jimmy Durante's exuberant illiteracy kept on convulsing America for many years after he left Broadway and moved to Hollywood. In the same year, Joe Cook sauntered in and out of *Fine and Dandy,* explaining with an earnestness that became more and more insane why he could not imitate four Hawaiians playing the ukulele. He also demonstrated an ingenious machine that cracked walnuts, filled paper bags with air, punctured a toy balloon, scratched his back, and punched his stooge, Dave Chasen, in the jaw. Joe was amazingly accomplished: he could pitch knives, shoot clay pigeons, walk the slack wire, juggle Indian clubs with his hands and feet, rope steers, play the banjo, and blow the trumpet.

In 1924, *André Charlot's Revue* came to New York from London and brought, among other gifts, Gertrude Lawrence, an inexhaustible virtuoso actress, and Beatrice Lillie, a comic genius. A slight, elegant lady with sharp features, a modish personality and a small, tight, abashed grin, Miss Lillie had an incomparable gift for raillery. She overwhelmed the audience, not by broad strokes, but by gleams and grimaces. Her mind was hard, and it was always far ahead of the audiences. It hated sentimentality, pretentiousness, and buncombe. Standing a little to one side of the main action, she undermined everything by the bright irradiations of her intelligence. She could turn a sentimental ballad about the fairies at the bottom of her garden into a devastating comment on the whole range of culture. The standard musical show was the most comfortable home she ever had, and it was a privilege to visit her there. There is something both frustrating and paradoxical about the fact that, after the musical stage became more intelligent, there was less and less room for the most intelligent comedienne Broadway ever had.

It is difficult to discuss the career of Irving Berlin without a certain awe. Son of a poor immigrant family that came to New York to escape the pogroms of Russia, a vagrant on the Bowery who sang for nickels, dimes, and meals, a songwriter who never had a musical education and never learned to play the piano except in the key of F sharp, he is nevertheless America's first songwriter. No one else has written so many songs that have set so many Americans joyfully singing over so many years. There is some sort of mystery here. Why should one man without a musical background, without training or guidance or formal education in his youth write with such universal eloquence and speak so directly to the hearts of so many Americans, while hundreds of better prepared music writers reach no one? His colleague, Jerome Kern, once made some comments that define the nature of Berlin's talents: "He honestly absorbs the vibrations emanating from the people, manners and life of his time and in turn gives these impressions back to the world—simplified, glorified, clarified."

On Cherry Street, Berlin was known as Izzy Baline. When he was fourteen years old, he ran away from home and bummed around the Bowery. He became a singing waiter at Nigger Mike's saloon at 12 Pell Street. When the saloon was empty at night, he tried to teach himself how to play the piano. By 1909, he was close enough to the fringes of songwriting to publish the first song for which he wrote the lyrics. (Total royalties, 37¢.) It was called "Marie from Sunny Italy," and the first verse was as follows:

> Oh, Marie, 'neath the window I'm waiting,
> Oh, Marie, please don't be so aggravating.
> Can't you see my heart just yearns for you, dear,
> With fond affection and love that's true, dear. *

Two years later, Berlin was in show business. He was writing both the music and the lyrics for popular songs. He wrote "Alexander's Ragtime Band" and "The Grizzly Bear" that year. Having begun with songs that appealed to everyone, he went on to "When the Midnight Choo-choo Leaves for Alabam'," "My Wife's Gone to the Country," "I Want to Go Back to Michigan," "The International Rag," and many others. In 1914, he wrote the songs for *Watch Your Step*, in which Vernon and Irene Castle, were starred; and in 1915, for *Stop, Look and Listen*, in which the sizzling Gaby Deslys appeared. "I Love a Piano" and "The Ragtime Melody" were parts of that show.

By the time the U.S.A. shocked Broadway by drafting Berlin into the army, he was so rich and eminent that he had a personal valet. He did not take his valet with him to Camp Upton, where he had the rank of an enlisted man and access to a piano; the valet waited on him in New York whenever Berlin got a pass. Although he did not trouble the Germans, he

* "Marie From Sunny Italy," words by Irving Berlin, music by M. Nicholson, copyright 1907 by Jos. W. Stern & Co. Copyright renewed 1934 by Irving Berlin. Reprinted by permission of Irving Berlin Music Corporation.

was able to carry on his profession without being court-martialed. He wrote "Oh, How I Hate to Get Up in the Morning" and "K-K-K-Katy," which were among the songs in the revue he wrote called *Yip, Yip, Yaphank*, which appeared on Broadway in 1918, just in time to win the war.

Berlin was then and for the rest of his life an important man in show business. But he has always been songwriter for the nation. When he was anxiously courting Ellin Mackay, who ultimately became his wife, he took America into his confidence. "What'll I Do?" "All Alone," and "Always" expressed his personal emotions and also the emotions of every romantic young man. Although he wrote "God Bless America" for one of the *Ziegfeld Follies,* he withdrew it because he thought a patriotic song was out of key in a spectacular girl show. Twenty years later, in 1938, Kate Smith sang it on the radio for an Armistice Night celebration, and it has been part of the musical literature of America ever since. Broadway was his workshop. But he has always talked directly to America. In some inscrutable fashion, he has the genius of America in his bloodstream and in his head.

The revue format suited him prefectly. In revues, some of which had topics but none of which had plots, he could retain the freedom of a songwriter to whom tunes and words were the first considerations. In 1919, he gave the *Ziegfeld Follies* its theme song in "A Pretty Girl Is Like a Melody." That had not been his intention, but again his instinct for the right song at the right time and in the right place gave it special significance. Berlin wrote the songs for four *Music Box Revues* in the next decade. In the dismal thirties, he captured the somber public mood in the most characteristic depression song, "Let's Have Another Cup o' Coffee," in Moss Hart's *Face the Music,* in 1932. The next year, he contributed several distinguished songs to Hart's *As Thousands Cheer,* which had a brilliant cast headed by Ethel Waters, Marilyn Miller, Clifton Webb, and Helen Broderick. The basic rhythm and the cocky style of "Easter Parade" epitomized that annual ritual; it became the theme-song of the Easter fashion show. Ethel Waters had frankness, vitality, and grinning good humor that gave audiences complete confidence in anything she did. Berlin wrote three superb songs for her—the mischievous "Heat Wave" (she started the heat wave by making her seat wave), the nostalgic, affectionate "Harlem on My Mind," and the poignantly tragic "Supper Time," in which the widow of a Negro who had been lynched had to tell their children that he would never come home again. Amid the jubilant festivities of an opulent Broadway show, that was a bitter number. But it was relevant; it showed taste and humanity in a man whose talent had room for everyone.

During the war years, Berlin did his bit for a second time by writing and appearing in *This Is the Army* ("This Is the Army, Mr. Jones" and a reprise of "Oh, How I Hate To Get Up in the Morning" were the most idiomatic songs). In 1946, he made the most important transition in his career. He accepted, not without misgivings, an assignment to compose the music for a modern musical play, substituting for Jerome Kern, who had died in November of 1945. Dorothy and Herbert Fields had written a rousing story about the adventures of Annie Oakley, the celebrated markswoman who performed in Buffalo Bill's Wild West Show. Rodgers and Hammerstein, who were to be the producers, asked Berlin to compose the music for *Annie Get Your Gun.*

Berlin was not sure that, after a long career as an independent song-writer, he could compose an integrated score that would define character, carry forward the momentum of a story, and retain the interest of the audience. The score he wrote turned out to be his richest and one of the most entertaining scores by anyone—"Doin' What Comes Natur'lly," "You Can't Get a Man With a Gun," "Anything You Can Do," "They Say It's Wonderful," "I Got the Sun in the Morning," and "There's No Business Like Show Business." Ethel Merman was the star. Her brass-band voice, her infectious sense of rhythm, and her razzle-dazzle perform-ing gave the songs remarkable beat and relish. But if Berlin had not written the songs with relish, as well as originality, she could not have overwhelmed audiences for 1,147 performances. That was the longest run of any Berlin show, and it came towards the end of his long and honorable career as a songwriter. His next two musical comedies, *Miss Liberty* and *Call Me Madam*, did not have such long runs, although "They Like Ike" in *Call Me Madam* opened the campaign for Eisenhower two years before his election. Songwriters have more political power than most delegates to the conventions.

Although Cole Porter's background was the opposite of Irving Berlin's, his experience was similar. He was a clever and inventive songwriter, who late in his career faced the challenge of scoring a well-written musical comedy in a modern format. He discovered, as Berlin had, that he had more talent than he had realized.

Cole Porter was born in Peru, Indiana, in 1891, son of a possessive and dominating mother, grandson of a rich lumber merchant who wanted an heir to his business. Porter's whole life was that of a pampered playboy. In his youth, his mother insisted on his studying the piano and violin. By the time he was ten, he was writing music, and his mother proudly published one piece called "The Bobolink Waltz." Since he was bored with Indiana, he was overjoyed when his mother sent him east to attend school at Worcester Academy in Massachusetts and then to Yale. He was not the soberest of students, but he did make one lasting contribution to the culture of Yale. He wrote a football song, with lyrics that are easy to remember: "Bulldog, bulldog, bow-wow-wow, Eli Yale."

To gratify his grandfather, who wanted a lawyer in the family, Porter went on to the Harvard Law School. A fellow student, T. Lawrason Riggs, and he put aside their law books long enough in 1916 to write a Broadway musical called *See America First*, intended to satirize the flamboyant jingoism of George M. Cohan. Although Clifton Webb, the dancer who ultimately became a comedy actor, made his debut in it, *See America First* got a bad press and only fifteen performances. Both of the authors were very much depressed. Riggs abandoned Broadway permanently and became a priest. Porter had a gayer idea. He went to Paris and joined the French Legion; when the United States entered the war, he transferred to the French Army. Stationed at Fontainebleau, he was close enough to Paris to escape the privations of war and to keep an eye on the kind of civilization that he found exactly to his taste. After the war, he studied music seriously with Vincent d'Indy and studied pleasure on his own time.

In 1919, he returned to America to ask his grandfather to increase his allowance. On shipboard, he met Raymond Hitchcock, who was sufficiently impressed with the songs Porter played and sang to commission him to write the music for the third edition of the *Hitchy-Koo* shows. It opened on Broadway in October, for fifty-six performances. One member of the cast was Joe Cook, who made his debut with a Porter song called "When I Had a Uniform On." One of the songs, "An Old-Fashioned Garden," was a hit. But Porter had no idea of wasting his talent on a Broadway career. Returning to Paris, he married a rich and congenial American woman, Linda Lee Thomas, and both of them devoted most of the next nine years to enjoying international society on a lavish scale. They were the avant garde of the jeunesse doré. They squandered talent, enthusiasm, and money on enjoying themselves and their friends. Porter entertained them with clever songs that he sang and played. He used his gift as a parlor trick. He put pleasure ahead of show business.

Porter had the best of two worlds—the giddy world of the rich on both sides of the Atlantic (he was willing to be called rich but he disliked being referred to as wealthy), and the giddy world of Broadway. While he was skipping from one party to another in Europe, he also wrote some brilliant songs for routine musical shows. His songs were pensive, clever,

THE GREATEST RIFLESH
IN THE WORLD

Catfish Row in *Porgy and Bess* (1935). (*Vandamm*)

Ethel Merman in *Annie Get Your Gun* (1946). (*Vandamm*)

and worldly by turns, with the romance bittersweet and the impudence brassy. No one could write lyrics as ingenious and naughty—and, on occasion—as civilized as he could: "I've Got Quelque Chose" and "Let's Do It" for the amorous Irene Bordoni, in 1928; "What Is This Thing Called Love?" for *Wake Up and Dream,* in 1929; "Night and Day" for *Gay Divorce,* in 1932. In 1934, in *Anything Goes,* which was a fabulous show, Ethel Merman collaborated with him: that is, she sang his music magnificently. For *Anything Goes,* he wrote a virtuoso portfolio of songs in varied style and with sophisticated lyrics: "All Through the Night," "I Get a Kick out of You," "You're the Top," "Anything Goes," and "Blow, Gabriel, Blow." When he was writing a song, Porter first decided on the rhythm and the lyrics, and then the tune to express them. No one else could play with rhymes as capriciously as Porter could; as in

> Flying too high
> With some guy
> In the sky
> Is my i-dea of nothing to do.
> Yet I get a kick out of you.*

His musical sources were fresh and extensive. While sailing around the world on a cruise in the *Franconia* with Moss Hart, in 1935, he heard an exotic native melody that resulted in "Begin the Beguine." Although Porter was the most sophisticated of songwriters, he had taste in art as well as knowledge of his craft, and he brought fresh ideas to Broadway from unexploited corners of the world. No one else could have written "The Kling-Kling Bird on the Divi-Divi Tree," based on music Porter heard in Jamaica.

He was saturated in luxury, success, acclaim, and enjoyment. His career proved that the legend of the industrious apprentice was a fraud. In 1937, fate struck him a foul blow. A horse he was riding on Long Island shied, reared up, and fell backwards. Porter could not extricate himself from the stirrups. The horse broke one of Porter's legs by rolling on it; then he broke the other by rolling on the other side. Both of Porter's legs were broken in so many places that the doctors recommended amputating both of them at once. But Mrs. Porter refused; she believed that amputation would destroy his morale permanently. She knew how much personal pride lurked under his insouciance. Throughout the next few years, he was in constant pain; eventually he had to submit to a total of thirty-one operations.

But Mrs. Porter was right. Whatever his private feelings may have been, Porter maintained his familiar demeanor of gaiety and friendliness. Both of the Porters continued their busy social life. When the casts were to be removed from Porter's legs, five hundred friends attended a festive "coming out party" at the Waldorf Astoria. He continued to attend first-night performances; two men carried him down the aisle to his seat. Later he was able to make his way slowly down the aisle on two canes, and then on one. He never gave up the life he believed in. In 1938, only a year after the accident, he wrote the score for *Leave It to Me*. It included the sardonic, disingenuous "My Heart Belongs to Daddy," with which Mary Martin began her Broadway career.

During the next ten years, never wholly free from pain, Porter wrote the songs for six Broadway musicals, living as splendidly as before. When he went on the road with a new show, he headed a royal procession. Every comfort was attended to. He brought paintings—Picassos and Dalis—to hang on the walls of his hotel rooms. He gave gifts on a princely scale. When his wife bought an estate in Williamstown, Massachusetts, he investigated rumors that an elderly farm woman who was painting original pictures nearby had considerable talent. Grandma Moses was only a local curiosity then. Porter bought twenty of her canvases and gave them as Christmas presents to friends. When the art world later accepted Grandma Moses as a genuine artist, some of the friends to whom Porter had sent her early works scrambled around to find them to hang in their livingrooms.

But the songs Porter was writing during this period had lost dash and impudence. He was no longer the wonderboy of the thirties, when his cleverness with music and lyrics had been almost blinding. In 1948, Sam and Bella Spewack, who had written the libretto for *Leave It to Me*, brought him the script of a thoroughly organized musical play based on Shakespeare's *The Taming of the Shrew*. *Kiss Me, Kate*, as it was called, was a complex prank in which three-dimensional characters were involved in a coherent story. Faced with the discipline of having to write to express characters in definite situations, Porter, like Berlin before him, was not certain that he could do the job successfully. But he wrote his liveliest and most enduring score for the superb cast that acted and sang it on December 30, 1948. The leading actors were Alfred Drake, Patricia Morison, Lisa Kirk, and Harold Lang, and the principal musical numbers were "Another Op'nin', Another Show," "Wunderbar," "So in Love," "Brush Up Your Shakespeare," "We Open in Venice," "I Hate Men," "Too Darn Hot," "Always True to You in My Fashion," and "I've Come to Wive It Wealthily in Padua."

Although Porter was a sensitive man, he was not shy or hypocritical. Since he enjoyed the gaudy rumpus of opening-night performances, he attended his own première at the New Century Theater with a phalanx of friends. Sitting in an aisle seat, he enjoyed the show as amiably as if it were all new to him and very much to his personal taste. *Kiss Me, Kate* had 1,077 performances. It represented the triumph of a small, delicate, agreeable gentleman who refused to let physical pain cripple his spirit. (His right leg had to be amputated in 1958. That was a blow to pride and body from which he never recovered, as his wife had foreseen.)

Although the Gershwin family was not wealthy, it had enough money, as well as an enterprising mother, to give George Gershwin piano lessons. They were originally intended for Ira, the older brother, but Ira preferred words to notes. As soon as George Gershwin sat before a keyboard, he became a prodigy and remained a prodigy for the rest of his life. After acquiring a solid musical education by studying the piano works of Chopin, Liszt, and Debussy, he created a style of his own, which became the sound of the twenties; it was bizarre, audacious, and exciting. He began as a songwriter; he used the worn formula of the Broadway song-and-dance show as a framework on which to hang tunes. But like his colleagues and contemporaries, he enlarged his field with the development of the old musical show into the new musical play, and wrote organic scores for *Strike Up the Band*, George Kaufman's savage satire on war, in 1927; Kaufman's and Morrie Ryskind's satire on the humbug of national politics in *Of Thee I Sing*, in 1931; and the Kaufman and Ryskind satire on the politics of the depression in *Let 'Em Eat Cake*, in 1933. Finally, he composed the music for the superb opera, *Porgy and Bess*, in 1935. Although he lived and worked like a Broadway songwriter, he was a pioneer in modern music. He touched and enriched the musical life of the world in many places.

His father, whose original name was Morris Gershovitz, emigrated from St. Petersburg to New York in the 1890s and supported his family by running a restaurant and by operating other enterprises, including the Lafayette Baths. George Gershwin was born in 1898 at 252 Snedicker Avenue in Brooklyn. He was two years younger than his brother Ira, whose talents as a writer of lyrics and whose personal devotion became the most constructive influences in George's career. If George had followed the conventional line of a young Jewish prodigy, he might have become a concert pianist. But he was also fascinated with show business. All his life, he saw no incongruity between serious music and the theater. At fifteen, he was earning $15 a week for playing the piano and plugging songs for the firm of Jerome K. Remick, leading Tin Pan Alley publishers. (Incidentally, a 1916 photograph of 28th Street near Fifth Avenue shows the business signs of Jerome K. Remick & Co., William Morris, Whitney Warner, music publisher, and the *New York Clipper*. That is as close to a geographical base as the mythical Tin Pan Alley has ever had.)

In 1916, when he was eighteen years old, Gershwin wrote "Pretty Lady," which was interpolated into the Romberg score for the *Passing Show*. Max Dreyfus, a partner in the musical firm of T. B. Harms, employed Gershwin as a staff composer in 1918. Dreyfus was a wise and gentle man who loved music and talent; at various times he put Jerome Kern, Vincent Youmans, and Richard Rodgers on his staff. When Gershwin was twenty-one years old, he wrote the score for his first Broadway show, *La La Lucille*, which had 104 performances in 1919. His first hit tune, however, was written independently. After discussing an idea at dinner one evening, he and Irving Caesar wrote "Swanee" in fifteen minutes at the Gershwin home in Washington Heights. It was not generally noticed by most people when it was sung in a stage show at the Capitol Theater. But Al Jolson heard it and liked it. He put it into *Sinbad*, in which he was appearing at the Winter Garden across Broadway from the Capitol Theater. When he hurled it across the footlights with his customary vehemence, everyone recognized its merits, and the days of George Gershwin's apprenticeship were over.

Gershwin was a tall young man with long features that, Sir Osbert Sitwell said, composed a "handsome ram's face." He was all energy and music. He was also full of humorless self-confidence. Regarding himself as a historical figure, he used the third-person when he discussed himself. His self-confidence was neither vain nor overbearing. It was nearer to naïveté. He said that one of his mother's most admirable traits was her modesty about him. Oscar Levant, pianist, wit, and friend, once remarked sardonically, "Tell me, George, if you had it all to do over again, would you still fall in love with yourself?"

Once Gershwin had opened the doors into the theater, his head was full of musical ideas, and he filled notebooks with more musical phrases than he could ever use. Once *La La Lucille* and "Swanee" had acquainted Broadway with his talents, he wrote the music for a whole series of musical shows that were conventional in form though interesting musically. His brother Ira started writing the lyrics to George's tunes in *Lady, Be Good!*, in 1924. Ira wrote lyrics with the virtuosity of his brother, tossing around internal rhymes with the sophistication of his brother's subtle changes in tempo and key. During the next few years, the Gershwin shows were *Lady, Be Good!,* for Fred and Adele Astaire, who were just beginning their career together, *Tip Toes,* with Queenie Smith and Jeanette Mac-Donald, in 1925; *Oh, Kay!,* with Gertrude Lawrence and Victor Moore, in 1926; *Funny Face,* with the Astaires and Victor Moore, in 1927; *Treasure Girl,* in 1928, with Gertrude Lawrence, Clifton Webb, Mary Hay, and Constance Cummings; and *Girl Crazy,* with Ethel Merman, Ginger Rogers, and Willie Howard, in 1930. Miss Merman made her Broadway debut in that merry-go-round by singing "Samson and Delilah," "Boy, What Love Has Done to Me," and "I Got Rhythm" in a clarion voice that bowled Broadway over. After listening to her treatment of "I Got Rhythm," one admirer noted that she could hold a note longer than the Chase Manhattan Bank.

All these productions, and one or two others, were part of show business. Gershwin worked on them like a songwriter. At the same time, he was writing concert music that serious musicians all over the world recognized as original and significant. His concert career began in Aeolian Hall on the evening of February 12, 1924, when Paul Whiteman played Gershwin's "Rhapsody in Blue" (Ira's title) as the twenty-second piece in a program of twenty-three. When a clarinet blew that rising scream in the introduction to the rhapsody, modern music acquired a new voice. It sounded like a wild and exciting improvisation that leaped freely around the musical staff and expressed the ecstasy of jazz. The audience had not been conspicuously attentive during the first part of the concert. But it cheered "Rhapsody in Blue" and accepted Gershwin's contention that jazz is legitimate—something that many people had not agreed on at that time. "Jazz is music; it uses the same notes that Bach used," Gershwin declared. "Jazz is the result of the energy stored in America. . . . I believe that it can be made the basis of serious symphonic works of lasting value."

He turned out to be his own best example. A year later, Walter Damrosch conducted Gershwin's "Concerto in F" at Carnegie Hall. In 1928, Damrosch conducted the New York Philharmonic-Symphony Society in Gershwin's "An American in Paris." Three years later, Serge Koussevitzky conducted the Boston Symphony Orchestra in Gershwin's "Second Rhapsody." Gershwin appeared as the piano soloist in all of these pieces. His concert music revealed such command of and ingenuity in the composition of modern music that he was urged to abandon Broadway and devote all his talents to serious music. But he saw no conflict between the two. He had always enjoyed writing popular music, which brought him in touch with the kind of people he enjoyed working with. He characterized himself as a "romantic Modern."

The year 1927 was a climactic year in the Broadway musical stage. That was the year Jerome Kern's *Show Boat* opened and made a profound impression on everyone who saw and heard it. That was also the year Gershwin wrote a mordant score for George Kaufman's *Strike Up the Band*, an independent, purposeful musical satire that portrayed the United States as making war on another nation for the purpose of expanding American trade. Ira Gershwin wrote the lyrics, one of which ran as follows:

> Whoops, what a charming war,
> Whoops, what a charming war.
> It keeps you out in the open air.
> Oh, this is such a charming war, etc.
> We're glad that we're over here over there,
> We sleep in downy feather beds,
> Our contract calls for ice cream soda when the weather's hot
> And a helluva lot of publicity if we get shot.*

* "Strike Up The Band" (G. & I. Gershwin) © MCMLXX by New World Music Corp. All rights reserved. Used by permission of Warner Bros. Music.

The virulence of *Strike Up the Band* offended so many people during its two-week road career that it was taken off. America was not ready for such acid iconoclasm yet. Three years later, Morrie Ryskind revised and softened the book. Blanche Ring and Clark and McCullough were engaged to appear in it and it had 191 performances. Several of Gershwin's songs, like "A Typical Self-Made American" and "Mademoiselle in New Rochelle," had saucy rhythms that expressed the mood of the piece. But the revised book was so loose and ineffectual that the Gershwin songs and the horseplay of Clark and McCullough provided most of the entertainment.

It was not until the next year that Gershwin completely dropped the posture of songwriter and became the musical spokesman for a dramatic idea. His taut, lethal, jeering score for *Of Thee I Sing* epitomized the point of view exactly. "Wintergreen for President" ("He's the man the people choose/Loves the Irish and the Jews"), "Love Is Sweeping the Country" ("If a girl is sexy/She may be Mrs. Prexy"), "The Illegitimate Daughter" ("The illegitimate daughter of the illegitimate son of an illegitimate nephew of Napoleon"), "Of Thee I Sing, Baby" brilliantly fantasticated the vitriolic theme of the show. Gershwin's swift, complex score of chants, marches, songs, and mock serenades constituted the structure of the Kaufman and Ryskind cartoon and represented Gershwin's ability to think in terms of a disciplined musical composition.

The Pulitzer judges departed from custom by giving the prize that year to *Of Thee I Sing,* as the theater piece that best represented the "educational value and power of the stage." Since the terms of the award did not include the music, the committee did not include Gershwin's name in the official citation. The committee thought the effect of *Of Thee I Sing* would be "very considerable, because musical plays are always popular, and by injecting satire and point into them, a very large public is reached." But they ignored the music of a musical play. Although "Wintergreen for President" turned out to be more enduring than the libretto, the brilliant author of the music was not among those memorialized in the award festivities.

One night in 1926, when Gershwin came home from an unsatisfactory rehearsal of *Oh, Kay!,* he picked up and read DuBose Heyward's novel entitled *Porgy.* It exhilarated him so much that the next day he wrote a letter to Heyward to suggest making an opera out of it. Although Heyward liked the idea, he and his wife, Dorothy, were already making a drama out of it—a sort of lithograph of Negro life—which the Theater Guild staged triumphantly in 1927. Heyward suggested writing an opera after the play was done. Having many other commitments, Gershwin kept postponing work on the opera. In the meantime, other people got similar ideas. In 1933, the Guild proposed engaging Kern and Oscar Hammerstein II, to make a musical play out of *Porgy* for Al Jolson, who wanted to perform in it. Heyward declined that proposal when Gershwin agreed to get to work on the opera at once. He did. Since Heyward refused to leave South Carolina and come to New York to work on the libretto, Gershwin went to Charleston for a fortnight to discuss the plan, and then they collaborated by mail. Heyward wrote some of the lyrics; Ira Gershwin wrote others. In the summer of 1934, Gershwin left Broadway and spent two months in a rough shack on Folly Island off the coast of South Carolina where he steeped himself as much as possible in the life of the Gullah Negroes. It took him eleven months to write the score and another eight to orchestrate it. When the opera was finished, it consisted of 700 pages of music, which would have taken four and one-half hours to perform. Rouben Mamoulian, who had staged *Porgy,* was engaged to stage the opera, and Alexander Smallens was engaged to conduct the music. Since Gershwin regarded *Porgy and Bess* as his greatest achievement, he approached the opening night in a state of euphoria. After attending one of the early rehearsals, he told Mamoulian: "I always knew that *Porgy and Bess* was wonderful, but I never thought I would feel the way I do about it. I tell you after listening to that rehearsal today I think the music is so marvelous I really don't believe that I wrote it."

It opened at the Alvin Theater on October 10, 1935. It was considered to be of such importance that most of the newspapers assigned both their music and drama critics to review it. Although the reception was cordial, it was less ecstatic than Gershwin and his associates had hoped for. The drama critics were the more enthusiastic, although some of them growled about the opera mannerisms, which they regarded as pretentious intrusions on a splendid musical. The music critics, on the other hand, took exception to the preponderance of songs; most of them were inclined to regard *Porgy and Bess* as a hybrid work in which a Broadway song-writer had overreached himself. But no one took exception to the passion and skills of an inspired company that included Todd Duncan, Anne Brown, Georgette Harvey, J. Rosamond Johnson, and the popular team of John Bubbles and Ford Buck.

The original production, which cost $17,000 a week to operate, had 124 performances and lost $70,000—the entire production cost. But it illustrated better than any other of Gershwin's works his ability to sustain dramatic exaltation.

The opera tumultuously evoked the life of high-spirited, poignant, admirable human beings; and the songs were all Gershwin and all gold: "Summertime," "A Woman Is a Sometime Thing," "It Take a Long Pull to Get There," "I Got Plenty o' Nuttin," "Bess, You Is My Woman Now," "It Ain't Necessarily So," "I Loves You, Porgy," "There's a Boat Dat's Leavin' Soon for New York." The songs have lost none of their magnetism through the years. They are obviously the work of a city boy; there are Broadway accents in Gershwin's portrait of Gullah Negroes. But *Porgy and Bess* is an American classic, and is never forgotten. In 1942, it was successfully revived; subsequently, it was performed in other parts of America, and in opera houses in Denmark, Sweden, Russia, Germany, Austria, and in other parts of the world. The United States State Department sponsored a foreign tour of a splendid production of it as a good will mission. What Gershwin saw in *Porgy and Bess* was there originally, and is there now. He did not overestimate it.

Porgy and Bess was his last Broadway musical drama. In 1937, he died suddenly of a brain tumor in Hollywood at the age of thirty-eight. Since he was, as usual, full of musical ideas and plans and seemed to be midway in a bountiful career, his close friends could hardly believe that he had died; and Broadway, his real home, was stunned. At a memorial meeting,

Irving Berlin summarized Gershwin's career in the vernacular of the trade:

> As a writer of serious music
> He could dream for a while in the stars,
> And step down from the heights of Grand Opera
> To a chorus of thirty-two bars.

Plain words and true ones about an inspired writer of eloquent music.

Richard Rodgers, a short, roundish man with conservative tastes and considerable aplomb, had the most constructive influence on the transformation of the musical stage out of cant into art. Having worked with two lyricists who had completely different styles—Larry Hart and Oscar Hammerstein II—he had two careers, one brisk and cynical in the Broadway manner, the other humane and compassionate. But both of them were progressive, for even in the days when he was working with remarkable astuteness in the Broadway medium, Rodgers disliked hackneyed ideas and was impatient with the standard musical play.

Rodgers was born in 1902 into a family that loved music. His mother was a pianist. His father was a New York City physician whose hobby was music. When Rodgers showed remarkable facility at the piano, his parents and his older brother were delighted. They also encouraged him to attend musical shows on Broadway. Kern was his boyhood hero, but his musical background included Offenbach, Johann Strauss, Gilbert and Sullivan, Franz Lehar, and Victor Herbert—all in the European tradition. Rodgers composed songs when he was an adolescent. When he was fourteen, he wrote the music of the theme-song for Camp Wigwam at Harrison, Maine. In view of the songs Rodgers wrote in his maturity, and specifically in view of the excellent show he wrote in 1937 about summer camps, *Babes in Arms*, it might be interesting to note the lyrics of "Dear Old Wigwam:"

> Wigwam, your braves will love you while the moon shines o'er Bear Lake;
> We'll keep your campfires burning
> For each fleeting mem'ry's sake;
> Future years will bring us happy days in glad review;
> Each passing year makes you more dear;
> Old Wigwam we're true to you.

By the year 1919, Rodgers had become a restless student at Columbia University, where he was more interested in writing varsity shows than in distinguishing himself in the classroom. This was the time when he made the acquaintance of a former Columbia student, Larry Hart, who had congenial ideas about the musical theater. They did two varsity shows together before Rodgers left Columbia to study music at the Juilliard School. Hart, a complex young man with a sharp mind, a literary background, and a respect for intelligent literary work, wrote the lyrics to Rodgers' melodies. In their working arrangements, Rodgers' music came first, Hart's words second. But their collaboration was fundamental. It was impossible to separate the subtle, cleverly paced lyrics from the melodies.

Since Broadway was their environment, and since Broadway standards were also their standards, they wrote a long series of Broadway shows in the next quarter of a century, especially when they were collaborating with Herbert Fields, son of Lew Fields of the Weber and Fields team. They wrote popular shows with great facility—*Poor Little Ritz Girl* (1920), *Dearest Enemy* (1925), *The Girl Friend* (1926), *Peggy Ann* (1926), *A Connecticut Yankee* (1927), *She's My Baby* (1928), *Present Arms* (1928), *Chee Chee* (1928), *America's Sweetheart* (1931), and several others—basically song-and-dance shows, but lively and amusing, distinguished chiefly by a few songs of the first rank, like "My Heart Stood Still," "Thou Swell," and "With a Song in My Heart." Rodgers and Hart were writing primarily to succeed, like most people on Broadway.

But they were also impatient with the musical formula. In the two *Garrick Gaieties* they wrote in 1925 and 1926, they ridiculed the Broadway musical shows written by their elders, particularly *The Three Musketeers* and *Rose Marie*, which were the current hits and the kind of hokum they despised. Several of the regular Fields, Hart, and Rodgers shows tried to break out of the formula. *Peggy Ann* abandoned the traditional opening chorus and consisted of spoken dialogue for fifteen minutes before the first song was sung. *Peggy Ann* had 333 performances. *Chee Chee* consciously attempted to fuse the songs and book into a single instrument or expression: it had only thirty-one performances.

Although Rodgers and Hart always remained within hearing distance of Broadway, they were aware of other aspects of the theater. *On Your Toes*, in 1936, was a pioneering show that had an independent style. It included a genuine ballet, "Slaughter on Tenth Avenue," staged by George Balanchine and danced by Ray Bolger and Tamara Geva, at a time when ballet on Broadway was a coterie art-form. In 1938, *I Married an Angel* combined ballet, décor, music, and acting in an exuberant, humorous production. On the assumption that a musical play should be as well-performed as *The Philadelphia Story* and *No Time for Comedy*, which represented the best standards of the dramatic stage, Rodgers and Hart assembled a cast for *I Married an Angel* that included Dennis King, Walter Slezak, Vera Zorina, and Audrey Christie. The Rodgers and Hart standards were high in all departments of the theater. In 1938, their *The Boys from Syracuse* was an uproarious fantastification of Shakespeare's unactable *The Comedy of Errors*. Reversing the familiar Broadway formula in 1940, *Pal Joey* made a hero out of a nightclub blackguard. The score for that acrid antic included some of Rodgers' most luscious melodies: "Bewitched, Bothered, and Bewildered," "I Could Write a Book," "Happy Hunting Horn," "In Our Little Den of Iniquity." After twenty years together, Rodgers and Hart were still trying to liberate the musical stage from the stereotype, but they did not renounce Broadway. Broadway was their natural milieu.

After *Pal Joey*, and *By Jupiter* two seasons later, Larry Hart became increasingly difficult to work with. Progressively more neurotic, he mysteriously disappeared for long periods. At that time, Theresa Helburn of the Theater Guild was trying to interest Rodgers in a musical version of Lynn Riggs' *Green Grow the Lilacs*. Hart disqualified himself from that project; he did not believe that he could write the lyrics for an outdoor play set "on a radiant summer morning several years ago."

His health went rapidly downhill, and he died of pneumonia in 1943 at the age of forty-eight.

In the meantime, Rodgers had been fortunate enough to find a collaborator whom he had known ever since he was a boy. During Rodgers' career at Columbia, Oscar Hammerstein II had written the lyrics for one of Rodgers' varsity shows, and he had staged the second. As proof of the fact that great men frequently begin their careers as adolescents, here are Hammerstein's lyrics to Rodgers' "Room for One More" in the Columbia varsity show of 1920:

> My heart is an airy castle
>   Filled with girls I adore.
> My brain is a cloud of memories
>   of peaches galore.
> There was Jane and Molly,
>   And Ruth and Sue;
> Camilla, Kit, and
>   Patricia, too.

My heart is filled to the brim with you—
But there's always room for one more!

Like Rodgers, Hammerstein was steeped in the Broadway theater. He was a grandson of Oscar Hammerstein, the cigarmaker who became an opera producer and challenged—unsuccessfully—the Metropolitan Opera Company with his own company in his own Manhattan Opera House in 34th Street. The first Oscar Hammerstein also had built and owned the Victoria vaudeville theater in 42nd Street and Seventh Avenue, managed by his son, who was the father of Oscar Hammerstein II. Although Hammerstein II unwillingly studied law for a brief period and unhappily performed a few acts of drudgery for some patient law firm, his heart belonged to show business. Like Rodgers, he knew the theater as a total operation. He had written the books and the lyrics for Jerome Kern's *Show Boat, Music in the Air,* and others. But his last ten years had been a miserable succession of failures.

When he and Rodgers got to work on the script of *Green Grow the Lilacs,* they departed from the old forms completely. Through taste, freshness, and enthusiasm, they raised the artistic level of the Broadway musical stage to a point where it had to be taken seriously as literature. Hammerstein, a tall, cordial gentleman with an en brosse hair style, was seven years older than Rodgers, and equally sophisticated. In some remote corner of his heart, he was a humanist and idealist. To use some of the words he wrote for a character in a later play, he was "stuck like a dope with a thing called hope," and he believed that "you have to be taught to hate." Since he wrote the lyrics first and Rodgers wrote the melodies second his influence on the collaboration was positive. There was a considerable disparity in the relative time involved in their work. It might take Hammerstein several days to write a lyric. But it would take Rodgers only five or ten minutes, or on occasion three-quarters of an hour, to compose the melody. "When the lyrics are right, it's easier to write a tune than to bend over and tie your shoe laces," he remarked on one occasion. Notes come more spontaneously than words. It was his intention to write music that would give pleasure to ordinary people, and in that mission he abundantly succeeded.

When Rodgers and Hammerstein were working on the script of their musical comedy, their initial problem was technical. They could find no justification for an opening chorus. With some misgivings, they decided to open with a rapturous song first heard offstage, "Oh, What a Beautiful

Morning"; and they had hardly made that decision before the logic of the plot indicated a second song, "The Surrey with the Fringe on Top." It was all irregular, but it seemed to be the natural way of telling the story.

The preliminary troubles were massive. The Guild was close to bankruptcy. No one was eager to invest in the show, which at the time was known as *Away We Go!* Backers invested, not out of enthusiasm for the project, but out of loyalty to Miss Helburn, Lawrence Langner, and the Guild. The New Haven road production and the preliminary engagement in Boston were discouraging. After looking at the production in New Haven, one of Broadway's most expert handicappers reported: "No legs, no jokes, no chance." The title of the show was soon changed to *Oklahoma!*—the exclamation mark signifying desperation rather than confidence.

On the evening of March 31, 1943, the curtain at the St. James Theater on 44th Street rose on a glowing country scene. A farm woman on a porch was seated at an old-fashioned churn. Offstage, Alfred Drake, in the part of Curly, sang:

> There's a bright, golden haze on the meadow,
> There's a bright, golden haze on the meadow.
> The corn is as high as a elephant's eye
> An' it looks like it's climbin' clear up to the sky.

Sauntering onstage, he continued with the chorus:

> Oh, what a beautiful mornin',
> Oh, what a beautiful day.
> I got a beautiful feelin'
> Ev'rything's goin' my way.

Within ten minutes, a Broadway audience was transported out of the ugly realities of wartime into a warm, langorous, shining time and place where the only problems were simple and wholesome, and the people uncomplicated and joyous. The opening song seemed like a distillation of something that had been hovering in the air since life began on earth,

> All the sounds of the earth are like music—
> All the sounds of the earth are like music.
> The breeze is so busy it don't miss a tree
> And a ol' weepin' willer is laughing at me.

After a verse like that, sung to a buoyant melody, the banalities of the old musical stage became intolerable.

In the hands of Romberg, *Oklahoma!* might have been operetta; the relationships between the characters were conventional enough for operetta treatment. But the taste as well as the talents of Rodgers and Hammerstein translated the story into a humorous idyll about attractive outdoor people —the exultant melodies of Rodgers harmonizing with the rustic verses of Hammerstein, and the frisky ballets that Agnes de Mille staged expressing in physical images the mood of the occasion. The cast, as unpretentious as the material, did not consist of stars—that is, until the curtain went down when the audience thought of them as stars. In addition to Mr. Drake, the cast included Betty Garde, Joan Roberts, Lee Dixon, Howard da Silva, Celeste Holm, Joseph Buloff, Joan McCracken, and Bambi Linn.

After twenty-five years of superior songwriting, Rodgers suddenly emerged as a composer of literate, imaginative melodies in many forms. The original production of *Oklahoma!* had 2,212 performances. In its first ten years, it made a profit of five million dollars on an investment of $83,000. Many a new day of memorable musical theater began the night *Oklahoma!* opened.

Probably the success of *Oklahoma!* stimulated Rodgers and Hammerstein into putting their minds on something more difficult. They abandoned the primary axiom of the musical stage: that the boy and the girl must be united in the last scene, and composed a musical drama with a tragic theme. The happiness of their hero and heroine in their next musical was destroyed by a flaw in the character of the hero, as in formal tragedy. *Carousel* derived from Theresa Helburn's suggestion that Molnar's *Liliom*, in which Eva Le Gallienne and Joseph Schildkraut had starred in 1921, might provide the material for a notable musical play. In the operetta era, a composer and librettist would have instinctively retained the original Hungarian background of the drama as somehow more cultivated and plausible.

It is significant that Rodgers and Hammerstein, and Benjamin Glazer, who wrote the adaptation, transformed the romance of Molnar's European drama into a plain New England tragedy. They made none of the usual concessions to entertainment. Although the score of *Carousel* is the richest in the Rodgers and Hammerstein library, it is impossible to separate the songs from their dramatic function as portraits of character. The long, bemused, improvised soliloquy by the hero when he learns that he is to be a father is a superb piece of music that articulates a young man's vagrant imaginings, but it is meaningless off stage. And his braggart challenge in the scene in heaven, "Take me before the highest throne/ And let me be judged by the highest Judge of all," gives depth and dignity to Molnar's amusing fantasy. Throughout *Carousel*, Hammerstein's compassionate lyrics drew more deeply on Rodger's reservoir of melodies than anything he had written before, and every song is either delightful or moving or both: "June Is Busting Out All Over," "You're a Queer One, Julie Jordan," "When I Marry Mr. Snow," "If I Loved You," "Blow High, Blow Low," "This Was a Real Nice Clambake," "What's the Use of Wond'rin'," "You'll Never Walk Alone." They express a composer's belief in his characters and in his profession.

Like *Oklahoma!*, *Carousel* was cast and staged in terms of its inherent dramatic values and without star performing. It opened on April 19, 1945, at the Majestic Theater, just across 44th Street from the St. James Theater, where *Oklahoma!* was still flourishing. *Carousel* was the Rodgers and Hammerstein masterpiece: it best illustrated their dedication to the musical stage as a legitimate art form. It had 890 performances—less than half of the run of *Oklahoma!* But *Carousel*, with its somber theme, its pity, and its respect for a wayward character's individuality, has more pertinence. The point of view is timeless and universal.

Allegro, in 1947, was not based on a play or book. It was a completely original work about the corruption of success in the career of a young doctor. It did not corrupt Rodgers and Hammerstein, because it was not a success. But the next work, *South Pacific*, was a triumphant stage entertainment, written with gusto by two extraordinary theater men at the peak of their power. It was based on James Michener's *Tales of the South Pacific*. Since Joshua Logan had been in the Navy during World War II, he collaborated on the libretto and staged the production. The literary material on which the play was based was conventional romance—the courtship of a Navy nurse from Little Rock, Arkansas, by a mature French planter on the islands and a doomed romance between a native girl and an American navy lieutenant. It was standard operetta stuff. But Rodgers and Hammerstein gave it distinction by the characterizations they portrayed in the music—"I'm a Cockeyed Optimist" and "I'm Going to Wash That Man Right out of My Hair," sung and acted with charm and sincerity by Mary Martin; "Some Enchanted Evening" and "This Nearly Was Mine" sung and acted with warmth and power by Ezio Pinza, who came from the operatic stage. The secondary romance was described in two songs in different styles—"Younger than Springtime" and "You've Got to Be Carefully Taught," sung by William Tabbert as the lieutenant.

These songs show how ordinary material can be transfigured through the medium of fresh music. They create and sustain a golden mood by their musical eloquence. But Rodgers and Hammerstein had one other fundamental asset: they never lost the common touch. An exotic melody, "Bali Ha'i," and a side comment, "Happy Talk," created an uncompromising native character that Juanita Hall described in screeching voice and pugnacious performance. And "There Is Nothing Like a Dame," comic and knowing, expressed the frustrations of the enlisted men in an alien world:

> There is nothin' you can name
> That is anythin' like a dame!
> There are no books like a dame,
> And nothin' looks like a dame,
> There arc no drinks like a dame,
> And nothin' thinks like a dame,
> Nothin' acts like a dame
> Or attracts like a dame.
> There ain't a thing that's worng with any man here
> That can't be cured by puttin' him near
> A girly, womanly, female, feminine dame!

Staged like a humorous ballet of caged animals, this forthright ballad was not only uproarious theater, but it bluntly expressed the real genius of Rodgers and Hammerstein—their insight into character and their sympathy for the common dilemmas of people. More than any other pair, they mastered the technique of the modern musical theater. But they also believed in human beings. Even in a flamboyant stage entertainment like *South Pacific* they wrote from strength because they proceeded from principle.

When Hitler banned Bertolt Brecht's *The Threepenny Opera* in 1933, Kurt Weill, who had composed it, and his wife, Lotte Lenya, who had been the principal singer in it, escaped to Paris. Weill was in double jeopardy in Germany: he was a Jew, and he was also composer of a popular musical work that portrayed the moral depravity of the Nazi movement. He was also thc composer of another savagely satirical sketch of inhumanity with a libretto by Bertolt Brecht; *The Rise and Fall of the City of Mahagonny* berated the virulent materialism of America, where at that time neither Weill nor Brecht had ever been. *Mahagonny* (produced Off Broadway in 1970) equals *The Threepenny Opera* in pithiness and musical versatility, and the satire is more withering.

In driving•Weill out of Germany, Hitler inadvertently did Broadway a service. Weill was a virtuoso composer who found America a congenial place to work. A modest, friendly unassertive man, short of stature, bald, bespectacled like a professor, he understood the theater thoroughly and could organize a play in music better than most playwrights could organize it in words. Excepting "September Song" and "The Ballad of Mack the Knife," his songs could not be detached from the scores; they were not separate entities. But the scores he wrote for *Knickerbocker Holiday* (1938), *Lady in the Dark* (1941), *Street Scene* (1947), and *Lost in the Stars* (1949) spoke his mind eloquently. Although his operatic version of *Street Scene* failed on Broadway, it became part of the repertory of the New York City Opera Company. His music was understood and warmly admired by professionals.

Kurt Weill was born in Germany in 1900, son of a cantor. His musical ability was recognized by his family when he was a boy. They sent him to study under Engelbert Humperdinck, composer of the opera *Hänsel und Gretel*, who gave Weill a classical musical education. Before he started to work with the disaffected poet, Bertolt Brecht, Weill composed operas that were sung in Germany, and he directed a small opera company. He was the kind of professional who wrote the orchestrations for his scores. After he had worked with Brecht, he also became a man committed to the problems of his times—too modest, too scrupulous to be a propagandist, but a man of conscience who took a moral stand on public issues.

Max Reinhardt, the illustrious German producer, who was also a Jew, had escaped to America in 1935. He invited Weill to leave Paris and come to New York to compose the score for Franz Werfel's *The Eternal Road*. Like many of Reinhardt's productions, this one was fabulous; and since it constituted Weill's introduction to Broadway, it may as well be recorded in detail. It was the story of the Pentateuch contrasted with the story of contemporary Jews, and it was designed to arouse interest in the Jewish tradition at the time when Hitler was bent on crushing it. Reinhardt thought of the play in terms of a spectacle of epic proportions. To design the scenery, he hired another superman, Norman Bel Geddes, who despised anything less than ten feet tall. Putting their imaginations together, Reinhardt and Geddes reversed the usual practice of producing: they adapted the Manhattan Opera House to fit the show.

Since the orchestra pit was not deep enough to contain part of the spectacle, they deepened it by drilling into bedrock under the theater. Before they got down as far as they wanted to, a spring of water spouted twenty-one feet into the orchestra: they had punched into a flowing underground creek. It was some time before the creek could be capped and the water diverted out of the orchestra pit. This was the most serious of the obstacles, but it was not the only one. There were ten postponements before the play could open, and the costs rose to $540,000. Everything was on a colossal scale. The cast included forty-three principal actors and singers. The scenery represented not only the earth where Moses morosely trudged across sand dunes, but also a modern synagogue on the lower level, with heaven above where a choir of angels burst into song in the blue empyrean.

When the production opened on January 7, 1937, the four acts ran until three o'clock the next morning, and exhausted the audience. But the critics left at midnight after seeing the first two acts, and most of the notices were rhapsodic. Beginning on the second night, the last two acts were furtively discarded, and *The Eternal Road* was a hit. There was not an empty seat during the 153 performances. But after the play opened the producers discovered that the operating expenses were greater than the revenue from capacity audiences and the production lost $5000 a week.

This was Weill's first experience with Broadway production. During the rehearsal period, the orchestra pit had been taken away from him and assigned to the scene designer, and the orchestra had to find another location. Weill was the most inconspicuous figure in an assembly of egotists, and his score unified their work. His music was the most moving part of *The Eternal Road*. The composer of the raffish *The Threepenny Opera* endowed *The Eternal Road* with religious exaltation. Weill did for *The Eternal Road* what he was to do for other productions for the rest of his life: he provided the unity and the eloquence in a meticulously composed score that brought all the details of a production into focus. By losing himself in the work of other people, he became an inspired composer.

Weill seemed to need no introduction to America; he was busy as soon as he settled down. The freedom and the spontaneity of America stimulated him. While *The Eternal Road* was struggling along from one crisis to another, he wrote the music for Paul Green's antiwar drama, *Johnny Johnson*, in 1938. Collaborating with his New City neighbor,

Maxwell Anderson, he examined the original principles of America in *Knickerbocker Holiday*, a musical drama about Pieter Stuyvesant. Thus, during the third year of his life in America, Weill found himself composing the music for a song called "How Can You Tell an American?"

Weill's rushing score for Moss Hart's *Lady in the Dark* was the principal unifying force in that 1941 psychoanalytical fantasy. Ira Gershwin wrote the lyrics—the first he had written since the death of his brother George. Two years later, Weill wrote the music for S. J. Perelman's *One Touch of Venus*, with lyrics by Ogden Nash. That play had the extra distinction of making a star out of Mary Martin.

Weill's score for the musical version of Elmer Rice's *Street Scene* was his masterpiece. Fourteen years after he had fled from Berlin, he was able to write a musical microcosm of Manhattan, conveying the violence, the misery, the sociability, the cautious hope, the blighted romance, and the immense vitality of Cosmopolis. The lyrics were by Langston Hughes, a poet who knew the city intimately and loved it with humor and forgiveness. There was immense depth and scope in the score—an ice-cream ballet, a jazzy serenade called "Moon-Faced, Starry-Eyed," Mrs. Maurrant's skeptical "Somehow I Never Could Believe," and her affectionate appeal to her son, "A Boy Like You." With his insight, modesty, and humanity, Weill composed a work of art that did not evade the truth of a corrosive city but also retained a certain wistful beauty. From the contemptuous satire of *The Rise and Fall of the City of Mahagonny* to the affectionate portrait of *Street Scene* was the measure of Weill's happy experience in America.

Lost in the Stars, produced in 1949, was his last musical drama. It was Maxwell Anderson's adaptation of Alan Paton's *Cry, the Beloved Country*. Racial prejudice was a theme that Weill knew from personal experience, and his score communicated the fears and hatred, the wildness and anguish, and the heavy spirit of a contemporary evil. His music lifted a commonplace play to a high plane of spiritual experience.

Weill died in April 1950, only fifteen years after he had come to America. In Germany he had already had extensive experience in the kind of homogeneous musical drama that Broadway writers were thinking about. He was the contemporary of George Gershwin, not only in time but in craftsmanship; he already knew how to do what Gershwin did in *Porgy and Bess* and Rodgers did in *Oklahoma!*. Since he wrote scores rather than songs, he never had the personal acclaim of most of his colleagues. After he died, Marc Blitzstein's astringent adaptation of

The Threepenny Opera provided gratifying compensation. It had 2,611 performances off Broadway; and Weill's widow, Lotte Lenya, dressed in the slatternly costume of a bitter harlot, sang the part she had sung in the depraved Germany that led to Hitler.

But Broadway had not become a musical academy in which gifted composers and visionary writers transmuted the regulation song-and-dance show into artistry. Mediocrity struggled along, as usual. Broadway could not quite shake off the burden of the old operetta. In 1948, when *South Pacific* was flourishing, a maudlin operetta painfully assembled from Tchaikovsky's music, and called *Music in My Heart*, reissued all the old stereotypes. "Ah, Paris, what memories it holds for me," sighed the pre-revolutionary ballerina who had apparently left her virtue as well as her lover in Paris. And the baritone who acted Tchaikovsky was brimming over with sentimentality: "She's lovely—like a flower," he sang, sick with desire. There was always the danger in those days that a new operetta might creep in. *My Romance*, suffocating in luxurious costumes and baroque scenery, was Sigmund Romberg's 1948 idea of Edward Sheldon's *Romance*, in which Doris Keane had subdued most of the world. Romberg's stuffy song titles disclose the nature of his operetta—"Souvenir," "Desire," "Polka," "In Love with Romance," "Waltz Interlude," "Finaletto." The orchestrations were equally pompous; horns and drums crammed the Shubert Theater with bombastic sound and boredom. In 1947, a revival of Oscar Straus' *The Chocolate Soldier* opened on the night before *Brigadoon* opened—the one a bit of show-business banality, the other a charming fantasy by Alan Jay Lerner and Frederick Loewe. The contrast between the old and the new could not be more clearly stated than in the doggerel Stanislaus Stange assembled for the big tune in *The Chocolate Soldier*:

> How handsome is this hero mine,
> The tears within my eyes are burning,
> How true and brave that face divine,
> My heart for him is ever yearning.
> That forehead so high, the chin firm and strong,
> The eagle-like eye. For him how I long.
> How graceful his carriage, how noble and free.
> The day of our marriage, happy be.
> I have a true and noble lover,

He is my sweetheart, all my own!
His like on earth who shall discover?
His heart is mine and mine alone.
We pledged our troth, each to the other,
And for our happiness I pray;
Our lives belong to one another,
Oh, happy, happy wedding day!
Oh happy, happy wedding day!

Come! come! I love you only,
My heart is true.
Come! come! my life is lonely,
I long for you;
Come! come! naught can efface you,
My arms are aching to embrace you,
Come! come! I love you only,
Come, hero mine!*

Broadway gave up the cloying past reluctantly. For years, revivals of *The Student Prince* and *Blossom Time* kept appearing from out of nowhere.

But there were too many skeptics in town to tolerate that sort of gibberish indefinitely. Composers with talent and ideas were replacing the hacks. In 1944, Leonard Bernstein wrote a biting score for an original musical called *On the Town*. His joyless, suspicious theme song—"New York, New York"—expressed a sophisticated attitude towards a baleful city. Vernon Duke's *Cabin in the Sky*, in 1940, improvised Negro fantasy about heaven, hell, and a black man's earth. John La Touche, a genuine poet, wrote the lyrics; and Ethel Waters, who had caused a heat wave in 1933 in *As Thousands Cheer*, made playgoers very happy indeed with the gleam and gusto with which she sang "Taking a Chance on Love." Harold Rome turned the stage revue into a genial salute to union labor in *Pins and Needles*, which had 1,108 performances. "Sing Me a Song of Social Significance," the chorus demanded in the prologue, and Rome gave them "Chain Store Daisy," "One Big Union for Two," and "Sunday in the Park" in return. There was nothing heavy or pretentious in the various versions of *Pins and Needles*. Arthur Schwartz, collaborating with Howard Dietz, writer of lyrics, had composed the scores for two memorable revues in the thirties—*Three's a Crowd* and *The Band Wagon*, which represented the modern taste, light, agile, and concise in comparison with the gaudy upholstery of the standard Broadway revue. In 1948, he and

Dietz wrote *Inside U.S.A.*, in which Beatrice Lillie starred. It was as contemporary as a newspaper; it was a sharp comment on America. Harold Arlen's *Bloomer Girl*, full of comedy and nostaglia, and Burton Lane's *Finian's Rainbow*, full of political satire and comic caprice, helped to redeem Broadway from drudgery. All these alert people brought modern music and modern ideas into a tired business.

Frank Loesser's *Guys and Dolls*, in 1950, was a masterly achievement in the new tradition—music, story, characters, acting, and direction pouring out of the same crucible. Musical dramas with nobler themes have

Jo Mielziner's set for a Times Square scene in *Guys and Dolls* (1950).

been less perfectly composed than this breezy legend of an underworld derived from some of Damon Runyan's stories.

Loesser was born in New York in 1910, son of a piano teacher who disliked popular music. Loesser grew up in two environments—classical music, from which "Fugue for Tinhorns," was derived, and Broadway, the source of "Luck Be a Lady." He began casually by writing the words for tunes by other people. The first song for which he wrote both the tune and the words was a famous one—"Praise the Lord and Pass the Ammunition," in honor of a gallant wartime chaplain. In 1948, he wrote the music and the lyrics for his first Broadway show—*Where's Charley?*, in which Ray Bolger appeared for 792 continuous performances. "Once in Love with Amy" was in that show; and thousands of theatergoers will never forget it, because Bolger persuaded them to sing it with him.

But *Guys and Dolls* was in a different category. It was a portrait of characters by a man who knew them. The raffish people and the dowdy environment of *Guys and Dolls* had been in existence a long time before Damon Runyan put them in his stories. They were horseplayers, gamblers, showgirls, and petty gamblers who lived from hand to mouth in a closed community of simpleminded fantasy—a little below the borderline that divides lawlessness from civic virtue, but not far below. Although they looked worldly, they were basically naïve. Although they looked comic to Damon Runyan—and to Abe Burrows and Jo Swerling, who wrote the libretto—they had no sense of humor. They thought that they were smarter than people who worked for a living, but they were not.

Less original writers than Runyan, Burrows, Swerling and Loesser could have romanticized them into Bohemians. But the genius of *Guys and Dolls* was to portray them without glamour, and the genius of Loesser was to characterize them musically with candor and relish. In the day of *The Chocolate Soldier* or *Robin Hood*, one memorable tune was all a composer needed for a successful musical. The standards had gone up sharply by 1950. In *Guys and Dolls*, every song had to be just right, because every song defined a character. There was not a commonplace nor a superfluous song in the score. "The Oldest Established Crap Game," "A Bushel and a Peck," "Adelaide's Lament," "If I Were a Bell," "My Time of Day," "Take Back Your Mink," "More I Cannot Wish You," "Sue Me," "You're Rocking the Boat," and "Marry the Man Today" were both the structure and the pith of the story.

Guys and Dolls was a carnival of shoddy Broadway innocents lost in a furtive but fabulous world, and nothing George M. Cohan wrote had the insight, humor, compassion, and variety of Loesser's Broadway classic. The difference between *Forty-five Minutes from Broadway* and *Guys and Dolls* is the difference between opportunism and talent, between cleverness and maturity.

In the bright interval between the experiment of *Show Boat*, in 1927, and *Guys and Dolls*, in 1950, the Broadway musical drama became the best in the world and the one department of the theater in which Broadway excelled. In pace, skill, variety, and zest it was unrivaled. Occasionally it was also art. It excelled the self-conscious new works put on by the Metropolitan Opera Company, because of the superior professionalism of Broadway, the craftsmanship and style. When American actors sang American musical dramas abroad, they were recognized as incomparable. Even singers with better voices and more training lacked the crackle and zest of the best American musical dramas.

WELCOME TO THE PLAYERS

After the appearance of O'Neill, Broadway was no longer an actor's theater. It was a playwright's theater; it was the theater of Shaw, Pirandello, Ibsen, Chekhov, Behrman, Coward, Molnar, Howard, Sherwood, Kaufman, Maugham, O'Casey. There were stars, of course, and many of the best now and then allowed themselves the easy luxury of a popular vehicle. But what the dramatists said was, on the whole, more important than the personalities of the actors. It was no longer a theater in which Richard Mansfield, Mrs. Leslie Carter, and James K. Hackett could behave like royalty and treat the playwrights like clerks. Broadway audiences had become too sophisticated for that.

It was also a theater in which a few producers had taste and progressive ideas, and several directors brought imagination and integrity into their staging of performances. The hokum of Belasco was no longer tolerable. Philip Moeller, a temperamental young man, imposed design on perfor-

Helen Hayes in *Victoria Regina* (1935).

mances for the Theater Guild, carrying on the tradition of Ames and Hopkins with perhaps a little more cosmopolitanism. He found suitable and diverse styles for *Saint Joan, The Guardsman,* and *They Knew What They Wanted.* Guthrie McClintic, who had learned from Ames the importance of color and composition, staged many of the most distinguished productions. His staging of Katharine Cornell's *Romeo and Juliet,* in 1933, was his finest. Brock Pemberton, who had learned from Hopkins that drama is a criticism of life, produced an original and baffling play in 1922, unlike anything Broadway had seen before—Pirandello's *Six Characters in Search of an Author.* It questioned the nature of reality and presented the audiences with a series of provocative conundrums. There were excellent actors in the cast, but none that presumed to outshine the author.

Gilbert Miller, son of Henry Miller, an actor of the old school, started his producing career with a bit of old-fashioned fiddle-faddle called *Daddy-long-legs,* in 1919. By 1925, he had advanced to the wit of Frederick Lonsdale's *The Last of Mrs. Cheney* and, by 1936, the grandeur of Laurence Housman's *Victoria Regina.* Although Broadway looked—and was—crude and garish, it could improve the taste of the people who assembled there. Max Gordon, born Mechel Salpeter on the Lower East Side, son of Polish immigrants, was brought up in a Yiddish-speaking family that was not interested in American culture. As a boy, he was infatuated with Broadway. It educated him. By the time he was in his thirties and forties, he was producing plays and musical shows that had taste and modern significance —*Ethan Frome, Dodsworth, Design for Living, The Band Wagon.*

The Shuberts continued to produce their familiar rubbish, making their usual fortunes; and Al Woods, the most raffish of the showmen, continued to put on farces and melodramas and to stuff huge wads of paper money in his safe deposit boxes. But a new generation of restless theater people with congenial ideas was dragging Broadway into the modern age. Everyone was getting bored with the old war horses. Duse's final tour in 1923 (she died in Pittsburgh before she had completed it) marked the end of an era. There were to be no more royal progresses. Sothern and Marlowe's last Shakespearean production—*Cymbeline,* at the Al Jolson Theater in 1923—was pathetic and humiliating, and had only fifteen performances. A style of classical acting that had been admired as the finest and worthiest in the first two decades suddenly looked empty and patronizing. The most respected acting team had become obsolete.

Although the rank of the actor had been superseded by the importance of the playwright and the director, the general level of acting was high, particularly for native American plays. Serious theater people had been much impressed by Max Reinhardt's perfectly orchestrated troupe from Berlin and by the Moscow Art Theater, which communicated the themes of the dramatists rather than the glamour of stars. They were genuine artists. Leo Bulgakov and his wife, Barbara, seceded from the company when it returned to Moscow, and they carried on the same tradition as actors, producers, and teachers in New York. If Broadway had no companies as beautifully trained and organized as those from Berlin and Moscow, the level of acting was high because the actors were intelligent and progressive and were alert to the new movement. They rarely failed the playwright. Although they lacked the style and versatility of London actors, who knew how to play the classics, they had enormous gusto and vitality, and they instinctively believed in modern ideas.

To see an American play acted in London was to appreciate the strength and color of American actors; they had pace and drive and the common touch. On Broadway, the performance of *What Price Glory?*— direct, pithy, and fresh—filled the theater with excitement about the theme of the play. There was no ham acting in it. The performance of *Porgy and Bess*—selfless and exotic and erupting with emotion—enriched the experience of the audience. During the height of the season in the twenties, five or ten plays opened every week; and through normal methods of attrition, most of them turned out to be in error. But the actors rarely made the errors.

Broadway was a matriarchy. Most of the best players were women. With only a few exceptions, the most respected male actors were not so much stars as leading men. John Barrymore was the last of the illustrious male stars. But there were many gifted actresses who could possess the audience. Pauline Lord, known as Polly to her friends, was about the least theatrical woman on the stage. Her style was shy, soft, self-effacing, and defenseless—a projection of her own modesty and misgivings. But in suitable parts, she was a powerful actress. As the bewildered, homeless waitress in Sidney Howard's *They Knew What They Wanted*, she held the audience spellbound. As the bedraggled prostitute in O'Neill's *Anna Christie*, she gave a squalid waterfront play an overtone of purity. Her memorable Zenobia in *Ethan Frome*, in 1936, was not the hateful hypochondriac Edith Wharton had imagined in the original novel. From Miss Lord's tremulous acting, Zenobia emerged as a frightened, lonely woman entitled more to pity than to censure. Caught in an inhuman triangle with Ruth Gordon's courageous Mattie and Raymond Massey's tenacious

Ethan Frome, Miss Lord's Zenobia was the third part of a masterpiece. The qualities that Pauline Lord feared were lacking in herself she drew out of the audience's inexhaustible fund of compassion.

Physically some of the greatest actresses were small women—Lynn Fontanne, Helen Hayes, Lillian Gish, Ruth Gordon, and Julie Harris, for example. Judith Anderson was—and is—another, but she seemed ten feet tall in the tragic parts she played in classics or adaptations of classics. A diminutive woman, burning with passion, she gave heroic performances. Hell had no fury like Medea scorned when Miss Anderson played that ruthless part in 1947 with an evil grandeur that snatched Euripides' tragic drama out of the textbooks and poured it into the bloodstream of the audience. Offstage, mild and little: onstage, fierce and terrifying—that is the genius of Judith Anderson, an Australian who made her debut in Sydney in 1915 and came to New York in 1918. If Medea did not understand the temperamental convulsions of her own character, she would have done well to consult Miss Anderson. Although Miss Anderson's style was volcanic, her head was clear about what she was doing.

Gertrude Lawrence, a versatile British actress, first took the measure of a Broadway audience in *André Charlot's Revue of 1924*, with Beatrice Lillie as part of the cast. Miss Lawrence was a unique phenomenon—a superb performer in any medium, exuberant, supple, and animated, and a formidable craftsman in the arts of the stage. She did not act so much as she performed. Contrasted with the crisp, swift, understated acting of Noel Coward in *Tonight at 8:30*, her bravura acting was one of the events of the 1936–1937 season (a fabulous season, as other items in this chapter will indicate). A highly competitive woman, she was always "on" in or out of the theater: she was always giving a performance that was versatile, tireless, and larger than life.

Unless the playwright had as much energy and craft as she did, she could make a vehicle of anything he wrote, as she did with Rachel Crothers' *Susan and God*, in 1936, and with Samson Raphaelson's *Skylark*, in 1939. She was a star in the old tradition. She was a singer and dancer as well as a performer. When she had to follow an exciting song number by Danny Kaye in Moss Hart's *Lady in the Dark*, she sang and performed her ribald "Saga of Jenny" with a superhuman fervor that reminded everyone that she was the star. She took second place to no one. She concluded her career with a triumphant tour de force. She sang and played the part of Anna Leonowens in the Rodgers and Hammerstein's *The King and I* with unflagging energy and inexhaustible charm until three weeks before she died of cancer. To all good actors, the theater is the universe. Her unwilling departure from a hit show was the only time in which Gertrude Lawrence acknowledged the importance of anything outside the theater.

Having had a fabulous career in silent films in her youth, Lillian Gish turned upon Broadway in 1930 as Helena in Chekhov's *Uncle Vanya*, playing a fragile, pliant wife of a pretentious Russian scholar. The casting seemed to be perfect, but it was also deceptive. Miss Gish is a quiet, seemingly frail, unworldly lady, and she has a girlish voice. But she was born a professional and has been implacably professional all her life. Although she looks vulnerable, she has great strength of character and physical stamina. Her sister Dorothy once remarked that many people made the mistake of treating Lillian as if she were a defenseless woman. That, according to Dorothy, was like the old vaudeville trick in which the comedian kicked a hat that concealed a brick inside it. The kicker was likely to get a broken toe.

After her return from Hollywood (though not a withdrawal from the screen) Miss Gish played some parts that seemed to be outside her range —the amorous courtesan in *The Lady of the Camellias* and the gaudy whore in O'Casey's *Within the Gates*. But nothing was outside her range. She was equally well cast as the touching sister of charity in Philip Barry's *The Joyous Season*, in 1934, and Ophelia to John Gielgud's *Hamlet*, in 1936. Miss Gish has never failed the author or the audience. She believes that it is the duty of the actor to help make the play intelligible and interesting. She has no patience with the introspective school of acting. To her, what motivates the actor is a matter of no importance; what moves an audience is.

In Ruth Gordon's youth, no one would have believed that she had talent for the stage. A small, unprepossessing suburban girl from Wollaston, Massachusetts, she belonged to a family that knew nothing about the stage. No one encouraged her. After she had studied at the American Academy of Dramatic Arts in New York, she was advised to abandon hopes of a career on the stage. She now takes pleasure in recalling that the Academy director said: "We see no signs that you are in any way suitable for the acting profession, and you will not be allowed to come back next year." But the theater has been her lifetime obsession. By persistence, intelligence, shrewdness and fanatical work, she made the theater accept and appreciate her. More glamorous young people with more captivating personalities, lacking her ferocity of purpose, have passed across the stage unnoticed. After her joyless apprenticeship in the American Academy of Dramatic Arts, she made her first Broadway appearance in 1915, in the obscure part of Nibs in Maude Adams' production of *Peter Pan*. In 1919, she turned a minor part in a minor play called *Mrs. Partridge Presents* (Blanche Bates was the star; Guthrie McClintic, the director) into an original comedy improvisation. The most propitious thing imaginable happened: Alexander Woollcott gave her an appreciative comment in his notice the next day.

Since she is neither beautiful nor imposing, Miss Gordon has had to fight for recognition throughout her career. But when she was still in her youth, she gave highly personal and enjoyable performances in Booth Tarkington's *Seventeen* and Maxwell Anderson's *Saturday's Children* and suddenly emerged as a skillful and discriminating actress in difficult plays like Philip Barry's mystic *Hotel Universe*, S. N. Behrman's adaptation of *Serena Blandish*, and the political broadside of John Wexley's *They Shall Not Die*. She gave a first-rate performance as Nora in *A Doll's House*, which had been the exclusive property of established actresses like Mrs. Fiske and Alla Nazimova. In 1936, she acted a plain, shy, awkward, restless Mattie in *Ethan Frome*. In the same season, she gave a triumphant performance as Mrs. Pinchwife in Congreve's *The Country Wife*. Her fantastic acting of the asides was vastly amusing. She played Natasha in Chekhov's *The Three Sisters*, with Katharine Cornell, in 1942. Miss Gordon's acting was always fresh. There were no echoes of older parts in her performances and no repetitions of her personality. She also wrote two successful comedies—*Over 21* and *Years Ago*. *Years Ago* was a popular account of her own youth, when she was haunted with a determination to make that implausible transition from Wollaston, Massachusetts, to Broadway. Miss Gordon created herself as an actress. She proved that acting is a craft as well as an art and not a form of exhibitionism. She belongs to no tradition; she founded her own.

One of her most celebrated colleagues brought more and gave less. Tallulah Bankhead came to Broadway from Huntsville, Alabama, with spectacular personal beauty, a husky voice, inexhaustible energy, and the devastating personality of a wit and iconoclast. When she appeared in 1918 in a worthless comedy called *Squab Farm*, she was the perfect flapper —an uninhibited, footloose girl of independent manners and no recognizable morals. Later she appeared in two merchantable plays by Rachel Crothers—*39 East* and *Nice People*. (Katharine Cornell also had a small part in that play.) But it was in London that Miss Bankhead became a sensation. In the early twenties, when she, too, was in her early twenties, and when young people were tired of respectability and believed in nothing except themselves, Miss Bankhead captivated London by her reckless, mannered acting in popular comedies and her startling antics offstage. Her quick and deadly wit entertained the town.

She returned to New York in 1933 with a formidable reputation. Her play was a routine piece of persiflage called *Forsaking All Others*. It provided Miss Bankhead with space enough to undulate around the stage, turn a couple of handsprings, cry, laugh, and waggle her head. But Broadway did not succumb as London had. In successive plays, it was obvious that Miss Bankhead could act individual scenes with daring and bravura. But she could not act a character at full length. There was another factor that militated against her: Broadway audiences had higher standards for plays than London had. London audiences were still fond of stage humbug. The plays in which Miss Bankhead appeared did not break down the surliness with which Broadway invariably stared at smart stuff that did not dazzle the mob. Baffled by Broadway's reluctance, she appeared in a revival of *Rain*. Mannered, wobbly, aimless, her performance was inferior to Jeanne Eagels' tense, vivid, smoldering acting in the original 1922 production. When she played Cleopatra in Shakespeare's romantic tragedy, John Mason Brown delivered the bluntest comment. As Cleopatra, he wrote, "Tallulah Bankhead sailed down the Nile in a barge last night and sank." Broadway was delighted with the reports of her ribaldries and social heresies but did not take her seriously as an actress.

In 1939 she encountered a director of the first rank and she gave an overwhelming performance. The director was Herman Shumlin, mild of manner but formidable as a craftsman, and the play was Lillian Hellman's *The Little Foxes*. As a heartless Southern lady, Miss Bankhead stated the malevolence of the character with all the poise and pride of a notable actress. She made the audience respect the keen mind and the personal force of a hateful woman. And in 1942, Elia Kazan disciplined her again. As Sabina in Thornton Wilder's comic allegory, *The Skin of Our Teeth*, she put a solid core of strength in the spine of a philosophical caper. Being an actress of superior skill, she made the technical transitions between the burlesque and the dramatic scenes with great virtuosity.

Miss Bankhead's parents and her good fortune gave her everything essential to a stage career except discipline. To her, life was an endless party. Although she behaved like a modern, she was essentially a throwback to the period of Lillie Langtry, Anna Held, and Gaby Deslys. She was a nonstop talker. Howard Dietz, the librettist, remarked after one visit: "A

Pauline Lord, Ruth Gordon, and Raymond Massey in *Ethan Frome* (1936). (*Vandamm*)

day away from Tallulah is like a month in the country." When her marriage to John Emery was over, he said: "It was like the rise, decline, and fall of the Roman Empire." Since Miss Bankhead lived as she wanted to, there is no point in deploring the loss of a talented actress. Miss Bankhead was not really interested in the theater. She provided her own glamour. Except in two instances, she was a more interesting actress offstage than on.

In the early twenties, a lean and cool actress, also in her twenties, gave two performances that captivated New York audiences. Eva Le Gallienne's wondering Julie in Molnar's *Liliom*, and her distraught princess in Molnar's *The Swan* were honest and reticent portraits that moved everyone who saw them. With that much success to build on, Miss Le Gallienne could have continued in the familiar pattern of the commercial theater. But she had an original and restless mind. Daughter of the British poet

Richard Le Gallienne and of a Danish writer, Julie Norregaard Le Gallienne, she was dissatisfied with the casual mediocrity of show business, and she was independent enough to do something about it. In 1926, she organized and directed—offstage and on—the Civic Repertory Company in West 14th Street, where audiences, paying 50¢ to $1.50, could see many of the theater's classics. Since that theater was off Broadway, it does not come within the scope of this book; but the repertory made a profound impression on thousands of New Yorkers interested in dramas of distinction. The repertory included plays by Ibsen, Chekhov, Molière, Shakespeare, Andreyev, Barrie, and many others; and among the early members of the acting company was Alla Nazimova, a genius. Patrons subsidized the Civic Repertory to the extent of $100,000 a year. And thousands of theatergoers got their theater education in the battered, cheerless 14th Street Theater that always smelled of disinfectant.

The subject of Miss Le Gallienne's theater, after its failure, comes within the province of this book. During the depression, the subsidies were not renewed. In the hope of earning enough money to continue the Civic Repertory, Miss Le Gallienne moved one of her most imaginative productions, *Alice in Wonderland,* to the New Amsterdam Theater in 42nd Street. It failed, but she did not surrender. She and Ethel Barrymore then appeared in Rostand's *L'Aiglon* at the Broadhurst Theater, under the Civic Repertory banner. The acting was admirable, but the play was old-fashioned and failed. Returning to Ibsen, the dramatist she knew most thoroughly, Miss Le Gallienne appeared in *Hedda Gabler.* Broadway was not really interested in that kind of theater.

But Miss Le Gallienne does not give up easily. After World War II, she and Margaret Webster tried repertory on a big scale at the International Theater in Columbus Circle. As the American Repertory Theater it opened in November 1946 with Shakespeare's *Henry VIII* with Miss Le Gallienne as Katherine of Aragon and Walter Hampden as Cardinal Wolsey. The other plays in the repertory were Ibsen's *John Gabriel Borkman,* Barrie's *What Every Woman Knows,* and Shaw's *Androcles and the Lion.* None of them succeeded. By February of the next year, the company had lost $100,000, and it closed.

The quick failure of such a high-minded organization shocked Broadway and seemed ominous for the theater as a whole. Actors' Equity and the American Theater Wing made donations, as did many individuals. Several service organizations that are usually indifferent to the fortunes of the theater donated their services. After closing the repertory, Miss Le Gallienne reopened the theater with a new production of Sidney Howard's

Yellow Jack in the hope of re-establishing the company. It failed. Broadway audiences do not like repertory. They are not interested in acting. They are interested in hits.

At the American Repertory Theater, the acting was less stimulating than the idea. The performances were intelligent but unexciting. But Miss Le Gallienne confronted Broadway with a plausible, enlightened idea that it has never been able to forget. Her taste, breadth of mind, good will, and energy discovered one of Broadway's dreariest truths. It does not want its mind improved. It wants to be bewitched and entertained.

The great ones have a little something extra. To love of the theater, to intelligence and willingness to work, they bring a personal incandescence that cannot be acquired or imitated. Katharine Cornell was one of these. Something psychological happened when she made an entrance. Audiences could not be indifferent to her presence. Although she was not pretty, she was beautiful—dark eyes, dark hair, a somber, patient voice, and a slightly withdrawn personality. It was as if she could not quite let go. There was about her some strange foreboding that was not deliberate but was inherent in her personality and suggested inner resources of understanding and passion that could not be entirely liberated on the stage. She was not spectacular, but she was electric.

She is the daughter of a Buffalo doctor who renounced his profession to become the manager of a Buffalo theater. She was educated in a Westchester finishing school. She was infatuated with the theater, though unsure of her own talents, as she was to some extent throughout her life. She made her debut in 1917 at the tiny Comedy Theater on 41st Street in *Bushido*, put on by the Washington Square Players. She learned the craft of acting in the pitiless routine of a stock company, managed by Jessie Bonstelle, who in the course of a long stock career trained several talented actors.

Although Miss Cornell was the least aggressive of stage people, theatergoers were interested in her from the beginning. She was favorably noticed in the small parts she played for the Washington Square Players. When she appeared in a London production of *Little Women* in 1920, theater people were aware of some sort of elusive talent in her quiet acting. As a result of that engagement, she was given the central part in Clemence Dane's *A Bill of Divorcement*, in 1921. There were other Broadway openings on the night when *A Bill of Divorcement* gave its first performance at the George M. Cohan Theater before an audience dressed in the style to which the fashionable producer, Charles Dillingham, had happily become accustomed. Helen Hayes opened the same night in Booth Tarkington's *The Wren;* Florence Eldridge opened in Arthur Richman's *Ambush.* Only three of the top critics attended *A Bill of Divorcement,* and their reviews were different. Among the first-nighters was Carl Van Vechten, a former music critic for *The New York Times* and an avant-garde novelist. Bursting with enthusiasm for Miss Cornell and the play, he urged Alexander Woollcott to see the production. Tallulah Bankhead was also enthusiastic, as were Noel Coward and Winthrop Ames. By the end of the week, Burns Mantle and Kenneth Macgowan were making pleasant comments on the production in *The Evening Mail* and *The Globe,* respectively; and on Sunday, Woollcott cried "bravo" in *The New York Times.* Exercising a critic's prerogative to make smashing pronunciamentos on meager evidence, Heywood Broun described Miss Cornell as "an American Duse." *A Bill of Divorcement* was a trumpery piece in the bland Pinero tradition, but it made a star of Miss Cornell. She went on to play Mary Fitton in another play by Clemence Dane—*Will Shakespeare*—a maiden-lady's portrait of Elizabethan lust. Broadway audiences were fascinated with this serial story romance about the author of some formidable classics. A decade earlier, Bernard Shaw had discussed the frailties of Mary Fitton more caustically in his brilliant *The Dark Lady of The Sonnets.* Neither audiences nor author should have been so overawed by her in 1922.

Just before *A Bill of Divorcement* was acted, Miss Cornell married Guthrie McClintic. It was a propitious event for both of them as well as for Broadway. During the next thirty years, they significantly raised the standards of Broadway acting and producing. But not immediately. Except for an excellent production of *Candida,* directed by Dudley Digges in 1924, Miss Cornell squandered her talent for a decade on rueful romances of inferior quality. They were all more or less successful and gave Miss Cornell box-office appeal. In 1925, she made a sensational success in Michael Arlen's *The Green Hat*—a fashionable tearjerker, in which she wore a mannish hat pulled down over her eyes and suffered a good deal from the miseries of the twenties. Humorless, proud, elegantly decadent, the Iris March she acted was a lost lady who felt sorry for herself. *The Green Hat* confirmed the personal vanity of hundreds of young people who enjoyed feeling that the world was not up to their standards, and Miss Cornell's somber sophisticate with head thrust forward became the symbol of the well-heeled losers. She also played in Somerset Maugham's trivial *The Letter,* a squalidly romantic murder play called *Dishonored Lady,* and a sentimentalized stage version of Edith Wharton's *The Age of*

Innocence. For a decade Miss Cornell did not distinguish between the bogus and the genuine.

She felt most comfortable in romantic plays that included a dash of sin or depravity. In 1931, she found one that also had literary quality. Rudolf Besier's *The Barretts of Wimpole Street* had been rejected by twenty-eight Broadway producers. It portrayed the improbable romance of Elizabeth Barrett and Robert Browning; it was also piquantly seasoned with a hint of her father's incestuous interest in her. The disciplined fury that Miss Cornell had been squandering on rubbish now had a worthy object. The gloom and terror of the Barrett home, the tenderness and dignity of Elizabeth Barrett's character, the generosity and ardor of Robert Browning's suit composed a piece of theater that established the Cornell–McClintic style—excellent company, sensitively directed in a beautiful production. Jo Mielziner had designed it with glowing splendor. The part of Robert Browning was played by Brian Aherne, a handsome Englishman who soon became a familiar stage and film actor in America. Charles Waldron, an actor of recognized distinction, played Elizabeth's father. All the actors had talent—John D. Seymour, Brenda Forbes, Joyce Carey, Margaret Barker, John Buckler. *The Barretts of Wimpole Street* opened at the Empire Theater on February 9, 1931. When the audience stumbled out after the final curtain call, there was a general feeling of elation, because Katharine Cornell had abundantly fulfilled the promises of a decade, and a beautiful play had been performed with grace and skill.

Fortunately, *The Barretts of Wimpole Street* was a box-office success. Miss Cornell never again appeared in trash, and Broadway acquired standards from the McClintic brand of casting and staging. Her next play, a version of André Obey's *Lucrece*, in 1932, had no purpose except the creation of beauty. It failed; it was more rhetorical than dramatic. But it looked sublime. Robert Edmond Jones gave it a spacious setting and gorgeous costumes in a style of medieval splendor, and the actors playing the parts of the two commentators wore golden masks that lifted the production above reality. The cast, several of whom had appeared in *The Barretts of Wimpole Street*, helped in the creation of a great occasion, and Miss Cornell's tragic acting was above the level of anything she had done before. The limp terror of her scenes with Tarquin and her farewell to life in the last scene composed a shattering performance. The script was the only failure.

In 1934, she acted Juliet in a stunning production. Romantic parts most became her, and her Juliet—very young in years but mature in sensibility, in love with love and also Romeo, indifferent to anything not concerned with love—was the finest of its time. The standards were high throughout. Edith Evans, who has never had the success she deserved in New York, played a guileful, temperamental, bawdy Nurse that was as fresh as if the part had never been acted before. Basil Rathbone's handsome Romeo was too neat and compact, and Brian Aherne's Mercutio was too diffuse. But the sweep and color of Jo Mielziner's setting gave form to an imagined world. The next year, Miss Cornell, Mr. McClintic, Jo Mielziner, and some notable supporting actors—Brian Aherne, Charles Waldron, Maurice Evans, Arthur Byron, George Coulouris, Kent Smith—saw Bernard Shaw's *Saint Joan* well bestowed. Joan, the country girl and the incarnation of a religious legend, added a new dimension to a star who was dedicated more to the art of the theater than to the box office.

It was a glorious decade. A modest woman played constantly in various styles of theater—dramas with contemporary ideas like Sidney Howard's *Alien Corn*, S. N. Behrman's *No Time for Comedy*, and a freshly imagined *Candida*, brimming over with pity and wisdom. Miss Cornell surrounded herself with peers. In her third and final production of *Candida*, the actors were off the theater's top shelf—Dudley Digges, Mildred Natwick, Raymond Massey, Burgess Meredith. In *The Doctor's Dilemma*, she played the small part of Jennifer, and again surrounded herself with a brilliant cast. The play was not a criticism of doctors; it became a crusade for the life of a talented artist when Miss Cornell stepped on the stage.

She was no actress to play sluts or slatterns. As Cleopatra in Shakespeare's tragedy, her amorousness was not abandoned or wanton. She gave a gracious performance of a reckless Egyptian woman. In Miss Cornell's acting, there was a core of decency that could not be eradicated or disguised. When she revived Somerset Maugham's *The Constant Wife*, it was impossible to believe that the ladylike Constance Middleton would leave her husband and fly into the passionate arms of a lover. Miss Cornell was not a sophisticated actress. But she was one of the few who presided magnificently over Broadway's finest era.

Since it was impossible to discriminate between them, Broadway had two First Ladies in the periods just before and after World War II. They were Katharine Cornell and Helen Hayes—separate but equal. Miss Hayes was thrust into the theater when she was a child. She was the daughter of a traveling salesman in Washington, and a mother who was fascinated with the stage and eager to escape domesticity. From time to time her mother acted in an obscure stock company in Washington and dreamed of a life gleaming with glamour and grandeur. Miss Hayes attended Holy Cross Academy, where she had her first acting experience. At age five, she played Peaseblossom in the school production of A *Midsummer Night's Dream.* Although she was a small, plain girl, she radiated a sort of magic on the stage. In a later school show that parodied the *Ziegfeld Follies*, she precociously impersonated a Gibson girl in a bathing suit and sang a sophisticated lyric ludicrously alien to her age and experience:

> Why do they call me the Gibson Girl?
> Just wear a blank expression
> And a monumental curl,
> Walk with a bend in your back and
> They'll call you the Gibson Girl.

Lew Fields was in the audience and offered to find a part for her if she wanted to go on the stage. But she was already in the midst of a local career. She was a box-office draw in a summer stock production of *The Prince Chap*, and she was re-engaged for other productions by the same company.

When she was nine, her ambitious mother took her to Lew Fields' office in New York, and he put her in his production of *Old Dutch*, a Victor Herbert operetta that had eighty-eight performances. Among Helen Hayes' fellow players in that musical were Mr. Fields, Ada Lewis, Ada Davenport, and Vernon Castle. There is a photograph of her in *Old Dutch*—a tiny girl in a long coat that reaches her ankles and with sleeves that nearly cover her hands. A square-shaped face looks gravely out from under a peachbasket hat. Anyone familiar with Miss Hayes' stage appearance in later years would find something touchingly familiar in that photograph. The patient expression of the mouth—both receptive and inquiring —is still characteristic. In the photograph, the face is neutral. It shows brightness, discipline, and confidence in others, but it is a mask. Since 1909, the personalities of many women have been written across that face, which is like a reflecting mirror; and it is still the plain grave face of a woman who has worked all her life impersonating other women on the stage. Miss Hayes does not have a personality that dazzles the public; she does not behave like a star. Like Katharine Cornell, she is a modest woman. In her home in Nyack, New York, she looks and behaves like a housewife. But put her on the stage and raise the curtain, and something happens to the audience. She was perfectly cast when she played in Barrie's *What Every Woman Knows*—a mousy, unassertive woman who has a powerful influence on other people.

As a child actress, she toured America with the courtly John Drew in *The Prodigal Husband*. At nineteen, she played with William Gillette in Barrie's *Dear Brutus*. All the time she was trouping, she was also studying lessons that the good nuns in Washington mailed to her until she earned her diploma in 1917. She had no life of her own. As a girl, she was busy in a sophisticated profession that took her to places that most children knew nothing about. But she was isolated from the normal life of young Americans. She was surrounded by America, but she was separated from it by the instability of the profession. It was a form of child labor. Earning her own living and her mother's living, she toured in one-night stands in *Pollyanna*, the insufferable "glad girl." She and Alfred Lunt became stars in Booth Tarkington's *Seventeen*. She starred in *Babs*, another play about an unbearable maidenly egotist made from short stories by Mary Roberts Rinehart.

During her engagement as Babs, Miss Hayes began to realize that, despite a dozen years of experience on the stage, she did not know much about acting. She could not sustain a part, performance after performance. Since Mrs. Fiske was in a play that had matinees on afternoons when Miss Hayes was not playing, she studied Mrs. Fiske's technique, and realized that there was more to acting than performing. Ruth Chatterton told her that, although she had talent for the stage, she had no technique. Miss Hayes then started to take lessons in acting from Frances Robinson-Duff, a respected teacher. Miss Hayes began to make a profession out of an occupation.

At about the time she and Lionel Atwill were giving a soggy performance of Shaw's *Caesar and Cleopatra* at the new Guild Theater in 1925, Miss Hayes met Charles MacArthur, a talented, romantic, bizarre young writer who moved in cosmopolitan circles. Suddenly a young star who had had no life outside the theater fell in love with a man estranged from his wife and totally alien to the Hayes Catholic background. Everything was against this improbable alliance. Their financial situations were unequal. He did not want to marry a woman who earned a great deal more than he did. Moreover, the Catholic church would not recognize her marriage to a divorced man.

This part of Miss Hayes' private life is pertinent because it changed her fundamentally. She suddenly discovered that she wanted not only this fascinating man, but the sort of domestic life her precocious career had made impossible. In 1928, she was starred in a romantic drama called *Coquette*, which had opened the previous year. *The Front Page*, written by Charles MacArthur and Ben Hecht, was scheduled to open while

Helen Hayes and Vincent Price in *Victoria Regina* (1935). (*Vandamm*)

Coquette was playing. Since the success or failure of *The Front Page* would be a crucial factor in her marriage to MacArthur, Jed Harris, producer of *Coquette*, closed it for the night when *The Front Page* opened. She sat in the balcony. The authors huddled on the fire escape. At the end of each act, Miss Hayes reported how she thought it was going. After the last act, the prolonged excitement in the theater convinced everyone that *The Front Page* would be a hit. MacArthur proposed to Miss Hayes that night. (In 1970 she played a small part in an excellent revival of *The Front Page*.) After they were married they moved into a large, friendly house on the shore of the Hudson River in Nyack; and despite MacArthur's dissipations and irresponsibility, they had a rich domestic life. They had a daughter, Mary; and they adopted a son, James, who has had a happy career in Hollywood and on television.

Miss Hayes' heart was in her homelife and her family. But her great days in the theater came after she was married. In 1933, she made the crucial transition from popular star in popular comedies to a serious actress by playing the title role in Maxwell Anderson's *Mary of Scotland*. The character of Cleopatra in Shaw's play had eluded her in 1925; she did not have the worldly experience to play that part with insight. But she played Mary of Scotland triumphantly. She was a small woman playing a tall one. Whether or not she was suitably cast was not a factor at the opening performance, for she gave an impression of greatness. She played a queen in royal style.

Two years later, she gave a disarming portrait of Queen Victoria in Laurence Housman's *Victoria Regina*, which was her masterpiece. She made the theater larger than life: she transmuted a rather dull, prosy woman into an overpowering presence. She made a living person out of a myth. Miss Hayes modeled her Victoria on her Grandmother Hayes, who had stood on the street in London when Victoria and Albert passed on their wedding procession in 1840; through the years, Grandmother Hayes had adopted some of Victoria's mannerisms as her own. In Miss Hayes' acting, it was all vivid and intimate. The girlish innocence, the eager propriety of her wooing of Albert, the unaffected joy of her devotion to him, her pettish anger when her authority was challenged, the moving humility of her surrender from Queen to wife, her courage and her simplicity were parts of a memorable stage composition.

Miss Hayes never acted on that level again. As Viola in Shakespeare's *Twelfth Night*, with Maurice Evans, she lacked style. She missed Viola's high breeding; her lighthearted, unsophisticated Viola was more pathetic than romantic. Her succeeding plays were pleasantly trivial. For the theater became less a career than a refuge. When her daughter died of polio, she instinctively turned to the theater for support. Her appearance in Joshua Logan's *The Wisteria Trees*, in 1950, was a form of therapy, and Broadway audiences supported her in it, not only because of her gallant acting, but because they understood her problem. The relationship between actress and public became increasingly personal.

Her public relations have always been uncontrived and cordial. The public took a personal interest in her courtship and marriage. When she had to leave a play because she had become pregnant, the court hassle was an entertaining public topic. "Act of God" was her womanly defense, and everyone approved. Although she has kept her private life intact, she takes a spontaneous interest in public causes. Her husband used to say that she was at the head of the sucker list, and he was partly responsible for putting her there. Before America went to war in 1941, he and Robert Sherwood cozened her into making a speech that Sherwood had written in support of the proposed sale of fifty destroyers to Britain. Nothing could have been more comically inept. Miss Hayes made the uninvited speech from a lifeguard's platform on the beach at Far Rockaway before people in bathing suits who wanted to loll in the sun and swim, and who doubted her competence to instruct them in international polity. "Who do you think you are: Queen Victoria?" one of the swimmers growled as she made her exit up the beach. Miss Hayes looks back on that episode with some embarrassment and a lot of amusement. But it is characteristic of her. Without being either sanctimonious or omniscient, she consistently leads good causes in the theater and, when invited, in the affairs of the nation. Her willingness to serve derives from her philosophy of acting. The phrase "give a performance" she interprets literally. Acting is a form of giving, she believes. Every performer gives the audience the best of himself. The audience also gives. When the occasion is right, it gives not only its approval but its capacity to believe. In all these years, it has never been able to withhold itself from the unaffected star who began as Peaseblossom in *A Midsummer Night's Dream*. Peaseblossom has only two lines in that play. One of them is her response to a question Bottom asks her. "Ready," she says. Miss Hayes has been ready all her life.

It was the heyday of the Lunts. Brilliant actors with mischievous personalities and an insatiable appetite for the stage, they were the most exhilarating and enviable couple on Broadway. As artists, they outranked Sothern and Marlowe. Whether or not they outranked Henry Irving and Ellen Terry is a more difficult question to answer. Reflecting the tastes of

Eva Le Gallienne and Joseph Schildkraut in *Liliom* (1921). (*Vandamm*)

Brian Aherne and Katharine Cornell in *The Barretts of Wimpole Street* (1931). (*Vandamm*)

their time in London, Irving and Terry played many of the greatest parts. Reflecting the tastes of their time on Broadway, the Lunts for the most part gave crackling performances in ephemeral comedies. The opportunities to play the great parts from the Greek tragedies, Shakespeare, and the Restoration comedies are always fewer on Broadway than in London, which has a classical tradition, and the career of the Lunts was limited by Broadway's lack of interest in the classics. But they emerged on Broadway at a time when many congenial young people were shedding the old manners and forming a brighter and gayer stage. Noel Coward, Howard Lindsay, George Kaufman, Marc Connelly, and the Lunts were all well met in the early twenties, when Lindsay was directing Miss Fontanne in the Kaufman and Connelly *Dulcy* (he was also acting in it), and Noel Coward was loitering around the fringes of Broadway and dreaming of the volatile comic improvisations that he introduced in 1925 with *The Vortex*. Although these young people had no program, they had modern ideas.

Miss Fontanne began her career as a child, in a Drury Lane pantomime in London. A thin young woman ("a bag of bones," someone called her) when she began her acting career in London, she did not have much personal success in the parts she played in commonplace plays. But her acting did interest Ellen Terry and Laurette Taylor. There is a hasty note in Ellen Terry's journals: "Must get Lynn more money. It's wicked. . . . She is so intelligent."

She first acted on Broadway in 1910, in the English company of *Mr. Preedy and the Countess*. It lasted only three weeks, after which she returned to London. Six years later, Laurette Taylor cabled her to come to New York to play in J. Hartley Manners' *The Wooing of Eve*. She came; the play failed before it reached Broadway. But she had a considerable personal success in Mr. Manners' next comedy, *The Harp of Life*. Guthrie McClintic, a young, hopeful actor at the time, recalled her in that play as a "tall, dark, very thin and angular" woman who brought the house down with a brief emotional scene at the end of the second act. She emerged from obscurity with that scene. As drama reporter of *The New York Times*, George Kaufman saw her in her next play and thought that she was very funny. Then she played Anna in Eugene O'Neill's *Chris Christopherson*, which was withdrawn before it came to New York and became *Anna Christie* in a second version. In 1921, after twelve years of trouping and mixed failure and success, Miss Fontanne acted the scatterbrained Dulcinea in *Dulcy*. She became a star by making a hilarious part out of a dull character. The surface of the part was trite; Miss Fontanne gave it interior humor by the skill and guile of her acting.

Alfred Lunt was born in Milwaukee into an economically comfortable family. Since his mother loved the theater, he started theatergoing when he was small. Acting was his hobby when he was a boy; he established one of the "attic theaters" with which young people used to entertain themselves in those days. By the time he became a student in Carroll College, Wisconsin, he was a precocious actor and performer in school productions. He described himself as a "character artist" in a circular, which added: "will please any audience who is fortunate enough to hear him."

He began serious work in 1912, when he left school and joined the Castle Square Theater in Boston—a stock company directed with taste and standards by John Craig and Mary Young. (Ruth Gordon, from nearby Wollaston, was a regular patron at that theater, where Winthrop Ames had learned his profession. At matinees, good seats cost only 50¢, less good seats in the orchestra cost 25¢.) Lunt made his professional debut as a bumbling sheriff in a play entitled *The Aviator*. For the next three years, at $20 a week, he played a great many routine parts, most of them old men. After having served his apprenticeship in the grind of stock, he played with Margaret Anglin on the road in *Beverly's Balance*. It was directed by Howard Lindsay, who then regarded Lunt as "awkward, ungainly and ugly" and whose voice, Lindsay thought, was hollow and had an unpleasant break. Lunt was subsequently leading man with Lillie Langtry in a vaudeville tour.

In 1917, he made his Broadway debut with Laura Hope Crews in *Romance and Arabella*. The comedy was without merit. But Lunt played his part in an original style that resulted in his being engaged at $150 a week to play in Booth Tarkington's *The Country Cousin*. Lunt was never a conventional player. His comedy departed from the prevailing style by being basically realistic; it was fresh and forceful. Tarkington liked it so much that he wrote a comedy specifically for Lunt. Entitled *Clarence*, it opened on September 20, 1919, with a cast that included Helen Hayes, Glenn Hunter, and Mary Boland. Playing a wretched, inept war hero returning to civilian life, Lunt was a sensational success: no one else could play routine comedy with so much craftsmanship and detail.

Clarence was produced by George Tyler. One member of Tyler's company was Lynn Fontanne. While Lunt was rehearsing *Clarence*, she happened into the theater, admired his acting, and asked to be introduced to him. They first played together in 1919, as members of the Tyler stock company in Washington, in Richard Washburn Child's *Made of Money*. On May 26, 1922, they were married by the City Clerk of New York, in the Municipal Building. The public first became aware of their genius as a team when they played in Molnar's *The Guardsman* at the Garrick Theater under Theater Guild management, on October 13, 1924. That comedy had failed in 1913 under a different title. Robert Sherwood once said that the Lunts always seemed to have a better time at a play than anyone in the audience, and that was the case with *The Guardsman*. Apart from the brisk, realistic, subtle style of acting they were creating, they enjoyed *The Guardsman* enormously. They entertained the audience with their skill, but they also enkindled the audience with their enthusiasm. In *The New York Times* the next morning, Woollcott wrote that the audience "may well have been witnessing a moment in theatrical history. It is among the possibilities that we were seeing the first chapter in a partnership destined to be as distinguished as that of Henry Irving and Ellen Terry."

After their tumultuous success in *The Guardsman*, which ran forty weeks, the Lunts became leading members of the Guild's acting company. The workload was crushing. It separated them from the secular world. It was like taking holy orders except that, since one was male and the other female, they had certain built-in advantages. Someone observed that they had an advantage over most actors because they could rehearse in bed. Since the theater was their whole life, they were willing to work hard, and they did. During the period of the Guild repertory, they took potluck with the other actors and usually appeared in separate plays. He played in Franz Werfel's *Juarez and Maximilian* while she played Eliza in Shaw's *Pygmalion*—the finest of all the Elizas, realistic and unromantic. He played in Ben Jonson's *Volpone* while she played in O'Neill's *Strange Interlude*. Although they were known as comedians, they played—either separately or together—many serious roles: in *The Brothers Karamazov*, *Ned McCobb's Daughter*, *Marco Millions*.

They appeared together in Maxwell Anderson's *Elizabeth the Queen*, in 1930, and their acting was serious and superb. Although her Elizabeth was made up to look physically unprepossessing, Miss Fontanne gave her regal magnificence, and his Essex conveyed spontaneity, quickness of intellect, and vitality. Their performance had all the enthusiasm of a new generation on the threshold of great achievement. Although the programs always announced the names of the directors, the Lunts inevitably directed themselves; their acting in *Elizabeth the Queen* revealed the understanding of character and the attention to detail that made them great actors as well as technicians. After they had appeared in S. N. Behrman's *The Second Man* and Sil-Vara's *Caprice* in London, in 1929, they notified the Guild that they would never again appear in separate plays. Their style of acting was unique; it involved overlapping dialogue, interrupting each other, facing away from the audience, and turning the back to the audience. Their acting style was largely frittered away if they acted separately.

After 1929, the Lunts took charge of their careers, whether under the management of the Guild or not. The performances were invariably original and memorable: Miss Fontanne's willowy charm and springy step and Lunt's civilized slapstick in Sherwood's *Reunion in Vienna*; their bouncy *The Taming of the Shrew*, which was like horseplay in a hayloft; the honky-tonk style in Sherwood's *Idiot's Delight*; the outrageous masquerade that S. N. Behrman made from Giraudoux's *Amphitryon 38*; Coward's *Design for Living*, in which Coward and the Lunts declared an uproarious moral holiday; the lurid voluptuousness of Coward's *Point Valaine*, in which Miss Fontanne played a middle-aged bawd and Lunt an epicene waiter—all these were entertainments acted with superb professional skill. It is one of the paradoxes of the theater that the most trifling pieces are often the most priceless. Skill, art, clairvoyance, craftsmanship, experience, dedication, even erudition about the theater, can charge a superficial script with gaiety. "Playing" reverts to its original meaning—to take part in a game. In the sinful pranks on which they liked to squander their genius, the Lunts played their scenes together in the style of the chicken coop—balancing the strut of the rooster against the bland mischief of the hen.

Although their style was festive, they were not triflers. Although their acting was worldly, they were scrupulous people. After an exhausting tour in *The Taming of the Shrew* for Finnish War Relief in 1940, they headed home for Genesee Depot, Wisconsin, for a rest. On the train from New York, they read the script of Sherwood's *There Shall Be No Night*—an elegy on the Russian invasion of Finland, an appeal to the conscience of Americans, a declaration of faith in the human tradition. It was a play of special pleading by a high-minded American citizen. Within two weeks, the Lunts were back in New York in rehearsal. On April 29, 1940, they played this serious drama in a spirit of moral inquiry. The play was too overwrought to make good literature, but the earnestness and skill of the acting moved the audience. It also provoked the wrath of some politicians who wanted to defy reality a little longer, and who

denounced *There Shall Be No Night* as subversive to the national interest. After acting *There Shall Be No Night* in America, the Lunts took it to London during the ordeal of the buzz-bomb. Although one part of the Savoy Hotel, where they lived, was blown apart, they never missed a performance until a bomb demolished the Aldwych Theater. They were not present in either place when the bombs exploded. Someone asked Miss Fontanne if she was not terrified when performances were punctuated by bombs falling in the neighborhood. "An actor does not think of death when a performance is going well," she replied. "He thinks of the performance and the audience." Over a period of four years, the Lunts played *There Shall Be No Night* 1,600 times.

On January 23, 1946, they celebrated peace by returning to their familiar milieu. They gave an accomplished performance in a perfunctory comedy at the Empire Theater in New York, where their fashionable peers had been appearing for forty years. The comedy was Terence Rattigan's *O Mistress Mine*. It had 451 performances, the longest run the Lunts ever had on Broadway. Again, they were squandering subtleties of speech and movement on rubbish. In 1949—twenty-five years after their shining performance in *The Guardsman*—they squandered technique and comic spirit on a ramshackle play called *I Know My Love*, which S. N. Behrman had adapted from Marcel Archard's *Auprès de ma blonde*. It was not up to the level of *O Mistress Mine*.

Except Alfred Lunt, there were no American male stars equivalent to the female stars. There were none who could fuse an audience together as John Barrymore had done. Some of them made excellent leading men, but they lacked the fluorescence of the women, or perhaps those who had it departed for Hollywood. Walter Hampden, who had trained for the stage in London, was an actor–manager of considerable eminence. With his own company, he played many Shakespearean dramas conscientiously. In a production of *The Tempest* in which he played an able Caliban, a fiery particle named Fania Marinoff played an Ariel that shimmered with poetry. Being an element of poetry herself, she made Shakespeare sound like poetry. Hampden made him sound like verse. Hampden was the best Cyrano of his generation. His extravagant costume and his grotesque makeup, his agility, his bravura style, and his facility in the speaking of verse brought Cyrano to life in a respected tradition of contrived jauntiness. All Hampden lacked was spontaneity.

In the great parts, English actors were more accomplished, and it is interesting to speculate why. Because of their London background? That must do something to a young man contemplating a career in the theater.

ania Marinoff as Ariel in *The Tempest* at the
Century Theater (1916). Louis Calvert was Prospero; Walter Hampden, Caliban.

The life of London is steeped in theater. The institution of the royal family is theater. The ceremony of the changing of the guard is theater. The Lord Mayor's banquet is theater. The beefeaters at the Tower of London are theater. When a young man begins to work backstage there, he moves through the streets and alleys where Burbage, Betterton, Davenant, Garrick, Kean, Irving, and Forbes-Robertson worked. He becomes part of a tradition three centuries old and as integral to English culture as the Houses of Parliament and St. Paul's Cathedral. In London, acting is not a capricious, freakish, or Bohemian way of life. It is an ancient and honorable profession that is accepted by the public as a normal part of the life of London.

Maurice Evans from London was artistically no greater than New York's Walter Hampden. His taste was no more cultivated; his knowledge and experience, no greater and perhaps less great. But his acting had more bounce and style. He was not self-conscious in the classical roles; costume drama added theatrical color to his pale personality. In London, he had played in six Shakespearean and two Shavian plays as a member of the Old Vic–Sadler's Wells Company. That was an excellent training school that specialized in the classics. Katharine Cornell first brought Evans to America to play Romeo in her traveling company; he played the part with more brio than Basil Rathbone, his predecessor. He also played an amusing Dauphin in her production of *Saint Joan*.

But he acquired permanent status in the New York theater in 1937, when he acted the title role in *King Richard II*. The production was received with rapture and may have altered Broadway's feeling about Shakespeare. *King Richard II* had not been played on Broadway since Booth appeared in it in 1878. A minor play, it was new to nearly every member of the audience. Margaret Webster, imported from London, staged it with classical authority and modern bluntness. Evans' strutting Richard, who succumbed to his enemies with tattered dignity and pathos, was fresh and disarming and transformed Shakespeare out of respectability into a dramatic humanist. *King Richard II* had 171 consecutive performances—an astonishing record that considerably improved Shakespeare's commercial rating among the producers. In association with Miss Webster, whose knowledge of Shakespeare and the stage was and is formidable, Evans acted other Shakespeare plays—including a full-length *Hamlet* that ran from 6:30 to 11:15, with a half-hour coffee break. It had the longest run *Hamlet* had had on Broadway up to that time—131 performances. In his several productions, including Shaw's *Man and Superman* and *The Devil's Disciple*, Evans was never an inspired actor. He did not infuse his productions with wonder. But he was a meticulous workman: he spoke clearly (a rare virtue); and he invariably mastered the text in a way that made it seem intelligible and interesting. For many years Shakespeare had seemed like a tolerable duty. Evans made him a pleasure.

As an actor of traditional parts, John Gielgud had a special asset. He was a latter-day member of the Terry family, who was as used to the stage as they were to their kitchens and living rooms. Ellen Terry was his mother's aunt. As a boy, John Gielgud knew her as a visitor to his parents' home, occasionally saw her on the stage, and impertinently gave a negative answer to her question: "Do you read your Shakespeare?"

John Gielgud first appeared on Broadway in 1928, in Alfred Neumann's *The Patriot*. It lasted twelve performances. To console himself for the unpleasantness of failure, he and other British actors prowled around town visiting speakeasies. To the Londoners, that was a particularly gaudy experience. They enjoyed the felonious sensation of giving mysterious passwords to doorkeepers through iron grills and then being admitted to dark saloons where the Scotch whiskey was awful. It was melodrama and acting. Not being able to find any new parts in New York, Gielgud was glad to return to London where he had begun to have a career.

When he appeared for the second time, in 1936, he was thirty-two years old. He came with considerable aura and retained, or perhaps, heightened it. His production of *Hamlet*, with Judith Anderson as the Queen and Lillian Gish as Ophelia, was joyfully accepted as the leading *Hamlet* of its time. Being young, slender, and handsome, Gielgud portrayed a sensitive and cultivated Hamlet—a little overcivilized perhaps. He lacked fire and passion; the spirit of revolt was weak. But there was no one else who could play with so much delicacy of feeling and patrician authority. For a brief time, there were two English Hamlets in town in 1936. Leslie Howard, a youthful actor of incomparable charm, had long coveted Hamlet as the part to which he was ideally suited. A month after Gielgud had raised the spirits of the ticket speculators, Howard opened his own production. After Gielgud, Howard's amiable and accomplished young prince was an anticlimax. It lacked a point of view, and quickly failed. Gielgud's production had 132 performances—32 more than the Barrymore *Hamlet* of 1922.

After World War II, Gielgud was as familiar a figure on Broadway as he was in London. The acknowledged master of an esoteric style, he showed America how the English comedies of manners must be acted. No one could act Wilde's *The Importance of Being Earnest* with so much diffidence and disdain, or Congreve's *Love for Love* with such devastating hauteur. Gielgud illustrated one of Wilde's celebrated apothegms: "In matters of grave importance, style—not sincerity—is the vital thing." With his head high, his bony face expressionless, his voice dry and snobbish, Gielgud played comedy of manners brilliantly. He made artificial comedy look and sound witty, thin, immaculate, and accomplished. "Style is the way the chin is worn," says Lady Bracknell in another Wilde comedy. Gielgud wore his very high indeed.

The extent of Gielgud's Broadway involvement in 1947 indicates the confidence the American theater had in him. In October, he vividly staged Judith Anderson's tempestuous *Medea*—although his personal portrait of Jason was ineffectual, for Gielgud does not have the rude strength for parts like that. In December of the same season, he gave a memorable performance as Raskolnikoff in Rodney Ackland's version of Dostoevsky's *Crime and Punishment*. It was staged with sweep and drive by Theodore Komisarjevsky, and it included a crackbrained Katerina by Lillian Gish and a Sonia that Dolly Haas acted with a balancing of strength and meekness that was shattering. Raskolnikoff was just right for Gielgud, whose sharp, lean, tormented characterization composed a masterpiece.

Two years later, he made Christopher Fry's *The Lady's Not for Burning* look and sound more brilliant than the text. Under Gielgud's direction, the company played in the glittering style of artificial comedy—Pamela Brown and Esme Percy being especially adroit and polished. Richard Burton, then at the beginning of his career, gave an amusing performance as a baffled clerk. But it was Gielgud's play. His acting and staging were like a piece of expert rococo architecture on the surface of a vacuum—elaborate but empty, imposing but meaningless. If it were not for Gielgud, Broadway audiences would not know how double-edged the artificial style is. Lunt is also a superb actor, but there is a trace of sincerity in his acting. There is always something about Lunt that has to be believed.

Broadway made the acquaintance of Laurence Olivier long before he became the leading English-speaking actor of his era. Some of his apprentice work was done in New York. In 1931, he and Jill Esmond served the humiliating function of being straightman and straightwoman for the comic extravagance of Noel Coward and Gertrude Lawrence in *Private Lives*. It was not a glamorous engagement for Olivier, but it was experience. Within three years, it was obvious that Olivier had become a remarkable actor. He played one of the two leading parts in Mordaunt Shairp's *The Green Bay Tree*—a baleful, enigmatic drama about a homosexual relationship. Olivier acted a character who was in the process of disintegration—all of it subtle and delicate and some of it at a pitch of emotion that left the audience dazed. In 1939, with Katharine Cornell, in *No Time for*

Comedy, Olivier acted a tempestuous young playwright with a virtuosity that seemed to have one hundred ways of saying what the author had in mind. The spectacle of Olivier gaining stature year by year was exciting.

His next performance was a disaster that he would like to consign to limbo. By 1940, he and his wife, Vivien Leigh, were the darlings of their profession. Everything they did was a tumultuous success. After making a film in Hollywood, they visited New York to play the drama to which their youth, charm, and skill and personal enthusiasm especially suited them. Their preparations for *Romeo and Juliet* were extensive and meticulous. Following Olivier's orders, the English firm of Motley designed twenty-one scenes to be mounted on moving platforms; and, as if one group of talented artists was not enough, Robert Edmond Jones was engaged to design the lighting. Everything about the production was solid; the doors closed with a bang; the hardware rattled honestly. Bells rang offstage. The orchestra was busy all evening playing the "traditional airs," and the religious scenes were overlaid with Palestrina chants. The cast was of the best—Dame May Whitty, as the Nurse; Halliwell Hobbes, as Capulet; Ben Webster, as Montague; Wesley Addy, as Benvolio; Alexander Knox, as Friar Laurence. In Motley's splendid costumes, Olivier and Miss Leigh looked ravishing. But they had designed a production that crushed the performance. They had to play so far upstage that it seemed as if they were in another theater and that two strange actors were playing to some other audience. Shakespeare's casual "two hours traffic on the stage" lengthened to more than three. A gifted actor had ingeniously designed his own destruction. Olivier left New York in a desolate frame of mind.

He got ample revenge six years later. He visited New York at the head of an Old Vic Company that left a permanent mark on the memories of theatergoers who saw him. Within the space of a month, he and his colleagues played a repertory consisting of both parts of Shakespeare's *Henry IV*, Chekhov's *Uncle Vanya*, Sheridan's *The Critic* and W. B. Yeats's version of the Sophocles *Oedipus Rex*. The Old Vic visit was a good-will mission from one war ally to another, and it was a resounding success. The company included many of London's finest players—Ralph Richardson, Miles Malleson, Margaret Leighton, Joyce Redman, and George Rose. They gave gorgeous performances of five unrelated classics. They performed with grace, ease, resonance, and dexterity.

Olivier is one of the bright figures in a panel of male stars that consists of himself, Richard Mansfield, John Barrymore, John Gielgud, and Alfred Lunt—the Grand Panjandrums of the theater in English during the first fifty years of the century. Broadway used them all after their deserts, which were magnificent.

1939–1950

WORLD WAR II

One week after Germany invaded Poland in 1939, Rachel Crothers, a serious-minded playwright who had been head of the Stage Women's War Relief in 1917, called a meeting of theater women to organize the American Theater Wing of British War Relief. She and her colleagues knew what was about to happen, and they took up where they had left off twenty years before. Although Broadway is liberal in politics and morals, it is conservative in its loyalty to the nation; and by the nature of its profession, it has a special competence in the promotion of public causes.

When the United States declared war on Germany and Japan in 1941, the American Theater Wing separated from British War Relief and concentrated on American needs. It became a major Broadway industry very quickly. It performed many different services and drew on the talent and good will of hundreds of theater people. The Wing headquarters at Fifth Avenue and 57th Street were jammed day and night with volunteers who

Tony Pastor, Frank Humphries, Parker Lund, Bob Walters, Paul Lajoie, Al Sears, and Buddy Weed perform at the Stage Door Canteen. (*Culver Pictures, Inc.*)

Killer Joe and Shirley Booth at the Stage Door Canteen's third birthday party. (*Culver Pictures, Inc.*)

did everything from addressing envelopes to writing stage sketches on themes affecting the understanding and morale of the public and workers in war industries. As in World War I, the stars were in constant demand to address war bond and Red Cross rallies and to appear at all kinds of street meetings. It was soon apparent that there were not enough stars to go around. Members of the Wing solved this problem by writing expository sketches that could be played on any improvised platform by three or four actors of less than star rank. The sketches were pure theater. They were so vivid and persuasive that the Wing had to be cautious about promoting anything that was not part of the government program.

After representing the theater in two world wars, Miss Crothers withdrew as president and was succeeded by a former actress and a consistent friend of the theater, Mrs. Antoinette Perry. Mrs. Perry presided over a tumultuous organization ably and anonymously. The annual Tony awards for excellence in all branches of the theater memorialize her skill, energy, and generosity. She had many assistants, among them Mrs. Louise Beck, who gave the Wing a large slice of her life. But it was Mrs. Perry who administered and developed a huge service organization.

People accustomed to the cautious tempo of the theater were astonished by the speed and scope of the Wing. On March 1, 1942, only four months after the declaration of war, the Wing undertook its most difficult and utopian enterprise. It opened the Stage Door Canteen in the basement of the 44th Street Theater, and entertained servicemen of all nations from six o'clock until midnight for the rest of the war. Executives in established corporations might have hesitated before organizing a project that needed such detailed supervision by members of a volunteer staff and consumed so much food and drink. The Stage Door Canteen was a combination night club and soup kitchen.

Although Broadway could not manage its own affairs, it ran the Stage Door Canteen brilliantly. Nearly everything was free. The Shubert Brothers donated the premises, which had once been a nightclub and speakeasy. Stage designers contributed the décor. Caterers, restaurateurs, and food merchants gave the sandwiches, pies, cakes, and coffee. The hostesses were volunteers who served on a rotating schedule; and dance bands, singers, vaudevillians, actors, and night-club performers put on excellent shows. About 1,700 people from all branches of the industry in rotation cooked, washed dishes, swept the floors, and looked after the unpredictable affairs of a night club. Some of them worked every night, although most of them had schedules of about three and a half hours a week. The job was impossible, but it was done.

The Wing had expected to serve about five hundred servicemen a night.

The number turned out to be closer to three or four thousand, most of whom had to stand in line before there was room inside. Most of them were Americans, but British, Canadians, Australians, Dutch, Chinese, French, and Russians also dropped in. There was never a shortage of entertainers. Ethel Merman, Gracie Fields, and Ethel Waters sang. Al Jolson did his bit by singing "Sister Susie's Sewing Shirts for Soldiers," a memento from World War I. Jane Cowl, Lynn Fontanne, and Alfred Lunt served food, waited on table, and helped with the chores. Some of the men in uniform were also performers. There was a sensational sailor called "Killer Joe" who became almost as famous as the stars. He was a stupendous jitterbugger; he tossed his partners over his head, including a few prudent stars who danced with him only once. Shirley Booth was among the stars he uplifted. In *This Is the Army*, Irving Berlin wrote a rousing tune called "I Left My Heart at the Stage Door Canteen," expressing a common experience. On Broadway, the theater was overwhelmed with problems. But the Stage Door Canteen, which had no backing except good will, had a long and happy run. Give the theater a cause it believes in, and it is like a cornucopia. Everything good pours out. Money is not the basic ingredient of show business. Convivial people are.

In comparison with World War I, World War II was thoroughly professional, and the volunteer service organizations were recruited and supervised on a large scale. The United Service Organization was only one step removed from being an arm of the government. In April 1940, twenty months before America declared war, the USO spontaneously inaugurated Camp Shows to dispel some of the agonizing boredom of military life among drafted Americans. Theater and motion-picture stars began at that time the long chore of touring the camps where citizen soldiers were stationed. In February 1941, still nine months before the American declaration of war, the War Department formally asked the USO to accept the responsibility of entertaining the troops. Abe Lastfogel, a citizen who believed in public causes and was an executive at the William Morris Agency, took charge of Camp Shows and helped to raise the initial $16 million from private sources. Government support was formidable. In June, General George C. Marshall made a special trip from Washington to unveil a huge USO sign in Times Square, containing a portrait of President Franklin D. Roosevelt with a brief endorsement: "The USO deserves the support of every individual citizen." Since it dominated Times Square, it helped every day to remind every Broadway pedestrian of the nature and the extent of the national emergency.

Representing all parts of American show business on the West Coast as well as the East, USO was a huge, far-reaching, professional organization. In December 1945, there were only thirty productions on Broadway—less than half the number in the theater's happiest era. But USO had fifty-nine touring companies in the United States and 228 overseas; and it employed 2,200 actors, ninety-seven percent of whom had to be paid. The three percent who were able to volunteer included eminent people. Katharine Cornell and Brian Aherne took *The Barretts of Wimpole Street* to overseas bases, some of which were close to the front. Miss Cornell was not certain how combat soldiers would respond to a Victorian literary romance. They loved it. Maurice Evans took what he called his *GI Hamlet* to many remote bases in the Pacific. It was rapturously received. Helen Hayes, Raymond Massey, Jane Cowl, Ethel Barrymore, Judith Anderson, Fredric March, and Florence Eldridge (the last two actors long devoted to public causes) toured overseas bases in dramas and sketches, many of which seemed too cultivated for soldiers and sailors. It turned out that nothing was too good for them. Joe E. Brown and Marlene Dietrich were USO actors. Bob Hope made four trips overseas during the war, and made annual pilgrimages to remote bases for the next quarter of a century.

USO companies played in Labrador, China, the Philippines, France, Italy—wherever Americans were stationed. Some actors gave more than their talent. Tamara, who had sung "Smoke Gets in Your Eyes" in *Roberta,* was killed in the crash of a USO flying clipper over Lisbon in 1943. Roy Rognan, a dancer with the same troupe, also was killed. Gypsy Markoff and Jane Froman were seriously injured, and it was the end of Miss Froman's career as a singer. Although she underwent several operations afterwards, she never recovered the informal, pleasant singing style that had made her a star. During the war, seventeen USO actors died overseas.

After having performed its mission well and bountifully for seven years, the USO disbanded in 1947. But not for long. By force of circumstances, it became a permanent institution. When the Korean war began in 1950, it resumed the endless task of relieving the tedium of army life everywhere. Al Jolson made his last appearance on the stage as a USO entertainer in Korea. The Vietnam war became the third of the USO's major emergencies.

World War II changed the nature of the civilians who wandered up and down Broadway. They were primarily moviegoers. Some of them seemed never to have attended the theater before. They came in mufti: they wore mackinaws and windbreakers. Inside the theater, they departed from custom by sitting in their shirtsleeves. They had plenty of money, which they had earned in war industries. When buying a seat worth $5.23, some of them startled the box-office treasurers by tossing fifty-dollar bills on the counter.

As in the past, the tawdry Broadway booths still sold fruit drinks for 5¢ and live turtles for 50¢. But luxury merchandise was in constant demand in the shops. The men's furnishing shops sold shirts for $15.00 to $22.50, and handpainted ties for $10.00 to $15.00. (Nudes were the favorite emblems on the ties.) It was easier to sell nightshirts for $30.00 to $50.00 than for the more usual $7.50. Walgreens drugstore had no trouble selling bottles of perfume for $50.00. People casually dropped into a jeweler's shop and paid $1,500 for rings. In the lobby of the Astor Hotel, the flowerstand sold orchids for $6.00 to $18.00. When Frank Sinatra was making personal appearances at the Paramount Theater, bobby-soxers sent him bunches of flowers that cost $30.00 or $40.00.

Broadway was choked every night with servicemen looking for a good time. But it was supported by many unworldly people who for the first time in their lives had more money than they knew what to do with. There were hundreds of enterprising merchants ready to help them. At night, Broadway looked exciting. At the head of Times Square, at 46th Street, Broadway, and Seventh Avenue, the bank of three electric signs put everything in proper proportion: "Four Roses," at the top; "Kinsey's Blend," in the middle; "Pepsi-Cola," at the bottom. On Broadway, there was something for everyone.

WITHDRAWAL

SYMPTOMS

After the demoralizing ordeal of the depression, the ordeal of World War II was particularly agonizing. There had been a latent feeling after World War I that something could be done to solve the problems of human existence rationally. In the theater, Sherwood, Howard, and Wilder were essentially optimistic men; and although Behrman, Anderson, and Rice were more cautious, they were not pessimists. All of them looked outward at a flawed world they thought capable of being mended. But this was no longer a tenable point of view. It was obvious that the problems of America and the world were not being solved rationally. The economic depression of the thirties, which had shaken the foundations of the political and economic system, was not solved: it was concluded, and not by positive action, but by the desperate organization of the nation into a war machine to produce goods and armies to kill human beings. The irrationality of another world war superseded the misery of the depression and made

Howard Lindsay, John Drew Devereux, Richard Simon, Dorothy Stickney, Larry Robinson, and Raymond Roe in *Life with Father* (1939). (*Vandamm*)

the future look ominous. The tendency of thoughtful people was to look inward. Art began to feed on itself. Audiences began to see something they recognized as realistic in negative and inconclusive dramas.

During World War II, Broadway was more sophisticated than it had been during World War I. Dramatists did not make the eagle scream; they were no longer amateur patriots. There was considerable swagger in Irving Berlin's *This Is the Army* and Moss Hart's *Winged Victory*, which were produced to create good will for the Army and Air Force, respectively. To thousands of sympathetic theatergoers, this kind of fond propaganda seemed both reasonable and enjoyable. But on the civilian stage, the uniform was not a carnival costume, as it had been during World War I. It symbolized the most serious crisis of the day.

There were no catchpenny spy melodramas like *Three Faces East* during World War I, or maudlin romances like *Marie-Odile*, which capitalized on the war. During World War II, Arthur Laurents' war drama about a Jewish soldier, *Home of the Brave*, was a serious discussion of emotional paralysis. John Patrick's *The Hasty Heart* was set in an Assam hospital and seriously portrayed the emotional dilemma of a Scottish soldier. Paul Osborn's dramatization of John Hersey's *A Bell for Adano* recognized the military occupation of an enemy village, not as victory, but as an unhappy necessity. There were some delightful comedies that had war backgrounds. Taking a script by Franz Werfel as his raw material, S. N. Behrman made a humorous and witty play, *Jacobowsky and the Colonel*, about a clash of personalities in the German invasion of France. John van Druten's *The Voice of the Turtle*, in which Margaret Sullavan and Elliot Nugent appeared, was an essentially romantic comedy about a soldier out on pass. But the war plays were not jingoistic shouts of victory. The two most popular after the war was over, *Command Decision* and *Mr. Roberts*, were antiheroic and depicted war as either horrifying or boring. The spiritual torment of *Command Decision* and the comic antics of *Mr. Roberts* recognized war as brutal or mad.

Some of the established playwrights instinctively attempted to lift the morale of the nation. Anderson wrote two missionary plays, *Candle in the Wind* and *The Eve of St. Mark*, but neither of them came to grips with reality. Sherwood's inquiry into the invidious motives of industrialists and newspaper writers during wartime, *The Rugged Path*, was a disastrous drama and, in fact, his last play. It was a painful conclusion to an honorable career. Of all the established playwrights, Sidney Kingsley, author of *Men in White* and *Dead End* in the thirties, acquitted himself most honorably. His *The Patriots* was not literature, but a thoughtful inquiry into the relationships among Jefferson, Hamilton, and Washington. It stated the American credo persuasively and received the Critics Circle award. "I believe, indeed, I know this government is the world's best hope," Jefferson said in the last scene. In 1943, when *The Patriots* was produced, that stated the national credo.

Since the theater is under no obligation to instruct, Broadway diverted theatergoers with some good comedies that had nothing to do with the war: Noel Coward's droll and impish *Blithe Spirit*, which involved a ghost in a worldly sex affair; Mary Chase's *Harvey*, in which Frank Fay impersonated a contented dipsomaniac; *The Late George Apley*, a sardonic portrait of a proper Bostonian, by George S. Kaufman and John Marquand, with a deliciously comic performance by Leo Carroll as the pettifogging gentleman; and Garson Kanin's *Born Yesterday*, in which a new, enchanting actress, Judy Holliday, played the impudent part of a gangster's moll. She was reformed and educated by the Washington correspondent of *The New Republic* in mufti, or so Kanin contended.

Since the energies of the nation were concentrated on the war, the decline in dramatic creativity did not seem surprising. Everyone was living from day to day in a common mood of anxiety; and writers did not have the excess of vigor needed to produce original work. But Broadway did not remain exclusively superficial; the revivals were numerous and had stature both as literature and acting. There were three notable productions of Shakespeare, all of them staged by Margaret Webster, who, beginning with Maurice Evans' *King Richard II*, had discovered how to make Shakespeare not only respectable but intelligible. Her productions had phenomenal runs. Evans and Judith Anderson gave 131 performances of a sensual, haunted *Macbeth*. *Othello*, with Paul Robeson as a slack and ponderous Moor, and with José Ferrer, Uta Hagen, and Margaret Webster giving color and tension to other roles, ran for 296 performances—a very high score for any Shakespeare production. Canada Lee, an excellent Negro actor, played Caliban to Vera Zorina's effortless, dancing Ariel in a first-rate production of *The Tempest*. During wartime, Shakespeare seemed like a pertinent writer; he knew how human beings behave.

But there were other revivals far above the average rank, and they gave Broadway interludes of distinction. Chekhov's *The Three Sisters* had a lustrous cast—Katharine Cornell, Judith Anderson, and Ruth Gordon, all of them radiant women. Miss Cornell, Raymond Massey, Burgess Meredith, Mildred Natwick, and Dudley Digges appeared in a rich and beautifully composed *Candida* that was the finest in Broadway history. The abundance and the splendor of the revivals turned out to be more than a wartime stopgap. After the war was over, they continued to compensate for the short supply of original scripts. In 1946–1947, the original plays included O'Neill's *The Iceman Cometh*, Lillian Hellman's *Another Part of the Forest*, and Maxwell Anderson's *Joan of Lorraine*, with Ingrid Bergman. Note that all these dramas were somber; the mood was melancholy. But in the same season, the interesting new plays were outnumbered by a series of excellent revivals—*The Front Page, Cyrano de Bergerac, The Duchess of Malfi, Lady Windermere's Fan, Androcles and the Lion, Lysistrata, The Importance of Being Earnest, The Playboy of the Western World*, and Eva Le Gallienne's repertory productions of *Henry VIII, What Every Woman Knows, John Gabriel Borkman*, and *Yellow Jack*. The literary standards of Broadway were remarkably high.

During the war, the public mood had changed. Plays in styles that had

Ethel Waters and Julie Harris in *The Member of the Wedding* (1950). (*The New York Public Library*)

Judith Anderson as Olga in Katharine Cornell's production of *The Three Sisters* (1942). (*Vandamm*)

Mildred Dunnock, Arthur Kennedy, and Cameron Mitchell in *Death of a Salesman* (1948). (*Culver Pictures, Inc.*)

Eddie Dowling, Laurette Taylor, and Julie Haydon in *The Glass Menagerie* (1945). (*The Lester Sweyd Collection, The New York Public Library*)

been acceptable before the war no longer interested the public. *Life with Father*, the ideal popular American comedy, ran for 3,224 performances after it was produced in 1939. But the sequel, *Life with Mother*, written by the same authors, and with Howard Lindsay and Dorothy Stickney applying the same humorous charm to the leading parts, failed in 1948. The material was as droll and affectionate as in *Life with Father*. In some respects, the sequel was more beguiling. But the public was no longer amused. It was difficult to know what the public attitude was. In a world that was playing with the atom bomb, Broadway was out of tune, and the familiar schism between Broadway and the adult world became so wide that playgoers could hardly see across.

During the forties, musical drama flourished both as entertainment and as literature. In musical drama, Broadway led the world. But, despite a few creative plays, the spoken drama was beginning to lose the confidence and drive it had before World War II. The theater no longer dominated show business. Commenting on the character of the postwar years, Sherwood remarked: "The American theater is today bristling with potential talent in all departments save one: playwriting. It is a melancholy fact that one needs few extra fingers to count the young and even the middle-aged playwrights who have so far made any valid claim on public recognition."

There were two happy exceptions to this bill of disconsolate particulars. Tennessee Williams and Arthur Miller, whose first Broadway productions occurred during the war, brought new ideas and styles and fresh energy into the theater. They dominated it so completely that the postwar years could be called the Williams–Miller era. What ten or twelve vivacious dramatists were to Broadway after World War I, Williams and Miller were in the years after World War II. They were natural theater men. They regarded the theater as a medium in which ideas could be stated.

Williams' wistful *The Glass Menagerie* was produced in the spring of 1945 and won the Critics Circle award at the end of the season. (The Pulitzer Prize went to *Harvey*.) Miller's first Broadway production was *The Man Who Had All the Luck*, in 1944. Although it lasted only four performances, many people recognized the talent of the man who had written it. Amid all the mumbo-jumbo of show business, neither Williams nor Miller had to wait for recognition. Their talents were needed.

If it is true that all modern playwrights are descended from either Ibsen or Chekhov, Miller and Williams are the perfect examples. Miller is concerned with things that can be defined or stated, with facts and ideas. His plays are tangible; they arrive at conclusions. Williams dramatizes impressions; he does not bluntly state either the premises or the conclusions. He is a poet at heart. There is no division between him and what he writes; everything is an emanation of himself.

Tennessee Williams was born (Thomas Lanier Williams) in Columbus, Mississippi, on March 26, 1914, the second child of Cornelius Coffin Williams, a smart shoe salesman, and Edwina Dakin Williams, daughter of an Episcopal clergyman. When he was eight, the family moved to St. Louis, where he spent his formative years. His father was a caustic, overbearing man who constantly belittled his son, calling him "Miss Nancy." His mother was a Southern lady full of social gambits and irrelevant conversation. After Williams had studied at the University of Missouri and Washington University, he submitted to his father's order to go to work as a clerk in the International Shoe Factory. The job was monotonous; life at home, unbearable. Finally Williams fled from both.

The depth of human understanding in the plays, the clarity and sensitivity of the characterizations, and the variety of the scenarios represent the range of his experience during the years when he was in flight and living on the fringes of society, working as a waiter, a night elevator operator, and a theater usher. He was one of the original hippies, whose sensuous world consisted of "hot swing music and liquor, dance halls, bars and movies, and sex that hung in the gloom like a chandelier and flooded the world with brief, deceptive rainbows," to quote from *The Glass Menagerie*, an autobiographical play. His experience was limited in scope but not in intensity. While battering around the country, he was escaping the kind of life he could not tolerate. In the act of writing plays, he escaped the pressures he could not endure within himself.

Before *The Glass Menagerie* was produced, he had one especially painful experience. After putting on his first professional production in Boston, *Battle of Angels*, the Theater Guild abruptly closed it; and, taking notice of the nature of the criticism, apologized to the subscribers for having afflicted them with an obscene play. (Sixteen years later, Williams revised it, called it *Orpheus Descending*, and tried it again in New York. No one was shocked. After sixteen years, he was accepted as a serious dramatist who was entitled to develop his own career in the styles most personal and characteristic.)

In his words, *The Glass Menagerie* was a "memory play." Without being a literal record of what happened, it recaptured the torment and insecurity of his life and the life of his sister and mother in St. Louis. In the context of the spring of 1945, when playwriting was at a low ebb, the intuitive form of *The Glass Menagerie*, the tender insight into character, the delicate symbolism, the familiarity with the environment, and the sustained tone of elegy were like a revelation of what superb theater could be. Fortunately, the play was staged perceptively, and acted by a cast that became a legend—Laurette Taylor as the overbearing mother full of social cant and clichés, Julie Haydon as the crippled daughter, Eddie Dowling as the rebellious son, and Anthony Ross as the gentleman caller full of amiable truisms.

With the quick success of *The Glass Menagerie*, Williams escaped from poverty and obscurity for the rest of his life. Although he has written other excellent plays, he has never again written a play as lovely and merciful as his first Broadway success. It contains the most personal parts of his background.

In the order of the writing, but not of the production, *Summer and Smoke* was his next play. Both plays had much in common. The structure of both was tenuous and poetic. The author looked on from a distance in the role of a sympathetic observer who watched the characters moving through the shadowy labyrinth of life. He put their hopes and frustrations into idiomatic words that had cadence and melody. The social status of the characters did not concern him, nor was he interested in their cleverness, skill, or accomplishments. Loneliness was the sovereign theme. He was concerned with what separated them. The epigraph he chose for *Summer and Smoke* stated his point of view. It came from Rainer Maria Rilke: "Who, if I were to cry out, would hear me among the angelic orders?" In *Summer and Smoke*, the two chief characters, Alma Winemiller and John Buchanan, had been neighbors all their lives and ought to have been able to meet on casual terms. But they were always at cross purposes. Her hysteria and his masculine bravado separated them. *Summer and Smoke* had the soft texture of *The Glass Menagerie* and the same languid doom. Despite a glowing performance and a shimmering production, the play failed on Broadway—partly because it was produced after *A Streetcar Named Desire*.

For it was *A Streetcar Named Desire*, in 1947, that took Broadway by storm and established Williams as a theater writer of the first rank. The episodes in *Streetcar* were concrete and tangible, and the momentum of the story was melodramatic. Like the women in the other plays, Blanche Du Bois was hysterical. Cooped up in a tiny, squalid apartment with her sister and brother-in-law, she pursued the silly fantasy of her emotional life. Only a writer who had survived in the lower depths of a sultry Southern city could know the characters as intimately as Williams did and be so thoroughly steeped in the aimless sprawl of the neighborhood life. The swinish poker game, the drunken quarrel, the banal courtship, the brutal sexual encounter in the last act, the homely pathos of the conclusion, and the simplicity of the dialogue were elements of a modern masterpiece.

Williams writes superbly actable parts. Like the cast that played *The Glass Menagerie*, the cast of *A Streetcar Named Desire* became a legend. Elia Kazan's direction was sensitive and scrupulous, and the confrontations and climaxes were overwhelming. The tenderness and the brutality were woven into a single strand of panic and doom. Marlon Brando became a star on the basis of the sullen, brutish brother-in-law he played vividly; and Karl Malden's portrait of the homely drudge named Mitch began the illustrious part of his career. Jessica Tandy's desperate, shrill, terrified Blanche and Kim Hunter's contented sister were sharply imagined and acted, and the baleful moods rose and fell in the acting of a perfectly balanced cast. The audience was both moved and elated by the performance, and *A Streetcar Named Desire* received both the Pulitzer Prize and the Critics Circle award.

All these plays had a similar tone of rejection; all the characters succumbed to tensions and hostilities. But they do not represent the whole of Tennessee Williams. He, too, longs for peace and companionship. There are three lines in a later play (*Cat on a Hot Tin Roof*) that round out the Williams sensibility: "Time goes by so fast. Nothin' can outrun it. Death commences too early—almost before you're half-acquainted with life—you meet with the other—Oh, you know we just got to love each other and stay together, all of us, just as close as we can." That's how Williams wishes it were.

The two playwrights who dominated the postwar theater could not be more unlike. Tennessee Williams is a short man, full of misgivings. Arthur Miller is a tall and remarkably self-assured and very articulate. If Williams is always in flight, Miller faces situations head-on. He believes that life has a meaning. He is a concerned citizen; he takes an active part in political and professional causes, and he is a persuasive polemicist. He was born in New York on October 17, 1915, but raised in Brooklyn, which has had a fundamental influence on his point of view. For it has given him his perspective on the American system. He sees the tyrannies and the inhumanities of the city from the viewpoint of neighborhood life just outside the city. He is aware of the system, without having been absorbed by it. He was educated at the University of Michigan, where in two successive years he received the Avery Hopwood Award for Playwriting—established by the expert writer of farce who regarded serious playwriting as a pose. Miller also received the Theater Guild's Bureau of New Plays award. After graduating from college, Miller joined a Federal Theater writing project that lasted only four months before the Federal Theater was purged by an astigmatic Congress. He wrote radio scripts for a time. During the early part of World War II, he worked as a steamfitter in the Brooklyn Navy Yard—a source of considerable knowledge about the habits and points of view of laboring people. For six months, he was attached as a reporter to the infantry to gather material for Ernie Pyle's film, *The Story of GI Joe.* This experience was the source of a book called *Situation Normal,* published in 1944. He published a novel about race hatred, *Focus,* in 1945.

While the war was still going on, a friend told him the story of a girl she knew who had informed the government against her father for selling defective machinery to the Army. That anecdote became the germ of *All My Sons,* a powerful play about a manufacturer who knowingly sold the government some faulty airplane engines that resulted in the death of twenty-one pilots. The thrust of the play was less against the crime than against the lack of social responsibility. Joe Keller, the manufacturer, was an ardent family man. Of his son he said: "I'm his father and he's my son, and if there's something bigger than that I'll put a bullet in my head." When the son, back from the war, decided to inform the government against his father for the defective engines, Joe Keller did kill himself. The son's concluding remark to his mother stated the theme of the play: "Once and for all you can know that there's a universe of people outside, and you're responsible to it."

During his early years in New York, Miller had admired the Group Theater as a socially useful organization. Although the Group Theater was no longer in existence in 1947, the production of *All My Sons* was very much a Group Theater enterprise. Harold Clurman, who had been one of the Group Theater leaders, was one of the three producers of the Miller play. Elia Kazan, of the Group Theater, was a second (Walter Fried was the third), and Kazan also staged the headlong performance. The shrewdly chosen cast included Ed Begley, Arthur Kennedy, Beth Merrill and Karl Malden, all of whom were part of the Group Theater movement in acting. *All My Sons* won the Drama Critics Circle award.

After it had settled down to a long run, there was some thunder on the right, echoing the political pathology of the day. Since Russia and the United States had been allies in a long war, they hated each other more than usual. In America, there was another psychosis: Russia was and is a Communist state. Jingoistic Americans who did not trust democracy suspected any criticism of the system as a Communist plot. They denounced Miller as a Communist. They berated *All My Sons* as a smear on the American business community. The Civil Affairs Division of the American Military Government refused to give *All My Sons* a license to be performed in the occupied areas of Europe. It licensed Wilder's *Our Town* and *The Skin of Our Teeth*, Robert Ardrey's *Thunder Rock*, O'Neill's *Mourning Becomes Electra*, Sherwood's *Abe Lincoln in Illinois*, Behrman's *Biography*, and van Druten's *The Voice of the Turtle*. But not *All My Sons*. Although the war had been fought for, among other things, freedom of speech, America was beginning to imitate the ideology of the enemy. A branch of the War Department reduced art to the level of propaganda. But Broadway, as usual, was not intimidated by crackpots and demagogues and continued to support a play it liked. On Broadway, "How's your second act?" is a more pertinent question than "Who's that liberal I seen you with last night?"

Miller's finest play, *Death of a Salesman*, was produced in 1949 and made unforgettable dramatic use of most of what Miller had learned in Brooklyn and in his experience in business. Willy Loman was a classic American figure—the chump who believed all the slogans and dreamed all the banalities. Fundamentally, he was a good man. His home was the center of his life. He was devoted to his wife and loved his two sons. Around the house, he was a good amateur craftsman—a good man with a batch of cement and ceiling panels. His wife said there was more of him in the front porch he built with his own hands than in all the merchandise he sold on the road. But outside the home, he bluffed and postured—a minor actor in the great mythology of sales promotion. He was betrayed by his vocation. In his old age, he was tossed aside by his boss because he was no longer an asset to the firm. The system rewarded one of its believers with the sack—nothing having led to nothing at the end.

Although Miller and Williams differ from one another completely, they had a common point of view, in one respect, in the forties. They suspected the social organization of American life of being unreal. Miller never identified the nature of the merchandise that Willy Loman sold, for the nature of the merchandise was irrelevant. Miller questioned the reality of the institution of salesmanship. In the last scene of his play, one of Willy's friends analyzed the nature of the business: "Willy was a salesman. And for a salesman there is no rockbottom to the life. He don't put a bolt to a nut, he don't tell you the law or give you medicine. He's the man way out there in the blue riding on a smile and a shoeshine." In Williams' *A Streetcar Named Desire*, Blanche Du Bois was also separated from reality. She was out there in the blue riding on false gentility and drugstore cosmetics. Blanche would have scorned Willy Loman as crude and stupid, but they were the same kind of people. It might be remarked here parenthetically that Williams' father was a shoe salesman in the braggart tradition. In one of Williams' early one-act plays, *The Last of My Solid*

Gold Watches, he memorialized the dreary conclusion to a flashy shoe salesman's career.

At one time, the form of *Death of a Salesman* would have been described as experimental. The various scenes were realistic in the Ibsen tradition; the situations were recognizable as imitations of life, and the play had a definite conclusion. But the form of the play was loose and expressionistic: the scenes flowed like improvisations that shuffled time and place and developed the theme with the moodiness of a tone poem. Kazan staged the play with power and theatrical conviction. The scenes slipped through the luminous maze of Jo Mielziner's transcendent setting, and the acting was overwhelming. Lee Cobb's weary, plodding, crushed Willy and Mildred Dunnock's tired, gallant wife were deeply moving characterizations, and Arthur Kennedy's portrait of the glib, alienated son was candid and touching. At the end of the 1948–1949 season, there was no doubt about the best American play. *Death of a Salesman* won both the Pulitzer Prize and the Critics Circle award.

Although the words Miller's characters spoke were in the vernacular of life in the streets and on the front porches of dingy neighborhoods, they had a firm hold on fundamental truths. The commonplace dialogue had a weary eloquence. Towards the end of the first act, Willy's wife, defending him to his disgruntled sons, spoke what amounted to the epitaph on the ordinary man: "I don't say he's a great man. Willy Loman never made a lot of money. His name was never in the paper. He's not the finest character who ever lived. But he's a human being, and a terrible thing is happening to him. So attention must be paid. He's not to be allowed to fall into his grave like an old dog." In the original production, Mildred Dunnock read that speech with a quiet conviction that gave it universal dimension. It was also Miss Dunnock who read Tennessee Williams' appeal for love and companionship quoted earlier in this chapter. An actress of modesty and great purity of spirit, Miss Dunnock has thus spoken the minds of the two leading dramatists of the forties. They are lucky to have been so scrupulously deputized.

The success of Tennessee Williams plays broke down resistance to emotional improvisations that dispensed with the conventional dramatic forms. Playwriting was becoming freer. Anyone who had read a textbook on the techniques of drama would have realized that Carson McCullers' *The Member of the Wedding* was not a standard play. For three immobile acts, it reiterated the foolish trivialities of an adolescent girl who, to escape loneliness, proposed to accompany her brother and her brother's fiancée on their wedding journey. Although the structure of the play was inept, it filled the theater with charm and understanding in 1950 because Harold Clurman, the director, staged it like a ballad, full of tenderness, childish audacity, and humor. It was endowed with inner life by the spontaneity of the acting.

At an early stage of her career, Julie Harris, an actress compounded of light and spirit, played a rumpled, unstable, egotistical girl who was both maddening and irresistible. As the cook and mother surrogate, Ethel Waters was a mountainous mass of patience and sense; and Brandon de Wilde, a little boy with a pair of glasses almost as big as he was, wandered through the play in an inquisitive daze. Out of nothing but air and genius, an affecting play was made. If *The Member of the Wedding* had overtones of Tennessee Williams, there was a logical reason. Both Mrs. McCullers and he were Southern writers concerned with the disaffected. Also, he worked on the script with her during a summer vacation on Nantucket Island. The loneliness of the harum-scarum girl in Mrs. McCullers' play was also the affliction of the mature women in the Williams plays. Blanche Du Bois, Alma Winemiller, and Laura Wingfield were mature versions of little Frankie Adams who looked into the mirror and naïvely said to the cook: "I don't know what to do. I just wish I would die."

Williams was the host to another play. When *The Glass Menagerie* was being staged in Chicago in the autumn of 1944, he revisited St. Louis, and the critic for the *Star-Times* interviewed him. The critic was William Inge, a former teacher at Stephens College in Columbia, Missouri, when Maude Adams supervised the drama department there. Inge went to Chicago to see *The Glass Menagerie*. It excited him. He thought that Williams had created a beautiful and moving play out of the private impulses and dilemmas of ordinary characters, and he thought that Williams' remembrance of things past gave the theater distinction as a literary medium. It encouraged him to complete a play of his own. Williams recommended it to Margo Jones, who had co-directed *The Glass Menagerie*. Miss Jones, a woman with great force of personality, operated a small theater in Dallas, Texas. In 1947, she produced Inge's first play, *Farther Off from Heaven*. The Tennessee Williams influence was widening the theater's awareness of obscure people, and Inge began to write in that mode of spontaneity and subjectivity.

Come Back, Little Sheba, was Inge's first Broadway play; it was staged by the Theater Guild on February 15, 1950. It was a fresh and fruitful occasion. The first act of Inge's script was a dull record of a dull marriage in a house presided over by a slovenly housewife and a mediocre chiropractor who was also an incipient alcoholic. In the second act, a disturbing episode plunged him back into a bout of drinking, and the rest of the play was explosive. An obscure, toneless, suburban home became a house of agony and remorse. Two characters whose relationship had been negligible were caught up in a savage encounter; two undramatic characters became painfully dramatic. Like Williams, Inge found extraordinary spiritual significance in ordinary people.

Come Back, Little Sheba changed three careers. Until Shirley Booth played the slovenly housewife, she was invariably cast as an expert character actress of sardonic hussies, and Sidney Blackmer had been a leading man drifting towards the fringes of obscurity. The two solidly written parts in the Inge play gave them new careers. The depth and range of her housewife, the anguish, defeat, and remorse of his chiropractor raised them several grades in the hierarchy of the theater. The play also established a Middle-Western newspaper writer as a major Broadway dramatist.

Although the postwar period was not prolific, it was not without enterprise. It attracted some enterprising new producers—Robert Whitehead, Alfred de Liagre, Jr., Dwight Deere Wiman—who were tired of the safe and the familiar and had the courage to sponsor new styles and ideas. They were not conservative people. In 1948, if the political demagogues and the crackpots had really been perceptive, they ought to have sounded an alarm over a witty play by a cultivated French bureaucrat—*The Madwoman of Chaillot*, by Jean Giraudoux. It ridiculed profit. The madwoman frustrated promoters and prospectors who were about to destroy the lazy contentment and charm of her neighborhood by drilling down to the pool of oil that was under it. She and her wacky friends successfully defeated a scheme to exploit natural resources for private profit—a fundamental factor in all capitalist societies. Giraudoux, a French diplomat who was the official spokesman for France during the early days of World War II, wrote this ironic fable in 1943 while the Nazi army was occupying Paris. Since he died in 1944, he never knew the pleasure the French took in his witty lampoon in 1945, nor the delight of Broadway three years later. In the dingy Belasco Theater, it was played with gusto and whimsical humor by Martita Hunt, as the presiding madwoman, and by Clarence Derwent, Vladimir Sokoloff, Estelle Winwood, Nydia Westman, Leora Dana, and John Carradine. By choosing kindness and beauty over riches and power, the crazy individualists of the Giraudoux play enchanted thousands of amiable New Yorkers who struggled for profit and power every day of their lives. *The Madwoman of Chaillot* was so droll and bizarre that no one noticed that it was undermining the philosophy of the western world.

At a time when the prevailing impulse was to try something new, T. S. Eliot exercised the prerogative of a royalist and high churchman by stepping backward. Having written a towering drama in liturgical form in 1935, he wrote a maundering play in the style of drawing-room comedy in 1949. *Murder in the Cathedral*—part pageant, full of religious faith and passion—is a permanent item in dramatic literature. It seemed particularly inspired when the Federal Theater played it in 1936 for 50¢ a ticket. But Eliot lusted after the popularity of the second rate. In *The Cocktail Party*, a major poet wrote verse intended to sound like prose. A man of articulate religious convictions discussed salvation in terms of social etiquette. He also substituted a psychiatrist for God and sanctimoniously prescribed martyrdom for a fashionable lady involved in a modish infidelity. Eliot condescended to the second rate, under the impression that he could be more effective on the level of his inferiors.

The Cocktail Party opened in New York on January 21, 1950, with a skillful British cast that included Alec Guinness, Irene Worth, and Cathleen Nesbitt. Since it combined religion with psychiatry and was written by the leading poet in English, audiences sat before it respectfully all winter and were able simultaneously to save their souls and eavesdrop on the follies of the upper crust. No one understood the play, but everyone assumed that it was important. The author of *The Wasteland*, which had been the rallying point of disaffected young people in the twenties, and *Murder in the Cathedral*, which reverently searched the conscience of Thomas Becket in the thirties, succeeded in discarding all distinction in *The Cocktail Party*. By rejecting his own genius, he contrived his own disestablishmentarianism. To judge by the happy mood of the box office all winter, theatergoers thought he was right.

Nothing could better illustrate the irreconcilable difference between the first decade of the century and the decade of the forties than a few devastatingly negative dramas that came from Europe. In form, they were dogmatic and ambiguous. They made no attempt to beguile the audience; on the contrary, they challenged the audience to accept them. In mood, they were savage and bleak. They came from European countries that were totally disillusioned. They were scornful of the commercial theater, which they regarded as decadent. In New York, the commercial theater took no interest in the émigré German playwright, Bertolt Brecht, especially since the failure of his *The Threepenny Opera* on Broadway in 1933. But on December 7, 1947, the Experimental Theater produced Brecht's *Galileo* for several special performances at Maxine Elliott's Theater, with Charles

Laughton in the leading part. This was the time when the House Un-American Activities Committee was looking into th erils of independent thinking in Hollywood. Since Brecht was living there as an émigré, the House Committee took a furtive peek into his mind. Although the Committee found nothing it could understand, Brecht too the hint and fled to Switzerland as fast as possible.

He had written *Galileo* during the rise of Nazism, when he thought the intellectual had a particular responsibility to stand up for the truth. The ordeal of Galileo represented in the play the moral problem of a thinker who was willing to compromise with tyrants. *Galileo* was suspected of being Communist when the Experimental Theater produced it after Nazism had been defeated. It was branded as "controversial"—a weasel word that soon became a permanent part of the American vernacular because it expressed a national passion for being safe and commonplace. *Galileo* was written in the form of objective scenes. It was epic theater— a simple, direct unemotional style invented by the German director, Erwin Piscator. To Charles Laughton, *Galileo* was a mission. In order to introduce Brecht's work to New York, he acted Galileo for $10.00 a performance— the standard fee for Experimental Theater actors. (There are sixty-six parts in *Galileo*.) But it was impossible for Laughton to be simple, direct, and unemotional about anything. He was a showman at heart. His pompous acting and his overbearing attitude towards the drama reduced epic theater to the level of exhibitionism. Many years later, *Galileo* emerged as a sharp-witted play of high ethics when Anthony Quayle played it without egoism.

For about two seasons, Jean-Paul Sartre was the recognized prophet of the bleak, depersonalized world that represented the extreme pessimism of postwar philosophy. *No Exit*, which was produced on November 26, 1946, was the first, the tightest, and the most ravaging of his dramas. Inside a vividly claustrophobic setting by Frederick Kiesler, two men and two women faced one another in hell. They were looking to one another for help. But there was no help. They were doomed to confront one another eternally. In the existential philosophy of Sartre, every person is responsible to himself and can expect nothing from other people. *No Exit* was ruthlessly staged by John Huston and acted with great vehemence and bitterness by Claude Dauphin, Peter Kass, Annabella, and Ruth Ford. On Broadway, it had to compete for audiences with *Born Yesterday* and *Happy Birthday* and it lost. It lasted a month before the production was consigned to the hell that receives all stage failures.

Nothing could have been more alien to the taste of Broadway, where people do not go to hear arguments or to be depressed or instructed. But *No Exit* made such a profound impression on a few theater professionals that Broadway continued to produce Sartre's plays for about two more years. *Red Gloves (Les Mains sales)* was staged in 1948, with Charles Boyer making his Broadway debut. *The Victors (Morts sans sepulture)* was produced the next year. Only one of his plays succeeded—*The Respectful Prostitute (La Putain respecteuse)*, which was transferred to Broadway after it had begun to draw audiences Off Broadway. But Sartre was not a hero to Broadway. Although the United States was low in mind after the cataclysm of World War II, it had not abandoned hope, as Sartre had.

He was an abstract writer. He was not interested in individual people but in objective psychological situations from which no exit was possible. Character, the basis of art, was outside his domain. "The difficulties in international relations do not derive from the characters of the men leading us," he wrote in a magazine article at the time. "The strikes in the United States do not reveal conflicts of character between the industrialists and the workers." He proposed to write short, severe plays about the situations that obliterate the free will of human beings.

The characters in *No Exit* may have seemed like human beings because the acting was so desperate and passionate. Sartre's later plays were like textbook exercises; with the exception of *The Respectful Prostitute*, the characters had no personalities. The dramatic form was mechanical. A brilliant philosopher, afflicted with the psychosis of intellectualism, wrote melodramas like those that had flourished thirty or forty years before. In lieu of characters, Sartre provided a rich diet of horrors, as had Owen Davis, Eugene Walter, and Edward Sheldon. It was primitive theater. The old became the new. Sartre was the forerunner of Samuel Beckett, Eugene Ionesco, Edward Albee, and Harold Pinter, whose dramas of the absurd or of hostility, disgust, and nothingness found audiences later on, partly because Sartre had opened the door. What he had to say was valid. His plays could be rejected, but his ideas could not be dismissed.

In the musical theater, Broadway was producing such robust and independent works as *Finian's Rainbow, Brigadoon, South Pacific, Kiss Me, Kate, Guys and Dolls,* and Kurt Weill's operatic version of *Street Scene.* But the equivalent exultation was missing in the spoken drama. Except for Williams, Miller, and a few others, the spoken drama was beside the point. The cruel futility of the outside world was catching up with Broadway, which is a holiday promenade not equipped to cope with intellectual problems.

NO PROFIT
ALLOWED

During the war years and for a few years afterwards, some liberal people began to take a new approach to the Broadway theater. They established three public enterprises that could never make a profit.

Mayor La Guardia, a humanist as well as a politician, was the catalyst of a New York people's theater, in the tradition of the Federal Theater and after the style of respected theatrical organizations in London, Paris, Berlin, and Moscow. Since the war was going on, a concern for the best interests of human beings was perhaps more spontaneous than usual. For it is one of the evil paradoxes of life that wars, which destroy life and property on a colossal scale, also bring out the best in many people, and the welfare of the nation as a whole takes precedence over private achievement. That may be the reason why La Guardia found members of his administration, theater people, and public-minded citizens enthusiastic about his scheme for turning a tax liability into a cultural profit. Mecca Temple in

The New York City Center. (*Alix Jeffry*)

55th Street between Sixth and Seventh avenues had reverted to the city because of unpaid taxes. It seated 2,700 people in a wide, cavernous auditorium. Instead of selling it at auction, La Guardia persuaded the City Council to lease it for a token rent to a group of private citizens to operate as an institution for the performing arts. In 1944, it became the City Center of Music and Drama and opened with a concert by the New York Philharmonic Orchestra at ticket prices of 55¢ to $1.65. Gertrude Lawrence then inaugurated the theater program by acting in Rachel Crothers' *Susan and God*, which she had played on Broadway at standard prices in 1937. That was the beginning of an admirable institution of the first importance.

Because of its immense size and awkward design, the City Center has always been better adapted to opera, ballet, and concert music than to the theater, which needs a more intimate environment. In terms of originality, the theater has been the least creative of the arts that have flourished there. But La Guardia's mind, as well as his heart, was in the right place: a people's theater could exist and serve a great many New Yorkers. Morton Baum as the chief administrator set the standard. A tall, cordial tax lawyer who served the Center for the rest of his life without pay, he ran his own business with his left hand and the Center with his right, and turned it into a public meeting-place like the Public Library and the Natural History and Metropolitan Museums. Hundreds of people have worked for the Center fanatically; and although the Center has always been a deficit operation, the standards of performance have been high. Jean Dalrymple, a tireless woman with plausible ideas and total invincibility, has administered the theater season by reviving good dramas with able actors on thrifty salaries. Although the Center is quixotic, theater people never have had a patronizing attitude towards it, and it has proved that audiences for good plays are unlimited if the box office rates are moderate. By 1949, the ticket prices had nearly doubled. The best seats cost $3.00. But during the two weeks engagement that is standard for dramas, the revival of *She Stoops to Conquer* that season drew 45,066 people, who paid $76,000 to get in—not enough money, incidentally, to pay all the expenses. Judith Anderson drew audiences almost as large when she played *Medea* at the Center after her national tour. Maurice Evans was paid nothing for his services as producer of all the plays that year; as a volunteer, he became one of hundreds of benefactors. But he did receive the regulation fee of $50.00 a week when he played in Shaw's *The Devil's Disciple*, which was so enthusiastically received that he moved it into a Broadway house afterwards. Without the respect and the cooperation of the theater people of Broadway, the City Center would have lacked professionalism and artistic distinction.

During this interlude of charitable feeling, the Broadway theater for the first time took a paternal interest in the welfare of unrecognized actors. John Golden, who had made a fortune by producing blameless comedies like *Lightnin'* and *Seventh Heaven,* subsidized the Equity Library Theater to give unestablished actors an opportunity to be seen by managers, agents, and other people who might be of use to them. George Freedley, curator of the Theater Collection at the New York Public Library, arranged the bookings in the available halls in branch libraries, and Golden paid $100 towards the expenses of each production. In the first season, there were fifty-six productions of dramas that could be played without royalty. To thousands of theater people, a goodwill enterprise of this nature and scope seemed too good to be true. In a measure, it was. For it soon appeared that the Library had no legal authority to donate its premises to members of a labor union. Although the Equity Library Theater could no longer use Public Library rooms, it became a permanent organization that leased a theater of its own and has relieved many good actors of their chronic obscurity.

Nothing was more utopian than the American National Theater and Academy, which lived on the fringes of Broadway and proposed to elevate the theater all over the United States. It began in the thirties with a national charter that Congress magnanimously bestowed on some Philadelphia worthies who breached all the congressional defenses by not asking for money. When the members discovered that they could not do anything with the charter because they knew nothing about the theater, the Dramatists' Guild prudently took possession of it, and Robert Sherwood accepted the presidency. He proposed organizing national tours of reputable plays with tickets scaled at a $1.00 top. Stars with whom he consulted agreed to serve. Since ANTA had no money to spend on anything, Sherwood personally paid all the expenses of mailing circulars to more than a thousand theaters in all parts of the country to solicit support and counsel. As it happened, the Germans invaded Norway on the very day the ANTA board had a decisive meeting. The extra editions of the newspapers were on the street when the directors emerged from the Playwrights' Company offices on Fifth Avenue. Everyone agreed with Sherwood that the idea of a $1.00 top theater was no longer feasible. Sherwood took leave from the theater as a whole and administered the Office of War Information in Washington.

After the war, ANTA acquired a dedicated executive secretary, Robert Breen, who regarded an empty treasury as an inspiration, never worried about his salary because he drew none, and never worried about the landlord because he and his wife installed the ANTA headquarters in the apartment they occupied over the Lyceum Theater. ANTA introduced an attitude of sustained cultural enlightenment to show business. ANTA gave advice to theater people in other parts of the country who looked to New York as a source of wisdom. ANTA read scripts. By default, it became an unofficial branch of the State Department, which was trying to improve international relations. It gave the State Department information and advice about the theater—a form of life as alien to the State Department as Albania. ANTA accepted a State Department directive to send an American production of *Hamlet* to the Elsinore Festival in Denmark.

Since no one on Broadway was cosmopolitan enough to maintain social relations with theaters in other parts of the world, Rosamond Gilder, former editor of *Theatre Arts* and an ANTA board member, became the American representative of the International Theater Institute and surprised a number of puzzled Broadway people by getting them to attend theater conventions in Europe and the Near East as if they were citizens of the world. It was a startling idea. Although many American plays were produced abroad and the American theater had considerable influence abroad, Broadway had no facilities for dealing with foreigners on cultural matters. During a long period of traveling abroad and proselytization at home, Miss Gilder made Broadway look less uncouth to foreigners. In matters involving cultural civility, Broadway lacked style.

ANTA estimated that it would cost $25 million to establish a national theater. Since that was an impossible sum of money to raise, ANTA did something else that seemed to be in harmony with the new mood of mutual good will in the theater. It established the Experimental Theater to stage interesting and promising plays that Broadway did not regard as financially plausible.

But the idea of a theater that did not conform to all the union regulations and that asked concessions nettled the unions. They felt threatened by altruism. ANTA leased the charming little Princess Theater and started paying the rent. But for three and a half sullen months, Actors' Equity and the Dramatists' Guild—the two most literate unions—wrangled over inequities in the contracts, each one suspecting that the other was getting an advantage. All the unions were suspicious of non-profit theater.

But even while the contract wrangling was going on, the public took a progressively enthusiastic interest in the project. There were 1,460 names on the first year subscription lists. Three years later, the list increased to 5,054, and the Experimental Theater had to move into Maxine Elliott's Theater, which had more room. During three feverish seasons, which were consistently threatened with sudden death, the Experimental Theater staged more than twenty new plays, including Bertolt Brecht's *Galileo*, in which Charles Laughton appeared; Jan de Hartog's *Skipper Next to God*, in which John Garfield was starred; a Negro version of Gorky's *Lower Depths* called *A Long Way from Home*; Robinson Jeffers' *Tower Beyond Tragedy*, with Judith Anderson giving a magnificent performance; and a highly original musical called *Ballet Ballads*, in which John La Touche, author of the text, and Jerome Moross, who composed the music, gave a new dimension to the ballet form. The Experimental Theater performed its mission so successfully that the deficit was more than $50,000. But Broadway did not trust an idealistic institution; it suspected the Experimental Theater of being a scheme for trying out scripts at the expense of the unions.

A few of the Experimental Theater productions were transferred to Broadway with standard contracts. That was not a simple maneuver. There was a price to pay. To penalize work that had been done at a discount, the craft unions compelled the Experimental Theater to build an exact duplicate of the original set and then destroy it—or to destroy the original set, it made no practical difference which, for something had to be built and destroyed in order to preserve the rights and dignity of union labor. But that was only a technical problem. The basic problem was the fact that all the Experimental Theater plays failed on Broadway. The general public was as skeptical as the unions. In 1950, the Experimental Theater paid its debts and went out of business—effectively eliminating the threat of high-mindedness on Broadway.

THE
LEVELING OFF

For years, "Broadway and 42nd Street" was a glamorous address that brightened the spirits of New Yorkers and made them feel homesick when they were in other parts of America or abroad. The exact geographical location was a little misleading. "Seventh Avenue and 42nd Street" would have been more exact. After the Knickerbocker Hotel removed its sidewalk canopies and closed the Old King Cole bar with its cheerful Max Parrish mural, the Times Tower was the only notable building at the Broadway corner, and *The New York Times* was no longer published there. It was published a half block away at 229 West 43rd Street, where there was enough street room for flatbed trucks to dump rolls of newsprint into the basement by day and delivery trucks to pick up the printed papers at night.

In the thirties and forties, the block of 42nd Street between Seventh and Eighth Avenues looked less and less like a theater street and more

Movie houses at 46th Street and Seventh Avenue, 1937. (*Culver Pictures, Inc.*)

and more like a midway. Theater business was declining all over the city. There were not enough productions in a season to support the available playhouses. The Shubert Theater Corporation had been valued at $25 million during the boom days. It went into bankruptcy in 1931. Four years later, Lee Shubert bought it back for $400,000 at a public auction on the steps of the subtreasury building in Wall Street. Looking over his familiar domain, he challenged logicians with an inscrutable remark: "These theaters would be dark today if I hadn't built them," he said.

In 1930–1931, the number of productions was 187, in comparison with 264 in 1927–1928. Then productions declined rapidly. In 1940–1941 there were only 72. Employment in the theater was down sharply. In 1939, the average member of Actors' Equity worked only ten weeks and earned only $800.

For thirty years, the block of 42nd Street had been a pleasant esplanade. On hot nights, Al Woods used to tip back his chair in the front of his Eltinge Theater and watch the audience go in. Audiences were well dressed and in a party mood. But the 42nd Street block was the first part of Broadway to disintegrate. The American Theater, which had been built in 1893, was pulled down in 1932. Both the Apollo and the Times Square, major houses, were sold or leased to motion picture exhibitors in 1935 and became grind houses, where old films were shown to audiences on the prowl. Wallacks, a distinguished house with a distinguished name, began to show movies in 1932. In 1940, the front wall was pulled out and rebuilt and the name was changed to Anco.

The New Amsterdam was the most patrician theater on the block and had the most distinguished record. In 1903, Nat Goodwin opened it with a decorous and amusing performance of *A Midsummer Night's Dream*. Henry Irving—a titled British actor—played repertory there. Beerbohm Tree —also titled—acted *Henry VIII* on that stage. Forbes-Robertson—titled— and his handsome wife, Gertrude Elliott, appeared there in Shaw's *Caesar and Cleopatra* in 1906 before Shaw had been universally accepted at his own value as a genius. The New Amsterdam was the headquarters for the *Ziegfeld Follies* and other extravaganzas until Ziegfeld built his own theater in Sixth Avenue with Joseph Urban's expansive plan. (The Ziegfeld was torn down in 1969.) When Ziegfeld needed a second house, he often returned to the New Amsterdam. During the early days of the depression, the New Amsterdam began to look seedy and the florid uniforms of the ushers, tarnished and worn. The last legitimate production there was Walter Huston's dispirited *Othello*, in 1937. After that, the New Amsterdam became another grind house. The elegant façade was disfigured with a

Lee Shubert. (*Culver Pictures, Inc.*)

bulbous-shaped excrescence; the expensive wood paneling inside was neglected, and the New Amsterdam became a slum.

The whole block degenerated into a combination of carnival and sex
bazaar. The Republic Theater, built in 1900 by Oscar Hammerstein in
Italian Renaissance style, had housed *Abie's Irish Rose* for 2,327 performances. But that was the end of the Republic's respectability. When *Abie's
Irish Rose* withdrew permanently, it became Billy Minsky's burlesque
house. Huge photographs of ravishing sex queens on the houseboards outside promised incredible licentiousness inside, and a uniformed barker
stood at the entrance bellowing, "gurls, gurls, gurls." There was a second
burlesque house across the street along with a shooting gallery for Broadway marksmen in need of practice.

The brightest emporium on the block was Hubert's Museum, popularly
known as the Flea Circus. Admission—10¢ to a box-office woman who was
startled by anything that interrupted her dreaming. When the customer
strolled inside, he was astonished to see grotesque images of himself in
distorting mirrors on the walls, and he was promptly assailed by Karoy,
"the man with the i-run tongue," who was a pitch-man extraordinary. In

addition to Professor Hubert's learned fleas, which had been the original attraction, there were tempting sideshows. After paying 15¢ more, the customer could watch three half-starved strumpets perform an "Ulgerian" belly-dance. Customers over eighteen were permitted for an additional 15¢ to probe the "Hidden Secrets" of sex that had been exclusively consigned to the Flea Circus by the French Academy of Medicine, Paris, France—or so the billing said.

When the culture quotient of 42nd Street began to decline during the thirties, the Flea Circus was blamed. It was rated as one step lower than the burlesque houses, which, in turn, were the poor farm of the theater. In 1940, Mayor Fiorello La Guardia, in an outburst of morality, shuttered all the burlesque theaters because he thought they were too sinful for New Yorkers. The culture of 42nd Street collapsed rapidly. But since the cultural standard of the Flea Circus remained constant, it gave the illusion of rising. By the time 42nd Street had become the most depraved corner of the Broadway district, patrolled day and night by male and female prostitutes, Hubert's Museum was the ranking cultural institution. The trained fleas turned out to be the finest performers on the block.

In the meantime, the spoken drama was a declining part of show business. Having dominated Broadway for half a century, the theater took second place to the screen with a feeling of reluctant incredulity. It could hardly believe that a branch of show business that was established on the West Coast was beginning to outrank the branch of show business that had created Broadway in the first place. The sensational openings were for the screen, and they were spectacular, for the screen industry had the resources to make Broadway conform to big-business standards. Screen openings became municipal events under the benevolent supervision of the police. The sidewalks were blocked with barricades and barricades poked into the streets. Searchlights mounted on trucks cut the sky with beams of light and flooded the lobbies of the theaters with a pitiless glare. Extravagantly dressed stars managed to look surprised and embarrassed when they stepped out of long limousines and were cheered by the populace. On Broadway, every Hollywood opening was a success although many of the films failed.

Most of the theaters on Broadway in the forties were film houses. All the huge houses—like the Paramount, Capitol, and Loew's State—were also office buildings and parts of the business complex of New York City. The screen was big business. But the traditional theater could hardly believe what it saw. When a film opening blocked the streets, the people of the theater were inclined to feel supercilious. To them, film openings were vulgar, pretentious, and bogus. But the crowds in the streets hardly knew that the spoken drama existed. They had no gods save the stars of Hollywood.

As an industry, the theater was obsolete. Rising real-estate values had made theater buildings uneconomical. In the first decade of the century, a new theater building had seemed to be not only a good investment but a symbol of gaiety. Most of the new theaters were beautiful buildings that improved the quality of the neighborhood. But after World War II, theater owners became acutely conscious of a pitiless fact of life: a theater could earn an income for only twenty-two hours a week, making only meager use of the expensive land it occupied. It earned nothing during most of the day, and usually nothing during the summer, but the taxes were continuous. An obsolete building code was largely responsible.

After the grisly Iroquois fire in Chicago in 1902, theaters were classified as dangerous buildings, and the Building Department in New York drew up an exacting code to minimize the dangers of fire. The code specifically prohibited construction above theater auditoriums. Film theaters were built later when fireproof materials were available, and film theaters were accordingly permitted to include office space that produced additional revenue. New York discriminated against the theaters that had created Broadway and had contributed to New York's attraction as a tourist city. Howard Cullman, an enthusiastic backer of plays and a consistent friend of the theater, inaugurated a campaign to get the building code revised, and he succeeded. But no one took advantage of the new code in the years that remained of the first half century. As an investment, a theater was too risky to attract real-estate promoters; and the Broadway theater gradually became a luxury operation that appealed to a small segment of the public. To go to the theater was like going to a minor, subsidiary, social event.

In 1947, the television industry for the first time covered the presidential conventions. If that event can be accepted as the beginning of the TV industry as a national medium, the theater then had to face another formidable competitor. Television was giving the public entertainment it did not have to pay for. It also gave steady and lucrative employment to writers and actors whom the theater no longer supported. Throughout the nation, general employment was high. But in 1948, eighty percent of the Broadway actors were unemployed. For the first time in its history, Broadway called a general emergency meeting for all the unions and all the theater people. Morton Baum, one man everybody trusted, presided; and everybody had an opportunity to propose methods for increasing employment. Several speakers suggested making better use of theater buildings by scheduling productions during the afternoons and the one evening when the occupied theaters were dark. There was also a wistful hope that the government would subsidize the theater. At about this time, Actors' Equity commissioned the Robert R. Nathan Associates to make an industrial survey of the theater from the point of view of modern management. No one was surprised to learn that the theater had no visible relation to modern industry, except that large sums of money were made and lost continually. "The theater is an organized calamity," Boris Aronson remarked with doleful affection. "I think that even the theater's mistakes are deteriorating." During this period of anxious soul-searching, nothing inside or outside the theater was changed except that the state law was revised to make Sunday performances legal. Producers of hits were not interested in changing familiar practices; they saw no reason to change a system that seemed to be making them rich. Producers without hits lacked influence. If a producer is not making money, his colleagues do not take him seriously.

If the theater were a rational industry with long-range capital and management and if it were operated primarily for profit, logic would have pronounced it a failure. Costs of production had increased from about $10,000 for dramas, in 1920, to about $50,000 or $75,000, in 1950, and it was impossible to stage a musical play for less than $200,000 or $250,000 in 1950. Theater tickets were about twice as expensive as they had been when costs of producing were five or six times lower. The annual number of productions was ominous. In 1950, there were 87 productions—exactly the same number of productions put on in the 1899–1900 season. (In 1900, the population of New York was 3,500,000. In 1950—7,900,000.) In 1927–1928—264 productions; in 1950—87. Those were signals of disaster. After the business expansion of the first two decades, and after the artistic achievements of the twenties, the Broadway theater had dropped to the level of the first years of the century. In similar circumstances, Studebaker and Packard automobiles went out of business.

But the theater is, among other things, a bright enigma. What it produces is not a "product." It produces moods, dreams, ideas, beauty, imagined characters. It is a form of incantation. If the dialogue in a play, if the movement of the actors, if the personalities of the actors, if the scenery and sound do not lay a spell on the audience, they have no value, no matter how admirable they may be in themselves. A successful production has to beguile several hundred strangers every performance into becoming a community of believers. Although the theater is not life, it is

Times Square in 1948. (*Culver Pictures, Inc.*)

The Times Building. (*The New York Times*)

composed of fragments or imitations of life, and people on both sides of the footlights have to unite in making the fragments whole and the imitations genuine. The theater is both *Abie's Irish Rose* and *Mourning Becomes Electra*, both *The Student Prince* and *Carousel*. The theater cannot survive without money, but it does survive without money because every production begins with a vision of something that never existed before. The writers, actors, directors, scene designers, and their assistants begin with a dream of impossible perfection. Although there are hundreds of cynics in the theater, the theater is not a cynical institution.

All the economic facts of 1950 were gloomy and portentous. But the theatergoer that season had several rich experiences—Laurence Olivier and Vivien Leigh in alternating performances of Shakespeare's *Antony and Cleopatra* and Shaw's *Caesar and Cleopatra*, which expressed the minds and emotions of two great writers; Tennessee Williams' *The Rose Tattoo*, which passionately involved thousands of theatergoers in the private belief and the anguish of two obscure, harum-scarum people; a dramatization of Melville's *Billy Budd* that came to grips with some of the ambiguities of life and balanced the power of evil against the vulnerability of life; Louis Jouvet, one of the great actors, and his Parisian company in Molière's satire on human sagacity, *L'École des Femmes*; expert, witty performances in the immaculately written comic operas of Gilbert and Sullivan, carrying on an elite tradition more than a half-century old; Gertrude Lawrence and Yul Brynner ruefully exploring the differences in national pride and beliefs in Rodgers and Hammerstein's *The King and I*. In that dwindling season, there were several other productions that helped to make life more interesting and more understandable, and deepened the experience of thousands of people. The theater of 1900 was not concerned with human experience. On the contrary, it assumed that theater was an escape from life. It regarded human experience as irrelevant.

Not being an industry but rather a loose array of individuals, the theater on Broadway in 1950 had certain valuable assets. At a time of increasing intolerance and political persecution, it was not afraid of unorthodox opinions or of dissenters. In a time of malicious official spying, it was not afraid of the government. Hollywood had so much investment at stake that it tossed overboard some of its best writers and actors to appease the smalltown bullies in Congress who had no respect for the principles of America. Within the next few years, the TV industry totally capitulated. On Broadway, there were conservatives as well as radicals, and they distrusted each other, but no one muzzled another. The anarchy of Broadway was a valuable asset in a time of intellectual crisis. Nor was the Broadway theater prudish. It was easily bored, but it was not easily shocked. In the early years of the century, theatergoers, the mayor, and the police were outraged by the mind of Ibsen and the morals of Shaw. Independent ideas alarmed and disgusted the establishment. In 1950, the temper of society was more wholesome; Broadway was no longer provincial. It listened to anything that was not dull.

Nor did theater people or theatergoers desert a form of show business that was declining. Although most theater people were not regularly employed and some of them were never employed but were reduced to forming committees and writing resolutions and cursing the darkness, they remained believers. The theater seemed to them the most important thing in life. Broadway composed a large reservoir of alert and sentient people who somehow seemed to give off more light than other people did. A few of them had burning beliefs about life and contributed to the intellectual life of the nation; many of them had extraordinary talents. All of them were alive and free. Although the theater on Broadway had lost scope, it had not lost its inner gaiety. Broadway was no longer a convivial neighborhood: it was more like a street fair. But in a corporate world that required conformity, the people of the theater constituted a little community of individuals who honored and observed the freedom of speech and the freedom of action on which the nation was founded.

They also preserved a sense of humor, which made it possible to go on year after year, despite the painful risks involved. On Broadway, boredom is the only malady that is fatal.

BILTMORE THEATRE

MICHAEL BUTLER

presents

HAÏR

The American Tribal Love-Rock Musical

Book and Lyrics by
GEROME RAGNI & JAMES RADO

Music by
GALT MacDERMOT

Executive Producer
BERTRAND CASTELLI

Directed by
TOM O'HORGAN

Dance Director
JULIE ARENAL

Musical Director
GALT MacDERMOT

Costumes by
NANCY POTTS

Scenery by
ROBIN WAGNER

Lighting by
JULES FISHER

Sound by
ROBERT KIERNAN

with

STEVE CURRY   RONALD DYSON   SALLY EATON   LEATA GALLOWAY

STEVE GAMET   WALTER HARRIS   PAUL JABARA   DIANE KEATON

LYNN KELLOGG JONATHAN KRAMER EMMARETTA MARKS MELBA MOORE

SHELLEY PLIMPTON JAMES RADO GEROME RAGNI LAMONT WASHINGTON

and

Donnie Burks   Lorri Davis   Hiram Keller

Marjorie LiPari   Natalie Mosco

Suzannah Norstrand   Robert I. Rubinsky

Original Cast Album by RCA-Victor

Musical Score Published by United Artists

POSTSCRIPT

1950–1970

The original plan of this book was to chronicle Broadway during the first fifty years of the twentieth century. Now it seems advisable to add a postscript about the years since 1950. This is more difficult. No generalizations and no rational conclusions are completely true.

After 1950, the theater business continued the disintegration that had begun in the thirties. In 1950–51, only eighty-one productions seemed an ominous number. But in 1969–70, there were only sixty-two, fifteen of which were revivals of past successes. And for the first time, both the Critics Circle award and the Pulitzer Prize for the best American play went to Off-Broadway dramas—Paul Zindel's *The Effect of Gamma Rays on Man-in-the-Moon Marigolds*, in the case of the Critics' Circle, and Charles Gordone's *No Place to Be Somebody*, in the case of the Pulitzer. The number of theaters in the fifties was slowly dropping. The Empire Theater, built in the best of taste and with great expectations by Charles

Gerome Ragni in *Hair* (1967). (*Dagmar*)

Frohman in 1893, went out of existence in 1953. The last production was Arthur Laurents' *The Time of the Cuckoo,* in which Shirley Booth gave a warm and gallant performance. After the final performance, the curtain did not fall, and actors and audience stood and sang "Auld Lang Syne." During its sixty years, the Empire had been host to thousands of the theater's most beautiful people—onstage and out front; it had preserved the amenities; it had maintained a patrician personality. But after *The Barretts of Wimpole Street* and *Life with Father* had completed their runs and become Broadway legends, the Empire was not earning enough to make the owners as rich as they felt they ought to be. In 1953, they surrendered their L-shaped plot of land at 40th Street to a perpendicular building that had a bank on the first floor and no personality on any floor and took no interest in the community and represented nothing more human than a sound investment. Howard Lindsay and his wife were among the many theater people who salvaged seats out of the old Empire and took them home as mournful souvenirs.

Theaters were disappearing all over town. Forty-eighth Street, once known as "the street of hits," gradually went to pieces. The Playhouse, the 48th Street Theater, and the Vanderbilt disappeared, leaving only the elegant Cort as a reminder of pleasant neighborly evenings; and the Cort was leased to a television show. In 1969, there were only thirty-six playhouses left—two of which were actually on Broadway. In the twenties, the number of theaters was loosely reckoned as seventy or eighty. There were half that number or less than half that number in the sixties.

In the fifties, the theater community—that is, the number of people connected with the theater—was estimated to be 20,000. That included about 10,000 members of Actors' Equity, 1,326 members of Local 1 (the stagehands' union), forty scene designers, ninety-six producers and theater owners. There was no reliable way of counting the theatergoers. But in 1956, the publishers of *Playbill* distributed 8,400,000 copies of their programs. They estimated the number of individual playgoers as 1,287,000 on the assumption that most of them went to the theater more than once during the season. Most of the playgoers were between the ages of thirty and fifty.

The Broadway theater continued to attract the interest of thousands of people in other parts of the country. One-third of the audiences were visitors from out of town. Going to the theater, according to a municipal survey, was one of the reasons for their coming to New York; and while they were visiting New York, they attended four or five productions. Gloomy news did not discourage them; they were in a festive mood before they walked into the theater. At a time when New Yorkers were beginning to drift away from the theater, something pleasantly inconsistent happened. The *Louisville Courier-Journal* and the *Columbus (Ohio) Citizen* organized "show trains" to bring some of their readers to Broadway. Their drama critics, Boyd Martin of the *Courier-Journal* and Norman Nadel of the *Citizen*, advised their readers about the nature of the productions available on Broadway; the newspapers arranged the transportation and hotel accommodations and purchased the theater tickets. The "show trains" gave the visitors better service than most New Yorkers had. One New Yorker took advantage of the system by going to Louisville and returning to New York on the "show train" with the tickets in his hand. It saved him time and vexation. "Show trains" were gala occasions. In later years, "show planes" have provided the same service for groups from many parts of the country. To visitors with a holiday at their disposal in the 1950s, Broadway did not look like a sick community.

But it was. Apart from its business problems, the theater of the fifties and sixties was affected by the disillusioning political experience of the nation. Most of the negative factors that made theater festivity impossible were external. Life was out of control. The cold war froze the American disposition. The hydrogen bomb, and its inhuman implications, was a chilling influence on everybody. Only five years after World War II, another war broke out, in Korea, and thousand of Americans were shipped to that divided land. The Vietnam war, in which more than forty-four thousand young Americans have died, has been the most horrifying and divisive influence on the American spirit in the last years of the 1960–70 decade. The American spirit had always been essentially optimistic. But it was no longer possible to be optimistic about a world that was under the pressure of so many disparate alarming events—military despotism in Europe, three wars between the Israelis and the Arabs, a futile invasion of Suez by France and Great Britain, race riots in Little Rock, Arkansas, the Castro revolution and the mindless Bay of Pigs debacle, the Vietnam war, the assassinations of President John Kennedy, Martin Luther King, and Senator Robert Kennedy. These awful events, and others, set the mood of the world. It was not conducive to the kind of cocky and irresponsible theater that Broadway was used to.

There was another negative influence. In the early fifties, the nation was stupefied and terrified by the recklessness with which a Wisconsin hoodlum, Senator Joseph McCarthy, turned the federal government into an instrument for harassing the citizens. He dominated the political and cultural life of America from 1950 to 1954, when the Senate mustered up enough courage to call him a liar. When McCarthy was on the loose, many Americans were afraid to speak their minds, and many who did were vilified. The cowardly phrase "controversial person" has become the permanent residue of McCarthyism: it slyly denigrates people who have independent ideas. Although McCarthyism did not paralyze Broadway as it paralyzed the film and television industries, congressional committees dominated by bigots harried a few obscure actors who were not humble citizens, and it charged Joe Papp, the public-spirited founder of free Shakespeare in Central Park, with slipping Communist propaganda into *Coriolanus*—a very difficult sleight-of-hand operation. To preserve the security of the nation, the State Department refused to give Arthur Miller a passport to see a production of his *The Crucible* in Belgium. It kept him home where it could intercept his mail. In this barbaric era, a few actors who had belonged to radical organizations in the thirties produced a tender, imaginative, wholesome folk program called *The World of Sholem Aleichem*. It became the focal point of McCarthyites all over the nation. They stigmatized the actors as traitors; they excoriated the critics who had praised the production. They tried to make a national scandal out of it. Externally the feud looked alarming. But Broadway theatergoers liked *The World of Sholom Aleichem* so much that it had to be revived the next season. As usual, they went to see what interested them.

McCarthyism was the most vicious aspect of a depressed cultural period. But the intellectual and artistic life of the nation as a whole was flattened or morose, and writers lacked the enthusiasm that is part of the creative process. Until 1962, when Edward Albee's *Who's Afraid of Virginia Woolf?* was produced, there were no new American dramatists of significance—about two decades after Tennessee Williams and Arthur Miller first appeared. Broadway was sustained by older dramatists, all of whom had done their best work in the past, and by several stimulating foreign dramatists who had fresh ideas and the audacity to state them. Plays of originality in form or theme were more likely to be produced Off Broadway, where a good production could be made for $5,000 up to $20,000 in comparison with the $75,000 to $200,000 on Broadway. Edward Albee's first play, *The Zoo Story*, was produced in 1960 in the Provincetown Theater Off Broadway, where Eugene O'Neill had begun his New York career a quarter of a century earlier. Although *The Zoo Story* was received with admiration and excitement, history did not repeat itself. Mr. Albee's career did not flourish as O'Neill's had.

These are some of the vital statistics—both business and artistic—of the Broadway of the fifties and sixties. They seemed to indicate that the theater was declining.

But this is the place where the paradox begins. For some memorable plays enriched the lives of thousands of theatergoers in this dismal period. A person concerned exclusively with the pleasures of going to the theater could have had a very good time. O'Neill died in 1952 in a tiny suite in the Shelton Hotel in Boston, overlooking the beautiful Charles River Basin. But he was alive for many years on Broadway. In addition to occasional revivals of *Anna Christie, Desire Under the Elms,* and *The Great God Brown,* four of his unproduced plays were put on posthumously in the fifties and sixties—one of them, *Long Day's Journey into Night* (1956), being one of his masterpieces. The other three were *A Moon for the Misbegotten,* in which Franchot Tone and Wendy Hiller appeared in 1957; *A Touch of the Poet,* in which Helen Hayes, Kim Stanley, and Eric Portman acted in 1958; and *More Stately Mansions,* played by Ingrid Bergman, Colleen Dewhurst, and Arthur Hill in 1967.

A Moon for the Misbegotten was a rambling, verbose drama derived from O'Neill's youthful days and retaining some of the sophomoric class consciousness, insolence and petulance of his youth. *A Touch of the Poet* and *More Stately Mansions* were adapted versions of the first and second dramas in his proposed cycle of plays about a family in America from the days of the Revolution. He had not come even close to finishing the cycle. Incompleted versions of these two plays somehow escaped the holocaust to which he thought he had committed all his unfinished work. The improvised version of *More Stately Mansions* that finally reached the stage turned out to be a maundering drama, interesting chiefly for Miss Bergman's stately acting in contrast with the passion and animation of Miss Dewhurst's stimulating performance. In *A Touch of the Poet,* there were many welcome echos of the familiar O'Neill style—the "pipe dreams," as he had called them in *The Iceman Cometh,* the clash of temperaments and egos, drunkenness, family intrigue. The acting of Miss Hayes, Miss Stanley, and Mr. Portman brought a random script vigorously alive.

But *Long Day's Journey into Night* was a major event when Fredric March, Florence Eldridge, Jason Robards, Jr., and Bradford Dillman opened it at the Helen Hayes Theater on November 7, 1956. Since it was a recognizable portrait of the O'Neill family life in New London in 1912 and referred to other people who might still be alive, O'Neill had specified that it was not to be acted until twenty-five years after his death. But his widow, Carlotta Monterey O'Neill, concluded in 1957 that there was no reason for keeping it locked up. Three and one-half hours long, it told the remorseless story of an adolescent boy and his dissipated older brother who tormented and sneered at their father, whom they accused of being parsimonious and stupid. They behaved with puzzled decorum in the presence of their mother, who was a secret drug addict. People who knew the O'Neill family in 1912 took exception to the ruthlessness of O'Neill's portrait of the character who represented his father. In life, they said, he was not the stingy despot depicted in the play. But O'Neill invariably over-dramatized his own life. By the time he wrote *Long Day's Journey*, his past and his family life had become a morbid obsession that had distorted his memory. With a kind of paranoid frenzy, he transferred his own defects of character to others. By 1956, the nostalgic comedy of the ingratiating *Ah, Wilderness!* had hardened into the thunderous anathemas of *Long Day's Journey into Night*. It also represented America's first dramatist at the peak of his power. It won both the Critics Circle award and the Pulitzer Prize and had 390 performances in New York. It concluded O'Neill's career triumphantly three years after he had died.

Some of the insurgents of the twenties and thirties continued to write for Broadway. Maxwell Anderson's character study of Socrates, called *Barefoot in Athens*, opened in 1951, with Barry Jones, an amiable, light-weight British actor, in the chief part. Like Mr. Anderson's previous pseudoclassics, it was literate and high-minded; but, unlike them, it was pedestrian. The Anderson energy and singleness of purpose were missing. Since there were some plausible analogies between the careers of Anderson and Shakespeare, *Barefoot in Athens* might be described as Anderson's *Pericles* or *Timon of Athens*. Mr. Anderson's final Broadway play was a commercial adaptation of William March's *The Bad Seed*, produced in 1954 with commercial success. As a craftsman Mr. Anderson was ingenious and able. He died in 1959.

S. N. Behrman, the treasured annalist of iridescent worldlings, wrote a charming autobiographical play called *The Cold Wind and the Warm* in 1958. Sensitive, loyal, humorous, and wondering, it portrayed family life in a provincial, Jewish tenement flat in the early days of the century, and the cast included three actors of notable sensibility—Eli Wallach, Maureen Stapleton, and Morris Carnovsky. In all his previous work, Mr. Behrman had made common cause with people of sophistication and gaiety. *The Cold Wind and the Warm* memorialized the modest, homely, orthodox origin of his sparkling career.

In 1953, Robert Anderson's *Tea and Sympathy*, beautifully acted by Deborah Kerr and John Kerr in the leading parts, introduced a new playwright to Broadway so vividly that he was elected a member of the Playwrights' Company the next morning. *Tea and Sympathy* was a poignant drama about the agonies of an adolescent boy in a private school who was suspected of being a homosexual. In the last act, the wife of the headmaster relieved him of his private agony by mercifully seducing him. Her curtain line has become famous. Placing one of the boy's hands on her breasts, she said: "Years from now—when you talk about this— and you will—be kind." This was commonly regarded as an uncommonly titillating scene, and *Tea and Sympathy* ran for 712 performances—the longest run of any Playwrights' Company production. (John van Druten's first play, *Young Woodley*, in 1925 had had a similar theme, and was also delicately acted in the two principal parts—by Glenn Hunter and Helen Gahagan, who several years later was promoted to United States representative from California.) None of Mr. Anderson's following plays were successful, until a program of one-act plays, whimsically entitled *You Know I Can't Hear You When the Water's Running*, was produced in 1967.

In 1954, Clifford Odets, whose Hollywood career had been floundering, returned to Broadway with an ingratiating folk fable called *The Flowering Peach*. It was the story of mankind told through the character of Noah, who performed his maritime duties under the benevolent eye of God. Unlike the tense and petulant families in Mr. Odets' previous plays, Noah's family was loving and dependable, despite a certain amount of domestic bickering—particularly over Noah's addiction to the jug. The family performed God's work with a kind of lumbering gallantry. The part of Noah was played by a fabulous Yiddish comedian, Menasha Skulnik, whose gnomelike presence, plaintive voice, and congenital mistrust were both funny and admirable.

In this period there were also any number of clever entertainments, like *A Majority of One*, in which the well-loved Gertrude Berg proved that a Jewish housewife had more sense than a professional diplomat, and Jean Kerr's *Mary, Mary*, which was an explosion of witty remarks about humorless people. It was also the golden time of Neil Simon, whose thin and agile comedies, *Come Blow Your Horn*, *Barefoot in the Park*, *The Odd Couple*, *Plaza Suite*, and *Promises, Promises* suited Broadway audiences completely. Mr. Simon was the success story—the Clyde Fitch— of the sixties. In attendance on his plays, audiences started laughing before a line was spoken. At the end of 1969, Simon's *The Last of the Red Hot Lovers* was produced amid a whirlwind of bravos when *Plaza Suite* and *Promises, Promises* were still drawing audiences. Thus, he had three plays on Broadway simultaneously, in addition to a touring company of *Plaza Suite*. His annual income from royalties was estimated at over two million dollars—illustrating the maxim that Broadway is a great place to make a fortune but a bad place to make a living.

Tennessee Williams and Arthur Miller, who had dominated the drama of the previous decade, were still the most imposing American dramatists of the fifties and sixties. Mr. Williams continued to turn out plays with a kind of desperation, as if, like many of his characters, he were in

Florence Eldridge, Bradford Dillman, Fredric March,
and Jason Robards, Jr., in *Long Day's Journey into
Night* (1956). (*Museum of the City of New York*)

Gloria Jones, Gusti Huber, Dennie Moore, David Levin,
Joseph Schildkraut, and Susan Strasberg in *The Diary
of Anne Frank* (1955). (*Museum of the City of New
York*)

Boris Aronson's set for *J.B.* by Archibald MacLeish, produced in the 1958–1959 season.

ETHEL BARRYMORE
THEATRE

PHILIP ROSE and DAVID J. COGAN

present

SIDNEY POITIER

in

The New York Drama Critics' Circle Award-winning play for 1958-59

a raisin in the sun

A New Play by
LORRAINE HANSBERRY

with

CLAUDIA McNEIL	RUBY DEE
LOUIS GOSSETT	DIANA SANDS
IVAN DIXON	JOHN FIEDLER

Directed by
LLOYD RICHARDS

Designed and Lighted by
RALPH ALSWANG

Costumes by
VIRGINIA VOLLAND

Lorraine Hansberry. (*Gin Briggs*)

flight from some nameless terror. The list of his plays after 1950 is astonishing—*The Rose Tattoo*, in 1951; *Camino Real*, in 1953, a long incantation of a no-mans-land surrounded with death and cruelty, marvelously well acted, as if it were an evil mirage; *Cat on a Hot Tin Roof*, in 1955, in which the joyless members of a plantation family told lies to one another because they could not communicate normally; *Sweet Bird of Youth*, in 1959, a portrait of degradation and cruelty with smoldering performances by Geraldine Page and Paul Newman; *Period of Adjustment*, in 1960, a commonplace comedy in which Mr. Williams attempted to be less repellent than usual and sounded like an avuncular marriage counselor; *Night of the Iguana*, in 1961, a bizarre panorama of the dispossessed in a tropical inn, acted with an eerie sense of foreboding by Margaret Leighton, Bette Davis, and Alan Webb.

In all these plays, Mr. Williams' sense of doom and defeat and his gifts for sensuous scenes and lyrical writing created powerful theatrical works that were eminently actable and that overwhelmed large audiences. But then his control of style and substance began to dissipate. In view of all he had done for the Broadway theater, it was a melancholy resolution of an illustrious career. Two different versions of *The Milk Train Doesn't Stop Here Anymore*, in 1963 and 1964, proved to be irresolute and boring; *Slapstick Tragedy*, which consisted of two short plays about "the tragicomedy of human existence on this risky planet," in 1966, was weak; and *The Seven Descents of Myrtle*, in 1968, represented a collapse of talent. It was as if his basic theme had turned out to be the truth of his own experiences. He was damned, like his characters.

Although Arthur Miller was less prolific, he was more a man of his times. He was eminently rational. He was also a moralist with a broad vision of the function of the theater as a social institution. "The stage is the place for ideas, for philosophies, for the most intense discussion of man's fate," he wrote in 1951. In 1950, when McCarthyism was just beginning to congeal the spirit of the nation, he adapted Ibsen's *An Enemy of the People*. It was entirely pertinent; it dramatized the spectacle of one man standing against the mob—to Mr. Miller, the only honorable stance. The production lasted only thirty-six performances, for Broadway is never much interested in polemics. But it provided an occasion when a number of actors of probity—Fredric March, Florence Eldridge, Morris Carnovsky, Art Smith, Lou Gilbert, Fred Stewart, Bob Lewis—could stand up and be counted in public.

Three years later, Mr. Miller met McCarthyism head-on. He dramatized the Salem witch-trials of 1692, in a tumultuous drama called *The Crucible*. Although the play drew no specific analogies, since the circumstances of 1692 were different from those of 1953, everyone knew what Mr. Miller had in mind. The play was generally admired; it ran for 197 performances on Broadway and has since been acted all over the world, including Moscow. The cast had some of Broadway's finest actors— Walter Hampden, Arthur Kennedy, E. G. Marshall, Madeleine Sherwood, Jean Adair, Philip Coolidge, Beatrice Straight, Joseph Sweeney—proud to be part of Mr. Miller's crusade.

After *The Crucible*, Mr. Miller's theater career was less startling. The themes were smaller; the sense of urgency, missing. *A View from the Bridge* and *A Memory of Two Mondays* were warmhearted dramatic sketches of shipping clerks in a warehouse and dock-laborers in Brooklyn— observant and compassionate plays. Such was the hubris of the time, they were produced solemnly like major works of art, as if Mr. Miller were already a classic author. During the next several years, Mr. Miller was more concerned with Hollywood than Broadway; he was the husband of Marilyn Monroe, who was a major industry in addition to being a complex woman. When the Lincoln Center Repertory Theater was founded in 1964, Mr. Miller contributed the first play—*After the Fall*, a character study of a young man who married a casual, uneducated girl and lived to regret it. Despite Mr. Miller's denials, *After the Fall* was generally accepted as an accounting of his marriage to Marilyn Monroe. Directed by Elia Kazan on an open stage, it was acted with great authority by Jason Robards, Jr., Salome Jens, and Barbara Loden. It was a better play than most people were willing to admit because the autobiographical implications embarrassed them.

Mr. Miller's two remaining plays in the sixties were *Incident at Vichy*, a well-written and well-acted drama about the Nazi assault on Jews (resented by some New York Jews because the noblest character in it was not a Jew); and *The Price*, produced in 1968—a delightful comedy that bogged down in a hackneyed conclusion about the ethics of success. By this time, Mr. Miller had many other interests; he was international president of the P.E.N. Club and was active in the P.E.N. defense of freedom of speech in all parts of the world. He took an active part in American politics; he had become a respected citizen of conscience and broad concern. Broadway no longer fascinated him as it had in the late thirties, when he was a tenderfoot playwright and attended the Group Theater productions in a spirit of hope and wonder.

In a disaffected cultural era and on a crumbling Broadway, there were other exalting or delightful episodes in the theater. Many of the plays transcended the environment and the period. William Inge, whom *Come Back, Little Sheba* had introduced to Broadway in 1950, wrote three more beguiling dramas about the private dilemmas of obscure people—*Picnic*, in 1953; *Bus Stop*, in 1955; and *The Dark at the Top of the Stairs*, in 1957. *Bus Stop* was the finest play of his career. Set inside a dingy restaurant in Kansas on a night when a snowstorm had marooned the bus, Mr. Inge's play was a comic and often poignant story of an impromptu romance between a third-rate nightclub singer (she called herself a chanteuse) and a dazzled, inarticulate cowboy. It was sensitively staged by Harold Clurman, who relished both the humor and the humanity; and it was acted with gusto by Kim Stanley, Anthony Ross, Albert Salmi, Elaine Stritch, Phyllis Love, and Lou Polan. After seven lush years, Mr. Inge wrote his first failure—*A Loss of Roses*—in 1959. It closed after twenty-five performances.

In any period, *The Diary of Anne Frank* would have been a splendid achievement. Written by Frances Goodrich and Albert Hackett, it told the haunting story of an adolescent Jewish girl who, during World War II, hid with ten other Jews in an Amsterdam attic for over two years. Eventually they were discovered by the Nazi police, and most of them were exterminated. The story of this restless and imaginative girl—"little bundle of contradictions," she called herself—could easily have been obtuse and melodramatic. But out of the brassy milieu of Broadway, Garson Kanin, the director, assembled a cast of actors with taste as well as skill, and they broke the hearts of a sophisticated public for 717 performances. Susan Strasberg began her career as Anne Frank. The other actors also played their parts with special benevolence: Joseph Schildkraut, Lou Jacobi, Gusti Huber, Jack Gilford, Gloria Jones, Dennie Moore, David Levin, Eva Rubenstein, and Clinton Sundberg. It seemed remarkable that ten years after Anne Frank's obscure death in a German concentration camp, Broadway could recover the grace and bloom of her spirit. *The Diary of Anne Frank* received all the prizes—Critics, Pulitzer, and Antoinette Perry. When the United States was invited to send representative stage productions to an international theater festival in Paris, the State Department banned *The Diary of Anne Frank* on the theory that it might offend Parisians. It never offended anybody anywhere. When it was produced in Germany later, it was received with the greatest respect and considerable contrition.

Despite the external circumstances of American life and the many uncertainties of Broadway, the 1955–1956 season was bustling and stimulating for no identifiable reason. In addition to *The Diary of Anne Frank*, the significant plays that lively season were: Anouilh's *The Lark*, in which Julie Harris gave an inspired performance as Joan of Arc; *Tiger at the Gates*, in which Jean Giraudoux anxiously argued the futility of war;

The Chalk Garden, an acidly witty comedy about the upper classes, written by Enid Bagnold, a British stylist; *Waiting for Godot,* Samuel Beckett's ruthless cartoon of an empty life; *The Matchmaker,* Thornton Wilder's old-fashioned comedy, in which Ruth Gordon gave a broadly comic performance as a cunning, nineteenth-century marriage broker; *No Time for Sergeants,* Ira Levin's adaptation of a novel about the comic crises of a country boy (played by Andy Griffith) drafted into an army he does not understand; and finally *My Fair Lady,* the melodious adaptation of Shaw's *Pygmalion,* which ranks with the finest musical dramas ever done on Broadway. It also made a national heroine of Julie Andrews. It might be remarked incidentally that in the three serious plays—*The Lark, Tiger at the Gates,* and *The Diary of Anne Frank*—the leading characters stood for principle. They took ethical stands. They were not so much acted upon by external circumstances as they acted against external circumstances. They were, no doubt unconsciously, carrying on an old tradition that *Waiting for Godot* quite consciously superseded.

A major American poet contributed a play of stature and vision in 1958. It was Archibald MacLeish's parable of life in a barbaric age—*J.B.,* the story of Job adapted to modern times in biting modern verse. Elia Kazan staged an inspired performance that had rhythm and pressure. Boris Aronson's setting swept a ghostly roof up into the awful void of the universe; and the cast included some of the theater's ablest actors— Christopher Plummer, Raymond Massey, Nan Martin, Pat Hingle. *J.B.* was Mr. MacLeish's version of both *The Book of Job* and *Everyman.* Like Job, J.B. made his peace with God and declared his faith in the continuity of life. Unlike the modish plays of the era, it ended on a note of hope. The Pulitzer judges gave their prize to *J.B.*

But the Critics Circle award went to *Raisin in the Sun.* In 1959, a talented and beautiful young Negro lady, Lorraine Hansberry, gave Broadway a blunt play about Negroes that avoided the stereotypes; it was free of sentimentality and innocent of revolution. The title came from a poem by Langston Hughes, another gifted Negro who was not a racist:

> What happens to a dream deferred?
> Does it dry up
> Like a raisin in the sun?

he said in a speculative poem about the plight of the American Negro;

> Maybe it just sags
> Like a heavy load
> *Or does it explode?*

John Golden Theatre

Masonic Corp.

FIRE NOTICE: The exit indicated by a red light and sign nearest to the seat you occupy is the shortest route to the street. In the event of fire please do not run—WALK TO THAT EXIT.
EDW. F. CAVANAGH, JR.
FIRE COMMISSIONER

Thoughtless persons annoy patrons and distract actors and endanger the safety of others by lighting matches during the performance. Lighting of matches in theatres during the performances or at intermissions violates a city ordinance and renders the offender liable to ARREST.

THE   PLAYBILL   A · WEEKLY · PUBLICATION · OF · PLAYBILL · INCORPORATED

Week beginning Monday, May 7, 1956   Matinees Saturday and Sunday

IN THE EVENT OF AN AIR RAID ALARM REMAIN IN YOUR SEATS AND OBEY THE INSTRUCTIONS OF THE MANAGEMENT.—ROBERT E. CONDON, DIRECTOR OF CIVIL DEFENSE.

MICHAEL MYERBERG
by arrangement with
Independent Plays Limited

presents

BERT LAHR

and

E. G. MARSHALL   KURT KASZNAR

in

WAITING FOR GODOT

A Tragicomedy
by SAMUEL BECKETT

with

ALVIN EPSTEIN   LUCHINO SOLITO DE SOLIS

Directed by HERBERT BERGHOF

Scenery by LOUIS KENNEL   Costumes by STANLEY SIMMONS

That poem expressed the forbearing attitude of Miss Hansberry, a young woman from Chicago who lived in Greenwich Village and enjoyed its freedom and variety. She wrote a turbulent play about a Chicago Negro family that bought a house in a white neighborhood and had to cope with white resistance, the problems being both personal and social. Sidney Poitier, who had become a Hollywood star, played the leading part in his effortless style with personal magnetism and professional deftness; and the cast included several other notable actors—Claudia McNeil, Ruby Dee, Diana Sands, and Louis Gossett. *Raisin in the Sun* had 530 performances on Broadway—a record for that sort of socially conscious drama. In 1965, Miss Hansberry wrote another drama, *The Sign in Sidney Brustein's Window*, which was more complex and diffuse and was not enthusiastically received. But it was admired and supported by many people who could not bear to see it fail. It had 101 performances during the agonizing time when Miss Hansberry (Mrs. Robert Nemiroff in private life) was dying of cancer. She died on January 12, 1965, depriving Broadway of a talented writer and a thoughtful woman.

Before World War II, American plays, both in style and content, made a considerable impact on the theater abroad. They were leaders in fashion. But in the fifties, the tide began to turn in the other direction. Most American plays seemed old-fashioned. The plays that set the trend came from abroad. Samuel Beckett's *Waiting for Godot* (1955), was the herald of disenchantment. Beckett said that there is no hope for anything, that the nature of life is irrational. No one presumed to understand Beckett's play literally—least of all, the men like Bert Lahr, who acted in it with power, and Herbert Berghof, who directed it ably. It was a seemingly formless, enigmatic scrawl, in which two vagabonds loitered onstage, making inconclusive remarks, and a fabulous monster drove a roped slave with a whip and many epithets, and a timid messenger boy meekly blundered around. What Mr. Beckett said was desolate and devastating. But the production and the performance were simultaneously bitter and comic. It took great ingenuity to express nothing with so much virtuosity. Bert Lahr made the play possible. His animal vitality, his clownish, helpless leer, his imbecilic grin, his ludicrous groans and his tentative movement stated Mr. Beckett's theme eloquently; and the other members of the cast—E. G. Marshall, Alvin Epstein, Kurt Kasznar, and Luchino Solito de Solis—completed the glowing performance of a play about nothingness. The concluding lines of *Waiting for Godot* conveyed the essence of Mr. Beckett's malevolent jest. "Well? Shall we go?" asked Vladimir (E. G. Marshall). "Yes, let's go," answered Estragon (Bert Lahr). They did not move.

Waiting for Godot had only fifty-nine performances. The non-drama is non-commercial. But after that fabulous evening of staggering conundrums, it was impossible to conduct business in the old ways. *Waiting for Godot* began a new cycle. Since Broadway audiences do not enjoy paying money to be told that they are nothing, all Mr. Beckett's other plays were done Off Broadway where the costs were less rapacious and the audiences more adventuresome.

Among the disaffected, Jean Anouilh presented the biggest problems. Like Mr. Beckett, he believed in nothingness. But perhaps because he was a native of France, not an immigrant in France like Mr. Beckett, he had more agility. Gaiety kept breaking in. Parisian audiences may have been better attuned to his wry fusion of intellectual desolation and comic caprice. It took Broadway several years to accept him as a discerning critic of his time. The aura of Katharine Cornell and an imposing production did not reconcile Broadway to his austere view of *Antigone*, in 1946. It had only sixty-four performances. Despite the personal magnetism of Tallulah Bankhead, *The Eagle Has Two Heads* gave only twenty-nine

Al Hirschfeld's drawing of Zero Mostel as the man who becomes a rhinoceros and attacks Eli Wallach in Ionesco's *Rhinoceros* (1961).

performances in 1947. Oscar Karlweis and Lili Darvas, two sophisticated actors, tried *Cry of the Peacock* in 1950—two performances. Richard Burton, supported by a good cast, played *Legend of Lovers* (*Eurydice*) in 1951—twenty-two performances. Julie Harris appeared as a flagrantly wanton wife in *Mademoiselle Colombe* in 1954—sixty-one performances. After eight years of consistent failures, Broadway would have been forgiven if it had abandoned a talented French misanthrope to his own people (not all of whom, incidentally, approved of him).

But the indomitable figure of Joan of Arc—drawn between worldly security and unworldly martyrdom—compelled Broadway to capitulate to M. Anouilh in 1955. In Julie Harris' guileless acting in *The Lark*, the religious mystery of Joan made hundreds of believers out of thousands of Broadway agnostics. M. Anouilh may have had a worldlier Joan in mind, for he was no believer, but no one could resist Miss Harris' gallant characterization. The entire cast was noteworthy. Boris Karloff, more celebrated for his supernatural fiends in the films, balanced Miss Harris' Joan with a quietly heroic Cauchon; and Christopher Plummer, Theodore

Bikel, and Joseph Wiseman were members of the cast. *The Lark* had 229 performances, and M. Anouilh's pessimism about life was rewarded with optimism at the box office.

In *The Waltz of the Toreadors*, M. Anouilh wrote a savage lampoon of a man of honor, which had 132 performances in 1957 and was revived with a different cast the next season. His view of the difference between the innocuous code of polite society and the cruel realities of social behavior amounted to contempt verging on hatred. M. Anouilh never truckled for favor. He took pleasure in shocking the bourgeoisie. Like most of his works, *The Waltz of the Toreadors* was eminently actable. Staged by Harold Clurman, with humorous relish of its grotesque animosities, it had the sort of polished acting that a literary stylist deserves. Ralph Richardson and Mildred Natwick in the opposing roles gave his iconoclastic drama great resonance. In the same year, *Time Remembered*, a tongue-in-cheek, Alice-in-Wonderland romance—always just on the edge of some fine romantic fulfillment—also had a splendid cast: Helen Hayes, Richard Burton, Susan Strasberg, Sig Arno, and Glenn Anders; it had 248 performances. In 1960, Laurence Olivier and Anthony Quinn made a popular success of M. Anouilh's *Becket*—a ferocious annihilation of the chivalrous legend of Thomas Becket and Henry II. They were portrayed as gross and heartless opportunists. Thanks to the cast and the performance, it had 193 performances.

Sitting once more in the center of his meaningless universe in 1959, M. Anouilh improvised a rancorous comedy he called *The Fighting Cock*. It recorded the humiliating dilemma of a man of honor who could not recognize the essential viciousness of civilization. Staged with characteristic bounce and vigor by Peter Brook, it presented Rex Harrison as master of the ghoulish revels, but it had only eighty-seven performances. The coldness of M. Anouilh's wit repelled audiences.

Whatever the right word for the new drama might be—"theater of the absurd" was the term most frequently used—it shifted the crucial responsibility to the director and the actors. The plays were not "actor-proof" plays, like those of Augustus Thomas, Edward Sheldon, and Avery Hopwood. The scripts were like the scores of operas and symphonies; they were guidelines for the director (conductor) and actors (instrumentalists). No one could take much pleasure in reading *Rhinoceros* by Eugene Ionesco, a Roumanian who lived in Paris, where he wrote many lucid prefaces to many ambiguous plays. *Rhinoceros* argued that human beings could be turned into anything, including rhinoceroses, if they submitted long enough to the prevailing psychosis of conformity. It was not much of a play. But it did provide a great clown and actor, Zero Mostel, with a chance to change from man to rhinoceros before the eyes of the audience, and Mr. Mostel accomplished that impossible transubstantiation magnificently—for 240 performances. All the other Ionesco plays were done Off Broadway, where variations from the norm were routine.

In 1961—one season after *Rhinoceros*—Harold Pinter, a British actor and playwright, brought to Broadway his first bizarre drama in an individual style that reflected the irrationality of the period. Since *The Caretaker*, as he labeled his first play, took no ethical or intellectual stand and seemed to have no theme, it belonged to the genre of plays alienated from the theater as well as life. But Mr. Pinter's report of the psychological experience of a shiftless, scheming, self-destructive tramp was actually naturalism carried to the point of absurdity—an almost unedited version (so it seemed) of irrelevant conversations; and they gave a British actor, Donald Pleasence, a part that he translated into a graphic performance. *The Caretaker* had 165 performances, and some people considered it the best play of the year.

Two of Mr. Pinter's plays appeared in 1967—*The Birthday Party* and *The Homecoming*. As author, he seemed to be an uncommitted observer, personally removed from the scene, looking on from a cool distance. Some undefinable sense of doom hovered over both plays, for that was his stance as a writer. In a grotesque and faithless period of history, both plays isolated some part of the hidden truth. *The Homecoming* was Mr. Pinter's only commercial success—the happy reward of its scandalous situation. It told the story—without emotion or moral overtones—of a gross father and his two sensual sons who made a family whore out of the wife of a third son, she laconically consenting. All the characters accepted this amoral situation without comment or external feeling. Staged at arm's length by Peter Hall and acted with imagined diffidence by the Royal Shakespeare Company from England, *The Homecoming* attracted many incredulous playgoers who enjoyed Mr. Pinter's cosmic joke on his characters and his audiences.

England's remorseless and exuberant existentialist, Peter Brook, directed the two most momentous dramas of alienation and contempt—Peter Weiss's *Marat/de Sade*, in 1965, a horrifying masque set in an insane asylum during the French revolution; and Friedrich Dürrenmatt's *The Visit*, in 1958. The full title of Mr. Weiss's play illustrated the extent of his rebellion against both life and conventions of the theater: *The Persecution and Assassination of Marat as Performed by the Inmates of the Asylum of Charenton under the Direction of the Marquis de Sade*. It was given an expertly disciplined performance by the Royal Shakespeare Company, and it included the first of the mandatory Broadway nudes— a comely gentleman viewed by the audience from the rear, where he was most presentable. In *The Visit*, Lynn Fontanne and Alfred Lunt concluded an illustrious career with a masterpiece of acting. Mr. Dürrenmatt, a Swiss, was not light-minded about anything. *The Visit* was the story of a woman who had become rich by whoring and who had corrupted the town where she had begun. She offered to make the town rich if it would murder the townsman who had seduced and abandoned her in her youth. The town consented. "The world made me into a whore," the rich woman said. "Now I make the world into a brothel." *The Visit* was a horrifying indictment of a cruel and greedy culture, staged with ingenuity and bravado by a gifted heretic and acted with subtlety, insight, and coolness by America's greatest actors. When the Lunts played in a worthless comedy called O *Mistress Mine* in 1946, they had 452 performances. In Dürrenmatt's *The Visit*, the joke was grisly and the play had only 189 performances. Broadway exacts a penalty for self-flagellation.

Being destitute of serious new American dramatists of comparable skills and originality, Broadway tended to put all its hopes in Edward Albee in the early sixties. His first play, *The Zoo Story*, done Off Broadway in 1960 when he was thirty-two years old, was welcomed not only for its intrinsic merits but for its freshness of talent; and some of Mr. Albee's other one-act plays—*The American Dream, The Death of Bessie Smith, The Sandbox*—seemed to confirm the original opinion. Two years later, Mr. Albee's first full-length play, capriciously entitled *Who's Afraid of Virginia Woolf?*, acted on Broadway, was rapturously received. It had the originality, pressure, and momentum of a first-rate modern drama. It was a contemptuous cartoon of marriage. Meticulously staged by Alan Schneider, who had already mastered the Samuel Beckett style, and who became Mr. Albee's most congenial interpreter, it was acted with exuberant rancor and corrosive wit by Uta Hagen, Arthur Hill, Melinda Dillon, and George Grizzard. An expression of hatred, it suited the mood of the day—alienation and contempt for the establishment; and although many people winced, it became the dramatic success of the season.

A year later, Mr. Albee fulfilled expectations by making an admirable dramatization of Carson McCuller's languid, moody story of unromantic love in a Southern community—*Ballad of the Sad Café*. Like *Who's Afraid of Virginia Woolf?*, it was sensitively staged by Mr. Schneider, and it was given a soft, brooding, basically malefic performance by Colleen Dewhurst and Michael Dunn. Although it failed, it was further proof of

George Grizzard, Uta Hagen, and Arthur Hill in *Who's Afraid of Virginia Woolf?* (1962). (*Museum of the City of New York*)

Mr. Albee's exceptional talents. But then Mr. Albee and Broadway began to part company. *Tiny Alice*, which was produced in 1963, with John Gielgud, Irene Worth, and William Hutt in leading parts, puzzled just about everyone, including Mr. Gielgud, who complained that he never knew what it was about and that Mr. Albee would not tell him. *Tiny Alice* was a preposterous allegory, signifying something portentous about the vulnerability of human beings. The avant-garde screen director, Andy Warhol, liked it: "I liked it because it was so empty," he said with the assurance of a mid-Manhattan guru. Mr. Albee also liked it. He called a press conference to upbraid the critics for writing unfavorable reviews and for being stupid enough not to understand it.

When he published the text, he again found himself satisfied with himself, and he rejected suggestions that he explain it. "I find . . . that I share the view . . . that the play is quite clear," he remarked in his foreword. Mr. Albee, who is a talented writer and a kind human being, was carrying alienation to its logical conclusion: he was alienating himself from his own profession. Two years later, he completed the alienation by writing a play that was totally inept and boring—*Malcolm*, dramatized from a novel by James Purdy. About this time, critics ceased reviewing Mr. Albee's plays; they started to psychoanalyze him.

Probably that was the inevitable way of dealing with a genuine writer and a generous-minded man who seemed to insist on his own destruction. Between *Malcolm* and the bill of *Box* and *Quotations from Chairman Mao Tse-tung*, Mr. Albee wrote two plays that were intelligible—*A Delicate Balance*, which clinically examined the hostilities of married life, and *Everything in the Garden*, adapted from an English play by Giles Cooper. *Everything in the Garden* was hardly more than a tabloid feature story about a suburban housewife who worked part-time as an afternoon prostitute to increase the family income—competent hackwork but not the sort of thoughtful drama people had been expecting from Mr. Albee. It left the Broadway situation empty and distressing. Without Mr. Albee, there was no serious playwright of sufficient rank to carry on the tradition of Tennessee Williams and Arthur Miller. Without any resident serious

Julie Andrews and Rex Harrison in *My Fair Lady* (1956). (*Friedman-Abeles*)

dramatists, Broadway settled back into being a midway for popular entertainment.

Although show business was depressed, there were many lavish musical shows in the 1950–1970 period. Two or three of them were memorable. They cost staggering sums of money to produce. In 1956, *My Fair Lady* cost $401,000, which seemed colossal. But in 1969, it cost more than $900,000 to produce *Coco*, in which Katharine Hepburn starred (at a $15 top ticket price it grossed $140,000 a week). *Jimmy*, a totally inadequate musical about Mayor Jimmy Walker, cost $900,000, and it lost a great deal more before it responded to public apathy. In a shrinking market, the costs of producing musicals escalated fantastically. But it was not money that made something memorable out of *My Fair Lady, Wonderful Town, West Side Story, The Music Man, The Most Happy Fella, The Sound of Music, Fiddler on the Roof, Man of La Mancha,* and *Hair.* It was enthusiasm. No one would undertake the intricate, painful, gargantuan, hysterical task of putting on a musical play unless he had more enthusiasm than most people have about anything.

All the good musicals had intelligible, coherent, and attractive books. In the case of *My Fair Lady*, the source material was Shaw's *Pygmalion*. In the case of *West Side Story*, it was Shakespeare's *Romeo and Juliet*. In the case of *Wonderful Town*, it was *My Sister Eileen*, which in turn had been dramatized from some humorous stories by Ruth McKenney. In the case of *The Most Happy Fella*, it was *They Knew What They Wanted*. In the case of *The Sound of Music*, it was *The Trapp Family Singers*. In the case of *Fiddler on the Roof*, it was some stories by Sholom Aleichem. In the case of *Hello, Dolly!*, it was Thornton Wilder's *The Matchmaker*, which was a new version of his *Merchant of Yonkers*, which in turn was an adaptation of a European comedy by Johann Nestroy. In the case of *Man of La Mancha*, it was *Don Quixote*. *The Music Man* and *Hair* began with nothing except the author's idea; there were no literary sources. But most musicals were assembled rather than written. The librettists and the composers had something on paper before they started work.

Alan Jay Lerner, librettist and lyricist, and Frederick Loewe, composer, of *My Fair Lady*, already had demonstrated superior talent and taste in two other excellent musicals—*Brigadoon* and *Paint Your Wagon*. Their choice of Shaw's *Pygmalion* as the theme for *My Fair Lady* was fortunate. It was a Cinderella story—a genre that has always been one of the staples of the musical stage. By learning to speak good English, an ignorant London slumdweller became a lady with acceptable social graces, and Julie Andrews triumphed in the part as Lynn Fontanne and Mrs. Pat Campbell had triumphed in the original play. But there was very little Shaw left by the time Mr. Loewe had written a captivating score in the melodic tradition of Rodgers, Kern, and Offenbach, and by the time Mr. Lerner had made a romance out of the meeting of Eliza Doolittle (Miss Andrews) and Professor Henry Higgins (Rex Harrison). When *My Fair Lady* opened at the Mark Hellinger Theater on March 15, 1956, the climax came, not when one of the two principal characters said or did anything romantic; it came when an ignorant flower girl mastered the pronunciation of a difficult English phrase: "The rain in Spain stays mainly in the plain." The audience cheered as if some great social issue had been solved.

Since Shaw had been dead for six years, he could not object to the violence done to his style. A militant antiromantic, he had never intended that Eliza Doolittle and Henry Higgins would progress from speech lessons to wooing. When the early audiences for *Pygmalion* jumped to that popular conclusion, he rebuked them by writing an epilogue in which Eliza married Freddy, a good-natured simpleton, and settled down to a dreary bourgeois life. But the logic and emotional momentum of *My Fair Lady* intimated a marriage between Eliza and Henry. Mr. Lerner took responsibility for what he had done to Shaw's whim of continence: "I have omitted the epilogue," Mr. Lerner wrote, "because in it Shaw explains how Eliza ends not with Higgins but with Freddy and—Shaw and heaven forgive me!—I am not certain that he is right." But *My Fair Lady* was never profligate: it may be the only musical play in which the hero and heroine never kiss or embrace.

It had another distinction. The score was not only infectiously melodious ("I've Grown Accustomed to Her Face," "Get Me to the Church on Time," "On the Street Where You Live," "I Could Have Danced All Night"), but it served the play with a kind of selfless dedication, as if it were more interested in the play than in its own success. It portrayed character; it accelerated the momentum of the narrative and also gave the audience enormous pleasure. *My Fair Lady* was brilliantly staged by Moss Hart at the peak of his ability; and the part of Henry Higgins was brilliantly played by Rex Harrison with virtuosity and subtleties of inflection that brought wit and humor into a romantic story. Mr. Lerner and Mr. Loewe wrote one more musical together—*Camelot*, produced with Julie Andrews and Richard Burton in 1960. It lacked the freshness and resonance of *My Fair Lady*. After that, Mr. Loewe withdrew from a fabulous partnership. He saw no reason for continuing to challenge the impossible.

If Leonard Bernstein had not deprived himself of a spectacular career by becoming conductor of the New York Philharmonic Orchestra, the musical stage would have been richer. A sophisticated young man, he had a special genius for composing music about New York City. In 1944, before he succumbed to serious music, he wrote the score for a delightful small musical called *On the Town*—brisk, gay and good-humored. In 1953, he wrote the score for an affectionately droll musical about the comic crises in the lives of two sisters in Greenwich Village. It was called *Wonderful Town*, and Rosalind Russell and Edie Adams played the parts of the sisters. The music was both astringent and amusing. Three years later, he wrote a vibrant modern score for Lillian Hellman's dramatization of Voltaire's *Candide*. His overture for that opera has become a standard musical item. From both the musical and theatrical points of view, *Candide* was a distinguished work—not only in the text and score, but in the quality of the singing and the musicianship of the conducting and the orchestra. Despite its artistic expertness and cultural value, it failed. In the meantime, the bumbling Metropolitan Opera Company was presenting a sloppy, hokum production of Offenbach's *La Périchole*, much to the delight of its humorless subscribers. The situation was painfully ironic: Broadway did an opera with distinction, and it failed; the Met did an operetta badly, and it succeeded. *Candide* had a cast of forty-three singers, a full orchestra, and seventy-three performances. Broadway had no interest in a musical drama that lacked romance.

West Side Story, in 1957, was Mr. Bernstein's finest work. By the standards of Broadway, it looked unpropitious. Instead of glamour, it offered the poverty-stricken life of Puerto Rican street-gangs, and it did not conclude with romance and the cliché of living happily ever after. It concluded with the violent death of the chief male character. Although it was deliberately patterned after *Romeo and Juliet*, it dispensed with the wit, poetry, gentility, and ceremoniousness of the Shakespeare drama. In the beginning, some theatergoers were repelled by the ignobility of the *West Side Story* scene and complained that Broadway had betrayed them.

But enthusiasm travels fast and infects theatergoers everywhere; and it was not long before *West Side Story* was recognized as an achievement of the first order. Mr. Bernstein's third city score (the fourth if the ballet *Fancy Free* is counted) was sui generis—a harsh ballad of the city, taut, nervous, and flaring, the melodies choked apprehensively, the rhythms wild, swift, and deadly. Since Jerome Robbins, the director, had been trained in ballet, the staging had a breathtaking pace, and the ballets were explosive. Carol Lawrence and Larry Kert played the leading parts with passion and wonder. Everything was superbly blended in this exotic work—the blunt text by Arthur Laurents, the lyrics by Stephen Sondheim, the pitiless city sets by Oliver Smith, in addition to Mr. Bernstein's score. *West Side Story* dispensed with the familiar charms of musical theater and relied solely on talent and artistic conviction. It had 732 performances on Broadway. The next year, Leonard Bernstein capitulated to respectability by accepting the post of conductor of a famous symphony orchestra.

When *Fiddler on the Roof* opened in 1964, just about everybody received it joyfully and especially liked the whirligig performing of Zero Mostel as a Russian Jewish peasant. But no one imagined that it would still be playing on Broadway six years later and long after Mr. Mostel had gone on to other parts. It became a staple item in the theater; it appealed to something fundamental in human nature. Since the music was commonplace and the libretto was routine, what was the quality that proved to be so durable? It must have been the folk genius of Sholom Aleichem, who created the folk hero, Tevye, the impoverished, devout dairyman who was forever arguing with God. Tevye was the core of the play; his skeptical piety amounted to realism. In one of his prayers Tevye blended the divine with the worldly in a characteristic side-remark: "Blessed are they that dwell in Thy house. (I take it, O Lord, that Thy house is somewhat more spacious than mine)." Unschooled, penniless, tormented in his own house, derided by his neighbors, Tevye was the perfect realist. He had a wholesome nature and no illusions.

There was nothing glamorous about *Fiddler on the Roof.* Tevye, his shrewish wife, his guileless daughters, and his fellow townsmen lived in a slovenly Jewish community in Russia in 1905; they dressed in rags, torn coats, and battered hats, and the men wore scraggly beards, and they all lived in a worn-out community—all of these things being the opposite of conventional showmanship. But there is a certain beauty in ugliness when enlightened artists deal with it. Boris Aronson's unadorned settings had vitality and aspiration; and Jerome Robbins, who had staged *West Side Story*, made a vivid composition out of the materials of the story. The sounds and the movement became the portrait of a civilized people—realism tempered with common sense, valor without heroics, and all of it suffused with warmth and humor. Beneath the façade of a big Broadway show, there was a core of human truth about some vigorous people.

When Sholom Aleichem settled in the Bronx in 1906, having fled the grisly Kishinev pogroms, no one could have imagined that, in 1964, some audacious Broadway operators would invest $375,000 in a musical drama based on his fugitive stories and that New York theatergoers would buy $650,000 worth of tickets before the show opened; or that theatergoers would still be buying $60,000 to $90,000 worth of tickets a week five years later. Tevye would not have believed it. He would have expected God to compensate for commercial success with some awful and humiliating disaster.

In the sixties, the quality of music deteriorated into a kind of standard monotone, as if it were a job but no longer a pleasure to write for the theater. The range of the music was narrow, the themes mechanical, and the melodies tight and introverted. Music in the films, nightclubs, and on Broadway all sounded alike. It was difficult to distinguish Jerry Bock, who wrote the *Fiddler on the Roof* score, from Jerry Herman, who wrote the score for *Hello, Dolly!*, and Jule Styne, who wrote the score for *Funny Girl* in 1964, and Burt Bacharach, who wrote the score for *Promises, Promises* in 1968. A kind of musical cant prevailed, as if the times were too stereotyped for individuality. Music was standardized on a level of mediocrity.

There had been plenty of joyous music in the fifties from composers who took pleasure in what they were doing. Although *The Flower Drum Song*, in 1958, presented two titillating Oriental actresses, Miyoshi Umeki and Pat Suzuki, it brought no memorable music from the opulent studios of Rodgers and Hammerstein. But *The Sound of Music* the next season contained some of their finest songs, one of which, "Climb Every Mountain," with its evangelistic theme and somber melody, became part of the national repertory. The music in Frank Loesser's *The Most Happy Fella* in 1956 was also imaginative and rich in the finest tradition of character description; and the nostalgic, brass-band score of Meredith Willson's *The Music Man*, in 1957, said "yes" to life with ebullience. In 1954, Gian-Carlo Menotti, who had written and composed *The Medium* and *The Consul*, gave Broadway a powerful and exalting operatic score in *The Saint of Bleecker Street*—far above the level of most musical dramas. It explored the spiritual dilemmas of simple Bleecker Street Italians who were caught up in a religious mystery they could not understand. Sung, performed, and staged with mastery of the musical theater, it was the most powerful drama of the season. It had only 92 performances. Nothing but a profoundly moving recording remains of that gallant work in a bountiful style that was strange to most theatergoers.

There were two musicals in the last half of the sixties that did contain music with character—Mitch Leigh's score for *Man of La Mancha* and Galt MacDermot's blaring rock score for *Hair*. *Man of La Mancha* expressed a kind of wistful admiration for the foolish gallantries of Don Quixote; and, among many songs played and sung with skill and freshness, it presented one song, "The Impossible Dream," that made a universal statement. It celebrated hope for a better life. *Hair* was populated with a harum-scarum band of hippies who turned out to be innocent and likable young people. "Beside disheveled what do you want to be?" one puzzled parent asked her child. The joke was good-natured, like the whole phantasmagoria of this hippie cartoon. *Hair* also discreetly displayed a few front-view nudes as evidence of its good citizenship. Both *Man of La Mancha* and *Hair* were enduring successes. Both had character; both were alive.

Since art theaters were manifestly uneconomic on Broadway, two valiant attempts were made to establish permanent acting companies by means of subsidies. In 1964, the Phoenix Theater, which had begun on Second Avenue in 1953, combined with Ellis Rabb's repertory company; and after a year of preliminary producing Off Broadway, the Phoenix–APA, as they called themselves, took up residence in the Lyceum Theater, where Dan Frohman had once presided over an excellent stock company. At the time of the combination, the Phoenix consisted almost exclusively of T. Edward Hambleton, the most indomitable gentleman in New York, one of the most indomitable impresarios on Broadway. He had devoted all his energy and a lot of his money for more than a decade to the Sisyphean labor of trying to make the public share his devotion to the high-minded Phoenix Theater. Mr. Rabb belonged in a similar category. Since 1960, he had been organizing, training, maintaining, and booking a company that called itself the "Association of Producing Artists" and trouped through the eastern parts of the nation.

The word "repertory" is synonymous with virtue. Ever since 1905, when a few wealthy patrons of art proposed what eventually became the New Theater, repertory has been the ideal of discriminating theatergoers—a kind of talisman or shibboleth. With the support of some anonymous donors, Eva Le Gallienne operated the Civic Repertory Theater on that basis for seven years, and her public made the acquaintance of many great dramas that the commercial theater was not equipped to produce. Mr. Rabb and his company opened at the Lyceum with the same objective. He headed a versatile and dedicated company that on an alternating schedule acted many plays that Broadway was not likely to put on for runs—a dramatization of Tolstoy's *War and Peace*, Marlowe's *Doctor Faustus*, Sheridan's *The School for Scandal*, Ghelderode's *Pantagleize*, O'Casey's *Cock-a-Doodle Dandy*, and others.

Not everything worked out on the lofty plane of the repertory ideal. Audiences did exactly what they did on Broadway: they attended the popular productions and ignored others that sounded worthy but not exciting. They did not pay much attention to two of the most triumphant productions—*Pantagleize* and *Cock-a-Doodle Dandy*, which were difficult and intricate plays that the Phoenix–APA mounted brilliantly. The real hits at

The Vivian Beaumont Theater, 1970.

The interior of the Vivian Beaumont Theater, showing the Lincoln Center production of *Camino Real* (1969). (*Martha Swope*)

Forty-second Street in 1970.

Times Square in 1970.

the Lyceum were not plays that could not be seen on Broadway but revivals of standard Broadway plays, like the Kaufman and Hart *You Can't Take It with You* and George Kelly's *The Show-Off*. As the caustic, vigilant mother in *The Show-Off*, Helen Hayes, who had joined the company as a friend of the theater, gave one of her most bustling and amusing performances. The next season, she took *The Show-Off* on tour and was able to send back a profit of $250,000 to the needy company in New York.

There was one more flaw in the repertory formula. Although the APA gave acceptable performances of Molière's *The Misanthrope* and Sheridan's *The School for Scandal*, the company lacked the polish, brio, skill, and style of the Comédie-française in Paris, Brecht's Berliner Ensemble in East Berlin, the Royal Shakespeare Company and the National Theater in London, and several companies in Leningrad and Moscow. After all the training and the artistic aspirations, the APA was most comfortable in popular American comedies.

Low ticket prices were a basic item in the Phoenix–APA plan. The deficits were correspondingly high. The 1968–1969 deficit was $900,000, which loyal patrons and foundations met. That was the final season, though not because of the deficit. For reasons never identified, the APA withdrew from the partnership, leaving Mr. Hambleton planning Phoenix Theater productions again and displaying again that familiar look of modesty, patience, and implacable will. In February of 1970 he set the Phoenix to bounding again with a jovial revival of Mary Chase's *Harvey* with Helen Hayes and James Stewart in the stellar roles. Their performance was more enjoyable than the original in 1944.

The most imposing effort to establish repertory on a permanent basis was the Repertory Theater of Lincoln Center at the Vivian Beaumont Theater. It regards itself as a Broadway theater. Although it is located thirteen blocks north of the theater district, and although it is actually located between Columbus and Amsterdam Avenues, the thoroughfare of Broadway does lunge through the neighborhood. In the newspaper advertisements, the Vivian Beaumont gives its address as Broadway at 65th Street. Perhaps it wants to detach itself from the gleaming cultural ghetto that includes the Philharmonic Hall, the Metropolitan Opera, the State Theater where ballets are performed, the Juilliard School, and the Library of the Performing Arts. They sound too genteel for a theatergoer.

The Lincoln Repertory represents a serious and deliberate attempt to establish an art theater immune from the crises of show business. Robert Whitehead and Elia Kazan, the original producing directors, started training a company in 1962—three years before the Vivian Beaumont Theater was built. Since the new theater was behind schedule, they also built a temporary theater with an apron stage in Washington Square and opened their first production there in January 1964—Arthur Miller's *After the Fall*, with an excellent cast.

Since New York invariably expects instant success, and, in this instance, expected instant repertory, and since Broadway instinctively takes a dim view of any theater with a mission, *After the Fall* was generally denounced as pretentious; and since the next two productions were badly staged, the Lincoln Repertory was criticized with mounting fury. S. N. Behrman's *But for Whom Charlie* was written for a proscenium stage and was in every way inept on the apron stage; and the revival of O'Neill's *Marco Millions* was maundering and chaotic. The second season included two interesting productions—Arthur Miller's *Incident at Vichy*, well acted and produced, and Molière's *Tartuffe*, which was ingeniously staged by William Ball. The prospects seemed brighter; three years of preparatory work seemed about to yield a good product.

But the Lincoln Center Repertory Theater was burdened with a board of directors that was composed of people generous with their money and competent in business management but totally incompetent in the theater. Their standards were those of Park and Madison Avenues and Wall Street. In January of 1965, they organized a snide management coup: in the midst of the season, they superseded Mr. Whitehead and Mr. Kazan with Herbert Blau and Jules Irving who had been operating The Actors' Workshop in San Francisco. Shocked by the thought that they might find themselves in charge of a failure, they hoped that Mr. Irving and Mr. Blau would rescue a project that had been established by two experienced producing directors who had been working on it with increasing competence for more than four years.

Mr. Irving and Mr. Blau had the good fortune to acquire a beautiful new theater that Mr. Whitehead and Mr. Kazan had helped to build. The Vivian Beaumont Theater, named for the woman who gave $3,000,000, is the finest in New York from both the stage and audience point of view. Eero Saarinen and Jo Mielziner were the architects; and Mr. Mielziner, after many years of practical experience, designed the stage. It can be used either as a proscenium or apron stage. It is the only apron stage on Broadway, although apron stages are common in other parts of the country. The seats are arranged in steep ramps on three sides of the stage. The acoustics are excellent. The lobbies and the public facilities are sumptuous and beautiful. Broadway people generally are contemptuous of the Vivian Beaumont Theater, and they regard the stage as disastrous. They think that entrances and exits are awkward on the apron stage, and that it is difficult for an actor to focus on an audience that is seated on the sides as well as in front and also on many levels. The criticism is provincial. Shakespeare had these difficulties to contend with, and still succeeded. The subscribers and the public in general find the Beaumont interesting and comfortable. They seem to be happy to be relieved of the austerities of the Broadway houses.

In October 1965, Mr. Irving and Mr. Blau opened the new theater with their first production—Buechner's *Danton's Death*. The production was amateurish and pretentious—flagrantly inadequate, played by untalented actors. For most of the next two seasons, the stage work was incompetent and the reviews savage. Mr. Blau resigned in 1967, leaving Mr. Irving in sole charge of a floundering organization. By this time, it included another theater that seats 299 people and is used for experimental plays. On the whole, the subscribers were patient; they believed in the objectives of the project.

And they were right. In 1967, the Lincoln Center Repertory Theater began to have a civilized personality. There was a tenderly staged production of Federico García Lorca's *Yerma*, which is more like a tone poem than a drama. Anthony Quayle, the British actor, appeared in the central part of a dynamic and well-organized production of Bertolt Brecht's *Galileo*. Both of these productions were directed by John Hirsch. In the spring of 1969, the Lincoln Repertory gave an impressively sober and responsible production of a provocative contemporary play—Heinar Kipphardt's *In the Matter of J. Robert Oppenheimer*. The first production the next autumn was a revival of William Saroyan's ragtime ballad *The Time of Your Life*, which was given a genial, humorous, affectionate performance. At the moment when it was produced in the autumn, it was the only bright spot in a dismal new Broadway season.

Since the Lincoln Center Repertory Theater was founded as a cultural institution that would not be expected to pay its way, no one is surprised by the size of the deficits. During the 1968–1969 season, the theater operated at ninety percent capacity and lost $800,000. The Lincoln Center is not a repertory theater in the classic sense, and for a very good reason: the American public will not adjust itself to a repertory schedule. It wants a succession of hits. The Lincoln Center is an art theater, with a resident company. By 1970, it was finding a place of its own in the hugger-mugger of Broadway. It was giving good performances of interesting plays for audiences who have taste and enjoy meeting in a cordial theater.

Oscar Hammerstein II's most visible legacy to Broadway was a statue of George M. Cohan. The statue was his idea; he hired the sculptor, Georg J. Lober; he solicited the money and made a generous personal donation;

he got the necessary permissions and arranged the dedication exercises in 1959. The statue symbolizes the endemic irony of Broadway: the greater man celebrates the lesser. At the tip of a tiny, slatternly park at Broadway and 46th Street, the old Yankee Doodle man carries a cane in one hand and a soft hat in the other and looks over the theater district with a leisurely air of approval.

But the Broadway that the statue looks at began to lose personality about the time the statue was erected (another irony). During the last five years of the sixties, the loss became massive and visible. Business corporations with monumental assets and no interest in people intruded on a neighborhood that had once been congenial to the public. In 1965, the Allied Chemical Corporation bought the Times Building that had presided over the neighborhood for sixty years. Modeled after a Renaissance Florentine tower, the Times Building had grace and elegance and seemed to take pleasure in being part of an affable community. The Allied Chemical Corporation stripped off the original stonework and junked the décor and covered the steel frame with blank marble slabs. It is a cold, self-possessed building that represents a cold, self-possessed industry and is totally detached from the crowds that stream through Times Square. In 1968, the Astor Hotel was pulled down to make way for a tall office building to be called One Astor Plaza. For more than a half century, the Astor had been host to theater people, who regarded the Astor's Hunt Room as their private luncheon club and who loitered in the gossipy barber shop in the basement. Actors' Equity used to hold its business meetings in the Astor. Theatergoers made appointments to meet one another in the lobby that was always crowded, or arranged assignations more discreetly in the balcony.

When One Astor Plaza is completed, it will contain a theater that will seat 1,600 people, and also a film theater that will seat 1,500. But an amiable, rather dowdy meeting-place for theater people has been carted off to the dumps. Economics dictate the disaster. Real estate values in mid-Manhattan from the North to the East Rivers make theater buildings obsolete. Individual theater buildings, with their proud but neglected façades and their cheerfully lighted lobbies, do not earn enough money to pay for the land they occupy. Eventually Times Square and Broadway will become aisles of tall office buildings. To preserve the theater industry, which is regarded as a New York asset, the city government gives builders an inducement to include theaters inside office buildings. The city grants them a bonus of twenty percent additional renting space. Six or seven theaters, ranging all the way from 499 seats to 1,700 seats, are already included in plans for future office buildings. If and when they are built, Broadway will continue to have places where dramas can be performed.

But a theater tucked inside an office building is a facility and not a home, and is not the equal of the comfortable old Winter Garden (the backstage areas of which were originally a car barn) or the equal of the arcade of theaters on 44th and 45th Streets, which are like old homes to thousands of theatergoers. They have personalities. They take pride in the profession. They are part of the culture of the world. They are not subservient to the kind of business that is congenitally unwilling to take a net loss of $6,000,000, as Broadway did in 1959–1960, or $5,000,000 as it did in 1967–1968.

The slow erosion of Broadway, however depressing, was inevitable. The colossal film theaters—Paramount, Capitol, Roxy's—had vanished. All the economic indices pointed downward. In 1968, the Broadway-Piccadilly Ticket Service, founded in 1916, closed shop. There were no longer enough tickets to sell to maintain the business. The number of ticket brokers was about two hundred in 1920; it was seventy-eight in 1967. Also, the number of new productions continued to fall. In the first six months of the 1969–1970 season, there were only eleven productions, and of these only two were hits. In November—traditionally one of the high points of the season —ten of Broadway's thirty-six theaters were dark. *Variety* reported that Broadway was operating at 46.5 percent capacity.

Nor were the artistic aspects of Broadway reassuring. Five of the eleven new productions were plays from the past: *The Front Page* (1928), *Private Lives* (1931), *Three Men on a Horse* (1935), *Our Town* (1938), *The Time of Your Life* (1939), and three of the best productions of 1970 were *Camino Real* (1953), *Harvey* (1944), and *Room Service* (1953).

Previously Broadway had assumed, with reason, that it dictated the taste of theatergoers in other parts of the country who saw Broadway plays in stock or in performances by road companies. But in the last three seasons of the decade the following plays came to Broadway from other parts of the country by institutions that had no Broadway affiliation: *We Bombed in New Haven* from the Yale Repertory Theater, *Red, White and Maddox* from Theater Atlanta, *The Sudden and Accidental Re-Education of Horse Johnson* from the Milwaukee Repertory Theater, *Does a Tiger Wear a Necktie?* from Brandeis University, *The Gingham Dog* from the Washington Theater Club, *The Great White Hope* and *Indians*, very aggressive and virtuoso dramas, from Zelda Fichandler's enterprising Arena Stage in Washington. One of the most searching dramas of the 1969–1970 season, Charles Gordone's *No Place to Be Somebody*, moved up to the ANTA Theater from Joe Papp's Public Theater in Lafayette Street. Off Broadway was beginning to service Broadway. Moreover, most of the daring plays that performed the primary function of criticizing life and that represented the thought and the mood of the time were produced Off Broadway with vary-ing degrees of success. There were more productions Off Broadway than on. It was not a subsidiary theater district. There was also a switch in film priorities. Broadway made new musicals out of old films. *Zorba*, a musical in which Herschel Bernardi appeared, was remade from the film *Zorba the Greek*. *Promises, Promises*, a generally odious musical that grossed more than $100,000 a week the same season, was made from a slightly odious film called *The Apartment*. It celebrated the senile assignations of aging business executives with their accessible secretaries. The odor of debauchery was not peculiar to *Promises, Promises*. In the lobby of the Rialto Theater, in the shadow of the Allied Chemical Tower, a television monitor showed voluptuous scenes from the squalid film inside, and Broadway rubes stood on the sidewalk gaping at it in dreamy contentment all day and evening. Nearly all the films on 42nd Street were billed as pornographic or licentious or both; and one redundant sign announced that the film inside the theater was for "Mature Adults" only. Immature adults would be barred. Sample invitations to orgies on the movie signs of 42nd Street: *Wall of Flesh, Too Much: Too Often, Lust in the Flesh, The Sensualist, This Sporting House, Girls That Do It*.

For several months, go-go girls in striptease attire danced as sensually as they could in the windows of an upstairs cabaret at 47th Street and Seventh Avenue. Crowds of dazed civilians in Duffy Square gawked at them all winter in a mood of sophomoric incredulity. At the close of the sixties, Broadway was on the downgrade as a form of art and as an amuse-ment emporium.

But that is not the final word. Again, the ironies prevail. The member-ship of Actors' Equity was in a constant state of flux, but it had a net in-crease of fifty to one hundred actors every season. At the end of 1960, the membership roll (including 3,000 members of Chorus Equity) stood at 16,000. The number of members who had maintained their dues payments was 12,407—a net increase of two thousand since 1950. During one sample week in August, when the summer theaters were flourishing, 4,584 were employed. Nearly four thousand members answered a survey about their income from the theater that year; 1,542 of them reported incomes of over $2,500. Equivalent figures from previous years are not available. But it may be noted that eighty percent of the members were unemployed in 1948; in 1939, the average income of the members from the theater was $800.

Despite the bleakness of the economic climate, there was another positive factor. The Broadway theater community was the most numerous in the nation, and it included the largest number of talented professionals— technicians as well as actors, directors, and designers. Give them a problem and they had not only the skill but the enthusiasm with which to solve it. They could perform the theater's most ancient ritual: they could entertain the public with gaiety and style.

To have a solid place in a community, theater has to be a criticism of life by writers with ideas and passion, like the leading writers of the twenties and thirties who were makers and shakers. In the late sixties, Broadway did not produce many plays that took positions on public issues or moral values. But when a play of that kind appeared, Broadway was equipped to stage and act it. It had the knowledge as well as the resources to express ideas creatively and to transmute something on paper into sound, movement, excitement, or exaltation. In 1968, it was impossible to be depressed about a theater that could translate the racial dilemmas of Jack Johnson into the vivid, human panorama of Howard Sackler's *The Great White Hope*. In 1969, it was impossible to be despondent about a theater that could turn the story of the exploitation of the American Indian into the somber, whirling elegy of Arthur Kopit's *Indians*; or to despair of a theater that could find the contemporary values of Shakespeare's *Henry V* with so much imagination and audacity as the young actors from the American Shakespeare Festival Theater did. After a long series of dreary productions, the form of musical entertainment seemed to have gone bankrupt. But in the spring of 1970, Stephen Sondheim's and George Furth's *Company* made the theater exciting again. In its acting, composing, and writing, it made a brilliant comment on the specious manners of the smart people of New York.

Since *Our Town* had a memorable performance by the original cast in 1938, the merit of the revival in the ANTA Theater thirty-one years later should not be regarded as surprising. But the sensitive and moving 1969 production with Henry Fonda, Mildred Natwick, Ed Begley, Elizabeth Hartman, and Harvey Evans in the leading parts confirmed an old conviction that, in addition to many charlatans, there are golden people on Broadway. Give them a humane script, like *Our Town*, and they can make it glow; they can give it an overtone of wonder. On the street, Broadway is tawdry; in many corners, it is degenerate. On the stage, it is usually bright and occasionally inspired. That's the eternal paradox of Broadway, still visible in the 1970 era of bad feelings. Broadway is artistically and technically proficient, but no longer creative.

ACKNOWLEDGMENTS

By neglecting to compile a bibliography, I'm sure I am being unfair to many writers whose books I have consulted. I have happily ransacked everything I could lay hands on—biographies and autobiographies, books of criticism from every era, newspaper and magazine articles, maudlin tributes to stars—all of them interesting and relevant and full of the bustle and fever of Broadway. There is a wealth of pungent material on the shelves of the Walter Hampden Memorial Library at The Players—including John Barrymore's prompt-book for his *Hamlet*. The Library of the Performing Arts at Lincoln Center is overflowing with newspaper clippings, diaries, letters, box-office records, and truculent pronunciamentos that preserve the passing moods of Broadway. I have taken everything within reach without giving thanks.

I have made consistent use of several books that provide a foundation for the continuing life of the theater. Harrison Grey Fiske's weekly *The*

New York Dramatic Mirror, which ceased publication in 1922, and Arthur Hornblow's monthly *Theatre Magazine,* which was founded in 1901 and expired in 1931, are full of essential material. They contain not only facts, but opinions and comments that retain the bustling personality of Broadway. In 1905, Sime Silverman, a journalist with a distaste for cant and humbug, founded a brash weekly called *Variety* that has been consistently honest, blunt, and factual about show business and has created a racy style of prose. Bit by bit *Variety* superseded *The New York Dramatic Mirror,* which took a stuffy attitude towards the stage. Jack Pulaski and his successor, Hobe Morrison, have made the theater section of *Variety* the essential fact-sheet and also a storehouse of juicy business scandals. Managers who give *Variety* dishonest information about their box-office receipts will never get into heaven. I could never conduct my writing profession without *Variety.* Burns Mantle's annual editions of *The Best Plays,* begun in 1919, have given the theater the dignity of a permanent institution. Nothing has been ephemeral on Broadway since he published the first book. Being a modest man, Burns Mantle began his service modestly; but with the help of a sister-in-law who kept the files and the records he steadily expanded the work to include additional material and make it the standard reference book about the Broadway theater. *The Best Plays* has had several editors since Burns Mantle died in 1948, and it continues to be invaluable.

Since John Gassner's mammoth *Masters of the Drama* is a history of the world theater from earliest times, the plays done on Broadway are only a small part of it. I have consulted it frequently. Apart from the scope of the information it contains, it always amazes me because it is written throughout in a style of sustained enjoyment. Since John Gassner was never a critic for a newspaper or publication of general interest, his work is not so well known as books by more celebrated writers. But no one has served the theater with so much insight, erudition, kindness, and good will. When he died in 1967, he left permanently an empty niche. Two other books have been consistently useful—Bernard Sobel's *The Theater Handbook and Digest of Plays* (1940 and 1959) and Glenn Hughes' *A History of the American Theater from 1700 to 1950* (1951). These books are packed with information.

I have helped myself liberally to Lehman Engel's *The American Musical Theater* (1967) and Stanley Green's *The World of Musical Comedy* (1962). Music is Mr. Engel's whole life; his long experience as a conductor in the Broadway theater has given him unique insight into the structure and style of musical plays. But he is absorbed in all kinds of music—serious as well as amusing; and, like a missionary, he is always off to Europe, Japan, the Near East, the West Coast of America, or the East Side of New York to spread the gospel among true believers. Mr. Green's cheerful and gossipy *The World of Musical Comedy* is the essence of Broadway. It takes equal interest in composers, lyricists, and performers and conveys the sensation of theater. It is a unique sourcebook of great value.

Ever since I was a boy, I have been indebted to librarians. In a greedy world, they have preserved grace of spirit. Although they know more than most people, they serve all kinds of people with equal respect; and although they are imposed on regularly, they do not object. In gathering the material for this book, I am in debt to several librarians who have accepted my problems as their own. Louis Rachow, the tall, quiet, selfless librarian at The Players, has enlarged my knowledge of the theater by tracking down obscure pamphlets as well as many useful books I had never heard of. I am grateful to him.

The busy staff of the Library of the Performing Arts accepted me as a permanent resident amid the silent uproar of their many duties. They are modest people with a mission. Nearly everyone else engaged in public service in the city is bored, surly, and inefficient, and regards the citizens as intruders. The Library of the Performing Arts is not only hospitable, but efficient, knowledgeable, and obliging. I owe particular thanks to Paul Myers, the amiable librarian, and to Betty Wharton, Dorothy Swerdlove, Maxwell Silverman, and Dorothy O'Connor. Sam Pearce of the Museum of the City of New York could not have been more hospitable and generous.

Two old friends, Max Gordon and Leah Salisbury, have read the manuscript and spared me the humiliation of making some conspicuous errors in public. The errors that remain are my own—unfortunately. I am grateful to Arthur Gregor, formerly of The Macmillan Company, for proposing this book to me, and to Richard Marek, formerly of the Macmillan staff, for his support and criticisms. I am much in debt to Jim Neyland for his meticulous copyediting and pitiless annihilation of errors. I want also to say thanks to my wife, Oriana, for her generous and helpful interest in this book. It's not the first time.

B. A.

INDEX